T0368374

GOD, GENDER, AND A FALLEN WORLD

JERRY FREDERICK

WESTBOW
PRESS®
A DIVISION OF THOMAS NELSON
& ZONDERVAN

WestBow Press books may be ordered through booksellers or by contacting:

WestBow Press
A Division of Thomas Nelson & Zondervan
1663 Liberty Drive
Bloomington, IN 47403
www.westbowpress.com
844-714-3454

ISBN: 979-8-3850-4155-8 (sc)
ISBN: 979-8-3850-4156-5 (hc)
ISBN: 979-8-3850-4157-2 (e)

Library of Congress Control Number: 2024927683

Print information available on the last page.

WestBow Press rev. date: 04/02/2025

CONTENTS

INTRODUCTION

I entered college in the fall of 1967. It seems like yesterday, and I remember it well. I was a frightened freshman waiting for my first class to begin at 8 AM; Inorganic Chemistry 105. It was held in a large old lecture hall with those desk/chair combinations which had the part you write on attached, so you kind of slithered into them and lifted the desk-part up. I slithered into mine, lifted the desk part up so I was ready to take notes, and stared at the empty stage. I was anxious to see what a real professor looked like. College professors were like animals in the jungle for me: I had heard that such creatures existed, but I had never actually seen one.

The clock chimed 8 AM; the door on the side of the stage opened; and out sprang Dr. Morrison. He bounded up the stairs to the stage and made a lame attempt at humor by asking if anyone wanted to plink out a tune on the old upright piano that sat to the side of the stage.

Silence.

OK, since there were no takers on the piano offer, he launched into Inorganic Chemistry, a course I would struggle through for the next two semesters.

About two months later, on a Thursday evening, I rounded a corner in a hallway in the dorm where I was living, and there was Dr. Morrison walking down the hall toward me. I felt awkward, like a third grader who sees his teacher in the grocery store. What do you say? I tried to make conversation by asking him what he was doing there. Probably he was trying to help some poor student who was already lost in Inorganic Chemistry, a condition hovering on the horizon for me.

He said he was leading a Bible study for some guys in the dorm, and would I like to join them next week?

I was stunned.

This man was a scientist. He was a college professor. He was smart. I knew that because I was in his class. He was way smarter than I ever hoped to be. What was he doing studying the Bible, and doing it with students? There was so much that did not fit.

Without making any effort to remember the time and place of the small study, I showed up the next week. I was not particularly interested in learning more of Jesus. I was not burdened with the hopeless weight of my sin and my need for a Savior. I did not consciously sense, in the trendy phrase of the time, the "Jesus-shaped hole in my heart" and was not looking for someone to fill it. Those would all come later with overwhelming weight.

But I was taken aback that a science professor would be studying such an outdated book as the Bible, that he would be willing to cross the student/professor barrier to do that, and that he would come into that bastion of sin, a men's dormitory, to do it. It was the *incongruity* that attracted me. So I went to the study, totally clueless as to the enormous change in my life that would happen as a result. It was, after all, a very accidental meeting in the hallway of a men's dormitory on a Thursday evening in the fall of 1967.

As I look back on that "accidental" meeting in a dorm hallway, I recognize that what attracted me to the small Bible study, which eventually led to my conversion to Jesus Christ, was the incongruity of an intelligent scientist studying the Bible. My mind had been made up concerning the uselessness of the Bible, and I was intrigued by the problem of an intelligent man studying it as though it had significance.[1] That was a problem for me. I needed to figure that out.

That is a pattern in my life. Puzzles have always attracted me.

---

[1] When I was a senior in high school, in a composition class, I wrote an essay on how uneducated and narrow-minded Christians were. They were so arrogant. How could they think they were right and nobody else was? In retrospect, they were right and I was wrong.

Because of that, the question of the relationship of men and women in the Kingdom of God has befuddled and held me hostage for some time. The Scriptures seem very contradictory. How could they all be true? How could God in one place say that women must be silent in church and in another place speak through a women prophetess? How could He say that "in Christ" there is neither male nor female and then say that wives must submit themselves to their husbands "in the Lord"? If there is neither male nor female "in Christ," then why would the same author say that wives should submit to their husbands "in the Lord"? Why would a woman be encouraged to learn but discouraged to teach or have authority over a man?[2] It sure sounded to me that God intended a difference, so how could He say there was no difference in Christ? I believe, as Einstein did, that "The Lord God is subtle, but malicious he is not."[3] He does not try to confuse us and then laugh at our confusion. But His truths are not always clear and easy. Behind these seemingly incongruous texts, my theology of Scripture now says, there must be some way they fit together like puzzle pieces and make a picture.

So for years I struggled to find a solution to that puzzle. Since I now believe in the inspiration and entire trustworthiness of the Scriptures, properly interpreted, there must be some way to make these pieces fit together to make a picture. This book is the picture I have discovered.

Bible-believing Christians are all over the place on this issue. It would seem, then, that this would not be an easily answered question. It is also true that, since we are all either men or women, we probably do not come without prejudice or vested interest. "All persons concerned with Biblical interpretation must admit the reality of an agenda other than simply a commitment to Biblical

---

[2] Galatians 3:28, Colossians 3:18, and 1 Timothy 2:8–12
[3] A quotation from Albert Einstein, which was inscribed in German over the fireplace in the faculty lounge of the math department at Princeton. It was actually said by Dr. Einstein to mathematics professor Oscar Veblen in May 1921. (Copyright the Hebrew University of Jerusalem. With permission of the Albert Einstein Archives.)

authority and Biblical teaching."[4] So says Dr. David Scholer. The interesting thing with that statement, and I agree with him, is that it condemns Dr. Scholer along with "all people"! He also must have an agenda. And it condemns me, also, as well as anyone reading this book. Complete objectivity is probably impossible. But with honesty and self-examination, perhaps we can all learn from the Scriptures, and hopefully God will expose our hidden agendas in the process. It is certainly with humility that such a person as I would presume to offer some sort of theological system for understanding what the Bible says on this issue.[5]

My reason for taking Inorganic Chemistry as a freshman in college was that I was on track to major in pharmacy, which I did. I sell drugs for a living. I am not a theologian. I have never been to seminary. I know no Greek or Hebrew. Any time I refer to original languages, it is because I am trusting someone else's understanding of the words.

But I love God's word. It may be refreshingly obvious to some readers and painfully clear to others that I am not a theologian. I claim no special revelation—only a desire to help God's church come closer to the wonderful organism He designed it to be. We are, after all, "away from home," and we currently live in a fallen world. The older I become, the more I see that God's church needs to be so different from the fallen world where we live that we will be attractive by contrast, not by similarity. We must not take this world's goals and values and put a God-coating on them and then offer them back to the world. The kingdoms are intractably different. Oil and water do not mix. I learned that in chemistry.

---

[4] Women, Authority and the Bible, edited by Alvera Mickelsen, from the article entitled "The Place of Women in the Church's Ministry," by David Scholer. IVP, p. 219, c. 1986.

[5] One note: The issue is gender. It is not the "women's issue." I am taken aback at how many people, including egalitarians who should know better, refer to this as the "women's issue." As if the men have no problem here. I think not. We all show evidence of living in a fallen world, and I think those who label the issue as "the women's issue" are showing evidence of the very patriarchy that is so often condemned. You cannot talk about one without talking about the other. This book is about gender, not just the women's issue.

So, after being held hostage to this puzzle, I offer what I have finally concluded to anyone who is interested enough to read this book. I find understanding to be satisfying. It *tastes* good. I believe God gave us minds to *find* Truth. C. S. Lewis is one of my favorite authors, and I make no apology for quoting him often. In his book The Great Divorce he describes a conversation between an angel from heaven and a visitor from Hell, who was a supposed intellectual, who was constantly searching for Truth but never settling on what he found. That is a disease many are infected with today. "You have gone far wrong," the angel from heaven says. "Thirst was made for water; inquiry for truth. What you now call the free play of inquiry has neither more nor less to do with the ends for which intelligence was given you than masturbation has to do with marriage."[6] The purpose for our God-given mind is to seek after and *find* truth. That's why God gave us brains.

We do not have the mind of God, however, so our understanding will always be partial. We should always maintain a willingness to re-examine our position until we get to heaven, where our understanding will be complete. So there is great cause for humility and none for arrogance. But we do need to settle on a position, even if we will often have to re-examine it.

I desire to offend no one, though that is probably not possible. Where I quote a brother or sister in Christ and disagree, it is intended, and I hope will be read, as done with respect and not disdain. I do this in the spirit of "iron sharpens iron" and expect myself to be sharpened by others, as I already have been. I see this debate as an intramural one, aimed at all of us growing in our understanding of Biblical Truth.

For what it's worth, here it is. If the reader becomes more confident of God and more hungry for heaven as a result of reading, that alone will make the book a success.

---

[6] C. S. Lewis, The Great Divorce, Macmillan Publishing Company, New York, NY, c. 1946, p. 44. Used by permission.

1

HERMENEUTICS

"Our beloved brother Paul wrote to you according to the wisdom given him, speaking of this as he does in all his letters. There are some things in them hard to understand which the ignorant and unstable twist to their own destruction, as they do the other scriptures."[7]

Misunderstandings happen.

I work in a retail pharmacy. The process of prescription writing is a good example of how misunderstandings happen. It often involves horrid handwriting that needs to be interpreted by the pharmacist. That's a job in itself. Then there are the abbreviations: letters are made to stand for whole words, and the words they stand for are often complicated medical terms. On top of that, many of the abbreviations are for words in Latin, a language which is spoken by no one today (except Latin teachers) and so is a "dead" language (and probably killed the Romans, as we said in my high school Latin class.) The potential for misunderstanding is enormous, and it does happen. All this despite the fact that the purpose of a written prescription is to *communicate* directions from a physician to a pharmacist so a patient can get the right medicine, take it correctly, and hopefully get better.

---

[7] 2 Peter 3:16

1

Communication is nearly always a multi-step process with potential for mistakes all along the way. We form a thought, entrust it to words, form words with our mouths, entrust the words to sound waves, or print on a page, or some other medium, and hope the hearer or reader will pick up the words, use the same definitions as we did (a crucial step), and end up with approximately the same meaning we started out with. That does not always happen! I remember well an embarrassing moment when I was working doing general labor at a castle in Austria. At my first meal with my fellow workers, after having worked outside all day in the heat, I announced to everybody at the supper table in my broken German that I was ready for sex. After a few stifled chuckles and snorts, one kind person explained to me that in German you do not describe yourself as being hot and sweaty the same way we do in English. It has a completely different meaning. I did not make that mistake again.

The apostle Peter acknowledged that this problem of misunderstanding may occur when referring to the letters of the apostle Paul in the quote at the top of the page. He acknowledged that there were "some things in them hard to understand" and that they could be twisted, even twisted intentionally. One of the pitfalls we may may fall into is intentionally twisting Scripture in order to *avoid* what it is saying rather than to *understand* and *apply* what it is saying. Rarely are we honest with ourselves about that.

Hermeneutics is the science of how we communicate and, particularly, how we understand. Understanding is done unconsciously; it is part of learning our mother tongue, which, of course, none of us remembers. It may seem strange to examine these unconscious processes: they may seem very obvious, but it is necessary when we read. It is particularly necessary when we read the Bible. When we open the Bible to read, we are reading a book that was written in a different language. What we hold in our hands is really a translation of the Bible. Translation is hardly an exact science. (Remember how I mis-communicated the fact that I was hot and sweaty, which meant in German that I was ready for sex.)

2

When we read the Bible, we are reading words that were written in enormously different contexts from ours, with very different worldviews. It contains figures of speech and illustrations from cultures foreign to ours, and so we may completely misunderstand the point of the author. My theology is that the words of the Bible were God-breathed, trustworthy, and true, and so are authoritative in our lives. Having said that, I do not intend to imply that understanding the Bible correctly is easy and simple. "The Bible says it so I believe it" is a bit simplistic. I have met many people who said those very words, but none of them greeted one another with a kiss, as we are commanded to do in the Bible. Since the words are God-breathed, it is critical that we understand those words properly before we submit to them.

The following principles may seem intuitively obvious or really weird, depending on whether they are part of your current practice or not. For example, if I say our local basketball team creamed the opposition, nobody understands that to mean all the opposing players were dead and made into some sort of macabre soup after the game. Everybody understands that as a figure of speech called hyperbole, a deliberate overstatement to make a point. To argue that it is not literally true, that the opposing teammates really were still alive after the game, is missing the point. The fact that they were alive does not take away from the *truth* that was intended by the speaker, even though the speaker said they were made into soup, which, of course, was *not true*. The point is clear to us. So *truth* was communicated through a statement that was *false*. That's how we use words. But if you're not a native English speaker, you might understand that there was an appalling carnage at an otherwise normal basketball game. After all, that's what the words said.

In reading and understanding the Bible, we want to understand what the author intended to communicate to his original audience. Since all languages contain figures of speech as well as non-literal usage of words, this can be a complex task and a less than exact science. When we understand what the author meant, somehow through the mystery of inspiration of Scripture, we hear God's voice. And then we attempt to practice the principle in our very different world. But that application may look very different from the application in the world of the original author.

So I submit the following list of principles for the (sometimes) confusing task of understanding the Truths of Scripture. It is not exhaustive but hopefully will be helpful.

1. All Scripture means something. All Scripture is inspired by God. Therefore, we do not have the privilege of picking and choosing texts that support our preconceived stance on a particular issue. There are a number of quite sophisticated-sounding methods for choosing Scripture texts to apply and texts to ignore. Doing so means we put ourselves *over* Scripture instead of *under* its authority. This is an extremely common error and comes in a number of disguises. For instance, if we give more weight to one side of a Biblical balance than the Bible does or choose texts that teach one side of a Biblical doctrine and ignore texts which teach the other side, we commit a serious error and end up with an unBiblically neat doctrine. I want to avoid that error.

While all texts, to be sure, are not equally important, we must avoid ignoring texts that "make us uncomfortable," that do not support our position on a particular doctrine, or that are culturally offensive. It was eye-opening for me to see how many authors who wrote on the gender issue completely ignored texts that did not support the position they were proposing. That was true of authors on both the egalitarian side and the complementarian side.

There are many examples of this that will come up as we examine the gender issue. One, however, that stands out in its subtlety comes from a book that is about how to interpret Scripture: Slaves, Women & Homosexuals by William Webb. There is much that is good in the book. He talks about "seed texts," which he defines as texts that "within the rest of Scripture suggest and encourage further movement on a particular subject… If later readers in another place and time draw out the implications of the seedling idea from the text, this can lead to taking other texts beyond their original-audience application and form to a more realized expression of the idea within."[8] He then goes on to list four "In Christ" formulas that he offers as examples of "seed ideas," which plant the idea that "in Christ" gender roles are discarded: Galatians 3:28, 1 Corinthians 12:13, Ephesians 2:15, and Colossians 3:11. Notably, three out of four of those don't even mention the male/female dichotomy.

First Corinthians 12:13 says that we all, Jews and gentiles, slaves and free, were baptized into one body. The apostle Paul, the author of all the texts listed above, teaches in First Corinthians 11 that Christ is the head of the male, the male is the head of the female, and God is the head of Christ. While Ephesians 2:15-16 says that Christ has broken down the dividing wall of hostility between Jews and Gentiles and brought us together into one body, the same author two chapters later in the same book, in the same context, calls for wives to be submissive to their husbands and for husbands to love their wives. And while Colossians 3:11 says that "there cannot be Greek and Jew, circumcised and uncircumcised, barbarian, Scythian, slave, free man, but Christ is all and in all," yet only six verses later the same author says, "Wives, be subject to your husbands, as is fitting in the Lord" (italics mine). I don't mean to be hyper-critical of Dr. Webb, and he does offer some helpful ideas to help us understand the Scriptures. But to understand correctly what a Biblical author means, we need to look at everything the author wrote and not just choose texts that support our position.

2. Some concepts in Scripture are beyond our ability to fit them into neat theological packages with no loose ends. Our minds are too small. How does one believe both the absolute sovereignty of God and the free will of mankind? They are mutually exclusive, yet the Bible teaches both. So we try to understand but we are not always able to understand.

---

[8] William Webb, <u>Slaves, Women, & Homosexuals</u>. InterVarsity Press, PO Box 1400, Downers Grove, IL, 60515, c. 2001, p. 83.

One of the characteristics of deacons in 1 Timothy 3:9 is that they must hold the *mystery* of faith with a clear conscience. They must have the maturity and the humility to acknowledge their intellectual limitations and so live with some ambiguity and be comfortable with that. While Biblical faith is not anti-intellectual (it does not make sense that God would create us with a mind, then ask us to ignore it in relationship with Him), we need to avoid the intellectual arrogance of demanding everything be understandable to us and fit neatly into our categories. In the gender discussion, and especially in the discussion on the nature of God, there are issues that are difficult for our limited minds to comprehend. That's our limitation. So just because a conclusion may seem difficult, if not impossible, to comprehend, it should not be automatically jettisoned because it leaves us scratching our collective heads.

3. Other languages, including the original Bible languages, contain figures of speech, some of which may be different from ours and so seem strange and difficult to understand. The Bible does use common figures of speech such as hyperbole, a deliberate overstatement to make a point. "If your eye makes you sin, pluck it out. If your foot makes you sin, cut it off." Probably (hopefully) Jesus meant these as hyperbole; they were deliberate overstatements to make a point. The point is this: act as if your eye were plucked out—that is, don't look. Act as if your foot were cut off—that is, don't walk to a place where you will be overcome by temptation. But, frankly, not everyone has taken those verses as figurative, and in the history of the church some have gone around with missing members in a (I believe) misguided attempt to obey this verse.

The Bible clearly says that the Earth does not move[9] and that the sun does move: it rises and goes down, though at one point it stood still in the sky.[10] It is a very natural and straightforward

---

[9] Psalm 93:1b, "Yea, the world is established; it shall never be moved…."
[10] Joshua 10:13, "And the sun stood still, and the moon stayed, until the nation took vengeance on their enemies" (implying that ordinarily the sun moved normally).

interpretation of the Bible to believe that the sun moves around the earth and that the earth does not move. The church excommunicated Galileo for postulating the opposite—that the earth moved around the sun, in direct conflict with (supposedly) clear Biblical teaching. In this instance, scientific discovery showed the church had been misinterpreting Scripture and taking as literal what had been intended as figurative. Such statements should give us pause and make us uncomfortable. They certainly do me. But the issue seems inescapable. It is possible to misunderstand Scripture as being literal when it was meant as figurative or the other way around. And sometimes science will help us see that. Our response needs to be not a lack of confidence in God's word or an over-confidence in science, but a humble willingness to re-examine our long-held interpretations and do the homework necessary for a proper understanding. Early Christians, after all, had to reinterpret their understanding of the Old Testament to include God's inclusion of Gentiles into His Kingdom from the very beginning. The Reformers had to reinterpret their understanding of what the Bible said about how to be right with God. And, to our shame, North Americans have had to acknowledge the sin of using the Bible to support slavery. Again, we all need to be humble enough to acknowledge we might be misinterpreting Scripture. There is plenty of historical support for this position.

Much has been made of the two creation accounts in Genesis (an issue central to my understanding of the gender issue in this book), as well as the supposed doublets found elsewhere in the first book of the Bible. Some have responded to this problem by proposing a theory of numerous authors of the first five books of the Bible instead of one author—Moses. Supposedly, several accounts were at a later date collated into our present book, but with some duplication of accounts of certain events. So the two creation accounts of Genesis 1 and Genesis 2 were supposedly written by two (or more) different authors, and later, when the whole book of Genesis was collated from various stories, both were included, even though they are clearly contradictory. However, there is evidence that the presence of seemingly contradictory accounts was a common figure of speech in ancient near-Eastern languages—a figure of speech that is foreign to us—and had a purpose of communicating *something*.[11]

In the illustration above, I mentioned a potential basketball victory where one team creamed the opposing team. What did we mean to communicate by saying that the opposing team was made into soup? The question to ask in the interpretive process (which is usually unconscious) is this: what did the author intend to communicate? Just as the losing basketball team was *not* carried off the court in a large bowl of "creamed basketball player soup" and so the meaning was *not* literally what the words said, so in Scripture the meaning may not be what the words literally say. Interpreting Scripture that way does not take away from its Truth any more than interpreting the basketball statement in a way that involves both teams being alive after the game takes away from the essential truth contained in the words that one team creamed the other. So the fact that the chronology of Genesis 2 is contradictory to Genesis 1 does not cause me a problem. It is a figure of speech, and the definition of a figure of speech is to use words in a non-literal way to communicate truth. We will discuss this more in chapter five on Genesis.

4. Interpret the narrative by the didactic. This is probably the most crucial principle of all and the most commonly ignored. The Bible contains various types of literature, and each must be interpreted according to the type of literature it is. One reads the front page of a newspaper differently than the editorial page, or at least one should. One does not expect the movie *Titanic* to be as historically accurate as the news accounts of what really happened. The type of literature determines how we interpret it.

The narrative portions of Scripture—that is, the historical portions, those that report what happened—report what happened correctly and reliably. They claim to be true. Jesus clearly believed

---

[11] More on this in the chapter on Beginnings about the book of Genesis.

8

them to be true. But that does not mean that everything that happened was good and is an example for us to follow. Solomon used slave labor to build God's temple. David had lots of wives, committed adultery and murder, and was a less than stellar father. Hosea married a prostitute, at God's direction. None of these men would be chosen as elders or deacons of a church today if the teaching of 1 Timothy 3 is followed. Yet God used them mightily. God even used a gentile king in the Old Testament, Cyrus, who did not even know God. "Thus says the LORD to his anointed, to Cyrus, whose right hand I have grasped to subdue nations before him... I call you by name; I surname you, *though you do not know me.*"[12] God can use *anybody* and *any* situation as He pleases. That does not mean we should base doctrine on that circumstance other than the doctrine of the complete omnipotence of God. The eleven remaining disciples chose a twelfth to replace Judas by casting lots, but Matthias, the one chosen, is never again heard from. What do we do with that? Should we make leadership decisions by casting lots? If we determine doctrine from the narrative texts of the Bible, we may conclude just that.

Jesus and Paul were both single. Should we follow their example? Peter was married and supposedly the first Pope, but now Popes must be single. Why do some Christians say the fact of Jesus choosing only males indicates that male leadership is the norm in the church, but do not follow His example of a single life when there is no explanation of either in the gospel accounts? God clearly used women in a wide range of positions of leadership and authority. Paul acknowledged that Timothy had been taught by his mother and his grandmother; many believers have benefited tremendously from the teaching of women. The best Bible teacher I have ever sat under was a woman. Deborah in the book of Judges was a leading woman, a judge, and a person of influence over men. Do we make doctrine from that? It is very easy, depending on your preconceived position

---

[12] Isaiah 25:1, 4

9

on the issue of gender relationships, to point either to how God has used women in positions of leadership and authority or to the fact that Jesus only chose males as his disciples, in order to use either of these true Biblical narratives to determine your theology. However, both texts are narrative, and the way we know what to do with them is to see what the Bible *teaches* on the subject, and not make doctrine out of what it *reports*.

The principle that I follow is to appeal to the didactic portions of Scripture and then interpret the narrative by the didactic. Then we can decide whether the narrative is normative or not, whether it is an example meant to be followed or not.

I recently sat in on a Sunday school class that was devoted to supporting women in leadership in our church. One of the sessions did a survey of the Old Testament and showed how women had functioned in various leadership roles in the Old Testament. That was done early in the class. But the interpretive question that went unasked, as well as unanswered, was how we were to know if this was an example to be followed or not. How, for instance, do we deal with Abigail, who clearly was a wise and intelligent woman and clearly out-maneuvered her lazy and incompetent husband in dealing with David and prevented David from sin?[13] She clearly had a lot more between her ears than her husband Nabal and did not ask or seek his permission for her bargaining with David. She was held up as an example in that by the teachers of the class. But it is also true that, when David sought Abigail to be his wife after Nabal apparently died of a heart attack, she bowed down to David and described herself as David's "handmaid" and "servant." Should we choose part of this narrative as positive and part as negative? Part to be followed and part not to be followed? What is our theological system to know the difference? But often that theological system is assumed, or not spoken, and so it is difficult to understand how we pick and choose.

---

[13] 1 Samuel 25:1–42

We will look at length at the first three chapters of Genesis, even though that passage is a narrative passage. However, it is referred to in the didactic portions of the New Testament. It is also a narrative that happened before the Fall, so contamination by sin had not happened. We will also look at 1 Corinthians 11, Galatians 3:28, 1 Timothy 2:1–15, 1 Peter 3:1–7, Ephesians 5:21–33, and Romans 16, and several other shorter texts. Romans 16 is a narrative passage, but it can be helpful to see how the principles taught in the didactic sections are carried out in the life and practice of the Apostle Paul.

Genesis 1 and 2 raise some unique issues in interpretation, because sin had not yet infected the world. So, even though these are narrative passages, we do not have to wonder if the events narrated are good or bad, like David's multiple wives and adultery. Those events were wrong. There is no wrong in Genesis 1 and 2. But that does not necessarily make the process of understanding and applying the events narrated in those chapters simple in our extremely different world. Adam and Eve walked around naked. Should we? Adam was a farmer. He was put in the garden to till it and keep it. Does that mean farming is the only Biblical vocation today? Apparently only Adam "worked." Does that mean today wives should not work outside the home?

As we attempt to understand and apply the narrative texts of Genesis 1 and 2, we should hesitate to go beyond how Scripture itself applies those texts. If Scripture does not make an application from these two chapters, we should be hesitant to do so.

5. In dealing with seemingly contradictory texts regarding the gender issue, it seems necessary to employ, either consciously or unconsciously, a technique to weight the texts in importance and so to interpret contradictory texts one in the light of the other. There are a number of ways this is done. However, the end result often boils down to picking and choosing texts to emphasize or ignore.

One technique is the "window-text" hermeneutic. What I mean is that one text is chosen as an overriding, summary text, and other, seemingly contradictory texts are seen or understood "through" the window text. Or sometimes they are just ignored. F. F. Bruce explains this in commenting on Galatians 3:28: "Paul states the basic principle here; if restrictions on it are found elsewhere in the Pauline corpus, as in 1 Corinthians 14:34ff, or in 1 Timothy 2:11ff, they are to be understood in relation to Galatians 3:28 and not vice versa"[14] David Scholer puts it this way in his article "Hermeneutical Gerrymandering," in which he responds to James Hurley's book Man and Woman in Biblical Perspective: "In the construction of a Biblical theology based on the New Testament, one important issue concerns the balance between various texts. Hurley's position is strongly influenced by the choice he makes concerning which text will provide the 'window' through which other texts must be interpreted. Hurley clearly makes 1 Timothy 2:8–15 *the* determinative text by which all other texts—including the gospels, Galatians 3:28, Philippians 4:2–3, Romans 16:1–16, 1 Corinthians 11:5—are ultimately evaluated. Any interpretation which correlates different New Testament passages will tend to have 'control' or 'perspective' texts. What must be made clear, however, is that the texts themselves do not tell us which passages should exercise control; we, the interpreter, make those decisions."[15] Now, it is important to see that different men who are much wiser than I am have arrived at opposite conclusions as to which text is the control text and so are at opposite ends of the issue. But they might very well be at opposite ends in their conclusion because they *started* at opposite ends, and their choice of a "window" or "control" text was determined by their beginning prejudice. Dr. Scholer is honest enough to acknowledge this issue in the quote above: "We, the interpreter, make those decisions." It is certainly possible that one could choose a "window" text that conveniently supports one's prejudice, and then since seemingly contradictory

---

[14] The Epistle to the Galatians, F.F. Bruce, Eerdmans, Grand Rapids, MI 49503, c. 1982 p. 190

[15] Hermeneutical Gerrymandering, David Scholer, Theological Students Fellowship Bulletin, May/June, 1983. p.12

texts do not support your "window" text, they are theologically discarded and we end up with a sophisticated-sounding method of picking and choosing what we will believe in the Bible.

A slightly different version of the same technique is to label some passages "clear" and others as "obscure." So Robert Johnson labels the text in 1 Timothy 2 as "the difficult text" that "needs to be read in the light of... Galatians 3:28."[16] Who determines which text is "obscure" or "difficult"? They both seem "clear" but seem also to contradict each other. Could it not be possible that our prejudice determines which text is "obscure" or "clear"? Maybe a text is "obscure" because it offends my prejudice. Or it may have been very clear to the original hearers but not to us in our modern culture. And so our cultural distance or personal prejudice leads us to ignore some texts.

Another example comes from Dr. David Scholer. He says that, because of "the exegetical and hermeneutical issues relevant to the so-called headship debate within evangelical circles, I am fully convinced that the Bible does not institute, undergird, or teach male headship...."[17] It is certainly true, as he points out in that article, that nearly all church fathers held terribly low and unBiblical views of women, that the headship of the male has created an enormous amount of abuse, both emotional and physical, of women by men, and that even today some interpret male headship wrongly and, I might add, loudly, to imply male superiority. But in spite of the misunderstandings of the concept, the fact is the Bible consistently calls the male the head, and there is not one example of the other way around. There really are no exegetical difficulties there, even though the definition of "head" is still to be determined. The Bible *always* uses the term "head" in the context of gender as referring to

---

[16] Robert K. Johnston, "Biblical Authority and Interpretation: the Test Case of Woman's Role in the Church and Home Updated" in <u>Women, Authority, and the Bible</u>, edited by Alvera Michlelsen. Downers Grove, IL: InterVarsity Press, 1986, p 31.

[17] From an article entitled "Dealing With Abuse," in the conclusion. Found on the website called God's Word to Women. See godswordtowomen.org/scholer.htm

the male, so it is hard for me to see how he can say the Bible does not say that.

That technique also may limit the application of God's word in any situation to my ability to understand. There is an awful lot that I do not understand. That was true in many of my classes in college! I don't need to be convinced that my mind does not have the horsepower to understand everything easily. The fact that a concept seems "difficult" to me says little about its legitimacy. It says a lot about *me*. It seems possibly a little bit arrogant to describe a text as "difficult" and then place it on the hermeneutical back burner.

Another example of the same technique is to label certain passages as "general principle" and others as "limited application." So, again, certain texts are eliminated or delegated to a minor role in understanding this issue. What criteria are used to minimize application of certain texts over other texts?

Another very similar version of this approach to Scripture is to refer to the "big picture" or "overriding themes" of the Bible and then disregard the texts that seem to contradict those overriding themes. Here are a couple of examples.

"I began to see that the passages that were barriers to my moving to a fully egalitarian position needed to be understood in terms of the big picture. It is the big picture that establishes the context for understanding the difficult passages. If one has the big picture right, it is acceptable to admit that for some passages there are several possible interpretations. It is alright to say, 'I don't know, but here are some possibilities.'"[18]

"I was shocked to realize that we as Christians had built an elaborate system of belief and practice on only a few difficult passages. These passages have loomed so large that we have allowed them to color everything else we read. We had lifted these passages out of their own context, out of the context of the broader themes

---

[18] Alan F. Johnson, editor, How I Changed My Mind about Women in Leadership, Zondervan, Grand Rapids, MI, c. 2010, p. 99, in an article by Stanley F. Gundry.

of Scripture, and elevated them to the point that they become more important than the overall message of Scripture on this topic."[19]

"But I believed that the proper interpretation of the Scriptures leads to equality even though I was not clear how to interpret a few isolated texts…. What became clearer to me, however, was that the overarching Biblical story led clearly to full inclusion of women in every aspect of church life and mutual submission in marriage…. There are two texts (1 Cor. 14:34–35 and 1 Tim. 2:11–12) that at first sight seem to suggest otherwise. To this day, I do not feel certain that I fully understand them. But since the broad sweep of revelation history moves from equality at creation through terrible brokenness in male-female relationships because of the fall to a radical departure in Jesus and the early church from typical first-century male prejudice against women, I conclude that these two texts probably refer to some local situation rather than a universal norm."[20]

"The number of 'mays' and 'possibles' in my own arguments indicates that I myself am not settled on every detail of cultural background I have argued, although I am convinced that the case as a whole is sound. But regardless of less crucial details, I trust that several basic themes have been argued persuasively."[21]

Now I want respectfully to disagree with the hermeneutic of the above four quotations. Three of them come from one of the books written from a strongly egalitarian perspective, which I found most compelling. The stories they tell of prejudice toward women and oppression of women are sobering and shameful. The modern church needs to confess and repent of some of the unBiblical practices in our past that indicate a painfully low view of women. I

---

[19] Alan F. Johnson, editor, How I Changed My Mind About Women in Leadership, in an article by Ruth Haley Barton, p. 45.

[20] Ron Sider, in the article titled "From Soft Patriarchy to Mutual Submission" in the book How I Changed My Mind About Women in Leadership, pp. 229-230.

[21] Craig Keener, Paul, Women, & Wives, Hendrickson Publishers, Inc. Peabody, MA, c. 1992, p. 225.

highly recommend the book for learning about the abuses, past and unfortunately very present, which women have suffered.

However, the point is a hermeneutical one. It seems to me to be a mistaken interpretive technique to determine the "broader themes of Scripture" or the "big picture" by selectively eliminating certain passages because they don't fit the "broader picture." How can you determine the big picture when you leave out some of the pieces? Will that not produce a skewed "big picture"?

Clearly, choosing a window text, or general principle text, or "clear" text versus an "obscure" text is not easy and is fraught with the possibility of being influenced by prejudice, bias, or plain self-interest. Because of the seemingly contradictory nature of the Biblical teaching on this subject, we need some tool for interpreting these texts without a sophisticated-sounding hermeneutic of choosing what you like and ignoring what you don't like. I will explain my choice farther on in the book, but for now, it is great cause for humility and self-examination to note that many wise, well-educated people have chosen opposite "window" texts. How do we explain that? And how do we avoid making the wrong choice, since obviously some of them must have?

6. It is common to hear people refer to the observation (a true observation, I think) that many, if not all, of the New Testament letters were *ad hoc* letters. By that it is meant they were written to very specific situations and so have quite limited application. The words *ad hoc* mean "to this," and so if we are not dealing with the "this" to which the letter is written, modern or universal application is questionable at best. Usually, for some reason, it is the texts that teach some form of hierarchy that are designated *ad hoc* letters. So the First Letter to the Corinthians and 1 Timothy and Ephesians are *ad hoc* letters. But Galatians does not seem to be considered an *ad hoc* letter, even though it also is written to a very specific situation. So Galatians 3:28, which says that in Christ there is neither male nor female, becomes the overriding principle, because, for some reason, it

16

is not considered an *ad hoc* letter. But the designation of 1 Timothy rather than Galatians as an *ad hoc* letter is up the interpreter. The fact is they are both *ad hoc* letters. We should be aware of arbitrarily designating *some* letters of the New Testament as *ad hoc* letters and then writing off their teaching as limited to that occasion.

7. A number of authors have introduced a dichotomy between creation and redemption. In Richard Longenecker's article, "Authority, Hierarchy & Leadership Patterns in the Bible," in <u>Women, Authority, and the Bible</u>, edited by Alvera Mickelsen, we find this: "A redemptive approach clarifies the fullness of the redemptive note sounded in the New Testament. Redemptive categories of thought are crucial to a Christian understanding of the status of women. Everything in the Bible has to do with either creation or redemption or both…. Early Christians generally, and Paul in particular, seemed to work from two categories of thought when facing questions related to the roles of the sexes: 1) that which emphasizes what God has done by creation, wherein hierarchical order, subordination and submission are generally stressed,[22] and 2) that which emphasizes what God has done redemptively, wherein freedom, mutuality and equality take prominence. By holding firm to what God has done by creation, they gave priority to what God has done redemptively in Christ Jesus. In 1 Corinthians 11:3, Paul speaks of a hierarchical order in creation and within the Godhead ('the head of the woman is man, and the head of Christ is God') but in 1 Corinthians 11:11 he tempers the subordination features of his creation category by a mutuality emphasis that springs

---

[22] Notice that an egalitarian author acknowledges that the Bible does imply (he uses the word "stressed") some sort of hierarchical order in creation; that is, in Genesis 1 and 2, in addition to freedom, mutuality, and equality. I think this is significant, and I don't want it to be missed. To be fair, not all egalitarians agree. Note also, farther on in the quote, that he acknowledges a hierarchical order in the Godhead. Jeanette Scholer says, "Salvation must be understood as both a work of grace for individuals and a work of grace in the process of restoring the *mutuality of creation* in human relationships"—this from her article entitled "Turning Dreams into Reality," in the same book, page 302. Notice that she assumes only mutuality in the Creation account, even though Richard Longenecker sees hierarchy in the Creation account. Both are egalitarians.

from his redemptive category ('in the Lord, however, woman is not independent of man, nor is man independent of woman')....
Therefore, we may take it that hierarchical order is built into creation by God and must be respected, but a hierarchical ordering of life is not always necessary and status in a functional hierarchy is not necessarily fixed, particularly when redemptive concerns overshadow what is true because of creation. In the Christian life, both creation categories and redemption categories must be taken into account, *though with priority given to the latter*" (italics mine).[23]

That dichotomy, to me, seems artificial. How does one choose one category in preference to the other? How is the hierarchical order to be "respected"? And why? If a hierarchical ordering of life is "not always necessary," how do we know when it is and when it isn't? The concept seems to raise more problems than it solves. Note also that he cannot see both hierarchy and mutuality as equally acceptable. It is one or the other. That supposed incompatibility is probably the central issue of this book and the central issue that needs to be resolved. As we'll see when we look at the texts themselves, the creation account contains *both* narratives of a completely egalitarian gender relationship *and* hints at a hierarchical relationship of complete equals. Importantly, this was before the fall of man and before the presence of sin. Significantly, the New Testament texts *also* contain both instruction on mutuality/egalitarianism and hierarchy/submission.

Here is another example from Grenz and Kjesbo's book, <u>Women in the Church</u>. "The argument [referring to the complementarian position] simply reverts to the question of the relationship of the sexes, which complementarians find embedded in the creation order. This appeal, however, is Biblically and theologically suspect. Even if God had built this principle in creation from the beginning (which he did not), it would not necessarily require that the church continue to practice male leadership and female subordination. Christ did not

---

[23] <u>Women, Authority, and the Bible,</u> Inter Varsity Press, copyright 1986, p. 82.

establish the church merely to be the mirror of the original creation but to be the eschatological new community, living in accordance with the principles of God's new creation and thereby reflecting the character of the triune God."[24]

This supposed dichotomy seems to invite a couple of questions: 1) What needs to be redeemed from the Creation? Was it not perfect? Was it not "good"? The Creator said it was. What is the theological system for preferring the eschatological community rather than the system embedded in the Creation? If there is subordination and hierarchy before the fall, before the presence of sin, what needs to be redeemed from that? Of course, as a result of the fall, there are fallen aspects of the Creation that need to be redeemed. To discern what those are is part of the purpose of this book. But if hierarchy and mutuality both existed before the fall, it would seem, then, that eliminating hierarchy is not what is necessary but instead correction of those aspects that were damaged as a result of the fall. We just need to try to get it right in this fallen world. Is there any other theological area where we talk of a creation hermeneutic and a redemption hermeneutic and then choose one over the other? If not, that whole hermeneutical dichotomy seems artificial. 2) How does one know what is a creation principle and what is a redemption principle, since both mutuality and hierarchy (although that point remains to be proven) are found in the Genesis texts *before the fall?* 3) By what criterion is it decided to give priority to the "redemption" category? Could it be that the choice was made because of bias toward the egalitarian position supposedly embedded in the redemption hermeneutic rather than specific evidence in Scripture? That is not

[24] Stanley Grenz and Denise Muir Kjesbo, <u>Women in the Church, A Biblical Theology of Women in Ministry</u>. Inter-Varsity Press, Downers Grove, Il, c. 1995, p. 192. Notice that they say God did not build the complementarian position into creation, but other egalitarian authors acknowledge something of a hierarchy in Genesis 1 and 2. See note 14 above. Also note that they assume the eschatological new community is to live with the principles of God's new creation, which, they assume, are different from God's perfect creation in Genesis 1 and 2. They do not say *what* is different, other than this particular issue. They also assume that the principles of God's new creation will reflect the character of the triune God, which they also assume to be egalitarian.

an accusation I can make, since I do not know motives. I don't know why the author would pick the redemption category over the creation category, but if one is given priority, then there must be some reason for that choice.

I do not accept this hermeneutic, because a) it seems to create a dichotomy where none exists in Scripture and b) it seems prejudicial in choosing one (redemption) over the other (creation). God is the author of both.

8. There must be a distinction between the authority of biblical teaching and the authority of the application of Biblical teaching. The purpose of hermeneutics, the science of understanding what is written, is to understand correctly what the author meant. When we understand that, because it is God's word and is "profitable for teaching, rebuke, correction, and for training in righteousness,"[25] then we need to take the step of application to our life and culture. The author's meaning carries the weight of God's authority. The application does not carry the weight of God's authority, as that may vary from person to person and culture to culture. "The interpreter should take care to distinguish between the author's intention and possible implications."[26] So we need to distinguish between a principle that is taught in Scripture and how it is applied to a particular culture.

9. Some have followed what I call, for want of a better description, a "trajectory hermeneutic" or a developmental hermeneutic or a "redemptive movement hermeneutic." The difference between this and the creation/redemption hermeneutic is not huge, and they may be in reality very close with only minor differences. Here is one example from Richard Longenecker: "In so doing, he set a pattern and marked out a path for Christian thought and action

---

[25] 2 Timothy 3:16
[26] Andreas Kostenberger, "Gender Passages in the NT: Hermeneutical Fallacies Critiqued," *Westminster Theological Journal*, 56:2 (Fall 1994), pp. 259–283.

after him to follow. And first-century Christians seem, generally, to have been prepared to move forward on that path."[27] In <u>Slaves, Women, & Homosexuals</u> by William Webb, we find: "As one might suspect from its name, a key component of a redemptive-movement hermeneutic is the idea of movement. The Christian seeking to apply Scripture today should examine the movement between the Biblical text and its surrounding social context. Once that movement has been discovered, there needs to be an assessment of whether the movement is preliminary or absolute. If it is preliminary and further movement in the direction set by the text would produce a more fully realized ethic, then that is the course of action one must pursue. The interpreter extrapolates the Biblical movement toward a more just, more equitable and more loving form. If a better ethic than the one expressed in the isolated texts is possible, and the Biblical and canonical spirit is headed that direction, then that is where one ultimately wants to end up."[28]

What I find troubling about that explanation is how we determine a "more just, more equitable and more loving form" which, apparently, is beyond Scripture. How do we define what a "more realized ethic" looks like? Could we go too far? I think it is a mistake to assume it is intuitively obvious that we all know what is a "more just, more equitable and more loving form" is. So, really, we have to return to Scripture to define that. Ironically, that hermeneutic seems to turn around and bite itself in the foot because it encourages us to move beyond Scripture to a more realized ethic but requires us to return to the Scripture we just moved beyond to define that ethic.

In addition to that problem, one has to admit the possibility, if not the probability, of determining the "more realized ethic" according to what is currently in vogue. So, in regards to the current gender discussion, Dr. Webb defines the "more realized ethic" as an

---

[27] Richard Longenecker, <u>New Testament Social Ethics for Today</u>, Eerdmans, Grand Rapids, MI. c 1984,p,88

[28] William Webb, <u>Slaves, Women, & Homosexuals</u>, InterVarsity Press, c. 2001, p. 36.

"ultra-soft patriarchy," or the current egalitarian position. How did he determine that? If one were using his principles during the early part of the 20th century in America, I suspect "ultra-soft patriarchy" or egalitarianism is *not* where one would end up, because neither of those were culturally in vogue. So the other irony of that hermeneutic is that in an effort to apply Scripture legitimately to a particular culture, it is very easy unconsciously to let culture determine your "more realized ethic" and thus rob God's word of its authority and application to whatever culture you are in. The purpose of the book is to enable us to apply God's word to our current culture, but we may well end up with a very culturally conditioned and not particularly Biblical application.

One more example comes from the book entitled Man as Male and Female by Dr. Paul K. Jewett: "In its implementation, the New Testament church reflects to a considerable extent, the prevailing attitudes and practices of the times. Because of this, we should look to the passages which point *beyond* these first century attitudes toward women to the ideal of the new humanity in Christ. Only thus can we harness the power of the gospel to make all history, not just first-century history, salvation history."[29] But how does one determine the "ideal of the new humanity in Christ" except by picking and choosing particular passages according to your bias, which may well be influenced by your culture?

Here is an example of how the "extrapolation" hermeneutic or "developmental" hermeneutic might work. The Old Testament shows an extremely low view of women. (Sometimes included in that is the second creation account where there seems to be some sort of vague orientation to the man—the woman is called the helper and so on.) Jesus' view of women was different: He spoke to them, taught them, allowed them to touch him, and in general treated them as equals. Paul's view, summarized in Galatians 3:28—"In Christ there is neither Jew nor Greek, slave nor free, male nor female"—is the

---

[29] Paul Jewett, Man as Male and Female, William Eerdmans Publishing Company, Grand Rapids, MI, copyright 1975, p. 148.

ultimate ethic. So we extrapolate from the Old Testament, to Jesus, to Paul, and extend the line to today and end up with an egalitarian position. So we, as modern Christians, have extrapolated to complete egalitarianism and mutuality.

There are problems with that hermeneutic. One is that the line is not that clear. The Galatians 3:28 text so often appealed to by egalitarians was one of the earliest Pauline texts. The two texts most often appealed to by complementarians, 1 Corinthians 11 and 1 Timothy 2, are later and, in fact, the 1 Timothy 2 passage was one of Paul's last writings on the subject. Surely he did not turn around and go backwards? To say the Old Testament had a uniformly negative view of women is not really true. Deborah was a judge in the Old Testament who clearly was in a position of leadership. As we will see, Abigail was a very intelligent woman and outsmarted her husband. So what we really have is not a clear ascending line of women being increasingly treated in a positive view as history "progresses" and our calling is to extend that to egalitarianism. What we see instead is a—let's be honest—confusing narrative of women sometimes represented as in no way subordinate and at other times called to subordination in certain limited instances. That is what we have to deal with, rather than a nice ascending history of redemption from the fall, when women were in subjection to men, to the present when, supposedly, there is mutuality. Or should be.

Having said that, everybody acknowledges that the Bible was written within the culture of the Middle East, and we all follow the practice of trying to live out the transcultural principles revealed in the Scriptures in our modern world. We do not greet everybody with a kiss. Most Bible-believing churches do not require women to wear veils—nor, I think, should they. However, it is one thing to try to discern a transcultural principle in a text and to figure out how to apply that in our very different world. It is another thing to try discern a direction Scripture might be pointing to and actually extrapolate beyond Scripture to some assumed "Biblical" position that the Bible may not actually teach. I do not accept the latter.

However, there is certainly *some* sense in which the Bible acknowledges some progressive revelation or developmental hermeneutic. Jesus himself acknowledged that certain aspects of the ceremonial law had passed away. Peter was commanded by God to go and eat unclean animals in the strange dream in Acts 11, which Peter interpreted as going to eat with Gentiles and to share the gospel of Jesus with them. That was an incredibly difficult concept for a Jew, even a Jew who believed in Jesus, to swallow (pardon the pun). So, again, humility is required to understand properly what exactly the words are saying.

10. Of course, we always interpret Scripture by Scripture. The assumption is that every text has the same Author. So all texts, *properly interpreted*, are equally true. The Bible was written over a 1,500-year time span, at least, and to many very different cultures and situations. Many of the New Testament letters, as stated above, were "ad hoc," meaning written to a specific situation. Just because they were written to a specific situation does not mean they have no applicability today. The challenge is to figure how to apply a principle in our culture, but that application may look very different from the application in Biblical culture.

11. Word studies are very helpful but can be limited. Exhaustive research into how a word was used in the secular culture of the time certainly helps us understand the meaning of the word. But the Biblical writers did not hesitate to take a word and use it with a very specific Kingdom of God meaning. In fact, if one thinks about it, how could *any* concept about the Kingdom be communicated except by using secular words, but with somewhat different (maybe radically different) meanings in the Kingdom of God context? For instance, the word *soteria* from which we get the term soteriology, the study of what happened when Jesus died on the cross, was really a word which meant wholeness or full health. "In the first century the word [*soteria*] had a much wider and more general meaning of rescue,

deliverance, and recovery, as well as referring to Christians being delivered from the penalty, power and presence of sin. A typical 'get well card' on first century papyrus would read, 'I have heard that you are ill and am praying for your salvation....' The word is used in Acts 27, describing a purely physical rescue from shipwreck.[30] In the first chapter to the Philippians, Paul prays that their 'prayer and the supply of the Spirit' will work out for his 'salvation' (verse 19, AV). He does not mean, of course, that he is not yet converted. He is, however, in prison and under possible sentence of execution, and he believes that through their prayers and God's enabling he will be delivered from his present situation."[31] It is the same verb used by Paul in Romans 10:9, which says, "if you confess with your lips that Jesus is Lord and believe in your heart God raised him from the dead, you will be *saved.*" He uses the noun form in Romans 1:16: "For I am not ashamed of the gospel: it is the power of God for *salvation....*" So, notice that the apostle Paul took a completely secular word and added a Kingdom of God meaning to it, and thus it became "salvation"—that is what happens to us because Jesus died a substitutionary death on the cross, the results of which will be completed in heaven. That is really Full Health and Completeness! He also uses the same word to mean rescue from a shipwreck. The secular definition does not contain the spiritual sense *at all*, and so we *must* let the Biblical context help define the word for us. We, as readers, need to be careful to distinguish between the secular meaning and the Kingdom of God meaning when we read. And the Bible contains both. To appeal only to the secular use of the word would severely limit our understanding of the Bible doctrine using that word.

So in Philippians 2:12, when Paul commands the Philippian church to "work out [their] salvation with fear and trembling," the context would indicate he is not talking about adding to what

---

[30] Acts 27:31, "Unless these men stay in the ship, you cannot be saved."
[31] Michael Griffiths, God's Forgetful Pilgrims, Wm Eerdmans, Grand Rapids, MI, 1975, pp. 46–47.

happened on the cross through some sort of works salvation. Instead, he was talking about working on a particular problem at that church. Paul desired that the church would grow to full health ("salvation") from the sickness that was troubling that fellowship, which the context indicates was selfish quarreling. That is indicated by the opening phrase, "Do nothing from selfish ambition [why would he say that unless they *were* doing things from selfish ambition?].... Complete my joy by being of one mind, one spirit, etc."[32] Then he gives the astounding example of Jesus who modeled the exact opposite of selfish ambition in coming to earth as a human, an obedient human, obedient even unto death. So, that church needed to come to full health (*soteria*) from their problem of quarreling and lack of unity. It is also helpful to recognize that the command to work out their salvation was a *plural* command, aimed at the whole church, not a singular command aimed at one person.

Now, that is all an example of how, in addition to the secular meaning, we need to let the Biblical context define a word, as Paul often added Kingdom of God meanings to secular words. So, doing an exhaustive study on what a word meant in first century Biblical culture may be helpful but will not conclusively determine what a word meant to the Biblical author.

The word studies on *kephale* (head) and *authenteo* (exercising authority) and helpmate in Genesis 2 are helpful but not final. Especially in defining the word *kephale*, we need to let the Biblical author use it in a different way than contemporary secular authors did, which I believe he does. So we need to define the word the way the Bible does, which may be, and I believe is, different from the secular definition.

12. I do believe that Scriptures, properly interpreted, are true even across cultural and historical lines. The important phrase in that sentence is "properly interpreted." There seems to be a view today

---

[32] Philippians 2:1 and following.

26

that Scripture may be interpreted as having different meanings in different contexts and the reader's interpretation is necessarily limited by his context. "One can no longer think of the Bible as a set of timeless, transcultural rulings or as propositions that speak in every age with one voice. The Bible can often be read in more than one way, even on important matters. This comment is incontrovertable because it is undeniable. History gives innumerable examples of learned and devout theologians who have differed from others in their interpretations of the Bible on almost every doctrine or ethical question.[33]

Now I readily admit (I hope I have made this clear) that the Scriptures may be misunderstood. They may be interpreted *wrongly*. There will always be the challenge of separating culture from transcultural truth, whether that be in interpretation or in application. But if you think about it, that means by necessity that there is a transcultural truth present that may be misinterpreted. Otherwise, one could never misinterpret. One cannot misinterpret if there is no correct interpretation to be misinterpreted. There are certainly different levels of meaning. There may be different levels of fulfillment, particularly of prophecies. There will be different applications in different cultures. Scripture is always written in the context of a particular culture, which complicates our ability to understand and, especially, to apply what is taught appropriately. The reason there are rules of hermeneutics is to help us understand *rightly*. I assume that there really is some transcultural truth present to understand and apply. Otherwise, why do the homework to figure out the original meanings of words, to figure out the grammar of original languages and figures of speech?

I am very comfortable in saying the church has historically misinterpreted what the Scriptures say about slavery, the structure of the solar system, the equality of the feminine gender, and its pre-Reformation doctrine of how salvation was obtained. But the reason

---

[33] Kevin Giles, <u>The Trinity & Subordinationism</u>, InterVarsity Press, Downers Grove, IL, 60515, copyright 2002, pp. 8, 9, 11.

I can say that is because there must be an underlying Truth present that has been interpreted wrongly. One cannot misinterpret unless there is a correct interpretation by which to judge.

13. In general, we will be going through the Scriptures in a linear manner, the way they were written. We will not be starting with the New Testament and interpreting the Old Testament in light of the New, but interpreting the New Testament in light of the Old. That is the way it was written.

14. Structure is a very important hermeneutical tool. Many have probably heard the phrase, "If you see a therefore, see what it is there for." That is an observation of structure in a passage. It indicates a conclusion based on some sort of premise. If you observe the word "however" or "on the other hand," that indicates that the concept taught is contrasted to what went before. Suppose one thought is clear, but the preceding thought is not clear. The fact that the author used a term like "however" indicates that the author believed the two thoughts connected by that term were opposites, and so that helps us understand the unclear thought. And it is this principle, the principle of interpreting structure, that makes it so important to read and interpret the Bible in whole books, the way they were written, instead of topically, in verses sorted by topic, which misses this very important tool of interpretation. I have heard too many sermons where the preacher decided on what he wanted to say and then picked Bible verses to support his agenda. I have always been a fan of, and as I grow older see the necessity of, expositional preaching. By that I mean preaching through at least whole passages and, preferably, whole books. That practice keeps the preacher honest— not letting him develop unBiblically neat doctrines and teachings. It is a mistake, I think, to approach the Bible as one might a bed of flowers, looking for pretty specimens or verses, which are then picked out of the bed, out of context, because you like them.

15. As I said in the introduction to this chapter, part of the process of communication is agreement on definitions for words. It is the job of the communicator to use words that the hearers (or readers) will understand. I remember once watching one of the pharmacists on my staff get into a heated argument with a patient because of the directions she had put on the vial: "Take one capsule daily for gerd." That's what the physician had written on the prescription and so those directions were correct. But the patient did not understand what *gerd* was and was quite irritated. The pharmacist countered with the statement that "gerd" was a perfectly acceptable medical term and he should not be irritated. But the point was that "gerd" did not communicate to the patient, and communication is the purpose of the directions on the prescription vial.[34]

So I need to define the way I will be using the terms "complementarian" and "egalitarian." I do not intend to imply my definition is the only correct definition. There really is no sense in arguing about what is the "correct" definition any more than arguing about the use of the term "gerd" to a patient who had no idea what the term meant. The point is to communicate, and that means we have to agree on the definitions we use. I realize there is discussion, even argument, about who "owns" the words "egalitarian" and "complementarian," and there are those who call themselves by both words. I want to define those words, not because my definition is necessarily right, but only so the reader will understand what I am saying. We need to use the same definition for communication to happen.

I use the term complementarian to describe one who believes the gender roles are not interchangeable and that there are at least some roles in the family and church that are unique to women and some that are unique to men. However, nearly all complementarians believe men and women are equal, theoretically, at least. I believe that very strongly. The terms "complementarian" and "egalitarian"

---

[34] It stands for gastroesophageal reflux disease—when you burp up acid into your esophagus. That should have been clearly explained by the pharmacist instead of being argued about.

do not describe monolithic groups, and so there is a fair amount of variation in definitions and applications.

I use the term egalitarian to describe one who believes all roles are open to women, and particularly, one gender does not exclusively fill a position of authority over the other. I do not intend to imply that egalitarians think the genders are interchangeable. I do not use the term egalitarian and feminist as synonymous terms. I can see how a person could be an egalitarian complementarian, and some have described themselves that way—one who believes the genders are complementary but there are no excluded roles in the church and family. Both groups are not monolithic groups, with everybody believing the same. Beware of assuming what a person believes just because he labels himself as a "complementarian" or "egalitarian."

I also want to be clear about the terms "hierarchy" and "patriarchy," because I will use the word "hierarchy" frequently. One person defined it this way: "This view holds that women are by God's design inherently disqualified from leading and teaching men. It goes against the creation order itself."[35] That is definitely *not* the definition I use. I use the term hierarchy to describe relationships between two or more individuals, where one has headship, properly defined, which is more than just mere authority, over the other. However, the other's value and significance as a person are *not* determined by where he or she falls in the hierarchy. It is not about competence or qualifications. It does not involve one serving another out of personal inferiority. It is very important to understand that concept. Patriarchy is a social system or governmental system in which men hold power and influence and women are largely excluded. Sometimes included in that is the view that men are the wise ones and women inferior in wisdom. I in no way consider the complementary position and patriarchy as synonymous.

---

[35] Editor: Alan F. Johnson, How I Changed My Mind About Women in Leadership, Zondervan, Grand Rapids, MI, copyright 2010, from an article by Stanley N. Gundry, p. 99.

16. This next-to-last principle is not so much a hermeneutical principle as a warning. I intentionally use the word humility in a number of instances in this book, particularly when we approach a controversial passage to interpret. By "controversial" I mean there is disagreement over how to interpret it. I am now old enough to remember when I was younger. I can now see how uneducated I was. I have regularly prayed that God would remove the memory from some people's minds of who I was and how I acted because I'm sure I brought dishonor to God. I say that because we are not always honest about what motivates us and as a result, our reading and interpretation of the Bible may be skewed. I am beginning to see the incredible pressure our culture puts on us to go along with the crowd, to fit in, to not be different, to be "trendy." The Bible calls that "being conformed to this world."[36] "When opinions and convictions suddenly undergo dramatic alteration, although nothing new has been discovered and the only thing that has dramatically changed is the spirit of the age, it is difficult to avoid the conclusion that the spirit of the age has had an important role to play in the shift."[37] We must be aware of the lure of going along with the current trends in the world as we try to understand the Scriptures. And we must be honest with ourselves that we do not like being different from the world, being looked down upon or ridiculed by those around us. Only the dead fish go along with the current. That temptation, the pressure not to be different from the world, can cause us either to re-interpret Scripture so we can fit into the spirit

---

[36] Romans 12:1. "Do not be conformed to this world, but be transformed, by the renewal of your mind, that you may prove what is the will of God, what is good, acceptable and perfect." The picture is that of a silver mold: the silversmith pours liquid silver into the mold, straps it together, and lets it cool. After cooling, he takes off the mold and there is a piece of silver shaped exactly like the mold. That's what the world may well do to us: we become "molded" and end up being just like the world, though claiming to be believers.

[37] Harold O. J. Brown, "The New Testament against Itself: 1 Timothy 2:9–15 and the 'Breakthrough' of Galatians 3:28," in Women in the Church: A Fresh Analysis of I Timothy 2:9–15, Andreas Kostenberger and Thomas Schreiner, eds. Baker Books, Grand Rapids, MI, p. 199. I am quoting Kent Hughes, pastor at College Church in Wheaton, Illinois, from a sermon delivered on March 29, 1998. He is quoting the book in this footnote, but to be honest I could not find the direct quote anywhere.

of the age or to harden our supposedly Biblical position and thus feel spiritually superior to those who shift their position. Both are wrong responses to the pressure to conform.

17. Since we live after the Fall of Humanity, we are all dwellers in a fallen world. That is a worldview derived from Scripture. It is necessary to understand how the Bible views the world in which we live in order to understand what it teaches. We are, in a profound sense, Away from Home. We were created to live in Eden. But now we live outside Eden in a profoundly fallen world, and we are profoundly fallen ourselves; yet our roots are in Eden. So we live after the Fall and before Heaven. Consequently, there is an ever-present hunger and dis-ease with life here in the fallen world. Most of the time it is deeply buried under culturally acceptable avoidance mechanisms to soothe the pain of this fallen world and make us feel good and successful.

One time I went on a hike with my son's Cub Scout pack in the national forest surrounding our town. Our assignment was to find "natural objects" and report back to the pack what we had found. It was a glorious autumn day: the sky was a deep blue with no clouds, and the whole forest glowed bright yellow and orange. It was one of those ideal autumn days you see captured on a postcard. The scenery was absolutely beautiful. The boys loved it. They were excited about everything they saw, and there was a lot to see. As we crested a small hill, we were unexpectedly confronted with the sight of a rusting hulk of an old car sitting there, surrounded by beautifully colored foliage. There was no sign of a road, path, or anything to show how it had gotten there. There were mature trees all around and so it had sat there a long time. The scene was quite bizarre and unexpected. How could it have gotten there? The boys swarmed over it like ants on a piece of sugar candy. This was by far the neatest "natural" object they had seen all afternoon. What kind of car was it? Where were the doors? What had happened? How did it get here? Was there a dead body inside? Were there any bullet holes? Was there any money in it? I found it interesting, also. There was so much missing on the car that it was nearly unidentifiable. But I recognized the general shape from my childhood. I grew up in the '50s, and cars looked vastly different then. I thought I knew what it was and looked mostly in vain for some nameplate that would make the identification sure. Finally, I found it. Cadillac. It was a mid-'50s Cadillac. I once had a roommate with a 1954 forest green Cadillac, which he named Amelia. That particular model was awesome; it was about a block and half long, and I think the front bumper and grill alone weighed more than most of today's cars. It was truly a tank. As I stood there looking at this discarded carcass of a car, I knew what it used it be. I knew what it looked like when it was new. I had seen cars like this in real life. But these young scouts were clueless as to what this piece of junk was when it was young. They had never experienced the glory of a '54 Caddy. And there was no sense trying to explain it to them. Trying to extrapolate from this piece of junk back to what it was when it came off the assembly line was beyond them.

In the same way, everything we experience in this fallen world is at its best a rusting hulk. There is a Reality that once was, from which we have fallen, and about which we only have a foggy, largely unconscious recollection. Sometimes something will happen: we will see a good movie, or read a good story, or see a beautiful natural scene, or we will feel particularly lonely, and something awakens in us from somewhere down deep, a hunger which reminds us that we were made for more. There is something missing. So we are filled with longing. C. S. Lewis identified the reason for this longing: "If I find in myself a desire which no experience in this world can satisfy, the most probable explanation is that I was made for another world. If none of my earthly pleasures satisfy it, that does not prove that the universe is a fraud. Probably earthly pleasures were never meant to satisfy it, but only to arouse it, to suggest the real thing. If that is so, I must take care, on the one hand, never to despise, or be unthankful for these earthly blessings, and on the other, never to mistake them for the something else of which they are only a kind of copy, or echo, or mirage. I must keep alive in myself the desire for my true country, which I shall not find til after death."[38] So we are stuck between two worlds, two realities. Don't miss what he is saying: when he talks about the deep longing that nothing in this world can satisfy, he makes this conclusion: that earthly pleasures were never *meant* to satisfy it but instead to *arouse* it. So earthly pleasures may well make us *more hungry* for heaven where the Real Thing is. They should.

After graduation from college, I worked in full-time Christian work with one of the parachurch groups aimed at reaching out to the secular college campus. After doing that for ten years, I returned to pharmacy and went to work full-time selling drugs, mainly because I sensed a call of God to live and work with non-believers. I wanted to live in the world but not be of it. I was willing to be *odd*. I wanted to show what that looked like.

It was a big adjustment. I was shocked at a couple of things. First, how decadent the world was. Second, how many sad people there were. We are a culture of sugar-coated humans, walking around trying to put on a happy face, looking happy and successful on the outside but empty inside. I say that because I see the drugs people take. I don't say that out of any sense of superiority, but actually out of a sense of relief at seeing that the rest of the world, like me, struggles with sin, sadness, loneliness, and a profound sense of failure. One gets a sense of how far we have fallen from C. S. Lewis's observation on Revelation 19:9, where the apostle John is listening to a heavenly being and drops down to his knees to worship him. The being says to him, "You must not do that! I am a fellow servant with you." It happens again in Revelation 22:8. "And when I heard and saw them, I fell down to worship at the feet of the angel who

---

[38] C. S. Lewis, <u>Mere Christianity</u>, Macmillan Company, New York, 1972, p. 120. Used by permission. His idea of something in this world being an "echo" or "mirage" is what chapter 3, "Fingerprints and Appetizers" is all about.

showed them to me; but he said to me, 'You must not do that! I am a fellow servant with you and your brethren the prophets and with those who keep the words of this book. Worship God.'" Lewis took that (and I agree with him) to mean that the Apostle John was seeing a regular person, one of us, but fully redeemed with the "new body," completely rescued from his fallen status. And John, mistakenly, fell down to worship! If we were to see ourselves as we really were, before the Fall or after our final Redemption in heaven, our natural response would be worship. In fact, apparently heaven is so unimaginably wonderful that we will be mistakenly falling down on our knees all the time to worship things that are only normal, in their unfallen state, instead of worshiping the Creator, the One True God, who *alone* is worthy of our worship. That means even that scum of a person who lives next door, that misfit who committed horrible crimes against his children, the mean parent who has ruined her kids, that customer who yelled obscenities at me because his prescription took too long to fill—these are all beings we would be tempted to worship if we saw them in their non-fallen status. I have one patient who takes tranquilizers all day long just to get through the day, and the directions read: "Take one tablet three times daily and take two if you visit your mom." What a sad statement about her mom. But if I were to see either of them fully redeemed, I would be tempted to fall down and worship them. "It is a serious thing to live in a society of possible gods and goddesses, to remember that the dullest and most uninteresting person you talk to may one day be a creature which, if you saw it now, you would be strongly tempted to worship, or else a horror and a corruption such as you now meet, if at all, only in a nightmare. All day long we are in some degree helping each other to one or other of these destinations.... There are no *ordinary* people. You have never talked to a mere mortal.... It is immortals whom we joke with, work with, marry, snub, and exploit—immortal horrors or everlasting splendours."[39]

---

[39] C. S. Lewis, <u>The Weight of Glory,</u> Wm. Eerdman's publishing company, Grand Rapids, MI. c. 1949, p. 15. Used by permission.

But the people we live and work with seem ordinary and dull because of the fallen state in which we all live.

So we need help from the Outside. We need God's Word to teach us, to tell us how to live in the here and now, and to make us hungry for the world to come. Since we are stuck here, in a fallen world and we ourselves are fallen people, the Bible seems obtuse, hard to understand, and foreign. It *is* foreign. We do not come to the Scriptures as unbiased beings, with a clean neutral slate, ready to be taught. The value system of the Bible and the Kingdom of God is not the value system of this fallen world in which we live and move and have our being, nor of selfish souls like me. The heavenly road-pavers are going to use gold instead of blacktop—that's how different the values of the Kingdom of God are from this fallen world where we live. So we need to choose which value system we will trust and follow. That choice is an "either-or" choice, not "both-and." The two are not even similar. It is crucial to understand the difference if you are to understand what I am saying in this book. I think much of the difficulty for us as Bible-believing Christians in comprehending the gender issue is that we try to comprehend what the Bible says about gender from the perspective of the values of this fallen world. We have the wrong color eye-glasses on. This issue is enormous for me in understanding what the Bible teaches about gender. It is a blind spot in our discussion. The only author in my reading who acknowledges this is Michelle Lee-Barnewell. "The ways of the kingdom are often at odds with a natural mind-set, since the Christian faith itself is based on the cross as foolishness to the world but the wisdom of God (1 Cor. 1:18). There are compelling reasons to ask whether the New Testament ethic for women and men might follow a similar pattern—something that turns the world's order upside down and is understandable only in light of a kingdom theology."[40]

The Scriptures say hard things to both men and women, things that will go against our fallen nature and the values of this world.

---

[40] Michelle Lee-Barnewall, Neither Complementarian nor Egalitarian. Baker Academic, Grand Rapids, MI, c. 2016, p. 7.

That is to be expected. Just because it goes against what I want, or think I want, or is currently the trendy position to take, does not mean it is wrong. So we should not be surprised at both the difficulty of understanding the Scriptures and the uncomfortableness we feel when we find our lifestyle challenged by the true words of God. Mark Twain said, "It ain't those parts of the Bible that I can't understand that bother me; it is the parts that I do understand." As I grow older, and the Bible becomes gradually clearer, I understand more the tension between where we live and where we will ultimately live. The two places are very, very different. So this journey into understanding will, I suspect and hope, both comfort and challenge us, just as it should. If the words we are reading really are "from the other side," this should come as no surprise.

C. S. Lewis said, "I believe in Christianity as I believe the sun has risen, not only because I see it but because by it I see everything else."[41] I find that the Biblical worldview fits life in its deepest sense in a way nothing else does. It does not fit my culture, though it explains my culture. If we are believers in Jesus Christ, we are citizens of the Kingdom that is to come, and as we increasingly shift our weight to that citizenship, we will find ourselves increasingly out of step with the world we live in. Increasingly odd. That is the choice before us. And I don't know about you, but I find the very best that this world offers pales into insignificance compared to what the Bible tells us about the feast awaiting us in heaven. I hope this book whets our appetite for that feast. If so, that alone will make it successful.

---

[41] C. S. Lewis, in the article titled "Is Theology Poetry," in the collection titled The Weight of Glory, p. 140, HarperCollins publishers, New York, NY c. 1976. Used by permission.

2

FINGERPRINTS AND APPETIZERS

"If I find in myself a desire which no experience in this world can satisfy, the most probable explanation is that I was made for another world…. Probably earthly pleasures were never meant to satisfy it, but only to arouse it, to suggest the *real thing*. If that is so, I must take care… never to mistake them for the something else of which they are only a kind of <u>copy,</u> or <u>echo,</u> or <u>mirage.</u> I must keep alive in myself the desire for my true country which I shall not find till after death."[42]

"Yes," said Queen Lucy. "In our world, too, a Stable once had something inside it that was bigger than our whole world."[43]

It is a daunting task to use words to describe something you can see but have never experienced. In the opening chapters of Ezekiel, the author attempts to describe a vision he sees, and by necessity he must compare what he sees to items in this world that are *something like*

[42] C. S. Lewis, <u>Mere Christianity,</u> Macmillan Company, New York, 1972, p. 120, used by permission.

[43] C. S. Lewis, <u>The Last Battle</u>, c. 1956, Collier Books, New York, NY. pp. 140-141, used by permission.

what he sees in the vision. So the passage bristles with phrases such as "Their appearance was like..." or "Their construction being as it were a wheel within a wheel..." or "I heard the sound of their wings like the sound of many waters...."

In the opening of the book of Revelation, we come across similar language: "His head and hair were white as white wool..." and "His eyes were like a flame of fire..." and "His voice was like the sound of many waters...."

Jump ahead with me to Revelation 19:7–9. "Let us rejoice and exult and give him the glory, for the marriage of the Lamb has come, and his Bride has made herself ready; it was granted her to be clothed with fine linen, bright and pure—for the fine linen is the righteous deeds of the saints. And the angel said to me, 'Write this: Blessed are those who are invited to the marriage supper of the Lamb.' And he said to me, 'These are true words of God.'"

In those examples, note the way that the vision is compared to something in *this* world. Or, to put it another way, something in this world is *like* something in the vision, in the other world. Even the end of history is described as comparable to, of all things, a wedding ceremony. Don't let the words whiz by you so quickly that you miss the profound comparison the author presents. The linens, the marriage supper, the Bride imagery, the wedding imagery—these are all hints of a Reality profoundly more real than the temporary items referred to in this world. To think of the final end of history and the consummation of God's relationship with His people as a wedding ceremony, even a wedding night, is almost embarrassingly intimate.[44] Yet that is what God has revealed; so it is true.[45] Those

---

[44] It is also profoundly unique among the world's religions. That the God of the Universe should reveal the end of His created world as a wedding, when His people, who had been rebellious sinners but now will have been redeemed by the shed blood of God Himself, would be presented as a Bride to the God who redeemed them, is almost beyond comprehension.

[45] "God gave us sex to give us the faintest whiff of what union with Him will be." From <u>How the Nations Rage: rethinking faith and politics in a divided age</u>. Thomas Nelson in association with Wolgemuth and Associates, Nashville, TN, c. 2018, p.45.

items in this world are given to us by God, created into His Creation to help us understand the Reality yet to come.

When you read the Bible, you get the distinct impression that there are two kingdoms we are living in: the Kingdom of God and the Kingdom of this world. One is temporary, will pass away, and is at its heart unfulfilling (though not without value). The other is eternal, will never pass away, and is at its heart fulfilling and therapeutic. One is Home; one isn't. The difficulty is that one is dissolved in the other, so that they are difficult to distinguish. On top of that, the ability to distinguish one from the other is not equally distributed. The ability to comprehend the spiritual kingdom of God belongs to spiritual people. It is spiritually discerned.

Many of us have been around people who manipulated the term "spiritually discerned" to mean that if you don't understand me, or if you disagree with me, then you are not able to discern spiritual things, you are not a spiritual person, and are spiritually uneducated. To put it bluntly, if you disagree, you're wrong. It is often said in the same tone of voice as the father talking to his daughter in the movie Matilda: "I'm big, you're small. I'm old, you're young. I'm smart, you're dumb." I have no intention of using the phrase "spiritually discerned" in that manner, as if to say, if you disagree with what I'm saying, you don't get it. Agreement with me is not a litmus test of your spirituality. However, the Bible is clear: there is such a thing as spiritual blindness, which would be an inability to understand and perceive the things of the Kingdom of God. The reason for that is that certain truths are spiritually discerned and not all people are spiritual people. It is not about IQ. It's about fullness of the Spirit.

In John 3, a man named Nicodemus came to meet Jesus. He was a Pharisee. The Pharisees were a very small but very influential group of people. In Herod's time, they numbered around 6,000, a tiny number compared to the whole population of Palestine. But they were extremely influential. That's why Jesus compared them to leaven or yeast. If you have ever made bread, you know that the amount of yeast compared to other ingredients is minuscule. As the yeast is heated up (not too warm or you'll kill the yeast and end up with a heavy brick instead of a nice, light loaf—I know; I have) in the presence of sugar and water, it grows and gives off carbon dioxide, a gas, which is distributed throughout the bread by kneading it, making it lighter because of the trapped gas bubbles. So the tiny bit of yeast affects the whole loaf. In the same way, the Pharisees exercised influence vastly beyond their numbers.

The text tells us that Nicodemus was a "ruler" of the Jews, probably a member of the Sanhedrin, the ruling body of the Jewish nation under Roman occupation. So he was an elite of the elite, which explains why he came at night to talk with such an outcast as this preacher named Jesus from the backwater town of Nazareth. He seemed to have a sincere interest in Jesus, as evidenced by his opening statement: "You must be a teacher come from God for no one can do these signs that you do, unless God is with him." But he was ashamed of that interest and so came at night. He asked no questions; he just made the very pregnant statement that Jesus must be from God because of the signs he does.

Jesus' response was obtuse. "No one can see the Kingdom of God unless he is born again." No chit chat. No verbal foreplay. There seems, as is often the case, to be no relation in the "answer" Jesus gives to the question that is asked or the statement made. But, as is often the case, Jesus is answering an unasked, maybe even unconscious, question. Nicodemus, the teacher, had no idea what Jesus was talking about. You can tell by his response: "How can a man be born when he is old? Can he enter a second time into his mother's womb and be born?" They talked some more and finally Jesus goes right to the core of the issue: "If I have told you *earthly* things and you do not believe, how can you believe if I tell you *heavenly* things?"

In the next chapter, John 4, a mirror image of the same story takes place, but with a different outcome. Jesus meets and requests a drink of water from a woman drawing water at a well called Jacob's well. There are two indications in the text that this was unusual. One is the woman's response in verse 9: "How is it that you, a Jew, ask a drink of me, a woman of Samaria?" Then the gospel writer explains to the reader who might not understand the gravity of the situation: "For Jews have no dealings with Samaritans." The other indication that this was an unusual situation was the disciples' response in verse 27: "They *marveled* that he was talking with a *woman*." It is difficult for us to imagine how low the status of women was in New Testament culture. They were considered so unreliable that their testimony was not given credibility in a court of law. And so the disciples *marveled* that he was talking with, of all things, a woman. She was also a Samaritan, a member of a group of people who were considered as half-Jews and were hated with vehemence.[46] So Jesus was making two serious social blunders: first, He, as a Jew, was talking to a Samaritan; and second, He, as a man, was asking help from a woman. If you look on a map, Samaria is tucked in between Galilee and Judea, and in New Testament times travelers from one to the other would take an intentional detour around Samaritan territory in order to avoid this distasteful people.

In addition to being a Samaritan and female, this woman appeared to be even an outcast among the other women. Getting water from the well was "woman's work" and was usually done in the cool of the day, morning or evening. It was a social event, a time to share news and gossip. This woman was at the well at mid-day, alone. Very much an outsider. Very alone. She was not a socialite, or she would have come with the other women. She was as much a low-life as Nicodemus was an elite.

Jesus strikes up a conversation with her about water: He wants some. She is surprised that He would even talk to her, a woman, a Samaritan, and an outcast among other women. Jesus responds by telling her that He could give her Living Water. "Whoever drinks

---

[46] You can get a sense of how much the Jews hated the Samaritans in John 8:48. In the midst of a very intense debate between the hard-line Pharisees and Jesus, they followed the debating technique so popular today: when logic fails, call your opponents names. "The Jews answered him, are we not right in saying that you are a Samaritan and have a demon?'"

of the water I give will never thirst again." "Great!" the woman responds. "I'll take some of that so I don't have to come back here anymore and get water out of the well." Probably she would have preferred to miss the constant reminder of her low social status. But Jesus was not talking about a sort of "permanent" water, one which quenched thirst once for all, at least not a physical "permanent" water. The woman did not get this earthly analogy to spiritual reality using water any more than Nicodemus did the analogy of birth and rebirth. They were both clueless. This nameless woman, as opposite as one can get from Nicodemus, is similarly out to lunch: she was thinking only of physical water, but an unusual water so effective that you did not get thirsty again and so never had to come back to the well. Nicodemus could not get beyond thinking of physical birth and asked the unintelligent question of going back into his mother's womb in order to be "born again." Neither one of them got it. The truth about heavenly things was hidden equally from both, so that neither the educated elite nor the uneducated outcast was able to perceive what Jesus was trying to reveal to them.[47]

Now, here is the point: there are heavenly things and there are earthly things. There is Another Reality out there. For us to understand what Jesus called "heavenly things"—that is, values, rules, and concepts from heaven—it must be revealed to us and we need to be spiritual people to perceive them. They are not merely academic. Otherwise Nicodemus would have understood. Such things are, as the apostle Paul said, "spiritually discerned."[48]

---

[47] Interestingly, in the course of her talking with Jesus, this outcast of a woman does come to see the light, forgets all about the physical water she came to draw, as evidenced by the fact that she left her bucket there and went to tell her friends about Jesus. Scripture tells us that many Samaritans in her city believed in Jesus *because of the woman's testimony.* Similarly, after the Resurrection, Jesus entrusted this most significant truth of all history—that of His being alive and raised from the dead—to one woman and she went and informed the male disciples and they believed *because of her testimony.* Josephus, in his *Antiquities* IV.219 (IV.8.15), stated, "from women let no evidence be accepted because of the levity and temerity of their sex." That's what the culture thought of the reliability of women. Jesus obviously disagreed and was not afraid to confront the culture where it was wrong.

[48] 1 Corinthians 2:14

In fact, that is the only way they may be discerned. So the Scriptures reveal truths of the other world by means of analogy, like birth or water, which are comparisons to *this world*, a sort of imperfect image of the reality of the Kingdom of God. And most of us, like Nicodemus or the woman at the well, just don't understand, because all our experience is of this world only and this world is a fallen world.

Now, to understand what I believe the Bible teaches about gender relationships, we need to be able to comprehend concepts and principles that really belong to the other world, the Kingdom of God. That may be difficult. In fact, it will be impossible, unless we can think in terms of that Other Kingdom, the Kingdom of God, instead of where we currently live. So we need to be like the woman at the well and be willing to have our minds opened to a whole different worldview with a very different set of values.

In one of the Narnia Chronicles, The Silver Chair, the four children are trying to explain to the Wicked Witch what the Overworld is like. All those living in the Underworld, under the earth, had never seen the Overworld. the surface of the earth, and so they knew nothing of what life was like on the surface. The sun, day and night, light and dark, were all a mystery to them. The Witch is speaking:

"What is this *sun* that you all speak of? Do you mean anything by the word?"

"Yes, we jolly well do," said Scrubb.

'Can you tell me what it's like?" asked the Witch.

"Please it your grace," said the Prince, very boldly and politely. You see that lamp. It is round and yellow and gives light to the whole room; and hangeth moreover from the roof. Now that thing which we call the sun is like the lamp, only far greater and brighter. It giveth light to the whole Overworld and hangeth in the sky."

"Hangeth from what, my lord?" asked the Witch; and then, while they were all still thinking how to answer her, she added with another of her soft, silver laughs. "You see? When you try to think out clearly what this *sun* must be, you cannot tell me. You can only tell me it is *like* the lamp. Your *sun* is a dream; and there is nothing in that dream that was not copied from the lamp. The lamp is the real thing; the sun is but a tale, a children's story."

"Yes, I see now," said Jill in a heavy, hopeless tone. "It must be so." And while she said this, it seemed to her to be very good sense."

In the story, the children began to believe the Witch: perhaps whatever they remembered from Above really was only an extrapolation of their experience from below. Then Jill goes on:

"There's Aslan."

"Aslan?" said the Witch. "What a pretty name! What does it mean?"

"He is a great lion who called us out of our own world," said Scrubb, "and sent us into this to find Prince Rilian."

"What is a *lion*?" asked the Witch.

"Oh hang it all!" said Scrubb. "Don't you know? How can we describe it to her? Have you ever seen a cat?"

"Surely," said the Queen. "I love cats."

"Well, a lion is a little bit—only a little bit, mind you—like a huge cat—with a mane. At least, it's not a horse's mane, you know, it's more like a judge's wig. And it's yellow. And terrifically strong."

The Witch shook her head. "I see," she said, "that we should do no better with your *lion*, as you call it, than we did with your *sun*. You've seen lamps, and so you imagined a bigger and better lamp and called it the *sun*. You've seen cats, and now you want a bigger and better cat, and it's called a *lion*. And look how you can put nothing into your make-believe world without copying it from the real world, this world of mine, which is the only world."[49]

---

[49] C. S. Lewis, <u>The Silver Chair</u>, Collier Books, New York, NY c. 1953, pp. 155 ff. Used by permission.

In the story, the Witch had it wrong. What the witch called the make-believe world was in fact real. She accused them of creating a fake reality by taking objects in her world and enlarging them to their "make-believe" world. And so some theologians today accuse us of the same thing: the reason we call God Father is because we need a Father-image bigger and better than our imperfect fathers, and so we create one to satisfy our longings. So they say. Gilbert Bilezikian coined an appropriate term for this: "anthropomorphic projection."[50] That would be taking something from our world and projecting it onto the heavens, expanding the concept to God's size.

However, just the opposite is true. Our longings often indicate another Reality that this world cannot satisfy. "If I find in myself a desire which no experience in this world can satisfy, the most probable explanation is that I was made for another world. Probably earthly pleasures were never meant to satisfy it, but only to arouse it, to suggest the real thing.... I must take care... never to mistake them for the something else of which they are only a kind of copy, or echo, or mirage." So said C. S. Lewis.[51]

Our fallen world contains finger-prints of the Creator's design and appetizers of the World to come, the other perfect world, for which we were created and where we will be perfectly "at home." But it seems foreign to us since nearly all our experience is living in a fallen, upside-down world, and the analogies are not always clear.

One of the main themes of the book of Hebrews is this very thing: that God designed a whole system of worship in the Old Testament, with a temple, priests, a curtain, in order to give us a taste of the Reality which is Heaven, where the Priest and Sacrifice both are Jesus himself and He opened the door (or tore the curtain excluding us), that we might walk into the Holy of Holies, a personal

[50] Gilbert Bilezikian, "Hermeneutical Bungee Jumping: Subordination in the Godhead," *Journal of the Evangelical Theological Society*, March 1997, p. 58.
[51] C. S. Lewis, <u>Mere Christianity</u>, Macmillan Company, New York, 1972, p. 120. Used by permission.

relationship with God. The author of Hebrews describes it this way: "They serve as a copy and a shadow of the heavenly sanctuary...."[52] The author uses the terms "copy" and "shadow" to describe how the Old Testament system foreshadows the Reality of Heaven. That is the idea I'm talking about: fingerprints, appetizers, shadows, or copies. They all point to *something bigger and more real.*

Since we are dwellers in this world, we find it difficult to comprehend the Reality of the Kingdom of God because we do not have categories in our experience to help us comprehend it. And the world around us is patiently teaching us as the Witch was trying to do in the Narnia Chronicles: teaching us that there is nothing more than what we see or experience in this life.

So we have to choose between labeling the possible representations of the Other World as merely "anthropomorphic projections" or we can treat them as opening a door to another Kingdom, dissolved in our world, which is radically different from this present world. The representations of that Other Reality, the Kingdom of God, dissolved in our world, take the form of, by necessity, items in this world. But those are only a mere shadow of the reality to come. Not all people see it. Nicodemus didn't. The disciples almost always didn't. The woman did. The Pharisees didn't.

And too often, we don't.

It seems to me there are two categories of representations of heavenly things in this earthly world. Actually, metaphor might be the better term, and Scripture just bristles with them. Our job is to figure out what they mean or to figure what the author intended to communicate by using that particular metaphor. I find it helpful to think in terms of fingerprints and appetizers. I know very little about art, but my sense is that each artist had his own style, and so, if one knows art, one can recognize a painting as the work of

---

[52] Hebrews 8:5

a particular artist, even if you've never seen the painting before. Musical composers do the same.

Those who create tend to leave evidence in their creations that reflect something of their worldview or personality. So our God has left fingerprints of who He is in his creation. The theological term for this is general revelation. It is what you can observe about the Creator by looking at His Creation if—and this is a big if—you have eyes to see. This is the inescapable reality that tugged C. S. Lewis, in his words, "the most dejected and reluctant convert in all England"[53] into the Kingdom of God. There were fingerprints that made no sense unless there was a Hand that made them. Lewis profoundly observed his thought process in recounting his conversion to Christianity: "My argument against God was that the universe seemed so cruel and unjust. But how had I got this idea of *just* and *unjust*? A man does not call a line crooked unless he has some idea of a straight line. What was I comparing this universe with when I called it unjust? If the whole show was bad and senseless from A to Z, so to speak, why did I, who was supposed to be part of the show, find myself in such violent reaction against it? A man feels wet when he falls into water, because man is not a water animal; a fish would not feel wet. Of course, I could have given up my idea of justice by saying it was nothing but a private idea of my own. But if I did that, my argument against God collapsed too—for the argument depended on saying that the world was really unjust, not simply that it did not happen to please my private fancies. If the whole universe has no meaning, we should never had found out that it has no meaning; just as, if there were no light in the universe and therefore no creature with eyes, we should never know it was dark. *Dark* would be without meaning."[54]

It was that kind of profoundly free *thinking* that caused Lewis to acknowledge God.

In addition to fingerprints, there are also items that God has

[53] C. S. Lewis, <u>Surprised by Joy</u>, Harcourt Brace & Company, c. 1955, p. 221.
[54] C. S. Lewis, <u>Mere Christianity</u>, Macmillan Publishing, New York, NY. c. 1945, pp. 45-46.

given which are appetizers[55] for the good and perfect Kingdom of God yet to come, which our grandfather and grandmother Adam and Eve decided to forgo in search of better and more immediate pleasures. For example, Ephesians tells us[56] that the gift of the Holy spirit is a "deposit guarantee" or a "down payment" of our inheritance that we will receive upon death and our entry into heaven.

I remember well when I bought my first house. I sweated mightily going $25,000 into debt (which shows how long ago that was and how small a house I bought.) The real estate agent was very patient with me as she explained the concept of earnest money. The buyer has to come up with an amount of money (for me it was $500) when he makes an offer on a house, just to show he is "earnest" about the purchase. It is to show he is not playing around, that this is really an "earnest" offer. If you, the seller, accept this "earnest," the full amount of money owed for the house is coming later. That's the same concept the writer of Ephesians uses to describe the gift of the Holy Spirit, and some translations even use the word "earnest" to translate the Greek word. Some use the phrase "down payment." It is evidence for us that God is serious. And there is a lot more coming for those who wait. In our culture, "wait" is a four letter word. We are so used to immediate gratification. But "waiting" is our situation. The rest will come later. So the "down payment" of the Holy Spirit himself in us is an appetizer of something much bigger yet to come and ought to make us *hungry* for the reality still awaiting us.

I did not marry until I was 36. There were a number of reasons for that, one of which was that I had a lot of growing up to do. During the times of singleness, which descended on me instantly upon graduation from college, there were some intensely lonely and low times. During one of those times, I was lamenting (maybe complaining would be a better description) that I would never experience marriage, the permanent intimacy and steadfast love,

---

[55] The difference is hazy at best, and I am not interested in being real precise on defining the difference.
[56] Ephesians 1:14

because of my circumstance. That seemed unfair. (Though where I got this idea of "unfair" is a mystery to me, and why I felt the audacity to hold the God of the universe to my standard of fairness is, in retrospect, embarrassing.) Then in my personal devotions I happened to come across the passage in Luke 20:27–40 where the Sadducees (who did not believe in the resurrection of the dead) were asking a question of Jesus meant trap him so that He could not answer and, as a result, appear simply uneducated. It was a question about an Old Testament custom. When a husband dies, the brother of the husband was to marry the widow and provide her with an heir. In their hypothetical situation, the woman marries seven times and each time the husband dies. (What a bummer!) Their question to Jesus was to whom would she be married in heaven, since she had married eight different men here on earth. Since their theology did not allow for any resurrection, this carried theological significance for them. And it appeared to be an embarrassingly difficult question for one who believes in the resurrection and heaven, as Jesus obviously did. Jesus' answer was unexpected: none of them would be married to the widow in heaven. In fact, in heaven there was no marriage! I choked on that for a while, thinking that I had missed my chance, and then came to a conclusion that satisfied me personally and seemed Biblical. As we have already seen, when the Bible talks about heaven, it bristles with language of marriage, wedding, wedding feasts, a bride and a groom, wedding garments, and the like. How could there be no marriage in heaven with all this talk of marriage? The only satisfying answer to me was that marriage here on earth is a tiny appetizer of the Reality in heaven, which is the marriage of the Church, the Bride of Christ, to Jesus Himself. So, if I never married, I would only miss out on the appetizer but the meal would be mine. And so I was "married," at least if I was a believer, in the marriage that really counts and eternally gives permanent satisfaction and intimacy. I do not mean to imply I will be physically married to Jesus, but that all the wonderful aspects of marriage in the here-and-now are appetizers for the Reality awaiting us in heaven, of which marriage in this world is merely an appetizer. So I had to live by faith and wait for the consummation that would be the Real Consummation, of which any marriage in this world was only a shadow of what is to come. I could live with the absence of the appetizer if the real meal were coming for sure. And so I could wait. Waiting is what Scripture calls "faith."[57] And it is absolutely necessary if you are going to walk with God is this fallen world.

Scripture bristles with appetizers and fingerprints. Here is a partial list. Probably you can come up with more.

Home
Vines and branches
Marriage
Sexual intercourse
Crowns
Gold and silver
Earnest money or down payment
Running a Race
Dung
Menstrual rags
Wedding
Wedding feast
Virginity
Bride
Groom
Adultery
Motherhood
Fatherhood

---

[57] This is the whole point of the great "faith chapter" in Hebrews 11. The point is definitely not that when we have faith, God will give us what we want. "These all died in faith, *not having received what was promised,*" says verse 13. The point of the chapter is that the lives of those great heroes of the faith were characterized by actions that only made sense if there was more to this world than what they *saw.* The text says, "These all died in faith, not having received what was promised, but having seen it and greeted it from afar, and having acknowledged that they were strangers and exiles on the earth. For people who speak thus make it clear that they are seeking a homeland.... But as it is, they desire a better country, that is, a heavenly one." Heb 11:13–16

Wedding garments
Childhood
Adoption
Grafting (as in plants)
Family
Baptism
Redeemer
Kinsman Redeemer
Tabernacle
Priest
Sabbath
Ransom
Fruit

There are probably more. Think about each one and what is implied or taught about the Reality in Heaven of which these are only appetizers. Those are all mentioned in the Bible, but they are representing Something profoundly bigger.

And there is, I believe, at least one more, which is a major focus of this book: gender relationships.

The nature of gender relationships, as outlined in the Bible, is a fingerprint and also an appetizer, or maybe image is a better word, of something much bigger—the very nature of relationships among the three persons of the Trinity, as well as the nature of the relationship between Christ and His church. I think that it is not "anthropomorphic projection" to label it as such. Just the opposite is happening; gender is revealing something: it is showing us something that we cannot see. That something is the nature of relationships among the persons of the Trinity. My reason for believing such is the repeated use of "created in God's image" and "male and female" in Genesis 1:26 and 27. That is territory that will be covered in chapter five.

In the New Testament there is a corollary verse: 1 Corinthians 11:1. That verse says the same word, headship, describes the

relationship of a husband to a wife and the relationship of Christ to
God. Not all Christians agree with this position. You, the reader,
will have to decide what you think the Bible teaches. It seems clear to
me from the repeated and unique use of the word *image* in Genesis
1:26 & 27, and from the direct statement that headship describes
both the husband/wife and the Christ/God relationship, that one
is a picture of the other. What makes this abnormally difficult
for us to comprehend is that the relationships among the persons
of the Trinity are very peculiar. They are very different from the
way things are done here in this world. They belong to another
Kingdom, a foreign Kingdom, one very different from where we live.
So those relationships among the Trinity and, theoretically, among
husbands and wives, are qualitatively different from anything we
have experienced in this world.

We live as people caught between two worlds, the kingdom
of God and the kingdom of this world. In the line of Biblical
history, everything after Eden and before Heaven is abnormal. It is
profoundly *bent*. It is no mistake, I think, that a baby's first response
to entry into this world is to cry. We were made by God to live in
the Garden of Eden, and our ancestors Adam and Eve blew it by
their disobedience to God. And so they were kicked out of Eden.
We have inherited their sentence. Since then, all our experience of
life is in a fallen world where we long, with a longing too deep for
words, for what we gave up as a race in one act of disobedience.
"Ever since Adam and Eve failed to remain within boundaries that
God had set with their happiness in mind, each of their descendants
has succumbed to the same temptation; to believe that God is not
good, that there is no relief in Him from the terror of isolation, that
we are therefore justified in doing whatever relieves pain and makes
life more immediately comfortable… and that effort leads either
to depression or addiction."[58] Let your mind digest that statement.
The difficult truth to understand is that living that way—looking

[58] Larry Crabb, "Who We Are and How We Relate," NavPress, Colorado Springs, CO, c.
1992, pp. 32, 21.

out for number one—seems so perfectly normal, because we have no other experience. So we attempt to manage life to make us feel better. Everyone does it. And the powers of this world tell us how to do that with an enormous amount of expertise. But they are feeding us lies, just as the serpent was feeding lies to Adam and Eve in the Garden. As Dr. Crabb told us above, doing whatever we can to relieve the pain of living in this fallen world leads either to depression or addiction. "We are to live with the ongoing cycle of anticipation/sorrow. If we admit that our deep desire is not fully met, then we can embrace the reality of a sojourner who has not yet found rest and peace. It is not "abnormal" to be empty, sad, and lonely at the deepest place in our souls, which were fashioned for eternity—to be dissatisfied with the empty provisions of this world, sad over the destruction of beauty, lonely for the companionship of lasting friendships. It is not only not abnormal, but wrong, to be otherwise."[59]

It is difficult for us to comprehend how different the values of the Kingdom of God are from the world we live in, which we unconsciously assume to be normal and right. Look with me at one area, the area of what authority looks like. Whether this is applicable to our study or not we'll decide later.

I love the gospel of Mark. It is short and packed with action. Jesus the King marches across the pages with majesty and power. And people constantly scratch their heads with astonishment when they meet Him. Go back with me to the geography of Jesus and live in this vignette of Jesus' life. Be thinking especially of the Kingdom of God and the Kingdom of this world. All italics, obviously, are mine.

"And they were bringing *children* to him, that he might touch them; and the disciples rebuked them. But when Jesus saw it he was

[59] Dan Allender and Tremper Longman, <u>Bold Love</u>, NavPress, Colorado Springs, CO, c. 1992, p. 142.

indignant, and said to them, 'Let the *children* come to me, do not hinder them; for to such belongs the kingdom of God. Truly, I say to you, whoever does not receive the kingdom of God like a *child* shall not enter it.' And he took them in his arms and blessed them, laying his hands upon them."

"And as he was setting out on his journey, a man ran up and knelt before him, and asked him, 'Good Teacher, what must I do to inherit eternal life?' And Jesus said to him, 'Why do you call me good? No one is good but God alone. You know the commandments: "Do not kill, Do not commit adultery, Do not steal, Do not bear false witness, Do not defraud, Honor your father and mother."' And he said to him, 'Teacher, all these I have observed from my youth.' And Jesus looking upon him, loved him, and said to him, '*you lack still* one thing: go sell what you have, and give to the poor, and you will have treasure in heaven, and come, follow me.' At that saying his countenance fell, and he went away sorrowful; for he had great possessions.

"And Jesus looked around and said to his disciples, 'How hard it will be for those who have riches to enter the kingdom of God!' And the disciples were amazed at his words. But Jesus said to them again, '*Children,* how hard it is to enter the Kingdom of God! It is easier for a camel to go through the eye of a needle than for a rich man to enter the Kingdom of God.' And they were exceedingly astonished, and said to him, 'Then who can be saved?' Jesus looked at them and said, 'With men it is impossible, but not with God; for all things are possible with God.' Peter began to say to him, 'Lo, we have left everything and followed you.' Jesus said, 'Truly, I say to you, there is not one who has left house or brothers or sisters or mother or father or children or lands for my sake and for the gospel who will not receive a hundredfold now in this time, houses, and brothers and sisters and mothers and children and lands, with persecutions, and in the age to come eternal life. But many that are first will be last and the last, first.'"

"And they were on the road, going up to Jerusalem, and Jesus was walking ahead of them; and they were amazed, and those who followed were afraid. And taking the twelve again, he began to tell them what was to happen to him, saying, 'Behold, we are going up to Jerusalem; and the Son of man will be delivered to the chief priests and the scribes, and they will condemn him to death, and deliver him to the Gentiles; and they will mock him, and spit upon him, and scourge him, and kill him; and after three days he will rise.'"

"And James and John, the sons of Zebedee, came forward to him and said to him, 'Teacher, we want you to do for us whatever we ask of you.' And he said to them, 'What do you want me to do for you?' And they said to him, 'Grant us to sit, one at your right hand and one at your left, in your glory.' But Jesus said to them, 'You do not know what you are asking. Are you able to drink the cup that I drink, or to be baptized with the baptism with which I am baptized?' And they said to him, 'We are able.' And Jesus said to them, 'The cup that I drink you will drink; and with the baptism with which I am baptized, you will be baptized. But to sit at my right hand or at my left is not mine to grant, but it is for those for whom it has been prepared.'

"And when the ten heard it, they began to be indignant at James and John. And Jesus called them to him and said to them, 'You know that those who are supposed to rule over the Gentiles *lord* it over them, and their *great* men exercise authority over them. *But it shall not be so among you.* But whoever would be great among you *must* be your servant, and whoever would be first among you *must* be slave of all. For the Son of man also came not to be served, but to serve and to give his life as a ransom for many.'"[60]

Children were powerless in that culture. They did what they were told. They had not learned the skepticism of adults. They were

---

[60] Mark 10:13–45

56

not "shakers and movers." Yet they are held up as a virtuous example of whom we ought to be like: "to *such* belongs the Kingdom of God."

In stark contrast to the children is the rich young ruler. Jesus was, as the gospel writer tells us, "setting out on his journey" (v. 17). We find out later exactly where he was going and what was to happen. But for now, we are presented with this young man who certainly, at first glance, *looks* spiritually hungry. He asks Jesus what must be done to inherit eternal life. We find out quickly, however, that he has closets in his life to which Jesus is not allowed entrance. Jesus answers the presented question with a list of several, but not all, the commandments. The rich, young, *proud* ruler states that he has done *all* of them, and not only done all of them, but done them all *from his youth*!

The three-word response from Jesus must have cut to the soul of this proud man like a knife: "you still lack...." Jesus enters the locked closet of possessions and riches of this young man, uninvited. "Sell what you have; give to the poor: and then your treasure will be in heaven." The young man looked down and went away in sorrow. He possessed too many things. Or they possessed him. His treasure was in the wrong place.

Let's understand what money is: it is the power to make others do what we want. That may be to bring us food in a restaurant, or a new car or house or a college education or whatever. Money is power to manipulate others. That's why it is so attractive: it gives the illusion of control.

Children are the opposite of the powerful. They have no control. So while the disciples were choking on what Jesus said to the rich young ruler, Jesus addressed *them* as *children*. Why would he do that? Obviously, they were not children. Why would Jesus call them children? In contrast to the rich young ruler, but like the children right before him, they had *not* gone away sorrowful at the invitation to follow Jesus. They followed him. They gave up *control*. Whatever the analogy of the camel going through the eye of a needle means, the point obviously is that it is very difficult for it to happen. So the same is true for a rich man to enter the Kingdom of God. Why? Because in the Kingdom of God, it is not about maintaining personal power and control—which comes through money. It is *different*. Part of becoming a believer is giving up *control*. The disciples had done just that in choosing to follow Jesus.

But don't stop there: follow Jesus all the way in his teaching on this. Jesus says that in this world, the great men "lord" their position over people. Pointedly, Jesus says, "It shall *not* be so among *you*." That is, for those who follow Jesus, in His kingdom, real greatness consists of serving people, not ordering them around to your own pleasure. In fact (and this tops everything), if you want to be really great in the Kingdom of God, you need to become a slave of all.

The position of a slave is not one most people in this world aspire to. President, yes. CEO, yes. Slave, probably not.

In contrast to the rulers of this world, who *lord* their position over others, in the Kingdom of God, *serving* others to the extent of being their slave is *virtuous*. In this world, to serve someone consciously to that extent would be viewed as psychologically pathological.

Now, this might be cheap rhetoric, were it not for the example of the person speaking. Remember that we know from verse seventeen that Jesus was setting out on a "journey." In verse 32, it says, "they were on the road, going up to Jerusalem." Jesus at this point tells them that they were, in fact, going to Jerusalem, and that he would be delivered to the chief priests, and he would be condemned to death, and he would be given to, of all people, Gentiles, and he would be mocked, spat upon, scourged, and eventually killed. Then He would rise three days later. We know from the accounts in the other gospels that this was not a particularly attractive scenario for Jesus. ("My soul is very sorrowful, even to death; remain here, and watch with me" [Matt. 26:38], or "And now my soul is troubled. And what shall I say? Save me from this hour? No, for this purpose I have come" [John 12:27].) Wouldn't it be for you? He went to the Garden to pray, taking three of his disciples for company, asking of the Father that there might be some other way. He sweat blood. The disciples, meanwhile, snoozed.

Here, He announces the coming Event in clear and exceedingly painful detail. There would be physical pain, emotional pain, as well as embarrassment. Clearly, the road to Jerusalem would have been a very dark time for Jesus.

The response of the disciples to this revelation of coming disaster for their leader and teacher is numbing. They ask, "Teacher, will you do for us whatever we ask?" From other gospel accounts, we know what was going on in their little minds during this whole time period leading up to the Crucifixion. They were *arguing* about who was to be regarded as the greatest (Luke 22:24). Jesus had just talked about greatness, so they decided to figure out who among them would best fit that description.

I don't think any of us would regard the impending death on the cross as a fun time. Jesus certainly didn't. His mind must have been heavy with sorrow and dread as he approached Jerusalem, the place where the sacrificial offerings had been made throughout history. Those offerings were just a foreshadow of the Perfect Offering that he was about to make. When Jesus got to Jerusalem, He went into the Temple, where the sacrifices for sin had historically been made, the sacrifices which were an appetizer of the Perfect Sacrifice that Jesus was about to make. He looked around. The silence must have been deafening. It must have been an incredibly heavy moment for Jesus. He was about to finish it all. A perfect sacrifice. Once for all. The Offering of His Life as a Ransom for such undeserving people as his disciples. And such an undeserving person as I am. As the time approaches, and as Jerusalem approaches, and as the dread grows, the disciples come to Jesus and ask him, of all things, to be their servant.

One of the reasons I believe the Bible to be true is because when the writers of the accounts, the eyewitness reporters, portray themselves as part of the story, which they were, they portray themselves as such spiritual numbskulls. And they were. Had they wanted to create a neat story and a new religion, surely they would have portrayed themselves in a better light. But they were about telling the truth: the truth about the nature of man and the nature of our Savior. And that truth is that one is ugly and the other beautiful. They tell the truth, even at their own cost.

Here is Jesus approaching the voluntary sacrifice of himself on the cross, and the disciples, completely caught up in self, offer him no sympathy, compassion, empathy, or even prayer. No, they want *him* to serve *them*.

Now, the absolutely stunning thing about the story is that He agrees to be their servant.

I would have stalked off in a self-righteous huff and discouragement at these incredibly self-centered men, especially after investing three years of my life into theirs. Not Jesus. How can you not fall down in worship at the feet of this man? What a hero! What an example! At the most painful moment of his life, he still thinks not of himself but willingly serves other people, people who do not deserve his service. How can you yawn in boredom at this most amazing person, as so many people do?

There are two Kingdoms doing battle here. Jesus lives in and displays the values of the Kingdom of God, where it is virtuous to be a servant. The Kingdom of this world is about serving self. Our world is so upside-down (and we are so used to it) that it has become normal to serve self. "You gotta look out for number one," we are told. "You have to look out for yourself." But in the Kingdom of God, it is good to be a servant of others. Don't let that breeze by you.[61]

[61] I have struggled with the accusation many have brought against Christians who supported slavery and used the Bible for that purpose. That is an accusation that is extremely unfortunate–and true. I can only make the following conclusions: 1) We must acknowledge the historical misunderstanding of what Scripture teaches on this subject. This is not the only time we have had to eat some crow. It is a perfect example of using Scripture to support our agenda and

I remember being at an elders meeting of our church, and we had asked a man to accept a certain role that needed to be done. I do not remember what exactly it was, but it was not glamorous. Our pastor had suggested him. As we talked it through with him, he seemed to become more and more agitated and finally blurted out that we were just asking him to be a "go-fer" and he was not willing to do that and, frankly, was a little insulted at being asked. He stood up and walked out. There was an awkward silence, and our pastor shrugged his shoulders and commented that apparently we had asked the wrong person. Yeah, I guess we had. As a pastor, he was used to working with people who were "still on the way" and so was patient with this man's stunning immaturity. This man clearly did not understand the values in the Kingdom of God, since he thought the job we were asking of him was "below him." It would have been perfectly legitimate not to have time. Or there would have been other excuses that would have been understandable. But to see a job as "below him" revealed an arrogant lack of servanthood, which showed a lack of understanding of the values of the Kingdom of God and was totally unbecoming for a follower of Jesus.

I know this raises all kinds of questions and confusion. It certainly does not promise success and victory in this world. But we need to comprehend that we live in a fallen world, and the kingdom of God, from what is revealed to us, is radically different—so much so that it seems strange, obtuse, and full of nonsense. Success and victory will be ours in Heaven, and we need to *wait* for that.

---

selectively appealing to certain texts and ignoring what we don't like. 2) Actually, Scripture *does* eliminate slavery by calling on owners to treat their servants fairly *as they would want to be treated*. In Colossians 4:1, masters are told to "treat your slaves *justly and fairly* knowing that you also have a Master in heaven." In Ephesians 6:9, masters are told to "do the same to them," meaning they are to treat their slaves in the same manner as their slaves act *toward them*. So Scripture does *not* allow for the inhumane treatment of slaves throughout human history. I believe that hierarchy in this world is a reflection of the perfect hierarchy in the Trinity. But in this fallen world, it has been horribly disfigured. The summary of the Biblical view is that, while it does not eliminate hierarchy, it eliminates the *unfairness and inequality* of hierarchy—and therefore the horror of slavery in this fallen world.

Let's make three observations from this text:

1. There are two kingdoms present, and Jesus, by verbal instruction and by example, is comparing the two kingdoms in one area—the area of what authority looks like. He uses the two words, "Gentiles" and "you"—using the "you" when he is speaking to the disciples. It is safe interpretation, I think, to take those two words as representing the kingdom of this world and the Kingdom of God.

2. In the Kingdom of God, Jesus does not deny hierarchy.[62] He does not say, "But it shall not be so among you. You shall all be equal and everybody shall be everybody else's servant." He pointedly does not say that. But he does say that authority in the Kingdom of God looks radically different.

3. Authority in the Kingdom of God does not preclude serving those over whom one has authority. In fact, part of the calling for the one in authority is to serve those he or she has authority over. Let's get that crystal clear: authority in the Kingdom of God is *not* self-serving. And serving others, like loving others, in the kingdom, has absolutely nothing to do with what kind of people they are or whether or not they deserve it. The disciples did not deserve to be served by Jesus. It is significant that Jesus is at the height of his sadness and sorrow as He approaches the Cross, and the disciples are at their zenith of ignorance and selfishness, when they

---

[62] It is significant that Jesus does not deny hierarchy. One of the themes of this book is that the God of the Bible is a God of three persons in perfect hierarchy where all the persons are completely equal, and so one of the fingerprints in His creation is also hierarchy. But the hierarchy among human beings, as a result of the fall, has become a hierarchy which conveys value. It is not a hierarchy of equals. And so slavery is hierarchy gone very, very bad. The Bible does not teach absence of hierarchy as the ideal, but a perfect hierarchy where value does not result from your position and where those in authority use that authority to serve. So slave owners should "do the same to them" in Ephesians 6:9. They do not have the freedom to treat slaves unfairly. Let me say that again-slave owners do *not* have the freedom to treat their slaves unfairly. That principle was sadly and horribly missed in the American slavery system and condoned by Christians.

ask Jesus to serve them. And He is willing. Does that not stun you into silence?

The experience of living in a fallen world is normative for us. It's all we know. We know nothing else but a fallen world. We know no kind of leader except the self-serving kind, though, if we are honest, there are certainly gradations of the degree of selfishness in all leaders.

But there is none like Jesus.

Well, of course, we say, is that not obvious? But don't be too quick to gloss over how our experience colors how we come to the Scripture. All our experience of leadership, of authority, of watching it, of being under it, is contaminated by being away from Home and by our own sinful soul. So when we hear the word "hierarchy" we may well unconsciously hear "higher-archy"—the state of one person being "higher" than the other. We assume that being submissive means being less than equal because that is all the experience we have. We *assume* that. So we bring that unexamined assumption into Scripture and struggle because our thinking has been fogged by living in a fallen world. Worse yet, we unconsciously misinterpret Scripture because it is so different from our experience. Or, worse still, we consciously misinterpret Scripture because it is to our advantage to do so.

So we need a great deal of help to comprehend the Kingdom of God. It is so foreign. We have been away from Home so long. What is in reality normal seems abnormal, unproductive, and, therefore, useless. So God has broken through into this fallen world in a number of ways—through Scripture, His Son, and also through the fingerprints the Creator has left in His creation and the appetizers He has given us to prepare us for the Kingdom to come. We need the tool of analogy in order to comprehend something incomprehensible to our unseeing eyes and uncomprehending soul. So God gives us pictures, things in this world, which are analogous to the Bigger Things above—the Real Things in God's Kingdom. That's what fingerprints and appetizers are all about.

As I have grown older and, hopefully, come to know God better in my older age, I have seen fingerprints and appetizers more often. I don't mean some sort of mystical, slightly out-of-focus image in the front yard. I mean seeing concepts in the Scripture which are clearly presented as "pictures" in the Bible that point to Something Bigger Above. "The Kingdom of God is in the midst of you."[63] It is dissolved in the world where we live, and sometimes we taste it. Sometimes lights go on inside us, or feelings too deep for words make us hungry for something more—even when we have everything this world has to offer. So Jesus says, "Blessed are those who *hunger* for they *shall be satisfied.*" What good news that is for those of us who feel correctly that we are out of place and out of step in this current world. We are, and, as followers of Jesus, we should be. The people around us, the citizens of this world, don't understand; their senses are too deadened by the continuous noise and extravagant consumption that surround us. But God has intentionally given us pictures, in this world, of heavenly things, things that we will not see unless we have God's help.

And I believe gender is one of those pictures.

---

[63] Luke 17:21

3

THE TRINITY, EQUALITY, AND HIERARCHY

One summer a number of years ago, we had a couple and their young son living with us for about six weeks since they needed a place to stay. They were both graduate students and did not have a lot of money. We live about six miles out in the country and so, in order to save gas, we car-pooled when we could. One night I got off work at 9 p.m. and picked up the husband, Gary, at the library on campus, and we headed out to our house. When we were within about a mile of the house, I remarked to Gary that someone must have a bonfire going (a common event in our neighborhood), as I could smell smoke. When we were within three houses of where we lived, I happened to glance over at my neighbor's garage and, to my horror, saw flames just licking along the peak of the roof.

Now, his garage was no ordinary garage: it was two stories high, and in it he stored all his tools, a couple of cars he was working on, and his favorite toy—an enormous four-wheel drive show truck he had built from the ground up just for exhibition. It was huge; he named it Max, and he had a habit of starting it up Sunday mornings about 6:30 a.m. and driving it up and down our road. It was very loud.

As we drove by and saw flames on the roof, I knew this was

serious. We got home as fast as we could, called 911, and then tried to wake up our neighbors and the owner of the garage. He was not there. We watched helplessly for what seemed like hours, even though it was only minutes, until we heard sirens in the distance and then the fire trucks arrived.

It was quite an education to watch the firemen pile out of the trucks and quickly set up a battle plan to attack what was now a roaring fire. Clearly, there was one man in charge, and he had a several others under him. The main guy barked out orders and they very quickly went to work like a well-oiled machine.

I have since thought a lot about that scene. (The garage was a total loss, by the way, to the tune of over three hundred thousand dollars. That was over 30 years ago. It would have been much more now. As I said, it was no ordinary garage.) Those firemen were amazing in how quickly they set up and ran an organized battle plan to fight the fire. They did not pray first. They did not take a vote. They did not talk with us, the curious bystanders, for our opinion about how to attack this fire. There was one man in charge, and he told the others what to do, and they did what they were told.

There used to be a fellow member of my church who loved birds. He majored in ornithology in college, and he was always noticing birds and commenting on them when you were with him. He also loved to climb trees. He would sometimes have his personal devotions in a tree. He worked for the state department of natural resources here in Indiana, and when they began a project to re-introduce Bald Eagles to the southern part of the state, it was Al they called upon. He was the one who climbed the trees in Alaska, retrieved the Bald Eagle eggs, and brought them back to southern Indiana to hatch them and re-introduce them to this part of the state. It was always a treat to ride with him in his rusty, beat-up pickup truck in the country and listen to him identify birds that were so far away they were just bobbing black dots. But he could identify them by how they flew or the sounds they made. He remarked once that he wished the church could be like a flock of birds. They seem just to mysteriously fly the same direction, turning this way or that, in unison, sensing the same inner voice together with no clear voice of authority or direction.

I have since thought of the contrast of those two pictures. In one case, the birds mysteriously flew the same direction, all following the same mysterious inner voice. Then there were the firemen who worked just as well together, but under a clear voice of authority. Why can people not function like the birds?

I have tried in vain to come up with even one human organization which is purposeful but not hierarchical. There seems to be something about human nature that requires hierarchy to function as a group. The more clear the purpose, the more clear the hierarchy. The armed services. An athletic team. *MS* magazine has an editor-in-chief. Any government, including even a Communist government that preaches a classless society and equality of all, has a strong leader. An elementary school staff. A pharmacy staff. A women's club. A men's club.

Why is that?

Some time ago, I attended a week-long Christian camp with the whole family, and during the week there was a regular daily small group Bible study time for the adults. There was no chosen leader ahead of time. At our first meeting somebody asked who the leader would be. One person said, "Let's just all lead instead of one person." That lasted about two minutes. Nobody really disagreed. It just happened that one person quickly assumed the role of leader and everybody followed his leadership. We had a list of questions we were supposed to work through as a group. It just was difficult to do without someone leading us. We could not function as a group without a leader.[64]

---

[64] I recently watched an excellent movie called *Defiance*. It was a true story about two brothers who helped a group of Jews survive in the woods for several years in Germany during World War II. A hierarchy immediately formed that functioned as their "government" and decision-making organ during their stay in the woods. So also, in the book <u>The Lord of the Flies</u>, which is a fictional story about some children stranded on an island, it was necessary for a "government" to form for them to function.

Why is that?[65]

The church has historically defined the nature of God as something like: One God, Creator of all things, infinite, perfect, and eternally existing in three persons: Father, Son, and Holy Spirit. That is a bare bones definition, and I want to lock arms with historic Christianity without hesitation in affirming the complete deity and equality of the three persons of the Trinity: Father, Son, and Holy Spirit.

Having made that clear, let's skip the verbal foreplay and go right to the heart of the issue. Does the Bible teach any sort of order in the Trinity? Is it possible to be equal and subordinate or submissive at the same time? These are not new questions; the church has debated the nature of God for thousands of years. But right now, especially, the nature of the relationship among the persons of the Trinity is a topic of much debate. There may be several reasons for that. Some say we are creating a theology to fit our approach to certain current issues. Dr. Gilbert Bilezikian correctly critiques this approach: "Some proponents of a hierarchical order between male and female attempt to use, as a divine model for their proposal at the human level, an alleged relationship of authority/ subordination between Father and Son. Then a parallel is drawn between a hierarchical order that makes the Son subordinate to the Father to a hierarchical order that makes women subordinate to men, thus claiming theological legitimacy for the latter."[66] He calls that "anthropomorphic projection," projecting our human nature onto God. Note that he seems to be saying that these people are starting with an agenda of hierarchy between male and female and

[65] C. S. Lewis stated this concept this way: "You cannot have a permanent association without a constitution." From Mere Christianity, The Macmillan Company, New York, NY. C. 1972, 16th printing, p. 102. Used by permission.
[66] Gilbert Bilezikian, "Hermeneutical Bungee-Jumping: Subordination in the Godhead," *Journal of the Evangelical Theological Society*, March 1997, p. 58.

then, he implies, they "create" a hierarchical relationship among the persons of the Trinity as a basis for that.

Now, I see no need to make a judgment as to whether "some proponents of a hierarchical order" have done that. I don't know their motives. I don't know if they "created" a hierarchy among the persons of the Trinity in order to legitimize a hierarchy of men over women. They certainly could have. It is also true that proponents of an egalitarian relationship between man and woman could have done exactly the same. So they see the relationship between the persons of the Trinity as completely mutual and non-hierarchical in order to promote an egalitarian approach to gender relationships.[67] That sword can cut both ways. We all have at least the possibility, if not the propensity, to develop our theology to fit our assumptions and desires, not only in this area but in any area.

A slightly different version of this error (and I agree with Dr. Bilezikian that it is an error) is committed by some who reason that, since submission of one party to another has negative effects here in a fallen world, it follows that there could be no submission of one person of the Trinity to another in the Godhead. That must be true since there can be no "negative effects" in the Perfect Trinity.[68] However,

---

[67] The 1999 Sydney Anglican Diocesan doctrine Commission Report states the following: "Statement 27: Given the issues at stake in debates about the nature of human relationships, there has been a move amongst some scholars to propose a version of the doctrine of the Trinity which is 'egalitarian.' It has been alleged that traditional teaching undergirds political, ecclesiastical and social injustice. Mutual submission of the Persons of the Trinity takes the place of subordination in relations." Quoted on page 130 in Kevin Giles' The Trinity and Subordinationism, c. 2002, Inter Varsity Press. So here, if this charge is true, which, frankly, I do not know, the opposite error is being committed by egalitarians. They make the nature of relationships among the Trinity "egalitarian" in order to support an egalitarian agenda in this world. This also is anthropomorphic projection and is also an error. We start with what is revealed in Scripture rather than an agenda in this world that needs support. Additionally, I find it interesting that the authors of that report apparently see "subordination of relations" as the "traditional teaching." Not everybody agrees on what the "traditional teaching" is. That is part of the debate in the area of relationships among the persons of the Trinity.
[68] So reasons Dr. Rebecca Groothuis: "Unlike the subordination prescribed for women, there could be no subordination in the eternal Trinity that would involve one divine Person acting against his own preference or best judgment under orders issued from the will of another divine Person. When the Father sent the Son, it was not along the lines of an earthly father who says, 'Well, son, here's what I'm going to have you do,' at which point the son learns what he had

that line of reasoning does not take into account the obvious but often forgotten fact that we live in a fallen world where everything is "bent." It was not designed that way. It does not necessarily follow that the negative effects of hierarchy between two sinners will be present in the perfect relationship of the perfect persons of the Trinity. That kind of negative anthropomorphic projection is also not legitimate. It does, however, fit consistently with the Biblical worldview that we live in a fallen world. So the image of God that is created into the genders and into their relationship with each other is bent and sometimes broken. We must not extrapolate backwards from our fallen world to the Triune God of the Bible. Our permanent residence in a fallen world muddies the waters considerably when it

---

better do or else." Page 330 in the book Discovering Biblical Equality, Complementarity without Hierarchy, published by InterVarsity Press. Of course not! That analogy is really very wrong. She fails to take into account that the marriage relationship between a man and a woman, or the relationship between an earthly father and son, are both *fallen images* of the *perfect* relationship among the persons of the Trinity that always functioned as a unity even though there are three different persons—even possibly three different persons with three different wills. That extremely inappropriate comparison fails to recognize that the three persons of the Trinity were always in perfect agreement with one another. They were perfectly One. No relationship on earth, in a fallen world, is like that. But that is our model, difficult though it may be to follow in a fallen world. Cynthia Long Westfall makes the same error in Paul and Gender, Baker Books, c. 2016, on page 87. She is referring to 1 Corinthians 11:3, where it says that Christ is the head of the man and the man is the head of the woman. It cannot mean authority, she says, because "Every man is not functionally subordinate to Christ in the present age." That *obviously* is true because we live in a fallen world, as she apparently hints at by saying, "in the present age." We cannot understand theological issues by extrapolating backwards from the conditions of this fallen world back to the Perfect Design.

Dr. Bilezikian follows the same line of reasoning on pages 147 and 148 of his book Beyond Gender Roles when he quotes a study that shows that "dominance and power are negatively associated with feelings of affection." So he concludes that hierarchy among the persons of the Trinity would have the same effect. This also is an example of anthropomorphic projection. Because hierarchy has negative effects here in a fallen world, among sinners, does not necessarily mean it would have the same effect in a perfect relationship such as the Trinity, or, for that matter, in a perfect relationship between two unfallen human beings. The pattern of reasoning in which a hierarchy among persons of the Trinity is *created* in order to support a hierarchy among the genders, or lack of hierarchy among the persons of the Trinity is *created* in order to support a lack of hierarchy among the genders, or the negative effects of hierarchy among fallen sinners in a fallen world are used to disprove the possibility of a hierarchy among the perfect persons of the Trinity—all three of those arguments are examples of anthropomorphic projection and are not valid arguments.

comes to trying to understand what the Bible says about the gender issue in God's creation.

There was a heresy in the early church called Arianism. This heresy taught that Jesus Christ was something less than God and was a created being. This actually made some sense, since Scripture uses words like "begotten" and "obeying the Father" to describe Jesus. This mistaken theology had one good effect: it required the church to define its doctrine of the Trinity, which it did at the Nicene Council. The result of that council was the Nicene Creed. Below are sections of the Creed that respond to the early Arian heresy.

"We believe in one God, the Father almighty, maker of heaven and earth, of all things visible and invisible.

And in one Lord Jesus Christ, the only Son of God, begotten from the Father *before all ages,* God from God, Light from Light, true God from true God, begotten not made....

And we believe in the Holy Spirit, the Lord, the giver of life; He proceeds from the Father and the Son, and with the Father and the Son is worshiped and glorified."

In those statements, it is affirmed that Jesus Christ, the Son, together with the Holy Spirit and the Father, are completely God. I affirm the same without hesitation.

The question before us is whether equality and equal personhood preclude hierarchy among the three persons of the Trinity. There are many very intelligent and spiritual people who respond strenuously that equality precludes order or any subordination of persons. To take that position based upon cultural assumptions—especially assumptions made in our fallen world—rather than the Bible is, of course, mistaken. I make no accusations but acknowledge how easy it is to think as our culture does rather than to think in Kingdom of God principles. That is true whether our culture is the secular culture we live in or a North American conservative Christian church culture. As we think about this issue, we all need to be aware of our propensity to determine our theology from our background, cultural assumptions, or even from blatant selfishness—the desire to want things to be what *we* want so *we* can be in control.

Here are some views about the Trinity and about submission and equality:

"In the previous chapter we saw that the position of evangelical women at the turn of the century cannot be neatly characterized as either 'equal' or being under 'authority.'"[69]

"It should be either equality and no hierarchy, or hierarchy and no equality."[70]

"Eternal subordination precludes equality."[71]

"Prior to the incarnation there had been no need for him [that is, Jesus] to be obedient since He was equal with God."[72]

"If one person on the basis of personal identity alone must always take the subordinate role, then he or she must be a subordinated person, less than his or her superior in some way."[73]

Speaking of the Trinity, Dr. Millard Erickson says: "Agape love makes each more concerned for the other than for himself. There is therefore a mutual submission of each to each of the others and a mutual glorifying of one another. There is complete equality of the three."[74]

[69] Michelle Lee-Barnwall, Neither Complementarian nor Egalitarian, Baker Academic, Grand Rapids, MI, copyright 2016, p. 35.
[70] "Hermeneutical Bungee-Jumping," p. 64
[71] Ibid, p. 64
[72] Ibid, p. 60
[73] Kevin Giles, "The Doctrine of the Trinity and Subordination," printed from www.cbeinternational.org, Christians for Biblical Equality, p. 4.
[74] Millard Erickson, God in Three Persons: A Contemporary Interpretation of the Trinity. Grand Rapids: Baker, 1995, p. 331.

"The ontological relationship of the pre-incarnate and submissive Sonship most certainly entails that Christ is inferior to God."[75]

"But the position that advocates women's spiritual equality but societal subordination—venerable though it may be—leaves unresolved the question of how one can speak of a necessary subordination of status without also implying a necessary inferiority of person."[76]

"In general, we have two basic groups to consider—men who believe in a traditional role for women and the women who accept that role. The former obviously have something to lose by granting full equality to women."[77]

"Does Paul teach a hierarchy of man over woman, or does he teach the full equality of man and woman in the church and the home?"[78]

"In a situation in which one member of a pair is always the one exercising the superior authority and the other one always submitting or obeying—and this relationship is fixed and necessary, not simply arbitrary or temporary—there is indeed something of a difference of the essence of the two, that the inherent superiority of authority is also a superiority in essence, and that, therefore, the latter is of an inferior or lesser essence."[79]

[75] C. H. Sherlock in "On God and Gender," from *Interchange 22* (1977): 93-104, who cites George W. Knight's statement. Quoted in Women, Authority, & the Bible, InterVarsity Press, 1986, p. 127.

[76] Women, Authority & the Bible, InterVarsity Press, 1986, p. 76, an article by Richard Longenecker entitled "Authority, Hierarchy & Leadership Patterns in the Bible."

[77] Women, Authority, and the Bible, p. 277, in a response by Frances F. Hiebert to an article entitled "Strategies for Change: Being a Christian Change Agent," by Joan D. Flikkema.

[78] From an on-line advertisement on the Zondervan web site for the book Man and Woman, One in Christ, by Dr. Philip Payne, November 2009. see faithgateway.com/products/man-and-woman-one-in-christ-an-exegetical-and-theological-study-of-pauls-letters?

[79] Millard Erickson, Who's Tampering with the Trinity? Kregel Publications, Grand Rapids, MI, c. 2009, p. 212.

"In Millard Erickson's most recent scholarly work on the Trinity, he seeks to provide a lucid and judicious answer to the question, is Jesus eternally subordinate to the Father, or is Jesus equal with the Father"[80]

"This tradition agreed that the Son of God was eternally equal with the Father in divinity, majesty and authority; only in the incarnation did the Son assume an inferior or subordinate status for our salvation."[81]

"When two people are true equals the permanent and necessary subordination of one party to another in being or in function/work is excluded."[82]

"If we are dealing with a person, the Son, who is eternally and necessarily subordinate to the Father, don't we have to ask whether the nature (or 'essence,' 'being,' or 'substance') of the Son is not somehow different and *lesser* than that of the Father?"[83]

"To my knowledge, he is the first evangelical theologian to face squarely the fact that if woman must of necessity be subordinate, she must of necessity be inferior."[84]

"But how can one defend a sexual hierarchy whereby men are over women—not just *some* men over *some* women, but *all* men over *all* women, because men are men and women are women—without

---

[80] Ibid., from the summary of the book on the back cover.

[81] Kevin Giles, <u>The Trinity and Subordinationism</u>, InterVarsity Press, Downers Grove, IL, c. 2002, p. 4. Why was Jesus considered "inferior and subordinate" in the Incarnation? It seems to me that to label Jesus as "inferior" during the Incarnation borders on Arianism, which is heresy.

[82] Kevin Giles, op. cit., p. 44.

[83] Millard Erickson, <u>Who's Tampering with the Trinity</u>, p. 175.

[84] Paul Jewett, <u>Man as Male and Female</u>, Wm. Eerdmans Publishing Company, c. 1975, p. 8. Actually in the foreword where Virginia Mollenkott is describing the author Paul Jewett.

supposing that the half of the human race which exercises authority is superior in some way to the half which submits?"[85]

"The difference of the woman from the man is beyond dispute. The issue is: Does this difference imply subordination? Can Barth (or anyone else) establish the mooted point—woman's *subordination to* the man—by underscoring the obvious point—woman's *difference from* the man—without the help of the traditional point—woman's *inferiority to* the man? The answer, it appears, is no."[86]

"Authority is a bond between people who are unequal."[87]

"All things being equal, servant leadership is a good idea. But in a world where all things are not equal—especially in matters of race, class, and gender—servant leadership has its limits…. Despite good intentions to serve, the leader retains the power. The inequality that often exists between the servant leader and the people being served remains unchanged."[88]

"Some egalitarians object to the complementarian interpretation of *head* as 'authority over' on the grounds that it requires that we not only view woman as subordinate to man but also view Christ as subordinate to God. By making the Son inferior to the Father, this interpretation introduces a heretical subordinationism into the Trinity."[89]

---

[85] Paul Jewett, Man as Male and Female, Wm. Eerdmans Publishing Company, Grand Rapids, MI, c. 1975, p. 71.

[86] Man as Male and Female, pp. 83, 84.

[87] Richard Sennett, Authority. London: Secker and Warburg, 1980, p. 10, as quoted by Stanley Grenz in Women in the Church, by Grenz and Kjesbo, InterVarsity Press, Downers Grove, IL, c. 1995, p. 225.

[88] "Lead Like Jesus," an article in *Christianity Today*, November 2015, by Christena Cleveland, p. 36.

[89] Stanley R. Grenz and Denise Muir Kjesbo, Women in the Church, InterVarsity Press, Downers Grove, Il, c. 1995, p. 114. The fact is that it does not *necessarily* introduce a heretical subordinationism. See page 66 in this chapter, where the difference is articulated. While I

"The equal standing of man and woman is incompatible with a subordinationist reading of verse 8." The author is referring to 1 Corinthians 11:8, which says, "For man was not made from woman, but woman from man. Neither was man created for woman, but woman for man" (1 Corinthians 11:8, 9).[90]

"Why would God call entirely equal sexes to deeply different roles? Why would one role be that of leadership and the other of submission if women and men were equal not only in status and dignity before God but in every other way as well?"[91]

"Is Jesus eternally subordinate to God the Father? Or are they coequal?"[92]

"Unless a scholar or interpreter assumes the superiority of men and inferiority of women as a presupposition for understanding the texts on gender, they cannot legitimately claim that his or her interpretation is in line with the traditions of Christianity.... Can they legitimately use traditional support for their interpretations and applications while they try to dissociate themselves from charges that they promote the ontological inferiority of women and superiority of men?"[93]

"Does the supposed subordination of the Son to the Father in eternity justify the *eternal subordination* of women to men in the heavenly church of the new creation? Are women to be *eternally* second-class citizens in the kingdom of God? Such specious arguments and misunderstandings of Scripture and tradition

---

definitely acknowledge the possibility of a heretical subordinationism, I believe there is such a thing as a non-heretical subordinationism.

[90] "Wild Hair and Gender Equality in I Corinthians 11:2-16," by Philip B. Payne, c. 2006 Payne Loving Trust. Can be located in *Priscilla Papers*, vol. 20, No. 3, Summer 2006.

[91] John G. Stackhouse, Jr., Finally Feminist: A Pragmatic Christian Understanding of Gender, Baker Academic, Grand Rapids, MI, c. 2005, p. 70.

[92] Alice Mathews, Gender Roles and the People of God, Zondervan, Grand Rapids, MI, c. 2017, p. 130.

[93] Cynthia Long Westfall, Paul and Gender. Baker Academic, Grand Rapids, MI, c. 2016, p. 4.

condemn women to positions of unending subordination, and worse still, *rob God the Son* of his coeternal and coequal glory, majesty, and lordship."[94]

"So, I ask again, why is it that subordination is never mentioned in any of these scriptural reflections on the immanent Trinity? The answer is very simple: subordination would absolutely throw into question the divine equality attributed to the Son."[95]

"What difference does it make for a woman whether she is 'equal' with men or is in a subordinate position to men?"[96]

What kind of assumptions do you, the reader, discern in those statements? Look over them again if necessary. I apologize for the quantity and repetitiveness in that list of quotes. My desire is to make a strong point, that point being the *pervasive assumption* that to be in submission implies inferiority and that hierarchy precludes equality. I believe the reason for that assumption is that we are living after the Fall of Man in Biblical history, and that affects how we understand relationships. That affects how we view hierarchy in relationships. It also affects how we function in a hierarchy. How we understand and function in hierarchy is a profound blind spot in the modern Christian worldview. Much of the blame for that lies in the way men have treated women throughout history, even in, and maybe especially in, church history. It's a bad sad story and we need to repent of that.

Complementarians bear a significant amount of blame for this bad sad story. Part of the blame is due to complementarians who consistently use the word "leader" as synonymous with "headship." I think that is a profound error. The word "leader" carries implications

---

[94] Alice Matthews, <u>Roles and the People of God</u>, Zondervan, Grand Rapids, MI, 49546, c. 2017, p. 144.

[95] Matthew Barrett, <u>Simply Trinity</u>, Baker Books, Grand Rapids, MI, c., 2021, p. 239.

[96] Alice Matthews, <u>Gender Roles and the People of God</u>, Zondervan, Grand Rapids, MI, c.2017, p. 48.

that the Biblical understanding of "head" does not, and the Biblical understanding of headship carries implications that "leader" does not. A second mistake complementarians have made is to define headship (*kephale*) as *synonymous* with authority, basically meaning the man is the boss. I think that does make women inferior. More on that later. I think much of the blame for the strident criticism of the submission of women to men in the quotes above is probably legitimate, and much of the cause is due, I believe, to a misunderstanding of headship and the concept of hierarchy among complementarians.

In addition to the above mistakes, we have to come to grips with the baggage that the word "subordinate" carries. For many people, unconsciously, part of the definition of "subordinate" is "inferior."[97] That is unfortunate, because it is not necessarily so and also because for many people that part of the definition is unconscious. So I will try to use to use the word "submissive" (but I may not always succeed), which seems to contain the same idea but hopefully without the sense of inferiority that "subordinate" implies.

For many people, it follows that since the three persons of the Trinity are equal, a very Biblical position and one I support without hesitation, role distinctions, especially authority distinctions, are precluded. The same line of thinking is also followed in the gender debate. In Dr. Philip Payne's book, <u>Man and Woman, One in Christ</u>, in chapter three, he lists twelve axioms of Paul that he says imply the equality of men and women. In the last one, he states that, especially in Christ, male and female are equal.[98] I know of few currently who

---

[97] "At this point it may be useful to distinguish between two English words often used as synonyms: submit versus subordinate. An Oxford dictionary distinguishes these terms in this way: submit has the sense of 'surrender [of oneself] to the control of another.' In contrast, subordinate as a noun means 'of inferior importance or rank, secondary.'" This from <u>Gender Roles and the People of God</u>, by Alice Matthews, p. 139. Also quoting the *Oxford Illustrated American Dictionary*, c. 1998, p. 827. Not being a linguist, I don't know if this is true, but I do want to use the words *submit* and *subordinate* in a way most people will understand. More on submission versus subordination later in this chapter.

[98] Philip Payne, <u>Man and Woman, One in Christ</u>. Zondervan, Grand Rapids, MI, c. 2009, pp. 69–76.

would disagree with that, although some, unfortunately, would. Very sadly, however, many well-known church fathers in the past have believed that women, compared to men, were inferior and shallow. Repentance is in order for that.[99] Dr. Payne believes that, since men and women are equal in Christ, there can be no submission based on gender either in the church or the home. In other words, equality precludes hierarchy.

The equality of men and women is really not the issue, or should not be. Both are created equally in God's image. The issue is whether role distinctions, particularly "hierarchical" role distinctions, are antithetical to equality. One of the theses of this book is that, as moderns and especially as citizens of a fallen world, we bring such a heavy load of bias and lack of understanding to this issue that we cannot accept both equality and hierarchy. And the fact is *all* hierarchy in this fallen world is controlled by sinful people, so all hierarchy is imperfect, to put it generously. Often it is incredibly evil and harmful to persons, especially to women, even in the church. The assumption that hierarchy eliminates equality seems present, consciously or unconsciously, in all of the quotes above. To be submissive or subordinate means, by definition, to be inferior. But the question before us is whether hierarchy in a perfect, unfallen world, precludes equality. If it is true that, in the Kingdom of God, it is possible that completely equal people can exist in a hierarchical relationship, then that is how we should live, or attempt to live, even in this fallen world. All the authors of the quotes above imply that hierarchy eliminates equality. And equality eliminates hierarchy.

That, however, is an assumption, and since we are trying to figure out if that assumption is true or not, you cannot use that assumption to figure out if people who are equal can still be in a hierarchical relationship. Let me put it another way: *if* it is true that

---

[99] Paul Jewett quotes Albrecht Oepke: "We never hear from the lips of Jesus a derogatory word concerning woman as such." And he makes the following observation: "If Jesus never belittled women, the theologians, to judge from such a comment, are hardly able to follow His example." That is a sad but true observation. See page 40 of his book, Man as Male and Female.

hierarchy can exist between two equal persons, then one cannot prove hierarchy does not exist, or should not exist, by proving their equality. That is important. It means we cannot disprove hierarchy among the persons of the Trinity merely by proving (or assuming) their equality, and it means we cannot disprove hierarchy in the gender issue by proving (or assuming) the genders are equal. What we need, and what is missing in the discussion, is a distinctly Christian understanding and *application* of hierarchy—where everybody is equal.

I recently had breakfast with my pastor, and we talked about the nature of the Trinity over scrambled eggs and bacon at Steak and Shake. He pointed out how words often carry hidden cultural meanings of which we may be completely unaware. This is part of the challenge and difficulty of communication I alluded to in the chapter on hermeneutics. He used the word "Waterloo" as an example. When we use the phrase, "He met his Waterloo," we are probably not consciously referring to a small town in Belgium. The word, to us, has a completely different definition from its original geographical definition; it just means a significant defeat. But the word has taken on a different definition from the small town in Belgium where Napoleon was soundly defeated, and so it now means to be soundly defeated in something, rather than to be introduced to the citizens of Waterloo. Likewise, a word such as "subordinate" carries with it, especially in the context of talking about the Trinity or the gender issue, baggage that implies "superiority" and "inferiority." In fact, in most people's minds, they are inseparable. This side of the fall, those words carry value assessments. They imply superior personhood and value or inferior personhood, value, and even competence. The word "hierarchy" even sounds like "higher-archy." One party is "higher" than another. We need to be open to the possibility that our thinking *might* be infected by the value system of this fallen world and *might not* reflect the values and definitions of the Kingdom of God. It is difficult, this side of Eden, to get beyond the personal value connotations of the word "subordinate," but I am convinced that issue is one of the "heavenly things," like being "born again," that caused Nicodemus to be so perplexed. I do not mean that as a condemnation of anybody but as a challenge for us to examine our thinking and the *possibility* of prejudice rooted in our current residence in a Fallen World. Definitions are crucial. By definition, it is true that assumptions, biases, and prejudices are not clearly thought out.

I very much appreciate this clarification in the 1999 Sydney Anglican Diocesan Doctrine Commission Report in Kevin Giles's book. "It [subordinationism] is a heresy. 'Subordinationism' is certainly the name given by historians of theology to a major heresy, that of suggesting that in substance or in being (ontologically) the Son is inferior to the Father. The classic form of Subordinationism is Arianism, the doctrine that taught that the Son was a secondary god, unlike and not of the same substance or essence as the Father.... *The question... is whether the subordinationism asserted in the current debate is the heretical form or not.*"[100] I want to be very clear that I am *not* talking about Jesus Christ or the Holy Spirit being any less than completely God. Neither Jesus Christ nor the Holy Spirit are "secondary" gods, in *any* way inferior to the Father. So the subordinationism I am talking about is *not* the heretical form. An important part of any communication is using the same definitions. I do not use the term "subordinate" to imply any sense of inferiority. Or lack of the same substance. I use it in the sense of "submissive," which, in the way I use the word, does not imply inferiority in any way. I cannot make that clear enough.

I believe the Scriptures teach that the Trinity consists of a hierarchy of equals. That does *not* make the Father superior to the Son or the Son inferior to the Father. Part of my purpose in writing this book is to begin to come to grips with the pain and scabs of living away from Paradise. It affects how we think. It affects how we

---

[100] Kevin Giles, <u>The Trinity and Subordinationism</u>. InterVarsity Press, p. 124, c. 2002, which quotes this study.

communicate. It affects our ability to understand and comprehend what the Scriptures teach. We need help to comprehend heavenly things. Not only do we need to be born again, as Nicodemus did, but our thinking needs not to be conformed to this world but instead be *transformed* by the renewal of our minds.[101]

Before we look at what the Scriptures teach, I want to be up front about several issues:

1. As creatures, we do not have the ability to understand our Creator. Our Creator is of such a different order of existence we will never be able to comprehend Him, or Her, or It.

2. As a consequence of the above assumption, any theological system we employ to try to explain our Creator will be inadequate. J. I. Packer wrote an excellent book entitled Evangelism and the Sovereignty of God, which I read as a young Christian. I still remember his paragraph about our minds being unable to hold certain seemingly contradictory concepts as having equal validity. That was very foundational to his topic, which invited the question, if God were really sovereign, why should we evangelize? He would bring those whom He wanted, so why should we do anything? Besides, how could we even recognize those whom He wanted? He exhorted his readers to realize we cannot put everything into nice neat theological boxes with no loose ends. Our minds are too small. That will always be true when we contemplate the nature of God. So there will be problems with *either* position. That is due to our limitations as humans.

3. Having said that, however, it is perfectly normal and healthy to try to contemplate the nature of God.

4. Since we are not sovereign, and since our minds do not have the mental horsepower to comprehend the nature of God,

---

[101] Romans 12:2. The image is that of a silversmith who uses a mold into which he pours liquid silver. When cooled, the mold is opened and the silver is now in the exact shape of the mold. So our thinking is not to be "molded" by this world.

we need to have the mental humility to submit to the way God has revealed himself in Scripture. The fact that it is difficult to comprehend should not automatically cause us to jettison the concept as unbelievable.

5. Our search must begin with observing the revelation of God in the Scriptures and determining our theology from that, rather than starting from some doctrine of relationships between human beings and extrapolating to the Trinitarian God of the universe. Theology is a one-way street.

We will look first at general revelation—what we can learn about the Creator from the creation. Then we will look at specific revelation, the Scriptures, and see what the Bible teaches, both about the submission of the Son and the Spirit and the complete equality of the Son with the Father and the Spirit. If we are interpreting both correctly, they will not contradict. We come as learners, not as imposers. We are under Scripture, not over it. Let's have a go at it.

The Nature of God as Revealed in His Creation (General revelation)

The first two observations are based upon general revelation. By that I mean what we can discern about the Creator from the creation, even though the first one comes from Scripture.

1. In Genesis 1:26 & 27, which are foundational verses for me, we have a picture of a plural God (later revealed to be a Trinity) who is (who are?) working together as a unity, as equal persons, making a group decision, to create the crown of their creation— human beings. When they are created, they are created also plural, that is, as male and female. They are given authority over the rest of God's creation. Nothing is said about either of them having authority over the other. The presence of one part of God's creation

83

having dominion over another part, the humans over everything else, should pique our interest. It invites the question: why is there hierarchy in God's creation? Why would God put into His creation such a thing as dominion of one species over the rest of everything? It was not necessary. The man and woman were not given the task of keeping order; that was not the purpose of dominion at this point in Biblical history: it was not even necessary. This was before the Fall, and authority was not necessary to keep order. In fact, there is no purpose mentioned at all. It's just there—I believe as a fingerprint of the nature of the Creator—who is hierarchical.

In Genesis 1, God "calls" certain parts of His creation by name. In verse 8 He "called" the firmament Heaven and so on throughout the rest of chapter one. In chapter two, God made the animals and brought them to the man, to Adam, to see what he would "call" them. And whatever he "called" them, that was its name. The same word is used in both instances. Just as God is higher than the creation, so, we should conclude, Adam is higher than the animals.

In Genesis 1:18, the narrator says that of the two great lights, the sun and the moon that God created, one was to "rule" the day, and the lesser light was to "rule" the night. They were set in the firmament of the heavens to give light and to "rule" over the day and over the night. It is the identical word to Genesis 3:16, where it says the man would "rule" over the woman, which is one of the effects of the Fall. The fact that "ruling" is present before the fall indicates that the concept of "rule" is not *necessarily* negative. However, since it describes the relationship of Adam and Eve after the fall, in that case it must be negative. That is an observation we need to revisit when we study Genesis 3. It is, however, not the same word as in Genesis 1:28, where the man and the woman together are to "have dominion" over God's creation and to "subdue" it. I don't want to be misunderstood: all I am saying is that there are several forms of hierarchy or order that seem to be built into God's perfect creation, before the Fall contaminated it. I am not saying that, since the sun "rules" the day and the moon "rules" the night, men should "rule" women. I am not at all saying that. There is no connection at all, except the same word is used. My point is that in God's perfect creation, before it was ruined by sin, we find words like "rule," "have dominion," and "subdue," and implied by the use of the same word "call" for God's naming the creation and Adam's naming of the animals, indicating Adam's superiority to the animals—all those words imply something we need to observe in God's creation: it bristles with hierarchy.[102] Since I believe the creation reflects something of the Creator, the presence of hierarchy invites a question: What aspect of the Creator is exhibited by the presence of several forms of hierarchy in the Creation? Or, to put it another way, how does one explain the pervasive presence of hierarchy in the creation by a creator who is, as some believe, non-hierarchical?

To answer my own question, I think that the order God has put into His creation is evidence of an order which exists among the three persons of the Triune God, the Creator. Thus, it is a form of general revelation. It is a fingerprint of the Creator. God could have created different life forms that were all equal and mutually submissive. He did not. Why did God create one part of his creation with authority over another part? It was not necessary. It was before the fall. It must have been by Design and reflects something of the Designer.

So there appear to be two kinds of diversity in God's creation. There is a "horizontal" diversity: there are a lot of different kinds of stuff in God's world. But there is also a "vertical" diversity: there is a diversity of authority. God has made it so that some parts of His creation have authority over other parts. That, I think, is significant. It reflects the diversity of the persons of the Creator.

---

[102] It may be significant that the same word "call" describes how Adam named his wife, Eve. If the use of that word is consistent, it would mean Adam is innately superior to Eve. But this happened after the fall and so seems consistent with the statement of consequence of the Fall, that Adam would "rule" over his wife. Now the hierarchy of perfect equals hinted at in Genesis 2, which we will observe in detail in chapter five on Genesis, has become a relationship of unequals where one is superior to the other.

2. One of the characteristics we observe about humanity, which uniquely is created in God's image, is that it is inescapably hierarchical. We need hierarchy to function.[103] I made this observation at the beginning of the chapter in the example of the firemen: there is no group of humans that is purposeful that is not hierarchical. Why does God's crowning creation, the only part of creation that is made in His image, *require* hierarchy to function? Could it be that this

---

[103] Even Richard Longenecker, an egalitarian, acknowledges this. "Certainly society requires order, with some people functioning as overseers and others as subordinates." This from a note on p. 76 of Women, Authority, and the Bible (InterVarsity Press). But he does not question *why* society *requires* order. That is a question that begs answering, and I believe it is because we, as humans, as male and female, are created in the image of a God who consists of a hierarchy of equals. As human beings, we cannot function outside our nature. But in a fallen world, the hierarchy has become something very different from what it was designed to be—and significantly uglier. Unfortunately, all our experience of hierarchy is in a fallen world. Nicholas Wolterstorff in the same book agrees: "I do not see how there can be human society without authority—understood here as the right to ask obedience. Furthermore, the Bible, so far from repudiating all authority, sacralizes at least a good deal of it. Governmental authorities, it says, are ministers of God. As for hierarchialism, God has inherent authority over us and parents have inherent authority over children.... The point is not that authority and hierarchy are to be entirely eliminated, but that gender is simply not relevant to the assignment of benefits and deprivations, neither within the church nor without." (From Women, Authority, and the Bible, an article entitled "Hearing the Cry" by Nicholas Wolterstorff, p. 291.) There are a couple of issues to observe: One is that he assigns "benefits and deprivations" to where one falls in the hierarchy. That is *very* significant and betrays a value system grounded in this fallen world rather than in the Kingdom of God. "Benefits and deprivations" in hierarchy are not part of the Christian understanding of hierarchy. Secondly, I think, is that he, obviously an egalitarian, recognizes that God's crowning creation, the only creation specifically made in His image, is inescapably hierarchical. He does not see how there can be human society without authority. That is a strong statement! I wish that Dr. Longenecker had not used the word "subordinate," as that particular word carries baggage implying inferiority. It is also significant, I think, that in the very next article in the book, "Understanding the Differences," J. I. Packer says that two passages, Genesis 2:18–23 and Ephesians 5:21–33, "continue to convince me that the man-woman relationship is intrinsically non-reversible. By this I mean that, other things being equal, a situation in which a female boss has a male secretary, or a marriage in which the woman (as we say) wears the trousers, will put more strain on the humanity of both parties than if it were the other way around. This is part of the reality of creation, a given fact, that nothing will change. Certainly, redemption will not change it for grace restores nature, not abolishes it" (ibid., p. 299). That is quite an amazing quote! It strains our humanity if the female is in charge rather than the male, he says! And that, he says, is part of the reality of our creation. To be honest, I have no problem with a female boss and male secretary in a secular environment. That is one way the equality of the genders can be manifested. The hierarchy I am talking about belongs to two distinctly Christian types of relationships—marriage and the church. And only there. At least for now. I do not know about heaven and am not willing even to debate that issue, as it is not only beyond our understanding but also, I believe, beyond what God has revealed to us.

also is a reflection of something in the nature of the plurality of the Godhead?[104]

Now it may be decided that hierarchy, as least among humans, is a result of the fall. After all, it does say the man would "rule" over the wife, and that is listed as a consequence of the fall for the woman. In that instance, it must be negative because all the effects of the fall were negative. We will need to make that decision after we have looked at Genesis in more depth. So let's put that question on hold and return to it in the chapter on Genesis. But for now we need to acknowledge that, in God's creation, hierarchy is pervasive, and in God's highest creation, the only one that is created in His image, that creature seems to be inescapably hierarchical. We cannot function without hierarchy.[105] Again, I do not want to be understood as saying more than I intend. I am just saying that we find evidence

---

[104] Dr. William Webb, in his book <u>Slaves, Women, & Homosexuals</u>, makes this statement: "It is much easier to argue that no human being should ever own another human being than to argue that no human being should ever exist in a hierarchical relationship to another human being. In fact, I cannot argue the latter. There are numerous social relationships where hierarchy makes good sense. The ultra-soft patriarchialists might be inclined to think that their argument is won. Having established the acceptability of hierarchy in *some* human relationships (and in divine relationships as well), they might be lulled into a false sense of confidence. However, any confidence at this stage of the dialogue is short-lived. The only thing that an ultra-soft position has really established to this point is that hierarchy in human relationships is not inherently evil" (p. 49). The author is in the midst of developing an argument, and this quote is mid-way in the development. But notice his two points: one is that hierarchy in human relationships is not inherently evil. I do not want to mis-represent him as if he favors one gender in hierarchy over the other. He doesn't. His second point is that he acknowledges hierarchy in the Trinity, as well. He also talks about patriarchialists having a "false sense of confidence." Frankly, I don't like the implication of that phrase. This is not about *me* supporting *my* position and winning *my* argument. It is about finding out what is *true*.

[105] Dr. Jim Belcher, in his book <u>Deep Church</u>, describes a new phenomenon among Christians in the emerging church movement called the "liquid church": "What would the liquid church look like? ... It would be characterized by no regular meetings, constant communication, limited or no formal structure, and no ordained ministry or offices.... The liquid church is about relationships, being connected in a myriad of groupings, activities and events. The goal is to live together every day.... When the group gathers, there would be no ordained clergy; everyone will have a chance to participate." (From <u>Deep Church</u>, InterVarsity Press, c. 2009, Downers Grove, IL, p. 166.) The interesting thing to me about this description is how it resembles my example of a flock of birds in the introduction to this chapter, flying this way or that with no discernible leadership, listening to some mysterious inner voice. I don't think humans are created to function that way, and the evidence is that they do not function that way.

in God's creation, and especially in human beings who uniquely are created in God's image, that, I think, points to a characteristic of the relationships among the Creator—the Trinity. The evidence is this: God's creation bristles with diversity and even a diversity of authority. And, frankly, I think the burden of proof is on the egalitarians who deny the possibility of hierarchy or diversity (at least a diversity or roles) among the persons of the Trinity to explain why such an egalitarian Trinity would create a world with hierarchy, diversity, and order infused into it instead of mutuality. It is so non-reflective of Him.

Dr. Millard Erickson asks a tough question in his book about the Trinity: "Does it follow from the necessity of differences of role that there must be superiority and subordination of role? ... Might it not be the case, however, that the Father, Son, and Holy Spirit perform different roles within the economy of the Godhead, and perhaps even that these are necessarily the roles they perform, without one having to be superior to the others?"[106]

Notice first how he uses "superiority" and "subordination" as a necessary consequence of the possibility of differentiation of roles in the Trinity. To be subordinate is the opposite of "superior," which would make one "inferior." That is some of the baggage we need to unload from our Christian worldview. In the last sentence, when he talks about "one having to be superior to the others," he means "be in authority over." So, firstly, I want to disagree strenuously that to be in authority over someone automatically makes one superior, in terms of personhood, to that person. That is very hard for us in a fallen world to understand.

Secondly, the question he is really asking is this: *if* there are differing roles among persons (and here he is specifically talking about the persons of the Trinity), then is it *necessary* for one to be in authority over the others to function as a group? To put it another way, is it necessary for hierarchy to exist among relationships if those

---

[106] Millard J. Erickson, Who's Tampering with the Trinity? Kregel Academic & Professional, Grand Rapids, MI 49501, c. 2009, p. 185.

relationships involve differing functions or roles? Perhaps God needs hierarchy in order to function as the Trinity because their roles are different. Could that be? Now, in terms of the Trinity, my answer to that question is very simple: "I have no idea." I would never say God can't function in a particular manner. But there seems to be plenty of evidence that God's crowning creation, the only part of creation created in God's image, *does* require hierarchy to function. I would not extrapolate that back to God and say that the diversity among the persons of the Trinity *requires* hierarchy for the Trinity to function. The three persons of the Trinity are always in complete unity. They are One. But experience seems to indicate that human beings, who, by Scripture's testimony, are created in God's image, *do* require hierarchy to function. We cannot function as group, whether it be a small group Bible study, a team of firemen, or a government, without an authority structure. We just don't function like a flock of birds, mysteriously turning this way and that, in unison. And that, I believe, is a reflection of humanity's creator, Jehovah God of the Bible. So I am clueless as to whether or not it is *necessary* for one person of the Trinity to be in authority over another; but it certainly does seem to be *necessary* for human beings. And that is a fingerprint of the Creator—the presence of hierarchy. Now, as we open the Bible, we will look to see if the three persons of the Trinity are just different, or maybe not, or if they exist and function in a hierarchy.

The Nature of God as Revealed in Scripture (Specific Revelation)

Submission During the Incarnation

So far, I have looked at what the Creation *indicates* is the nature of the Creator. Now I want to look at what Scripture *teaches* about the nature of the Creator. If we find Scripture teaching the same as we observed from the creation, then that is a good sign that we may be on track. As much as possible, we want to begin without prejudice, especially the prejudice of living in a Fallen World. I realize that is impossible, but I challenge us, as much as possible, consciously to try to leave behind life-long patterns of thinking and take a walk across newly fallen snow, making new tracks, as we try to understand Scripture without prejudice or bias.

1) Jesus was submissive during the Incarnation. Jesus frequently describes himself as coming to earth as a result of being sent by the Father. "My food is to do the will of him who sent me and to accomplish his work."[107] "And the Father who sent me has himself borne witness to me."[108] "No one can come to me unless the Father who sent me draws him."[109] "As the living Father sent me, and I live because of the Father, so he who eats me will live because of me."[110] "I bear witness to myself, and the Father who sent me bears witness to me."[111] "He who sent me is true, and I declare to the world what I have heard from Him."[112] "I can do nothing of my own authority but speak thus as the Father taught me."[113] He seemed to make it very clear that He was not here on earth of His own will, but by the Father's will. "My teaching is not mine, but his who sent me; if any man's will is to do his will, he shall know whether the teaching is from God or whether I am speaking on my own authority."[114]

Notice in those quotes from Jesus how He makes it clear that He did not come on His own authority but instead because the Father *sent* Him. In fact, He says that He could do *nothing* on his own authority. Dwell on that for a minute or two. The work He was doing was not His work but the Father's who sent Him.

---

[107] John 4:34
[108] John 5:37
[109] John 6:44
[110] John 6:57
[111] John 7:18
[112] John 8:26
[113] John 8:28
[114] John 7:16, 17

Part of the debate we will look at later is the meaning of the Greek word *kephale*, which some say means "authority," while others say it means "source." It is usually translated as "head." Dr. Phillip Payne makes an interesting statement in his book in the context of debating this issue: he says, "the meaning 'source' implies no inherent subordination of Christ. It simply affirms that Christ came from the Godhead in the incarnation."[115] That is the most common understanding by those who use the meaning "source" for *kephale*. Given how Jesus himself describes it, I don't understand how you can describe Jesus' incarnation as merely "coming from the Father." That does not seem to be a fair summary of the words in the texts listed above, in the very words of Jesus Himself. John 8:42, the text that Dr. Payne refers to, indicates Jesus "came" from the Father, says Dr. Payne. It says, "If God were your Father, you would love me, for I proceeded and came forth from God." That certainly seems to support Dr. Payne's and many others' position. However, in the same verse, in the same breath, in the very next words out of Jesus' mouth, He says, "I came not of my own accord but he sent me." Jesus did not "simply… come from the Godhead in the incarnation." He was *sent*. Dr. Payne seems to be shamelessly picking and choosing which words of Jesus to believe. In John 7:28, Jesus seems to be desirous of making that very clear: "I did *not* come of my own accord…." Just to "come" and to be "sent" are not synonymous, and we should not understand them as synonymous. Consistently, those who define *kephale* as "source" say, as Dr. Payne did in the quote above, that God is the *kephale* of Christ in that Christ "came from the Godhead in the incarnation." But if there is any period of time when the Son clearly was submissive to the Father, it is during the Incarnation. He said repeatedly that he was "sent." Those are His words. So to use the Incarnation as an example of a non-authoritative relationship between the Father and the Son just does not do justice to the words, especially the words of the Key Figure involved.

---

[115] Philip Payne, <u>Man and Woman, One in Christ</u>, pp. 134–135.

Jesus seemed desirous to make it clear that, even in the form of God on earth, He was submissive as a Son to His Father. Yet the church has affirmed the complete equality and deity of the Son while on earth along with the Spirit. I believe that affirmation to be completely true. Therefore, it would seem that it *must*_be possible to be equal and still submissive, because that characterized Jesus while He was on earth. Everybody agrees that, when Jesus was on earth, He was submissive to the Father. And everyone except heretics agree that Jesus was fully God when He was on earth. It may be possible, of course, that this submission of the Son to the Father was only temporary, a necessary[116] result of the Incarnation, which is a common position many believers take. Jesus, during the Incarnation, was both fully God and fully human, and so His submission can be explained away as being required because of His humanity. Of course, humans are to be submissive to God. And yet in Scripture Jesus is portrayed as submissive before the incarnation. We will tackle that difficult issue below. He was still a divine part of the Trinity when God "sent" Him. So you really cannot explain His submission as merely a result of His humanity.[117]

---

[116] There are a number of authors who use the word "necessary" in reference to the Son's coming to earth to accomplish our salvation. But that, to me, invites the question of why it was "necessary." It certainly is possible, and this would seem to be the simplest answer, that the submission of Jesus to the Father, or of the Son to the Father, was a *direct* result of His taking on human flesh. It is, of course, completely appropriate for humans to be submissive to their Creator. If submission by the Son to the Father were only a result of taking on human flesh, a *necessary* result of taking on human flesh, then we should expect to see some evidence for lack of submission among the persons of the Trinity, in the pre-incarnate Christ or post-incarnate Christ. That is missing. Jesus is *eternally* the Son, before the Incarnation and after. Some have said that the use of language like Father and Son referring to the pre-incarnate and post-incarnate Christ is anthropomorphic language, thereby admitting that the terms "Father" and "Son" do occur in pre-incarnate and post-incarnate descriptions. When an anthropomorphism is used, it is meant to communicate *something*. So that raises the question of what God is trying to communicate by using that anthropomorphism. Additionally, *if* there really is such a thing as some sort of hierarchy among the equal persons of the Trinity, even before and after the Incarnation, how could it be communicated to us without it being dismissed as merely anthropomorphic language? And if it is not "merely anthropomorphic language," then what is the reality in the Trinity which is represented by terms like "Father" and "Son"?

[117] The first chapter of the book of Hebrews bristles with this dichotomy that we have such a hard time accepting and understanding—hierarchy and equality. The Son is "appointed heir of

At this point, it seems to me, at least three questions arise:

a) Why is it acceptable that the Son was submissive and still equal with God during the Incarnation, but unacceptable that He could be submissive and equal with God for all eternity, as many who deny hierarchy in the Trinity believe?

b) If it is impossible that the Son is eternally submissive yet equal to the Father, does that mean that the Incarnation is not a true revelation of God, since the Son was clearly, by His own testimony, submissive and equal while on earth?

c) If Jesus' submission on earth was due only to his taking on of human flesh (which is a possible answer to questions a and b), why did He *consistently* describe Himself, as we saw above, as being submissive to the *Father*—that is, to *part* of the Trinity? It would seem that if He were modeling how we humans should live in submission to God, then He would describe His submission as being to God, as ours is (or should be), rather than just to the Father.

2) There are a number of passages where Jesus relates to the Father as someone who is in authority over him—both during the Incarnation and before and after the Incarnation.

In John 17, Jesus prays to the Father for his disciples. Lest we think that this is an activity of Jesus limited only to the Incarnation, remember that intercession is the only activity recorded of Jesus since his ascension. In fact, both the Spirit and the Son are listed as interceding for us in Romans 8:26, 27, 34: "Likewise the Spirit helps us in our weakness. But the Spirit intercedes for us with sighs too deep for words.... The Spirit intercedes for the saints according to the will of God.... Is it Christ Jesus, who died, yes who was raised from the dead, who is at the right hand of God, who indeed intercedes for us?" Notice that both the Holy Spirit and Jesus are

---

all things" and sent into the world by the Father, yet is addressed by the Father as "God." Being "appointed" implies authority, yet the one who is appointed is addressed as "God."

interceding for us. The nature of intercession is that one intercedes to a higher authority.

As we have already seen, the Gospel of John frequently records Jesus describing his coming to earth because He was sent by the Father (John 4:34, 5:37, 6:44, 6:38, 7:28, 8:18, 8:26, etc.). In fact, He seemed to want to make it very clear that he was not here on earth because of His choice or initiative, but because the Father sent him. John 5:19 says, "Truly, truly, I say to you, the son can do nothing of his own accord, but only what he sees the Father doing; for whatever he does, the son does likewise." John 7:17 says, "I have not come of my own accord, he who sent me is true." John 12:49–50 says, "I have not spoken on my own authority. The Father who has sent me has given me commandment what to say and what to speak.... What I say therefore, I say as the Father has bidden me."

The Bible clearly portrays Jesus as submissive to the Father during the Incarnation. Since the only recorded activity of Jesus since the ascension is to intercede for us, this would indicate submission after the Incarnation also.

In John 20:21, Jesus sends out his disciples with the following words: "As the Father has sent me, so I also send you." Clearly, Jesus had the authority to send His disciples out. This verse implies that the Father has the *same* authority over Jesus. The word "as" implies similarity. In the same way that Jesus was *sent* out by the Father, Jesus *sent* out His disciples. There was authority involved in *both* cases, a similar authority implied by the word "as."

3) The submission of Jesus to the Father is not limited to His time on earth alone. The same language is used describing both the Pre-incarnate Christ and the Post-incarnate Christ. If the submission of Jesus to the Father were only limited to the time of the Incarnation, which many theologians believe, then there should be evidence of a lack of submission, or evidence of mutuality, in the texts describing

the pre-incarnation or post-incarnation relationships in the Trinity. Is that true?

There are no instances where Jesus even hints that His submission to the Father was temporary and limited to the period of the Incarnation. There was also never a hint that his submission was due exclusively to His status as a human being. However, there is a question that needs to be examined. We asked above about the possibility that the Incarnation might not be a True revelation of God if Jesus' submission to the Father was only during the Incarnation and not for all eternity. Let's be honest. There were some unique characteristics of the relationship of the Son to the Father during the Incarnation. It is not typical of the eternal Trinity that one person (the Son) would be unaware of what the other persons are doing, as Jesus was about the timing of the Second Coming. It is not typical that one person of the Trinity would cry out to another person of the Trinity, "My God, My God, why have you forsaken me?"[118] However, both those observations can be explained by the fact that Jesus, in addition to being completely God, was also completely human, and at one point in history even took the penalty for *my* sin. That burden caused a jarring shake-up in the relationships among the Trinity.

Dr. Bilezikian brings up the interesting and somewhat difficult verse from Hebrews 5:7–9. The verse says, "In the days of his flesh, Jesus offered up prayers and supplications, with loud cries and tears, to him who was able to save him from death, and he was heard for his godly fear. Although he was a Son, he learned obedience through what he suffered; and being made perfect he became the source of eternal salvation to all who obey him."

Dr. Bilezikian says, "Whenever Christ is said to act in obedience, he fulfills his self-assumed destiny as Suffering Servant rather than obeying orders. In so doing, he displays an obedience not required of him, since he was a Son. He did not learn obedience *because* he

---

[118] Matthew 27:46

95

was a Son but *in spite of* the fact he was a Son ("Although he was a Son, he learned obedience" [Heb. 5:8]). His obedience did not derive from submission in sonship but from 'being made perfect' (Heb 5:9) in fulfilling his mission. He accomplished his task by being obedient to it, even unto death (Phil. 2.8)."[119]

This is a complex text with a number of issues that need interpretation.

First, it is not a fair description of the Incarnation to say it was "his self-assumed destiny." Look back again at the words Jesus himself used to describe His coming from the Father on page 90 in this chapter. Jesus consistently described His coming as being "sent" and made it clear that He did not come on His own authority. To describe the Incarnation as Jesus' "self-assumed destiny" is just plain inaccurate. But then, that understanding, although never mentioned in Scripture, follows from Dr. Bilezikian's denial of hierarchy in the Trinity. Jesus would have to self-assume his Sonship, since being "sent" would imply authority and Dr. Bilezikian cannot accept that among the persons of the Trinity.

Second, I scratch my head at his understanding of sonship. Did he say, "obedience was not required of Him *since* he was a Son"? The Scriptures are clear that children (including sons) are to obey their parents. How could he say obedience was not required of him *since* he was a son, as if sonship did not include obedience? That is one of the problems for those who deny hierarchy in the Trinity: why would God reveal himself using the words "Father" and "Son" if no submission were involved?

Third, there is also a problem with the word "learned." Why on earth would Jesus have had to learn *anything*, especially obedience, since He was sinless? Dr. Bilezikian's point is that Jesus learned obedience not because He was a Son but from being a Suffering Servant, his "self-assumed destiny." However, the words "suffering Servant" are not even mentioned in this text. That interpretation

---

[119] Gilbert Bilezikian, <u>Beyond Sex Roles</u>, p. 228.

seems to be more based on the assumptions that he brings to the text than on what the text says. Since Dr. Bilezikian cannot accept a hierarchy of equals in the Trinity; he has to assume that sonship does not include obedience (contrary to what the Scriptures teach about sonship) and so imports words and meanings that are not in the text. Fourth, the text seems to imply that the term "son" applies to Jesus before the Incarnation. Dr. Bilezikian seems to accept that implication or he would not have to come up with his "sonship does not require obedience" principle. Since he cannot accept that the Trinity is a hierarchy of equals, his only option in interpreting this verse is to conclude that sonship must not require obedience, which, when applied to earthly sons, is an unBiblical position. This is a complicated and difficult text, which we will re-visit in more depth in chapter ten.

The names given us for two persons of the Trinity, the Father and the Son, are not limited to the time of the Incarnation. Everything taught in the Bible about parenting makes it clear that children are to be submissive to parents and sons are to be submissive to fathers.[120] If there is no submission in the Trinity, it is mysterious, if not confusing, why *God* would choose these particular words as names for two persons of the Trinity and why those particular names would be used both at Creation and after the end of time. In Revelation 3:21, the Risen and reigning Christ says, "I myself conquered and sat down with my Father on his throne." Note that, not only does Jesus still use the term "Father," but He also describes the throne as his Father's throne, not "our" throne, which might indicate a lack of hierarchy. Another example is Hebrews 1:2b: "but in these last days he [God] has spoken to us by a Son, whom he appointed the heir of all things, and through whom also he created the world." So Jesus is described as the Son both at the creation of the world and in "these last days." Also, Jesus, the Son, is "appointed" the heir of all things. To be "appointed" implies authority. It seems to me difficult to hold

---

[120] Again, see Nicholas Wolterstorff, an egalitarian, in <u>Women, Authority, and the Bible</u>, p. 291: "parents have inherent authority over children."

97

the position that Sonship and Fatherhood describe the relationships among those two persons of the Trinity only during the time of the Incarnation. Otherwise, why is the term "Son" used to describe Jesus on the throne of His Father at the end of time and at the creation of the universe? Those are God's words, not man's. I believe words in the Scriptures are trustworthy. The chosen words Father and Son are not meaningless. God could have chosen the words brother and brother if complete mutuality were the principle. Or better yet: brother and sister.[121] But God chose Father and Son, which has implications both in terms of authority, and at the same time, equality.

The only activity recorded of Jesus since the Resurrection is His interceding for us. To whom? The idea of intercession is that it is done to someone of higher authority. You don't intercede to someone of lower authority. So that activity of Jesus that is done on our behalf implies hierarchy among the persons of the Trinity.

The writer of the book of Hebrews obviously had a very high view of Jesus. That is obvious from the way the book opens. We'll look at that in the next section as we examine the equality of the Son with the Father. Yet in verse five of chapter five, it says that Christ "was appointed by him who said to him, 'Thou are my son, today I have begotten thee.'" To be appointed implies order and authority.

Notice the strange contradiction even in the Great Commission at the end of Matthew 28: "All authority in heaven and earth is given unto me. Go, therefore, and make disciples of all people." Why do I use the term "strange contradiction"? If all authority on heaven and earth belongs to Jesus, then He is not *under* any authority. There is nobody to whom He needs to be submissive. But it is *given* to Him. By whom? How could He not be under any authority, but that position be *given* to him? And why does He use phrases like "I can do nothing of my own authority, but speak thus as the Father taught me"?[122]

---

[121] One of the problems with terms like brother/brother or brother/sister is they imply a pre-existing parent, which of course could not be true for the persons of the Trinity.

[122] John 8:28

There is an interesting quirk in the definitions made by several who deny any order among the persons of the Trinity. Some define the heresy of subordinationism as the view that the Son and Spirit "do not fully possess the divine essence." Another says, "The doctrine that in essence and status the Son is inferior to the Father, or the Spirit is inferior to the Father and the Son."[123] Those would both be the heretical subordinationism. These are written by people who do not see any sort of subordination or order in the Trinity as viable or Biblical. We should (and I do) consider it heretical for any person of the Trinity to be considered *inferior* in essence and status to another person of the Trinity. The question is whether or not the *role* determines the status, superiority or inferiority.

The Kroegers claim the heresy of Subordinationism "assigns an inferiority of being, status, or role to the Son or Holy Spirit within the Trinity."[124] It is significant to note that the Kroegers characterize the heresy of subordinationism as being defined by "being, status, or *role*" (italics mine). They said "role." Do they really believe that your role defines your being or status, your personhood? The practical implications of that error are enormous. I wonder if they would go so far as to say that being a servant of another makes one an inferior person—in *any* situation. Clearly in the Kingdom of God that is not true. Jesus said that if you want to be the best in the Kingdom of God, you need to be a servant.

Yet on the very same page quoted above, they say, "The Nicene fathers ascribed to the Son and Spirit an equality of being or essence but a subordination of order."[125] So it seems, if they are consistent, they would need to reject at least that part of the Nicene Creed, because it refers both to equality of being but subordination of "order." That is one of problems with the position that role determines

---

[123] The Concise Dictionary of Christian Theology. Baker Books, Grand Rapids, MI, 1986, p. 161, from the article on subordinationism by Millard Erickson.
[124] R. C. and C. C. Kroeger, "Subordinationism," in *Evangelical Dictionary of Theology*, ed. Walter A. Elwell (Grand Rapids, MI: Baker Book House, 1984), p. 1,058.
[125] Ibid.

personhood or equality of person. And that is the problem with an unBiblical understanding of hierarchy.

But, having said that, is it not telling that they *always* mention the subordination of the Son and the Spirit, but *never* of the Father? Why is that? Because the Bible *never* hints at the subordination of the Father. It would seem, if there were complete mutuality among the persons of the Trinity, as they claim, the Father would be included in the subordination. There would be "mutual subordination" among the persons of the Trinity somewhere. But the subordination *never* extends to the Father. And so they betray the truth they are attempting to deny in their definitions—that the order in the Trinity, as revealed in Scripture, always goes one way.

In her book, Men and Women in the Church, Dr. Sarah Sumner mentions complementarians hypothetically saying that men have exclusive access to higher status leadership "solely on the basis of their gender." Or again, "From their perspective, they are submitting to the mandate of Scripture. It is not men's gender per se that leads them to believe that men take the roles with higher status."[126] This is *very* important. She let the s-word slip out: status. She calls the supposed roles the males claim in applying their understanding of Scripture as roles "with *higher status.*" That is a very significant mistake and is, I think, the "elephant in the room" in the gender debate. It is an unBiblical understanding of headship or hierarchy. Dr. Nicholas Wolterstorff reveals the same misunderstanding when he says, "gender is simply not relevant to the assignment of benefits and deprivations, neither within the church nor without."[127] Did he really say "benefits and deprivations"? Which roles provide "benefits" and which provide "deprivations"? I wonder how much of the underlying energy pushing us towards egalitarianism in the church and the home is seeing certain roles as having more "status" or "benefits" and others, as a result, as having less "status" and

---

[126] Sarah Sumner, Men and Women in the Church, InterVarsity Press, Downer's Grove, IL, c. 2003, p. 278.
[127] Nicholas Wolterstorff, Women, Authority, and the Bible, p. 291.

more "deprivations." Or, on the other hand, I wonder how much of the pressure from the complementarian side of the debate is men wanting to be in control, or "in charge," desiring to maintain the "status" and "benefits" of being the leaders. If so, and I suspect that is true, then they have fallen into the same trap. If certain roles do contain such privileges, then to deprive one gender access to that "status" or those "benefits" or relegating that gender to the "deprivations" of not having equal access really is *unjust*. If certain roles really do have those qualities, then I agree that "equal access" is a matter of *justice*.

This is very important and one of the themes of this book. In our fallen world, hierarchy is perceived to confer importance, status, and superiority to those in the "higher" positions of the "hierarchy." I think that is a result of the Fall. I do not see that those "higher up" in the hierarchy as having more personal worth, status, or benefits, or are in any way superior in the Kingdom of God. And so hierarchy in the Trinity, which I believe the Bible teaches, does *not* imply superiority or inferiority of any of the persons of the Trinity. This is one of the heavenly things—values belonging to the Kingdom of God—that are hard for us to comprehend as members of this fallen world.[128]

Dr. John Stackhouse talks about feeling the pain of patriarchy, the pain of "being passed over recognition or promotion," on page 240 of the book, How I Changed My Mind About Women in Leadership.[129] I don't mean to minimize the pain of being treated as less than equal or as incompetent merely because you were born a woman. I don't want to minimize that at all, and the history of the church bristles with that sin. But he does use the words "recognition or promotion." Did he really mean "promotion"? That is not a neutral word. Felicity Dale says one of the goals for her

---

[128] I do not mean to imply that character or maturity are irrelevant in choosing leaders. Just that that does make them more valuable as persons in the Kingdom of God.

[129] John G. Stackhouse, Jr., in the article, "How to Produce an Egalitarian Man," in the book How I Changed My Mind About Women in Leadership. Zondervan, Grand Rapids, MI, c. 2010, p. 240.

book The Black Swan Effect[130] is to help women "reach their full potential," and the rest of the book is about the need of the church for women in leadership. Does that mean a woman, or a man for that matter, or some women or some men, cannot reach their full potential unless they are in a position of leadership? I fear that women may be following men down the wrong path, a path that men have followed for thousands of years, thinking that being a leader makes you "important." That being a leader makes you superior. In God's kingdom, that is not true. I hope, for both men and women, that being promoted or being recognized as a leader is not our goal or our vision of the "successful" Christian life, nor that it gives status or benefits. There are definite Biblical qualifications for choosing leaders, and these should not be ignored. But being in the position of leader does not make you superior. This is very much a gender-neutral challenge—for men and women both—to all Christians—to be different from the fallen world where we live. We must take to heart the words of Jesus on this topic in Mark 10:43: "but it shall not be so among you." In the kingdom of God, leadership and servanthood are seen very differently than they are in our fallen world. One does not have more status than the other. In fact, is that not one of the significant points of Paul's teaching in 1 Corinthians 12 on the nature of the Body of Christ—that all receive *the same* care and we do not give more care and attention to "our more presentable parts"? In other words, your value, your care from the Body of Christ, does not come from what role you fulfill in the Body of Christ. That is a profound truth we need to grasp. Do we really believe that?[131]

---

[130] The Black Swan Effect, by Felicity Dale and others, Kingdom Heart Publishing, c. 2014, p. viii.

[131] I am writing this at a time of a surprising evil resurgence of white supremacy in our nation. It makes me wonder what the root of that is, or what the cause of racism in general is. Why do we feel the need to be superior? To be better than another race? To put down another race so we can feel superior? I have listened to Christian homeschoolers speak critically of the world around us and positively about how they avoid the sins of the world, with an air of superiority. And then public schoolers criticize the homeschoolers for separatism, also with an air of superiority. Each political party in our country feels superior to the other. First Corinthians 1

The Scriptures seem to be consistent in presenting us with the picture of a Triune God of three equal persons, who exist in a particular order but who are completely equal. What else can you do with the names Father and Son, chosen by God, instead of brother and sister? What else can you do with the Biblical revelation that Jesus came because the Father "sent" Him, and that Jesus' promise that He would "send" the Holy Spirit? If you are one who believes in the egalitarian view of God, these are questions sitting on your plate.

That, however, is not the full picture.

The Equality of Jesus to the Father and the Spirit

Having said all this, it must be acknowledged with equal weight that the Son and the Spirit and the Father are completely equal persons in the three-person God whom we acknowledge. Everybody agrees on that. It is considered heresy not to. Having made the claim that the best way to understand the whole Biblical picture of order or hierarchy in the Trinity is to acknowledge some sort of order from the Father to the Son to the Spirit, we must also acknowledge their complete equality. Here is the evidence:

1. Jesus was often found dodging stones in the gospels—most often in John, the same book in which He most often describers Himself as being "sent" and as being under the authority of the Father. In John 10:30, Jesus makes the statement, "I and the Father are One."

---

describes a "party spirit" in the church there—where each party feels superior because of the person they follow. Germany, in World War II, was infected with a racial superiority complex. The church at Ephesus seems to be infected with this disease—the need to be superior or to be seen as superior. So we read in 1 Timothy 6:5 that there were some in that church who where "depraved in mind and bereft of the truth imagining that godliness is a means of *gain*." What is this "gain" that comes as a result of winning some theological argument? What is the root of this need to feel superior to others? I believe it is an ugly manifestation of hierarchy after the fall, infected by sin, with the need to be more important, superior, better than others. And especially for others to know about it.

The people listening understood exactly what He was saying. Jesus made no attempt to correct them. This was why they were throwing stones at Jesus: "We stone you because you, being a man, *make yourself equal with God.*" He also said, "If you had known me, you would have known my Father."[132] Or also, "I and the Father are one."[133] Again, "This is why the Jews sought all the more to kill him, because he not only broke the Sabbath but also called God his Father, making himself equal with God."[134] Never does Jesus try to correct their understanding of what He was saying. He fully accepts it. He clearly saw Himself as equal with the Father.

2. In Mark 2:1–12, Jesus seems intent on making that very point and even takes the initiative to do it. It takes place in the well known story of four men lowering down a paralytic through a hole in the roof directly in front of Jesus in order that he might be healed. Jesus mysteriously does not heal him at first, but instead pronounces his sins forgiven. (I suspect the four anonymous men who carried this paralytic to Jesus looked at each other in surprise and maybe frustration. This is *not* why they brought him to Jesus.) The scribes sitting there immediately light up. "Who can forgive sins but God alone? It is blasphemy!" Don't miss the seriousness of their accusation. Jesus' statement was worthy of punishment of death by stoning and the reason is clear: only God can forgive sins.

Forgiveness always rests with the person who is sinned against. If I dent a friend's car, the problem is between him and me. Forgiveness rests on him. But Jesus had never seen this paralyzed man before. The paralytic had done nothing against Jesus. So why would Jesus make this strange statement about forgiving this paralytic of his sins when He was not the one sinned against? Obviously, He was assuming He *was* one who had been sinned against—namely, God.

---

[132] John 14:7

[133] John 10:30

[134] John 5:18. Note that while calling God His Father implies hierarchy, it also implies equality with God.

The Pharisees were correct: Jesus was committing blasphemy. He was assuming the position of the person sinned against—namely, God. Jesus knew exactly what they were thinking. So He then asks them, "Why do you question thus in your hearts?" Then He attacked the central issue: "But that you may *know* the Son of man has authority on earth to forgive sins"—He turns and specifically addresses the paralytic—"I say to you, rise, take up your pallet and go home."

And the paralytic who had been lowered perilously down by ropes now stood up, picked up his mat, and made his way out as the crowd parted in stunned silence to let him go.[135]

This is pretty amazing stuff. Don't miss the unmistakable *intention* of Jesus to make it clear that He thought He was God. He could have just healed the man right off and been done with it. Instead he *instigates* the whole discussion by doing something that the four friends did not foresee: claiming to forgive the man's sins. Then Jesus makes clear his intention: "That you may *know* the Son of man has authority on earth to forgive sins...." He wants them to get it: He is doing what by their own admission only God could do. He is not committing blasphemy. He is proclaiming and showing them the Truth. Jesus clearly thought of himself as God.

3. In the names Father and Son—names that God chose, they are not our choosing—there is, as we have said, an implied submission of role. Otherwise we are faced with a very confusing choice of words by God himself, because Scripture itself says that sons are to be submissive to fathers.[136] But there is *also* implied in the Father/Son relationship an equality. They are the same stuff. They are not a

---

[135] I have to observe the *thoroughness* of Jesus' healing. As a paralytic, his muscles would have atrophied and he would lack the co-ordination necessary to walk, let alone carry the weight of his pallet. But he gets up, walks, and carries his pallet out of the house where Jesus was teaching to the amazement of those watching. And we also, hopefully, are just as amazed.

[136] Ephesians 6:1, "Children obey your parents"; or Colossians 3:20, "Children obey your parents." No doubt this implies fathers as well as mothers, since fathers are included as one of the parents.

man and his horse. They are not a man and his pickup truck. They are of equal being. Again, the Jews of Jesus' time wanted to stone Jesus because He called God his father, "thereby making himself *equal* with God."[137]

4. Paul wrote to the Colossians, "For in Him the whole fullness of deity dwells bodily."[138] The interesting thing about that particular text is that it was written to a church that was struggling with the beginnings of the heresy that eventually became the Gnostic heresy. Like the Arian heresy, it denied the full equality of Jesus with the Father. Clearly Paul could not accept anything less than full equality of the persons of the Trinity, even though he used the terms Father and Son.

5. In one of the most Christological passages in the Bible, Hebrews 1, the author wants to make it clear that Christ is divine—the very stuff of God. God has never done anything like He did when he sent his Son.

"In many and various ways God spoke of old to our fathers by the prophets; but in these last days he has spoken to us by a Son, whom he appointed the heir of all things, through whom also he created the world....

For to what angel did God ever say, "thou art my Son, today I have begotten thee?

Or again,

I will be to him a father and he shall be to me a son?

Or again when he brings the first-born into the world, he says,

Let all God's angels worship him;

Of the Angels he said,

Who makes his angels winds, and his servants flames of fire?

But of the Son he said,

---

[137] John 5:18
[138] Colossians 2:9

Thy throne O God is for ever and ever...."

And,

"Thou, Lord, didst found the earth in the beginning, and the heavens are the work of thy hands."[139]

Clearly, this "Son" is no ordinary being. It is through his Son that God created the world. That means the Son *must* be eternal. So the Arian heresy is destroyed. The Son was never created. The Son was there at the creation of the Universe. In fact, the Son was the agent of the creation of the World. God even addresses his son as God.

And yet, their relationship is still described as a father/son relationship. "I will be to him a father and he shall be to me a son."

Now, that is a short representative study of what the Scriptures say about both the equality of the Son and His submission to the Father. It certainly is not exhaustive, just representative—and, in my little mind, difficult to ignore. You, the reader must decide if the Bible teaches *both* the equality and the submission of the Son to the Father in all eternity.

That position, to be honest, raises a very thorny problem. If the Son is eternally submissive to the Father, does that imply that the Son is eternally *different* from the Father and the Spirit? And does that imply that the Father has some quality, eternally, that the Son and Spirit do not have? Or, to put it another way, does each person of the Trinity possess *all* the attributes of deity? That is what the Church Fathers have affirmed ever since the Nicene Creed. According to the creed, each person of the Trinity must be equally and completely God. Dr. Erickson puts it this way: "The problem is this: If authority over the Son is an essential, not an accidental attribute of the Father, and subordination to the Father is an essential

---

[139] Hebrews 1:5–8b, 10

107

not an accidental, attribute of the Son, then something significant follows. Authority is part of the Father's essence, and subordination is part of the Son's essence, and each attribute is not part of the essence of the other person. That means that the essence of the Son is *different* from the essence of the Father. The Father's essence includes omnipresence, omniscience, love, etc., and authority over the Son. The Son's essence includes omnipresence, omniscience, love, etc., and submission to the Father. But that is equivalent to saying that they are not *homoousious* with one another. Here is surely a problem for the gradationists,[140] for they want to affirm the *homoousious*, in order to reject Arianism."[141]

He raises a very real problem and, as a gradationist, I agree that it is a very real problem. I affirm the complete equality of the three persons of the Trinity with no hesitation. I struggle with this question, and it may be one of those issues where we have to accept our inability to understand. One of the qualifications of deacons in 1 Timothy 3:9 was that "They must hold the *mystery* of the faith with a clear conscience." We need to be humble enough to accept the limitations of our understanding. The fact is, God has revealed himself as three persons with three *different* names and uses those names throughout all eternity. What do you do with that? Are the three different names for the three different persons completely meaningless? Do their different names indicate *nothing?* Or does it just indicate different roles? This question is one all of us who believe that Scripture is True need to grapple with: what is the significance of the *different* names for the *different* persons of the Trinity? If the three persons of the Trinity are equal, why does Scripture call them by different, non-interchangeable names? Could that mean the three persons of the Trinity are different and non-interchangeable? That is a hill I am not willing to die on, as I could be wrong. I am struggling to understand what cannot be understood.

---

[140] Dr. Erickson uses the term "gradationist" to mean one who believes the Trinity is a hierarchy of equals.

[141] Millard Erickson, <u>Who's Tampering with the Trinity?</u>, p. 172.

As part of God's creation, as a dweller in space and time, I do not have an answer. As one who struggled through biochemistry, it doesn't bother me that I do not have an answer. I believe God is the author of all science. Since I cannot comprehend that part of God's creation called biochemistry, how can I expect to comprehend the author of biochemistry—namely, God? I could not understand the textbook.

Part of the answer is that, since the Father, Son, and Spirit are really *one,* we cannot talk about the Son or the Father or the Spirit in isolation, *separate* from the other two persons. God is an *indivisible One.* Separating God into three persons and then comparing them is impossible. They are not disconnected and cannot be disconnected and then compared. God is One.

There is also another possibility: look at what I believe might be a visual aid God has given us: husbands and wives. They are equal. They are different. *They are each fully human.* Yet each one has some characteristics which the other does not have, yet they are equal and complete. The male has physical organs a female does not and vice versa. In marriage, there is a oneness that comes from two different but equal persons. They are not interchangeable. Even though different, they are of the same essence. Could it be that this is the same among the equal persons of the Trinity, where they are eternally different but equal and *together* they make a unity of equals? So they are not interchangeable and they are not the same. But together they make up the one whole. It's more than just the role each fulfills.

That analogy is inadequate, I admit. Helpful, maybe, but inadequate.

Oneness

The word for "one" in the Hebrew in the famous Old Testament quote, "Hear O Israel, the Lord your God is One"[142] is an interesting word. It does not necessarily mean a homogeneous or monolithic unity. It can be used to describe one unit which consists of smaller units in the one unit, such as one tribe, one people, or one bunch of grapes, or an army that appears as one unit.[143]

In the New Testament, the Body of Christ is made up of people who all have the same personal value but have different functions. As we have already observed, that is the point in 1 Corinthians 12, where the teaching is that we are all different, with different functions, and, thus, dependent on each other. But we must have the *same* care for each individual—even those who might seem less important—our "less presentable parts," as Paul calls them. That is by God's design. It is not accidental. So it would seem that persons can be significantly different and still be equal members of a unit. They can still be One.

One of the more stunning passages in the Bible dealing with this topic is the high priestly prayer by Jesus to His Father as he contemplated His sacrificial death on the Cross for the sins of His people just a couple of days away. There are a number of profound concepts Jesus mentions that are easily missed. As before, this is holy ground and we should take our shoes off.

First, Jesus talks a lot about His relationship with his Father. "Father, glorify thou me in thy own presence with the glory which I had with thee before the world was made."[144] "All mine are thine,

---

[142] Deuteronomy 6:4

[143] The word is *"ehad"* and is used in Genesis 32:8, 34:16, 34:22, Deuteronomy 12:14, Numbers 13:23, 1 Samuel 11:7. It is used in Genesis 1 where, after there was evening and morning, it was described as *one* day, a one-ness made up of two parts. When God forms Eve out of Adam's rib, the two become *one*, again a one-ness made up of parts. In contrast to that is the Hebrew word *"yahid,"* which really means one, like the number. In Genesis 22:2, God tells Abraham to take his *"only* son" and sacrifice him. Or in Jeremiah 6:26, we read, "Make mourning as for an *only* son." Again, the word is *Yahid*, not *Ehad*.

[144] Again, notice that the terms Father and, by inference, Son apply before the world was made.

and thine are mine." "I am coming to Thee." "I pray... that they may all be *one*, even as thou, Father, art in me, and I in thee, that they also may be in us, so that the world may believe that thou hast sent me." "The glory which thou hast given me I have given to them, that they may be *one* even as we are *one*, I in them and thou in me, that they may become perfectly *one*, so that the world may know that thou hast sent me and hast loved them even as thou hast loved me." "Holy Father, keep them in thy name, which thou hast given me, that they may be one, even as we are *one*." "O Righteous Father, the world has not known thee, but I have known thee, and these know that thou hast sent me. I made it known, that the love with which thou hast loved me may be in them, and I in them."

Clearly, Jesus had an exceptionally close relationship with God the Father, as a son with his father, and that was not limited to the Incarnation. His own words indicated it was true "*before the world was made.*" Jesus' description of His relationship with the Father was that they were "one." It is significant that Jesus described his relationship as a father/son relationship, which implies both authority and equality.

Secondly, he does not describe the Incarnation as Him merely "coming" from the Father. Five times He says that He was "*sent.*" "And this is eternal life, that they know thee, the only true God, and Jesus Christ, whom thou has sent." "They know that Thou didst send me." "As thou didst send me into the world, so I have sent them into the world." "The glory which thou hast given me I have given to them, that they may be one even as we are *one*, I in them and thou in me, that they may become perfectly *one,* so that the world may know that thou hast sent me." "These know that thou hast sent me." Surely all of us would say that Jesus had the authority to send the disciples into the world. Yet in this text He says, "*As* thou didst send me into the world *so* I have sent them into the world." The process is the same.

Thirdly, Jesus also prays that his disciples—not only the twelve with him but also those who would believe through their word—*that would be we believers living today*—that we would also be *one*, just like He and the Father are *one*—"that the world may believe that thou hast sent me." So there should be something about how we Christians relate to each other that reveals to the watching world the same quality of relationships that exist among the Trinity. So "oneness," in all that word means in Scripture, is a means of revelation. Or should be. At least, that is what Jesus prays for.

Don't miss the obvious fact that how we relate to each other in the Body of Christ, in the church (and in marriage, though that comes from other texts), reveals something of the relationships among the three persons of the Trinity to the watching world. What is revealed by the words Father and Son and by Jesus' description as being "sent" is a hierarchy of equals. So that should be evident in church relationships and marriage relationships. That is on Jesus' mind as he turns his direction to the Cross. It should be on ours, as well.

In John 17:21 and 23, Jesus is nearing his sacrificial death on the cross for sinners like me. During His home stretch leading up the cross, He prays for His disciples—present and future—that they would all be "one"—"even as thou, Father, art in me, and I in thee." So the persons of the Trinity, specifically mentioned here as the Father and the Son, are perfectly "one," even though they are mysteriously separate and, maybe, different. The names "Father" and "Son" imply authority that goes in one direction only. The different names imply, at least, different roles, and yet they are represented as living perfectly in a hierarchy (as implied by their names) yet completely equal. Significantly, the Body of Christ, which presumably Christ is referring to when he refers to "those who believe in me through their word," should be the same; that is what Christ prays for. There are clearly elders who "rule." The teaching on the Body of Christ tells us that it is by God's design that the members in Christ's Body fulfill *different* roles. Yet they can still be "one," since that is what Christ prays for. Notice that Jesus seems very clear about the similarity of relationships in the Body of Christ and the Trinity: "Holy Father, keep them in thy name, which thou hast given me, that *they* may be one, even *as we* are one.... I do not pray for these only, but also for *those* who believe in me through their word, that they may all be one; *even as thou Father, art in me and I in thee*, that they also may be in us so that the world may believe thou hast sent me...."[145] The glory which thou hast given me I have given to them, that they may be one *even as we are one*."[146] Three times in eleven verses Jesus intentionally compares the "oneness" of his followers to the oneness present in the Trinity. I think the correspondence is intentional and therefore real.[147]

The Biblical view of marriage presents us with the same idea: two beings being one, yet still different. As we continue to study, we will observe a marriage relationship to be between two individuals, male and female, living in a perfect hierarchy but a hierarchy of equals. Significantly, the "head" in that hierarchy serves the other person, not himself. Just like Jesus. If that is true, there is an attractive and, I think, significant consistency in all three examples, a "oneness" that comes out of a number of equal *but different* parts. And I believe those parts function as a hierarchy of equals.[148]

---

[145] Note that part of what Jesus wanted the world to see through the "oneness" of His church was the authority of the Father over the Son—that they would see that "Thou hast *sent* me." The world needs to see the church functioning as a hierarchy of *equals*. This is one of the themes of this book—the unworldly type of relationship that the Bible describes as "one." But—and this is very important—it is a relationship of equals, where no position has more "status" than any other position. It is a type of relationship that has incredible diversity, including diversity of authority, but all positions have equal personhood. This is the relationship among the persons of the Trinity and, ideally, in Christian marriage and the Body of Christ.

[146] John 17:11, 20, 22

[147] In his book <u>Simply Trinity</u> (published by Baker Books, c. 2021), Dr. Barrett strenuously disagrees with this concept. In chapter three, entitled "Since when did the Trinity get social?" he quotes a theologian named Miroslav Volf: "Volf concludes there must be a direct correspondence between the type of community we see in the church and the Trinity" (p. 81). Dr. Barrett thinks that is badly mistaken. But isn't that what Jesus is praying for in John 17?

[148] I recognize that the New Testament is written in Greek, not Hebrew. Yet the idea is still there, in the Body of Christ and in marriage, of unity that is made up of plurality, just like the Trinity. In this passage in John the correspondence, stated by Jesus Himself, seems clear. That would also correspond with Genesis 1:26 & 27 where the man and woman are somehow said to be in the image of their God and I Corinthians 11:3 where Paul says that headship describes both the relationship of the husband to the wife and Christ to God.

While it is up to each person to interpret the totality of the Biblical teaching on this topic, I believe the concept of a hierarchy of equals best explains God's use of the terms Father and Son, with their implied authority and equality, the pervasive presence of hierarchy in the unfallen Creation, the quality of relationships in the Body of Christ, and the Biblical teaching on gender relationships in marriage.

And so I appeal to a bit of anthropomorphic projection, but a backwards anthropomorphic projection. In the two relationships on earth that are said to reflect relationships among the Trinity, marriage and the Body of Christ, there is present a hierarchy of equals. Yet the members are different. But also equal. That appears to be by design. Each person in the Body of Christ and in a marriage is *completely* human. But all are different. Yet these relationships are stated to be an image of the Oneness in the Trinity, in which each person is completely God yet possibly—dare I say it?—different. I say "possibly," because I fully realize I am skirting heresy in suggesting this. I am not intending to "push" this view of the Trinity but want to ask the question if Biblically we could view the Trinity as made up of persons who are different yet each *fully* God and *completely* One—inseparable. I think that presents us with consistency, which the egalitarian view of the Trinity lacks.

Of course, we cannot comprehend the Trinity and I absolutely want to distance myself as far as possible from "fighting" about this. *I could be wrong* and have been told I am wrong. To fight about this would be like two ants fighting about how the space shuttle is designed. But I do think this understanding best fits the big picture of who God is, who the Body of Christ is, and what marriage is. The Scriptures seem to present the last two as being reflective of the first. This makes me think of C. S. Lewis' words: "I believe in Christianity as I believe the sun has risen: not only because I see it but because by it I see everything else."[149] It fits the big picture in a way the egalitarian understanding of the Trinity does not.

---

[149] "Is Theology Poetry?" from a collection of essays titled <u>The Weight of Glory</u>, Harper Collins Publishers, 1 East 53rd St. New York, NY.10022, c.1976, p. 140. Used by permission

Dr. Stackhouse raises an interesting question in his book: "Why would God call entirely equal sexes to deeply different roles? Why would one role be that of leadership and the other of submission if women and men are equal not only in status and dignity before God but in every other way as well?"[150] That is a very good question. I want to make several observations in trying to answer that question.

First, I disagree with his use of the word "leadership." I think that the consistent use of that word instead of the Biblical term "headship" is very unfortunate. They are *not* the same. But he does ask a very good question. Actually his question should be worded as wondering why God would call only one gender to the role of headship. It is a significant question because the term "leader," as we normally use it, is not a neutral term. It does imply superior competence. Whom do we look to for leadership? Is it not those who have a better grasp of the situation and will take us down the better road? I agree with those who say that if only one gender is called to *lead*, then one gender is presumed to be more competent than the other. If I were a female and the Biblical position is that only males could "lead," I would feel inferior to males. I do not believe that. I think we should limit ourselves to the Biblical term, which is "headship" and not use the unBiblical term "leadership." They just are not the same.

Second, the fact that we ask that question shows our difficulty in comprehending the concept of a hierarchy of equals. Such a concept does not belong to this world. But I think the revelation of relationships among the Godhead shows it to be true. What's wrong with "differentness," even if that "differentness" includes hierarchy? Why do we have such a difficult time understanding different but equal?[151]

Third, the author grates at the call of God of the equal sexes to

---

[150] John G. Stackhouse, Jr., <u>Finally Feminist: A Pragmatic Christian Understanding of Gender,</u> Baker Academic, Grand Rapids, MI, c. 2005, p. 70.

[151] I realize this might be slightly suggestive of the stench of racism's "separate but equal" dogma and I in no way intend that or agree with that. It is truly a stench.

different roles. But surely he would say that the sexes are different. So different roles *might* be appropriate if the sexes really are different, which he does not acknowledge but must believe.

Fourth, the issue for him really is, I think, that he presumes that "leadership" or, what I think he means, "headship" implies a difference in status and even dignity. As you might guess, I disagree with him. His understanding, or misunderstanding, of roles crystallizes the difference between the world's understanding of hierarchy and that of the Kingdom of heaven. As I said before, if roles in the Kingdom of God imply status or dignity, then I agree that equal access to "leadership" or "headship" is a matter of justice.

It *is* hard for us to understand. It is a concept that belongs to the Kingdom of God and *only* to the Kingdom of God, and it is largely incomprehensible to those of us who are citizens of a Fallen World. But we see it sprinkled throughout the Scripture: in the body of Christ, in a Christian understanding of marriage, in what Jesus prays for His disciples, and, I believe, in the ultimate source of everything that is—in a plural God who functions in different roles and *possibly* is made up of different persons who are indivisibly One and equal. Yet the persons of the Trinity function in a hierarchy of complete equals. A unity made up of individual parts. God is *One*. In marriage, two become *one*. Jesus prayed that the disciples would be *one*. And in all those there is hierarchy—but an unoppressive, unselfish hierarchy of complete equals.

Current trends are not always bad—although the *desire* to be "trendy" probably is. "Diversity" is a current trendy topic, and it is really quite on the mark. Differentness does not make for more or less personal value. C. S. Lewis, as usual, has made some profound observations on this point: "I am afraid that when we describe a man as 'a member of a church' we usually mean nothing Pauline: we mean only that he is a unit—that he is one more specimen of the same kind of thing as X and Y and Z. How true membership in a body differs from inclusion in a collective may be seen in the structure of a family.

The grandfather, the parents, the grown-up son, the child, the dog, and the cat are true members precisely because they are not members or units of a homogeneous class. They are not interchangeable.... If you subtract any one member you have not simply reduced the family in number, you have inflicted an injury on its structure. Its unity is a unity of unlikes, almost of incommensurables."[152] His point is that, by design, our physical bodies that God has given us, the Body of Christ that God has given us, families that God has given us, are each made up of *equal* members who are *different*. (Well, I would not include a dog and a cat as members of a family in that generalization.) Perhaps that characterization fits the Trinity, as well? And so could these groups be given us as fingerprints of the Trinity? I think it is no coincidence that the Trinity is presented as a hierarchy of different persons and that the two genders which God has created in His image, and the group of people which are uniquely His, the church, all have this same characteristic. They all contain diversity, not only of role but also of authority, and yet all contain completely equal persons. All members are of the same essence. It is the way God has revealed Himself. For those of us who dwell in a fallen world, it is very difficult to comprehend and even more difficult to live out.

Both positions on the Trinity, the equivalent authority position and the gradational authority position, have their problems. You, the reader, will have to decide which you think best fits the totality of Biblical revelation. But, as I said in the introduction, we do not come at this problem as unbiased thinkers. As members of modern western culture, we tend to absorb values unconsciously from the world we live in and then view what we learn about the Kingdom of God through world-colored glasses. Let me suggest a couple of examples that affect our thinking.

---

[152] C. S. Lewis, "Membership," an essay included in the collection titled The Weight of Glory and Other Addresses, Wm. Eerdmans Publishing Company, Grand Rapids, MI, c.1949, p. 34. The essay is very challenging reading and ought to be read more often. Used by permission.

The Culture We Live in

The nature of cultural assumptions is that you are not aware of making them. They seem natural. It is difficult to believe anybody has ever believed otherwise. To challenge them is to challenge what is obviously Normal. Anything else is obviously abnormal or, worse yet, outdated. Lewis described a similar attitude as "chronological snobbery." It is "the uncritical acceptance of the intellectual climate common to our own age and the assumption that whatever has gone out of date is *on that account* discredited."[153] The key word is "assumption." As modern westerners, we are hardly unbiased on this issue of authority.

I work behind a cash register in a retail pharmacy. I have told the technicians I work with that anybody who does not believe in original sin has never waited on the public. I would never dream of treating people the way they treat those of us in the pharmacy where I work, and everybody I've worked with has said the same thing. Our economic system is a pervasive influence on everybody who has grown up in it, and we unconsciously perceive reality differently because of its influence on us. Because of the numerous advertisements and the emphasis on customer service in our system (which is good, not bad), most people have an innate and unconscious sense of the right to be satisfied. What that really means is that they have a right to get what they want. That is the right of the person spending the money, the consumer, and it is the duty of the person on the other side of the cash register to fulfill that right.

Now, as a pharmacist, I am completely committed to doing my utmost to take care of the sick people who come up to my register, whether or not their expectations or demands are reasonable. That is my calling—within the limits of our healthcare system and present state of knowledge of how the human body works.

But often people go beyond those limitations and unconsciously

---

[153] C. S. Lewis, <u>Surprised by Joy</u>, Harcourt, Brace & World, Inc, c. 1955, p. 201. Used by permission.

feel entitled to get not necessarily the best we can do, or anybody can do, but *what they want*—which may be, and sometimes is, more than the best we can do. If our present health care system cannot do what they think they are entitled to (and our healthcare system has its limitations), then the customer often ends up going to the manager, a victim of perceived bad customer service.

I recently watched a customer go totally ballistic with his insurance company because they would not cover an expensive sleeping medication without the physician calling them and explaining why the cheaper alternatives would not work. He was yelling and screaming and cussing at them over the phone in front of our counter about why they were "playing medicine" when the physician had already written the prescription. I tried to explain to him that the issue was not the legitimacy of the prescription but that his insurance company was not willing to pay for it without a prior authorization and that was part of the contract that his employer signed with the insurance company. No, he said, the health insurance premiums were paid and so he was entitled to get this prescription covered. (In other words, he wasn't listening to what I said.) I repeated that this was all part of a contract and that contract included what was covered, what was not covered, and the procedure for getting things covered that normally were not. No, he repeated back to me, he was the boss since he paid the premiums, and he was going to get them to do what he wanted and walked off in a huge huff. His understanding, skewed as it was, is common. If you pay for something, you have a right to get what you want, not necessarily what you paid for, or thought you paid for. As the consumer, you are the *boss.*

What has happened is that consumerism has become a worldview. I have the right to get what I want. I sit in the driver's seat. That worldview makes submission a very bad word.

Our political system has evolved to the same end point. I have been around long enough to remember political campaigns from the '50s. As I remember them, the questions presented to the voters at that time were something along the line of voting for what was best for the country. Each party certainly presented differing answers as to what was best for our country, but that was the question to be decided by an election. Now the question presented voters is what is best for *you*, the voter. "Are you better off than you were 4 years ago?" was the slogan in one recent campaign. And if your representatives don't do what you think they should, then the solution is to "vote the bums out."

As in our economic system, our political system also promises that the individual is entitled to get what he wants. That's a principle that goes unquestioned. And if you don't get it, you vote your self-interest in the next election. It's even written in the opening of the Declaration of Independence: that every human is created equal and *entitled* to "life, liberty, and the pursuit of happiness." That is endowed by our Creator. That is foundational to our thinking in this country. I'm afraid it may often be perceived by individuals, and in the collective mind of our culture, that each person has a God-given right to do whatever he wants to feel good. And nobody can tell anybody not to. My happiness is the ultimate good. What has happened is that our governmental system, constitutional democracy, just like our economic system, the free market system, has become a worldview. The government is here to serve me and I have the right to get what I expect from it or I'll just vote for somebody else next election. The Declaration of Independence says our Creator wants me happy. And that, again, makes submission a very bad word.[154]

Now, I appreciate my country and its governmental system, and I appreciate our economic system. I love my job. There is nowhere

---

[154] Here is what C. S. Lewis says on this sense of a "right to be happy": "Though the 'right to happiness' is chiefly claimed for the sexual impulse, it seems to me impossible that the matter should stay there. The fatal principle, once allowed in that department, must sooner or later seep through our whole lives. We thus advance toward a state of society in which not only each man but every impulse in each man claims *carte blanche*. And then, though our technological skill may help us survive a little longer, our civilization will have died at heart, and will—one dare not even add 'unfortunately'–be swept away." (From God in the Dock, in an essay entitled "We have no right to happiness." Wm Eerdman's publishing, Grand Rapids, MI, c. 1970, p. 322. Used by permission.)

I would rather live or work on earth. And the reason they work so well is that both institutions work fairly well in a fallen world. But when our government or our economic system define our worldview instead of the Bible, they have overstepped their bounds. They also may have stepped outside of reality.

As modern westerners, we automatically have a prejudice against authority. Submission is difficult for us. And there are many legitimate reasons for that—not the least of which is the ingrained worldview of our economic system, our governmental system, or the Declaration of Independence. I am not speaking to either gender. I am speaking to modern people—men and women. All of *us*. I use first person plural purposefully. I include *me* in that generalization. Submission requires that I give in to somebody else beside *myself*, *my* wants, and to somebody else's agenda besides *mine*.

Interestingly, in the Kingdom of God, it is actually *good* to do just that.

C. S. Lewis was describing his frustrations with Christianity (before he became a believer), which included ugly architecture, ugly music, and bad poetry. But that was not his biggest issue. "But, of course, what mattered most of all was my deep-seated hatred of authority, my monstrous individualism, my lawlessness. No word in my vocabulary expressed deeper hatred than the word *Interference*. Christianity placed at the center what then seemed to me a transcendental Interferer. If its picture were true then no sort of 'treaty with reality' could ever be possible. There was no region even in the innermost depth of one's soul which one could surround with a barbed wire fence and guard with a notice 'No Admittance.' And that was what I wanted; some area, however small, of which I could say to all other beings, 'This is my business and mine only.'"[155]

I suspect if all of us were as honest as he, we would say the same

[155] C. S. Lewis, Surprised by Joy, Harcourt, Brace, and Company, c. 1955, p. 172. Used by permission.

thing. If we all took time to reflect on our soul's condition, would we not all agree with him?

Since at the very center of the fall of man was *rebellion* against God's authority over us and choosing to believe one of His creatures instead of Him, it is not surprising that difficulty in *submission* would continue to be part of the fallout of the Fall. And if we do still live outside the Garden, in a fallen world, and especially if we are modern westerners, it is not surprising that to talk of submission is not only difficult, politically incorrect, foreign, but also deeply offensive. I am talking to both genders. I am talking to *me*. As we will see, both genders are called to submission—that is a gender neutral-calling in Scripture. And don't miss the fact that, even as egalitarians promote "mutual submission," that concept still includes submission.

As we observed in the chapter on hermeneutics, many people refer to the New Testament letters as "ad hoc" letters, meaning they were written to a specific situation. The words in Latin mean "to this," and if the "this" to which the letter was written is not what we are discussing, the letter is of questionable value and application to our current situation. We will look at 1 Peter later in chapter 9, but for now notice that the letter was written to "the exiles of the Dispersion." Those exiles were believers. We know that because they were described as "those who have been born anew to a living hope through the resurrection of Jesus Christ from the dead."

But they were scattered. They were scattered among the Gentiles. And in that world where they were foreigners, they were to be submissive. "Maintain good conduct among the Gentiles, so that in case they speak against you as wrongdoers, they may see your good deeds and glorify God on the day of visitation."[156] What does "good conduct" mean? See what follows in the text: "be subject for the Lord's sake to every human institution whether it be to the emperor as supreme, or to the governors as sent by him." "Servants,

---

[156] I love to read Mark Twain. He put it this way: "Let us endeavor so to live so that when we come to die even the undertaker will be sorry."

be submissive to your masters with all respect, not only to the kind and gentle but also to the overbearing." "Likewise you wives, be submissive to your husbands, so that some though they do not obey the word may be won without a word by the behavior of their wives." "Likewise, you husbands, live considerately with your wives."[157]

Submission is a word very foreign to our culture with its biases. It is foreign to our nature. It is foreign to our experience. If we are called to submit, we feel "put down" and inferior. We feel "lower" in the "higher-archy." But then, we also have to admit every hierarchy we have ever experienced is fallen. It is run by selfish sinners, and all of us, I suspect, have suffered in one. We all have very good reason for not liking the call of Scripture to submit. Not only does it carry enormous possibility for unpleasantness, if not suffering and abuse, but we feel put down, a lower, inferior person. But if our personhood does not come from our role, as is true in our example of the three persons of the Godhead, we are freed up to serve one another. The use of the words "one another" is intentional and Biblical. Both genders are called upon to serve. It is this mystery of a hierarchy of equals, of submission within the form of a hierarchy, that the church needs to model to a fallen world. Our culture certainly cannot comprehend such an animal without a picture, and even then it still may not be able.

And so, it is probably appropriate to avoid using words like "superior" and "inferior" and even the word "subordinate." While the words "inferior" and "superior" definitely are inappropriate, the word "subordinate" may be inappropriate, and, significantly, may carry baggage for some people, maybe unconsciously, that does not apply in the kingdom of God. The way our culture uses that word implies a value judgment that I (and I suspect they) do not intend to imply. I plead with you all, fellow-dwellers in this fallen world where things are messed up almost beyond comprehension, to try to get beyond the patterns of this world and look at the possibility of a very

---

[157] 1 Peter 2:12, 13, 18, and 3:1, 7

different revealed system for God's Kingdom. It is *very* different! To be submissive does not necessarily imply less value, at least in God's Kingdom. To be a servant is not bad. In fact, it is actually good. The stunning example of that is our Lord himself. If being a servant is an insult to your personal value, then what on earth do you do with *Him*? And He was a *male*. Clearly the positive nature of being a servant applies to both genders, to all people in the kingdom of God.

The husband "ruling" over the wife is one of the results of the Fall. It means the position of being in charge, the one making the rules, with no responsibility to care and serve and sacrifice for others. The only human relationship present at the time of the Fall was the husband-wife relationship, and with one person becoming the ruler, the "top dog." I recognize it is difficult to digest what existed before the Fall, that which, after the Fall, became *ruling*. We must not forget the example of Jesus, our *servant*, who was both submissive within the Trinity and yet a completely equal person along with the Father and the Spirit. This concept is one of those "heavenly things" that Jesus admitted was difficult for us to understand. It requires a completely different value system from a completely different Kingdom. The ability to see it requires leaving the system of this world behind. So, He told Nicodemus that he needed to be born again. It is questionable if he ever got it, at least at that point, although later he probably did.[158] This concept may well be *the* most significant issue to come to grips with in the gender debate, and it is one that, because of our position in a fallen world, is hard to comprehend. It belongs to Heaven. But as we scratch our heads at this strange concept, we must not eliminate it as being impossible, as many have, because we, like Nicodemus, are not able to comprehend it. And we must not let the Evil One use the church's ugly history of arrogant male dominance and an unBiblically low view of women

---

[158] But interestingly, he shows up again in a debate among the Pharisees in John 7:50, when he takes Jesus' side and after the death but before the Resurrection, he shows up with spices for the body of Jesus. It seems he could not ignore this amazing person and even defended Him to his own class of people—Pharisees. I suspect he became a believer.

to affect our thinking so that we cannot see the beautiful picture revealed to us.

C. S. Lewis put it this way: "The Nazi [that is, sinful, ugly, self-serving, hyper-authoritative systems] and the Nudist make the same mistake. [That is, both are seeking a misguided solution for the consequences of the Fall.] But it is the naked body, still there beneath the clothes of each one of us, which really lives. It is the hierarchical world, still alive and (very properly) hidden behind a façade of equal citizenship, which is our real concern.... Even in the life of the affections, much more in the Body of Christ, we step outside that world which says 'I am as good as you.' It is like turning from a march to a dance. It is like taking off our clothes. We become, as Chesterton said, taller when we bow; we become lowlier when we instruct. It delights me that there should be moments in the services of my own Church when the priest stands and I kneel. As democracy becomes more complete in the outer world and opportunities for reverence are successively removed, the refreshment, the cleansing, and invigorating return to inequality, which the Church offers us, become more and more necessary."[159]

Now, I disagree with his use of the word "inequality." He uses that, unfortunately, as synonymous for hierarchy. It is clear from the context of the article from which the quote originates that he does not believe position determines value, that to be a servant is not to be less of a person. This reminds us, I think, of how difficult it is, on this side of Eden, to understand and wrap words around this idea of equality and submission within a hierarchy. We have no real experience of it.

Before we leave this topic, I want to touch on several complex issues, at least for me. Since God, our creator, is the One in whom we live and move and have our being, it is good and natural and appropriate to want to know and to understand the One who made

[159] C. S. Lewis, "Membership," p. 37–38, in the book <u>The Weight of Glory and Other Addresses</u>, W. B. Eerdmans Publishing Company, Grand Rapids, MI, 1949. Used by permission.

us, even though that is impossible for our minds to comprehend. This God spoke into existence the galaxies, probably three trillion of them, some of which we have probably not even seen, they are so far away. But this God is the ground of our being, and so knowing and understanding him helps us understand who we are, what the purpose of life is, and the nature of reality.

I want to remind us that we start with God, not some agenda in this world. Some possible agendas might be gender relationships, family relationships, church relationships, or politics. In all cases, we do not start with our agenda and then make God into a form that will conveniently support our goals. Theology is a one-way street.

A subtle tendency to avoid, if possible, is to limit God to our earth-bound ability to understand. The wife of one of my previous pastors, a wise woman, once said to me that we need to be comfortable with some degree of ambiguity in our faith. In our competitive, humanistic, technology-oriented culture, that is tough. As I said before, one of the qualifications of deacons in 1 Timothy 3:9 is that they must hold the *mystery* of the faith with a clear conscience. On the other hand, we have probably all heard the comment that God does not want us to check our minds at the door to church. Those two concepts are an example of the ambiguity that is present in our faith, as well as the intellectual humility in our faith, and we need to hold both in balance. I appeal to the comment by C. S. Lewis I quoted in the introduction—that God gave us minds to seek and *find* truth. It makes sense that God did not give us minds and then ask us to ignore them in our relationship with Him.

That means we need to let God reveal himself the way He is and not limit Him to our preconceived ideas, human limitations, or the way we have been taught. Let me give an example. In his challenging book, Simply Trinity, Dr. Matthew Barrett talks about the characteristics and limitations of humanity being projected onto deity—his point being that is not a healthy thing to do, and I fully agree with him on that. "What occurs in the human experience of Christ is projected onto the divinity of the entire Godhead. At its root, this is a failure to distinguish between Christ in the form of a *servant* and Christ in the form of *God*. Christology has swallowed up the Trinity. *Our Triune God has been domesticated, created in our image*"[160] (italics are the author's). That is a healthy warning for us as we try to understand our Creator. What he is warning against, I think, is a kind of backward anthropomorphic projection, based on the earthly life of Christ. What he is referring to is seen in the immediately preceding statement. He says that "EFS [he is referring to those who believe in the Eternal Functional Subordination of the Son in relation to the Father—those who believe that the Trinity eternally exists as a hierarchy of equals] have taken a human quality during the incarnation—but in this case submission—and projected it back onto the divine person of the Son apart from the incarnation so that hierarchy defines the inner life of the Trinity in eternity."[161] He seems to think that those who believe in EFS have taken the submission of the Son to the Father, a quality which Dr. Barrett thinks can *only* be a human quality, and projected it onto the Trinity. He believes this human quality of hierarchy and consequent submission *cannot* be present in the Trinity because it is *just* a human quality. But what if it is true of humans *because* we were created in the image of a God, who is a hierarchy of equals, but that quality in humans has since been damaged by the Fall? Can we not let God reveal Himself as He really is without rejecting His revelation because He has some "human" qualities, qualities that we also have because we are created in His image, but qualities which in a fallen world are negative? In the perfect Trinity, the negative aspect of these qualities would not be present. It seems Dr. Barrett is doing exactly the same thing he is accusing others of doing—projecting the human experience onto the divinity of the Godhead. Except in this case, it is a negative human experience because of the Fall, and so, of course, the negative component would not be present in the Trinity, and so, he says, that cannot be true.

---

[160] Matthew Barrett, <u>Simply Trinity</u>, Baker Books, Grand Rapids, MI, c. 2021, p. 115.
[161] Ibid., p. 115

In another place, he says, "EFSers take what is said of Christ Jesus as man, (i. e., submission to the Father) and they transfer that concept to that substance of his which was everlasting before the incarnation and is everlasting still."[162]

He also says, "We've read creaturely characteristics like subordination back into the divine names."[163]

However, he then says, "But it is a step too far to restrict the temporal missions from revealing the eternal relations. While we should not project everything in the mission of the Son or the Spirit onto the eternal Trinity, nevertheless it would be too extreme to conclude that such missions do not mirror eternal relations in one specific way: the only reason the Spirit can be sent by the Father and the Son to save a lost humanity is because he proceeds from the Father and the Son from all eternity."[164]

But then who is to decide what "creaturely characteristics" or what characteristics of the "temporal mission" are appropriate or inappropriate to project back onto the Divine? By what criteria? Just the ones we like? Or the ones that make sense to our limited intellect? How do we distinguish between wrongly projecting "creaturely characteristics" back onto God but recognizing we have those characteristics because we are created in God's image, but an image that has been tarnished by the fall? We are left with the very real prospect, which Dr. Barrett so adamantly and rightly resists, of making God in our image, an image we like, or the image that will support our social agenda.

What if God really is, in eternity, a perfect hierarchy of equals? Is it legitimate to reject that because hierarchy among us fallen humans has negative characteristics? If that were true, how could He reveal a perfect hierarchy of equals, if found in the Trinity, in a manner that we would not reject because of our negative experiences of hierarchy in our fallen world? I think we need to let God reveal a kind of

---

[162] Ibid., p. 242
[163] Ibid., p. 255
[164] Ibid., p. 271

relationship that might be foreign to us who live in a fallen world, but that is true—a perfect, hierarchical, non-superior relationship between persons who are not the same but are nevertheless equal.

Another question to think about is the position held by many regarding the actions of the Trinity during the Incarnation. They explain what happened during the Incarnation by proposing a "Covenant of Redemption" among the persons of the Trinity. It explains how the three persons worked together to accomplish the redemption of mankind. Below is a definition by Matt Slick found on the web site Christian Apologetics and Research Ministry, dated May 23, 2010.

"In the eternal covenant, God the Father and Jesus the Son made an agreement with regard to the elect. This covenant was made before the universe was created and it consisted of the Father promising to bring to the Son all whom the Father had given Him (John 6:39; 17:2, 9, 24), to send the Son to be the representative of the people (John 3:16; Rom. 5:18–19), to prepare a body for the Son (Col. 2:9; Heb. 10:5), and to give the Son all authority in heaven and earth (Matt. 28:18). The Son would become a man (Col. 2:9; 1 Tim. 2:5), become for a while lower than the angels (Heb. 2:7), and be found under the Law (Gal. 4:4–5). The Son would die for the sins of the world (1 John 2:2; 1 Pet. 2:24) and the Father would raise the Son from the Dead (Psalm 2).

The Holy Spirit would empower Jesus to do the will of the Father and Christ's ministry on earth (Matt. 3:16; Luke 4:1, 18; John 3:34), and to apply the redemptive work of Christ to Christians (John 14:16–17, 26; Acts 1:8; 2:17–18).

Normally, Covenants are made between persons of different authority levels such as a king and a subject. But in the Eternal

Covenant, all the parties involved (the Father, the Son, and the Holy Spirit) are equals.[165]

Several observations are in order:

1. The Covenant is defined as an *eternal* covenant—made before the foundation of the world. Scripture in many places refers to the plan of redemption or the plan of salvation, that we were chosen before the foundation of the world, and so forth. I think we would all agree that God's plan to send Jesus for the salvation of the world was not a Plan B, hurriedly created after the fall of Man, but was instead an eternal plan. However, the very concept of a covenant implies *it was something entered into*, not eternal. We could say at this point the analogy falls short, and that is a legitimate thing to say. All analogies fall short when it comes to God. But it must be noted that all covenants by definition have a beginning, but this one does not—if it's eternal.

2. The author makes it clear that, although some covenants are made between persons of different authority, this one is not, even though the names Father and Son, names which God chose, imply both sameness and a difference of authority. In the Bible, sons are to submit to fathers. He believes that the three parties of the Trinity are equal, and I support that without hesitation. In the Covenant of Redemption, the Son, Jesus, is submissive to the Father. That is clear.

   The reason that is problematic is that the Covenant of Redemption is an *eternal* covenant. That would imply, then, that the Son is *eternally* submissive to the Father, a position to which I suspect the author of that summary would strongly object.

---

[165] See carm.org/about-doctrine/what-is-the-eternal-covenant-also-known-as-the-covenant-of-redemption/ in the article entitled "What is the Eternal Covenant?" on the Christian Apologetics and Research Ministry website.

3. While the author provides numerous Scriptural references to support his position, the fact is the term "Covenant of Redemption" never occurs in Scripture. But then, the term "Trinity" also never occurs, so that does not necessarily disqualify the concept. But all the references could just as legitimately be understood as explaining how the Trinity, as an eternal hierarchy of equals, has *always* functioned to accomplish the redemption of mankind. It would definitely help the case for such a covenant if there were *some* passage similar to Genesis 1:27 where the Triune God is pictured as making a group decision to create male and female. Such a passage portraying the persons of the Triune God making the Covenant of Redemption does not exist. I do not think such a covenant of redemption is a required understanding of Scripture. If we can accept that equals can exist in hierarchy, the concept of the Trinity existing and functioning as a hierarchy of equals from all eternity is just as reasonable an understanding of Scripture as is the Covenant of Redemption. Our interpretation depends here on our preconceived (and possibly unconscious) assumptions.

The fact is the three persons of the Trinity are One. You *cannot* separate them. One person cannot act individually without the other two. You cannot talk about the Son as "different" from the other persons because the Son is One with the other persons. So while it may cause problems for some to think of the persons of the Trinity having differing characteristics, or differing roles, yet still being One and indivisible, it does not for me. You cannot separate the persons of the Trinity and then compare them. Do I understand that? I do not.

And so I punt. I bow my head and accept a God whom I cannot comprehend. I have no need to understand everything about God. As I said before, I could not understand that part of God's creation labeled "biochemistry." So I have no problems with submitting to a God I do not understand.

I want to end by returning to the question brought up at the beginning of the chapter: is it possible for equals to be in hierarchy? Does being "higher" in the hierarchy confer superiority or status on a person? As dwellers in a fallen world, we will tend to answer or act unconsciously that yes, hierarchy does confer superiority of person and status. And we will tend to answer or act unconsciously that hierarchy eliminates equality. Was that not obvious from the long list of quotes at the beginning of our discussion? Who wouldn't answer that way? Who doesn't want to be "on top"?

My point is that Scripture does not present the concept that way. I have tried to present the picture, which I think is Biblical, of a unique relationship of equals—among the Trinity, the Body of Christ, and the highest creation of the Trinity—human beings, of diverse equals, even when part of that diversity is a diversity of authority. Yet all are equally significant and important.

To summarize quickly, here are the reasons it seems to me that a hierarchy of equals is the best way to understand what Scripture reveals to us about God.

1. Before the Fall of Man, in God's perfect creation, there were several forms of hierarchy. There was dominion, rule, the act of "calling," and authority. Normally, a creation reveals the personality of the creator.

2. Both Dr. Richard Longenecker and Dr. Nicholas Wolterstorff, both egalitarians, observed that we humans need hierarchy to function. See footnote 103 in this chapter. And so, human beings, who uniquely are described as being created in the image of God, seem to be inescapably hierarchical—at least according to these two egalitarians. That certainly conforms to my experience. Again, normally a creation reflects something of the nature of its creator.

3. Jesus described himself when He was on earth as submissive, not to God, which would have been characteristic of human beings, but to part of God—to the Father. He consistently described Himself as being "sent" by the Father and being under the authority of the Father. And then Jesus sent the Holy Spirit.
4. The terms Father and Son, which are the terms revealed by God, imply *both* equality as well as authority.
5. The terms Father and Son are used to describe these two persons of the Trinity before the creation of the world and after the end of time. They are not limited to the Incarnation.
6. "One" describes the Trinity, marriage, and the church of Jesus Christ. Marriage is a relationship of two different, but equal, persons. The church of Jesus Christ is *intentionally* diverse, but a diversity made up of equal persons. And the church of Jesus Christ does, like *all* human institutions, have an authority structure. Marriage and the body of Christ are described later in this book. Since "One" describes all three, and since marriage and the body of Christ are a hierarchy of equals, it would seem that the Trinity is also a hierarchical relationship of equal persons. I realize I have not yet defined marriage and the body of Christ, as such—that will come later.

The equality of the persons of the Trinity is really not up for discussion—at least, I hope not—so I have not included that issue in this summary.

As we'll see as we study Ephesians five, the authority described in the term "headship" is not self-serving but other-centered and sacrificial. Maybe the picture of the Body of Christ is the easiest for us to see. Paul teaches us in 1 Corinthians 12 that the more "unpresentable parts" are just as important as the more presentable. Yet there is still an authority structure in the Body of Christ. But those in authority are not superior in any way. Jesus prayed that

133

they would all be "one" just as He and the Father are "one." That concept is, I believe, rooted in the nature of the Trinity and is also seen in the Body of Christ, the church, and in a Christian view of marriage. That is the way I understand the Bible.

Before leaving this mind-numbing topic, I want to look quickly at two Biblical scholars who are firmly egalitarian, both in their approach to the Trinity and to marriage, but who acknowledge the Bible *could* be read to support a hierarchical view of the Trinity. The first quote is from Kevin Giles and the second from Millard J. Erickson.

"I concede immediately that the New Testament *can* be read to teach that the Son is *eternally* subordinated to the Father. I seek rather to prove that orthodoxy rejects this way of reading the Scriptures"[166] In other words, he says, the Bible *could* be read to support hierarchy, but he says that historically the church has not read it that way.[167] However, he also points out in his book that the church has historically made other interpretive mistakes, such as the structure of the Solar System, how salvation is grasped, and whether or not slavery is Biblical. So while I certainly do not want to ignore church tradition, history shows that the church has made errors in interpreting the Bible.

Dr. Erickson states:

"The very names of the persons, designated as Father and Son, indicate that, just as with human fathers and sons, God the Father is in the position of supremacy with regard to God the Son. The compilation of such texts is impressive and taken alone would have to be judged to have established the gradational-authority view as

---

[166] Kevin Giles, The Trinity and Subordinationism, InterVarsity Press, c. 2002, p. 25.

[167] I do not know church history well enough to judge his statement, but my sense is not everybody agrees with him.

true." Note how he, like so many, describes the position of being in authority as a position of "supremacy." I do not believe that, nor do I think the Bible teaches that.

"There are, *however* [italics mine], texts that seem to support the equivalent-authority position. Some of these are general in nature, such as the meaning of the names Father and Son, the variability of order in the listing of the three, and the variations of names used for the three persons...."

"On balance, then, we judge that the best interpretation of the full Biblical revelation is that no action of any person of the Trinity is an action done in isolation from the other two persons, even though one is primary in that action. This means that the texts that speak of the Father commanding and the Son obeying are to be understood as referring to the time of the Son's earthly ministry. The Father's will, which the Son obeys, is actually the will of all three members of the Trinity, administered on their behalf by the Father. While some texts, such as the I Corinthians 15 passage, favor the gradational view, it is our judgment that overall, the equivalence view does a better job of explaining more of the Biblical evidence and with less distortion of the texts."[168]

Notice, first of all, that he cannot in his mind hold both the gradational view and the equivalence view. He cannot accept that persons can exist in a permanent hierarchy and still be equal. That is indicated by the significant word "however" in the first line of the second paragraph. For him, it is "either/or," not "both/and." Yet he has to acknowledge what he calls the "primary" action of the Father. What does that mean? He says that it means that the obvious authority of the Father over the Son is limited to the Incarnation alone and is not applicable to all eternity. When the Bible speaks of the Son obeying the Father, it is the will of all three persons of the Trinity (which I would agree with) "administered" by the Father. That is the "primary" action of the Father. But he seems to be

---

[168] Millard J. Erickson, Who's Tampering with the Trinity?, Kregel Publications, Grand Rapids, MI, c. 2009, pp. 248–249.

dancing around the word "authority," which he cannot use because *to him* that implies inequality of personhood, which, we all agree, is not a true description of the persons of the Trinity.

And so, he must admit, the text in 1 Corinthians 15 ("When all things are subjected to him, then the Son himself will also be subjected to him who put all things under him, that God may be everything to everyone") is problematic for him since he believes in the equivalent-authority view. The context indicates clearly that it is talking about future eternity, not the temporary time of the Incarnation, and still it talks about the Son being subordinated to the Father in eternity.

I wonder to what extent the reason for the position that hierarchy eliminates equality is the unconscious *assumption* held by so many of the thinkers listed in the quotes at the beginning of this chapter: that to be in a hierarchy *does* eliminate equality. Consider the following: if it were *not* true that hierarchy implies inequality, could we accept the equality of the persons of the Trinity even though they are in hierarchy? If it were *not* true that hierarchy implies inequality, would we look at the Biblical evidence differently? If it were *not* true that being a leader gives one status and a sense of importance in the eyes of others, would we read the Bible differently? Let me ask again to underscore its importance, and, if possible, discard the common cultural assumption that hierarchy implies inequality. After discarding that assumption, then, would you, the reader, say that the Biblical evidence indicates hierarchy among the equal persons of the Trinity?

We're back to where we started. Is it possible for persons, even the persons of the Trinity, to be equal yet still in a hierarchy? Is it possible in a perfect world? The reader will have to decide which best represents the full Biblical revelation. But I challenge us, as dwellers in a fallen world, to leave behind the baggage of this fallen world and try to base our theology on God's revelation in the Scripture. I don't mean that as an accusation of those who disagree with me; I mean it as a challenge for us all to think differently than our fallen world. This is not a small issue for me. This understanding of the nature of relationships in the Trinity, a hierarchy of equals, is central to my understanding of gender relationships. Everything from here depends on that understanding. If I am incorrect in that, then the rest of this book is mistaken and a waste.

This whole issue is similar to the rusty, nearly unrecognizable wreck of an old 1954 Cadillac found in the woods by my son's Cub Scout pack, which I referred to in the chapter on hermeneutics. It was nothing at all like the beautiful original. In the same way, most of our experience of hierarchy is negative and nothing like the beautiful original Design. We've all been hurt by it. To suggest that the Originator of everything that exists consists of a hierarchy of equals, that his highest creatures, humans, the only creatures that bear His image, also consist of a hierarchy of equals, is difficult to swallow. It is difficult because of our prejudice against hierarchy and our dislike of submission. It is difficult because we have all suffered under hierarchy in a fallen world. It is difficult because our governmental and economic systems create a prejudice in us against it. It is difficult because we don't even have words that adequately express the concept; hierarchy just sounds too much like "higher-archy." It is difficult because it belongs to a distant Kingdom that is in reality our Home and for which we were designed and of which we are citizens. But we have been away from home so long.

I have several desires in writing this book. One is that we would come to understand something of how the damaged relationships we experience in this fallen world are different from the beauty of relationships in the Kingdom of God. Another is that we would begin to understand something of the wonderful world that will be Home, where we were designed to live, and to which we shall return, if we understand and accept the salvation Jesus offers through His substitutionary death on the Cross. And one more is that we would begin to understand some of the fingerprints and appetizers our Creator left in His Creation. God's Creation is so damaged by the Fall that it is often unrecognizable. One of those fingerprints is how the genders are designed to relate to one another. Another one is the nature and structure of the church. That is not easy, as we are talking about a completely different Kingdom and a completely different Reality. And a far better one. Additionally, we are all sinners. "The sufferings of this present time are not worth comparing with the glory that is to be revealed to us…. Because the creation itself will be *set free* from its bondage to decay and obtain the glorious *liberty* of the children of God."[169] But with God's help, perhaps we can begin to see a little more clearly that distant image that seems so blurry now.[170] I sincerely hope this book, as much as anything else, will make us hungry for Home, which is awaiting us in Heaven.

If so, I will be pleased.

---

[169] Romans 8:18, 20

[170] I in no way want to imply that a hunger for heaven means we can ignore our calling to feed the hungry and care for the fatherless, widows, and underprivileged in this fallen world, even at a cost to ourselves and our personal comfort. In fact, it is *because* our home is in heaven that we are freed up to sacrifice the temporary pleasures this world offers to help others, because we have incomparable pleasure awaiting us in heaven. So says Jonathan Leeman in his book How the Nations Rage (Nelson Books, Nashville, TN, c. 2018, p. 72): "Contrary to what people may think, it's the most heavenly minded people who are free to do the most earthly good. They are free to pour themselves out or give themselves away, because they are not trying to store up their treasure on earth."

4

BEGINNINGS

"I had heard that I was in the wrong place, and my
soul sang for joy, like a bird in the spring…. I knew
now… why I could feel homesick at home.[171]

"I must keep alive in myself the desire for my true
country which I shall not find til after death."[172]

Julie Andrews told us in the 1960s movie *The Sound of Music* that
"The beginning is a very good place to start." And so it is. As we
examine the issue of God, gender, and the implications of living in
a fallen world, we'll start at the beginning, in the book of Genesis.
From there, we'll go through the Scriptures in a generally linear
direction, from beginning to end. For the most part, we will examine
the texts as they were written, as part of a bigger piece of literature.
Approaching the subject that way instead of topically, looking at
isolated verses, helps avoid a skewed interpretation. It's too easy to
come up with the answer you want, choosing the verses that support
your position and ignoring those that don't. That has been known
to happen!

---

[171] <u>Orthodoxy</u>, by G. K. Chesterton, conclusion titled "The Flag of the World."
[172] <u>Mere Christianity</u>, by C. S. Lewis, Macmillan Company, New York, NY, c. 1972, p. 120.
Used by permission.

So we will start at the beginning by looking at the book of Genesis, the first book in the Bible. Since there are no videos of the creation of the Universe, we must limit ourselves to what the Creator has revealed to us. It is admittedly a selective account. We are not told everything, but we are told enough.

The Bible begins with the topic of the beginnings. The name of the first book in the Bible means "Beginning," and it bristles with them. The beginning of matter. The beginning of light and, by deduction, the beginning of darkness.[173] There is the beginning of plant life. The beginning of animal life. The beginning of marriage. The beginning of bad marriages! The beginning of death. The book starts with blossoming lifeforms and ends with Joseph being buried in a coffin in a foreign land. If all the reader had was the first chapter and the last chapter of Genesis, he surely would conclude that something had gone terribly wrong.

And so it did. The beginning of sin. The beginning of death. The beginning of betrayal. The beginning of murder. The beginning of weeds. The beginning of labor pain in birth. The beginning of broken, dysfunctional families.

However, the good news is there is also the beginning of Good News. The beginning of God's initiative into the lives of people. The beginning of a people uniquely chosen by God. The beginning of God's rescue from the consequences of sin. The beginning of redemption. The beginning of the experience of God's Patience and Forgiveness. And on and on.

But there is one entity that does not have its beginning in

---

[173] Interestingly, darkness is not the opposite of light but the *absence* of light. To make a room dark, you do not turn on a bulb that emanates darkness. You merely turn out the light and darkness happens. That tells us that darkness will never overcome light. It cannot. The Apostle John says, "God is light and in Him is no darkness at all" in 1 John 1:5. Just as there is no equal but opposite of light, there is also no equal but opposite of God, like positive and negative ends of a battery. Satan, who appears very early in Biblical history, is not equal to God, but Bad. Then we would have two equal but opposite powers at war, and nothing would ever happen because each would cancel the other out. So the good news at the very beginning of Biblical history is that God is in control and Satan will not and *cannot* stop God's purposes. At the very beginning of recorded Biblical history, we know who the eventual winner will be.

Genesis, and that is God. The contrast is striking if you catch it. "In the beginning, God created...." That's how it all starts. There is no beginning for God in the book of beginnings. The very first sentence in Biblical history introduces us to a God already there and functioning as the subject of the very first verb: "created." When history begins, God is already there, uncreated, doing verbs. And, thankfully, that does not stop.

The Serial Creation

Structure is an important interpretive tool, and so the structure of Genesis One is important. Chapter and verse divisions, of course, are not part of the original text but were added later, possibly, as one person remarked, by a medieval editor riding in a buggy and whenever it hit a bump in the road, the editor inserted a chapter division. Sometimes the verse and chapter divisions seem about that logical. The first narrative of creation probably extends through chapter 2:3: "So God blessed the seventh day and hallowed it, because on it God rested from all his work which he had done in creation." That verse seems to continue the pattern of "days" and brings to a conclusion the "days" of creation. From there, the author returns to square one and re-tells the whole story of creation but with a markedly different emphasis. More on that later. For now, notice that there are no "days" in the second creation account. Verse 4 ("These are the generations of the heavens and the earth when they were created") could be either a summary of the first creation account or an introduction to the second, and it does not seem critical to our understanding of the passage which it is.

The skeleton of chapter one, on which the flesh of the chapter is fixed, consists of the repeated phrases "and God said, "Let there be... And there was... and God saw... And God called it good." That occurs some ten times in the chapter. God fashions the Universe in a careful, orderly, progressive manner and presumes to be the judge of what He has made.[174]

I think words are important, particularly when God has chosen them. Seven times in the chapter we find the phrase "Let there be…," and in response to those words something happened: "and there was." The subject is *always* God. The word "created" is only used five times in three places in the chapter, again, always with God as the subject. "In the beginning God *created* the heavens and the earth" (verse 1). "So God *created* the great sea monsters and every living creature that moves…" (verse 21). And verse 27: "So God *created* man in his own image, in the image of God he *created* him; male and female he *created* them." The word "created" seems to be a word used sparingly by God to describe a unique event in the blossoming of creation. Since I believe the words in the Bible are there by God's design, then it would seem that not all creation is the same. Some creation seems to be the more passive "let there be… And there was." There are also verses 11 and 20: "Let the *earth* put forth vegetation, plants yielding seed, and fruit trees bearing fruit in which is their seed, each according to its kind, upon the earth" and "Let the *waters* bring forth swarms of living creatures…."[175]

It is in striking contrast to those phrases that we find at critical junctures in the text the powerful, majestic phrase: "God created." I am not sure what to make of the fact that plants are not described as "living" but animals are in verses 11 and 20. But taking the Bible at its word, the three uses of the word "create" are in the creation of

---

[174] It is interesting that on the last day, the day that God rested, there is no mention of evening and morning. Words are important and structure is important. I think that the author did not just forget to put in those words, but this is a hint of an eternity of *rest*, for which there is no beginning or ending, which is coming and will outlast creation. It does not have a morning or an evening.

[175] I think this is very significant in the debate on evolution, or theistic evolution. Sometimes God "creates" and sometimes He seems to let it happen. Why did the author of Genesis use different words instead of the same words? Interesting and, I think, very significant, but that discussion is not the purpose of this book. I was a science major in college, and there I came to believe that God is the author of science—of *all* science. So, as a result, any scientific principle has God as its author. In this text it is very important to remember that God is equally the subject of both the verbs "let there be…" and "create."

matter (verse 1), the creation of life (verse 20), and the creation of human beings (verses 26 and 27). The rest of the time, there is the more passive, "let it be" and it happened. I think that structure is significant.

I remember the first time I saw the original *Bonnie and Clyde* movie. It was great fun until the end when they were killed in a shooting carnage in their old car. Part of the reason I remember that part of the movie so vividly is that it suddenly shifted into slow motion at the point the shooting began. There were bullets slowly crashing through the metal of the car, bodies jumping around as they were hit with a shower of bullets, and blood spurting all over everything in ghastly slow motion. Why slow motion for that gruesome scene? Because that was a way to emphasize what was going on, and it was done intentionally by the author of the movie-script. For some reason, he wanted to emphasize that particular part of the story. The way he did it was to shift suddenly into slow motion. After probably fifty years, I still remember it vividly, even after seeing it only once.

The writers of the four gospels in the New Testament do the same thing. Each one spends several chapters on the last 72 hours of Jesus' life, documenting in careful detail what happened, while only selectively reporting on the first thirty or so years of his life. Think about that. Thirty years of ministry warrants spotty reporting, but the last week, and the last three days, warrant careful detail. All of Jesus' life and ministry is important, but not all is equally important. Clearly the death and resurrection of Jesus are what the gospel writers want us to digest, rather than what he looked like or did as a ten-year-old. The reader can discern that by the shift into "slow-motion" at the end of each of the gospels. That, incidentally, proves wrong the often heard comment that it wasn't the death of Jesus that was important; it was his life. "He came to show us how to live and how he died is not that important." Well, he certainly did show us how to live, but without the death and resurrection of Jesus, we would still be dead in our sins and rebellion against God and the possibility of living a life that comes anywhere close to the imitation of Jesus would be non-existent. The fact that all four gospel writers down-shift into slow motion at the death and resurrection of Jesus indicates what they thought was of supreme importance in Jesus' life: how it ended.

The author of Genesis 1 uses the same technique to focus our attention. There are 34 verses in the first creation account in Genesis. Of those 34 verses, five are devoted to the creation of man, in the form of male and female. That is really quite astounding in light of the fact that the other 29 verses of the chapter describe the creation of the whole universe and all its lifeforms! This is a universe that we know to be big beyond our comprehension; with our biggest telescopes we cannot see where it ends. The distances to the farthest galaxies are just mind-boggling. Why such emphasis on a mere two creatures compared to all the other creatures and everything else in the universe?

Simply because the man and woman are not a "mere two creatures." That is why five of the 34 verses of the first chapter are devoted to those two individuals. They are created, unlike the rest of the creation, *uniquely*, in God's image. Long before the movie *Bonnie and Clyde*, another author used slow motion to emphasize an event. Of the five times the word "created" is used, three of them are used in verses 26 and 27. Only the man and woman are described as being created in God's image, and that three times in two verses! And only in the creation of human beings is gender mentioned. Presumably the other animals were also created male and female, since they did reproduce. But only with the humans is it specifically mentioned, and that in the context of the reader being told repeatedly that the human species is uniquely created in God's image.

"Then God said, 'Let us make man in our image, after our likeness; and let them have dominion over the fish of the sea, and over the birds of the air, and over the cattle, and over all the earth, and over every creeping thing that creeps upon the earth.' So God created man in his own image, in the image of God he created him;

male and female he created them. And God blessed them, and God said to them, 'Be fruitful and multiply, and fill the earth and subdue it; and have dominion over the fish of the sea and over the birds of the air and over every living thing that moves upon the earth'" (Gen. 1:26–28).

In contrast to the rest of the chapter, like the slow-motion segment in the movie, the author focuses our attention on the creation of the male and female, in order that we see the high view of humanity, male and female alike, and therefore gender, that the Bible presents. It is inescapable. Created. Created. Created. Three times. Not just "happened" or even "Let them be... And they were." But the powerful "God created." Since the word is used only at the creation of matter, of life, and here, of humanity as male and female, it would seem to follow that these two humans, male and female, are a whole new order of existence.

As if that were not enough, the word "image" is used twice in these two verses, plus the word "likeness." No other creation warrants three uses of the word "created." No other creation warrants the words "In his own image." No other creation warrants God thinking and talking and musing about its creation.[176] No other creation is actually spoken *to* by the creator behind all the verbs in this chapter, and no other creature is blessed by the Creator. And not only were they created, but created specifically in God's image; *male and female* is how He created them. Only in the creation of human beings are both image and gender mentioned. This is holy ground and we should take our shoes off.

The name that is used exclusively for God in chapter one of Genesis is an interesting word. It is the word or name Elohim. In Hebrew, the ending -im is a plural ending, as -es is in English. One bench. Two benches. The interesting thing about this name of God is that, even though it is a plural word, it always takes a singular verb or singular adjective. In the whole chapter, the only name used for

---

[176] Genesis 1:26: "Then God said, 'Let us make man in our image, after our likeness, and let them have dominion over the fish of the sea,'" and so on.

God is "Elohim," and so we have revealed a God who is somehow plural yet always acts as a unity. Genesis 1:1 says, "In the beginning God (plural) created (singular) the heavens and the earth." The first five words of the Bible are actually quite stunning. We have already observed that, at the beginning of everything that is, God is already there doing verbs. He has no beginning. He is also there as a being of complexity, a plural being who somehow is acting as if he were singular but is, in reality, plural. This is pretty amazing theology, and all this in the first five words of the Bible.

There is in Hebrew (which was a real language used by real people in normal life) a construction which we do not have in English called a plural of majesty. The way this particular construction was used was very similar to what we have seen in Genesis one: a Hebrew king, in order to show his majesty, was always referred to in the plural (kings) but always took a singular verb or adjective. Could that be what is going on here in Genesis one? Many have said that, and they might be correct. But what happens in Genesis 1:26 and 27 is unmistakably unique. "Then God (plural) said (singular), 'Let us (obviously plural) make (singular) man (singular) in our (obviously plural) image, in our (obviously plural) likeness (singular) and let them (plural) rule (singular)....' So God (plural) created (singular) man (singular) in his (singular) image, in the image of God (plural) he (singular) created (singular) him (singular): male and female (plural) he (singular) created (singular) them (plural)."

While it might be possible to dismiss the plurality of God in Genesis one as merely a plural of majesty, there is never an instance in secular Hebrew similar to what is happening here. God talks and "consults" among himself (themselves) and comes up with a "group" decision to create a being in his (their) image, and when that being is created (described with a singular verb "create"), it is created plural—male and female—a being with two "forms" or genders. Twice repeated "image." Three times repeated "created." Male and female He created *them*. This is not merely a plural of majesty. This is a real plural being who acts as a singular, and when

He creates a being uniquely in His own image, that being is a plural being—male and female. It took a plural being, male and female, to reflect the image of a plural being—Elohim. And this plural creation of Elohim—male and female—later on becomes *one*—a unity.[177]

Significantly, in chapter two, when the separate creation of the woman is recorded, the plural "let us make" is recorded by singular "I will make." A singular creates a singular. Here a plural creates a plural—and very specifically says that one plural is the image of the other plural. Also, significantly, there is no mention of being created in the image of God in chapter two where the man and the woman are created separately and in a serial order. It seems to me inescapable that male and female, and therefore gender, the relationship between the genders, somehow reflects the plurality and relationships among the Godhead. I see no way around that. It is a foundational principle of this book that gender is a reflection of the plurality of the Godhead. Exactly what that means is yet to be seen.[178]

As we read through the Scriptures from beginning to end, it seems God's revelation is progressive, or gradual. This is not the same as extrapolation revelation, in which the interpreter extrapolates beyond what Scripture says. There is not sufficient information in Genesis one to validate our doctrine of the trinity. But the foundation is there. There is also not sufficient information to validate any detailed doctrine of gender from the opening chapters of Genesis. But the foundation is there.[179] Just as the Scriptures gradually develop a doctrine of the Trinity, so the Scriptures also

---

[177] Ephesians 5:31

[178] I do not intend to imply that the relationships among the persons of the Trinity are sexual relationships. That would be anthropomorphic projection—a term coined by Dr. Gilbert Bilezikian that I refer to on page 46 footnote 50. I do intend to imply that the sexual relationship between a husband and wife, the intimacy and totality of that relationship, body, soul, and spirit, is a fingerprint of the perfect, holy, and whole relationships among the persons of the Trinity.

[179] Some complementarian authors have looked at the second creation account in Genesis two and said that the chapter teaches that Adam was the head of Eve and that he failed in his headship calling by not being the "leader" in dealing with Satan's temptation. That seems to me to be reading more into the text than is obviously there. It may be true, but it is not *obviously* true.

gradually develop a doctrine of gender. Since gender is a fingerprint of the triune Creator, and since one is an image of the other, it makes sense that, if one is gradually revealed throughout Scripture, the other would be, too.

The thesis of this book is that Genesis 1:26 and 27 are central to understanding the Biblical view of gender. It lays a foundational principle upon which all the texts on gender are built. This is not a "window text" that is used to discount other texts that seem to contradict this verse. This is not a "clear text" that allows us to ignore an "obscure text," which may be "obscure" because we don't like what it says. It is an introductory text that other texts explain and expand upon as the fuller revelation in later Scripture comes along, just as later Scriptures define and bring into focus the doctrine of the Trinity.

Now, before we go on to the second and very different creation account, there are several observations to be made from this chapter.

1. There is no mention of any differentiation between the male and the female. None. Both are created in God's image—equally.
2. Since, as I said above, I believe gender relationships (particularly between a husband and wife) are a fingerprint of relationships among the three persons of the Trinity, that might appear to leave a single person out, not in the image of God. But just as the three persons of the Trinity are completely God, so a single person is still created in God's image. But it is the relationship between a husband and wife that uniquely mirrors the relationships among the persons of the Trinity.
3. Both the male and the female are given dominion over God's creation. The word "over" is mentioned three times in verse 28. This is a quality that makes the two humans different from the animals. To have dominion requires authority, and that authority is given both to the man and the woman

equally. There is no differentiation. They are co-regents, like a king and queen.

4. Even in a sinless world, there is hierarchy and dominion. The word "over" is present in a perfect world. It is a significant question to ask: why in God's perfect creation is hierarchy present? Why were they not all equal, able to live together in a "tree-hugger," "love-your-mother-earth" sort of way? Hopefully that was clarified in the chapter on "The Trinity, Hierarchy, and Equality." The presence of authority and dominion in God's perfect created world is, I think, a fingerprint of the Creator. However, in the fallen world in which we live, God's design is so disfigured by sin that it is hard to recognize.

5. Since dominion over God's creation was given to both the man and the woman equally, apparently both are capable of wielding and handling authority.

6. When God created the universe, significantly, He created a universe in which there was diversity, even diversity of authority. The man and woman were given dominion *over* the rest of creation. That, I believe, implies something of the nature of God who created it. God is a diverse God, and part of that diversity is a diversity of authority.

7. Lastly, before there was anything, any matter at all, there was relationship. The plural God, whom we understand from a later Biblical perspective to be a Trinity, had relationship among themselves, as a unity, in eternity before the creation of the universe. Since relationship came before matter, the essence of reality, then, is relationship, not matter. Because relationships are more significant than matter, a healthy relationship will be immensely more satisfying and fulfilling than anything material, like a new car. "He who finishes with the most toys wins" is just not true. He may well be the ultimate loser, an incredibly lonely and unhappy person

despite buying into the overwhelming media message that possessions bring you happiness.

Look at all the advertising. The people with the "things" are always smiling and happy. The clear message (and the intended message) is that the things make you happy. The advertiser wants you to *buy* his product and so implies that it will make you happy. It certainly is true God gives us things to enjoy. But what is foundational to deep personal wholeness is good relationships, first of all with God and secondly with fellow human beings, rather than a multitude of possessions.

I remember hearing a speaker deliver a stunning hypothetical illustration that brought this home to me. Imagine you are watching TV comfortably in your home and a news bulletin comes on. Scientists have just discovered that an asteroid will crash into the earth in thirty minutes, eliminating life as we know it. The authorities plead with people to avoid chaos and be sensible in these last thirty minutes. How would you respond? Would you think, "Oh, my. The car is so dirty for this event," or "My hair looks terrible," or "I cannot believe I won't be able to enjoy my new TV for very long. This is just not fair"? Is that what your soul would turn to as you unexpectedly face the last thirty minutes of your life? I think not. I suspect phone lines would be instantly jammed. Families would be running to be together. Spouses would be hugging. Apologies would be blossoming all over the place. When life is cut short, we automatically turn to what is really important, and for most people (in reality, all people), that is not "things." I believe in foxhole religion and deathbed conversions. Impending death has a way of clearing the air and bringing Reality into focus. The really unfortunate thing is that we go through everyday life avoiding reality and buying the lies of the world that tell us what is really important and what will really fill our soul is possessions. That is incorrect.[180]

---

[180] C. S. Lewis describes this unfortunate, late decision called "deathbed conversion," which ultimately shows God's Divine humility, in his book <u>The Problem of Pain</u>. "It is a poor thing

My wife loves funerals. I know that seems strange. But the reason is that for her (and for me also), funerals put things in perspective. We see what really matters. In the sharing about the deceased, which has now become a common practice, people never remark about how cool his car was, how stylish her hair was, or how nice their lawn was. A satisfying and memorable life is just not about things. It's about relationships. The reason is that relationship (among the Trinity) existed before matter and will outlive matter.

The Centrality of Gender

A modern reader reading through Genesis for the first time would probably scratch his head at what follows Genesis one. Genesis two comes next. That hardly seems remarkable until you read chapter two. Since two comes after one, the reader would expect that chapter two would follow chronologically what occurred in chapter one. But what follows is unexpected: the story starts over again. Back to square one. There is a repetition of the *same* story again, but it is *different*—strikingly different.

First, God creates the man, then the woman. In chapter one, they were created at the same time. Is the serial creation of man and woman significant? If not, why did God record it in chapter two? Astonishingly, in chapter two, the woman was created *out of* the man, because the man's being alone was "not good." It was God's own words that it was "not good" that the man should be *alone*. That is in striking contrast to the repetition of "God saw that it was good" in chapter one. Now, suddenly, before the fall—we are still in a sinless world—something is *not good*. Being Alone. It is worth

---

to strike our colors to God when the ship is going down under us; a poor thing to come to Him as a last resort, to offer up 'our own' when it is no longer worth keeping. If God were proud He would hardly have us on such terms: but He is not proud, He stoops to conquer, He will have us even though we have shown that we prefer everything else to Him, and come to Him because there is 'nothing better' now to be had" (p. 97). (Macmillan Publishing Company, New York, NY, c. 1962, 21st printing. Used by permission.)

reminding ourselves that the man had God plus the whole beautiful Garden of Eden. Was that not enough? Apparently not. It was *God's* judgment that the man needed something more, and it was not a new car.

In chapter one, the plants came before the animals and the humans. In chapter two, the order is reversed. In chapter one, the animals were created before humans. In chapter two, the opposite is true.

In chapter one, both man and woman were apparently created simultaneously. In chapter two, the man was created first, the woman some time after.

In chapter one, the creation of the human creature as male and female came as the last in a series of God's creations—God's crowning creation; in chapter two, everything else seems like background to the creation of the man and woman.

In chapter one, the man and the woman are given dominion over all of God's creation. In chapter two, there is no mention of dominion. In fact, they are told there is one part of God's creation over which they do *not* have dominion: "You may freely eat of every tree of the garden, *but* of the tree of the knowledge of good and evil you shall *not* eat, for in the day you eat of it you shall die."[181] These are strikingly new words: "you shall *not*...." There is one part of God's creation over which the man and the woman definitely did not have dominion. They were not allowed to eat of that one tree. In a sinless world, God still puts prohibitions on his human creations. He is God and they are not. They may freely eat of *any* tree of the garden... but one.

And if this is not enough, there are three dangerous new concepts introduced—"evil," "you shall die," and "ashamed." This is new stuff.

Now, a modern reader is tempted to throw up his hands in frustration, wondering how two such different accounts of the same

---

[181] Genesis 2:16, 17

event could be included in a book as supposedly reliable as the Bible, not knowing which account to believe, if either. And many non-believers have pointed to this contradiction as one of a legion in this unreliable book called the Bible.

In reality, this was a figure of speech common to ancient near-Eastern languages in which two stories of the same event are repeated, each one having a different emphasis and maybe even contradicting each other in peripheral issues. Dr. K. A. Kitchen makes the point that such duplication of texts was commonplace in ancient Near Eastern texts: "It is often claimed that Genesis 1 and Genesis 2 contain two different creation-narratives. In point of fact, however, the strictly complementary nature of the 'two' accounts is plain enough: Genesis 1 mentions the creation of man as the last of a series, without any details, whereas in Genesis 2 man is the centre of interest and more specific details are given about him and his setting. There is no incompatible duplication here at all.... Precisely this relationship of a general summary-outline plus a more detailed account of one (or more) major aspects—with different styles for the two accounts—is commonplace in ancient Oriental texts."[182]

A figure of speech is a non-literal use of words to convey meaning. "The home team killed the visiting basketball team." Not true, really. The point is the home team won handily. Notice that a statement that contains a *factual error* (one team killed the other) actually communicates *truth*. That is the way a figure of speech works. We must not get caught up with the factual contradictions between chapter one and chapter two, which are real, any more that we should get caught up with the factual error that one of the teams was not dead after the basketball contest, even though that's what the words said. I do not want to be understood as having a low view of Scripture's reliability, that we ignore the "errors" and try to see what the "real meaning" is. Not that. My point is that we use words sometimes in non-literal ways, but that doesn't take

---

[182] K.A. Kitchen, <u>Ancient Orient and the Old Testament,</u> InterVarsity Press, Chicago, IL. c. 1966, pp. 116, 117. He goes on to give examples from other literature from the same time period.

away from the truth we are trying to communicate, even if that is done by intentionally using a statement that is factually wrong. The point is this: what is the author trying to say? When I read the two creation accounts back to back, I assume purpose in the presence of two differing accounts: surely the duplication is not accidental and therefore meaningless. Properly interpreted, they are not necessarily untrue or unreliable. We can maintain our high confidence in the reliability of Scripture even though chapter two in many ways contradicts chapter one. That's just the way we use words. The question is, why did the author narrate the events *differently,* retelling the story, but differently? What was the author trying to communicate? What is present in chapter two that differentiates it from chapter one and why is it there?

1. First, and significantly, the man was made first. The woman came later. There is no indication in the text that being created first carries any significance at all. That issue arises later in Biblical history. But as a result, there are a number of activities that *only* the man did because he was there and she was not. The statement about being free to eat of every tree of the garden, along with the command not to eat of the tree of the knowledge of good and evil, was given only to him. In fact, it is brought up three times to his face and his alone: once in the giving of the command, once in the confrontation, and once in the judgment (Gen. 2:16, 3:11, and 3:17–19).

2. It was "not good" that the man was alone. If the woman had been created first and so also alone, presumably that would also be "not good," but that option is not presented us since the man was created first. If our understanding of Genesis 1:26 through 28 is legitimate, then the loneliness of the man is extremely negative. It is very "not good" that he should be alone.

3. The woman is created to be a "help-mate" to the man and not the other way around. They are not mutual helpers. However, we learn from later texts that this in no way means that "help" only goes one way and that being a "helper" does not make one inferior.

4. The man was created out of the dust of the ground. The woman was created out of man.

5. God brought the woman to the man, not vice versa. They did not come to find each other. But it is the man's role to leave, to cleave to the woman, and to become one flesh with her. There is no mention of the woman's responsibility in the relationship. This *may* imply that responsibility for the relationship lies with the man. Of course, the woman had no father and mother whom she could leave, but then neither did the man. I will leave the belly button issue—did they have one?—up to theologians brighter than I.

6. The man, not the woman, was given the task of naming the animals. Presumably, again, that is because he was created first and, had the woman been created first, she would have done it. But the animals did not name themselves. The man did it. So there are several activities that the man did because he was formed first.

7. The man's naming of the animals mirrors God's naming of the segments of the creation in Genesis one. The same word is used in both instances. God created the universe and named the various parts, and now, in chapter two, the man is naming some parts of the creation, the animals. The *implied* message seems clear: the man is in hierarchy over the animals just as God was in hierarchy over His creation.

8. The man also named the woman. Significantly, she did not name herself. She did not name the man. They did not name each other. In the first two instances of one party "calling" or "naming" another party, the subject is definitely in a position of hierarchy over the party being named. God

"calls" parts of His creation "good," and the man "names" the animals. The parallelism *implies* that the man is in a position of hierarchy over the woman. The word is the same word in Hebrew in all three situations: God naming His creation, the man naming the animals, and the man naming the woman. Is the repetition intentional? Is it significant? I think so.

9. When the woman is made out of the man, the sense of personhood or self-consciousness remains with the man. It is not equally divided between the two new genders, created out of the one. By that I mean it is the man who recognizes the woman and perceives what or who she is. "Bone of my bones, flesh of my flesh; she shall be called Woman because she was taken out of Man." Those are his words, not the woman's. If it had been equally divided, then they would have "recognized" each other. But that is not what Genesis two says. And presumably if the woman had been made first, she would have recognized the man as being bone of her bones, flesh of her flesh, having been made out of man.

10. There is nothing said in Genesis two about the man and the woman being created in the image or likeness of God. They are both created by God, and, significantly, the male is created out of dirt but the woman out of the man. The text uses a singular word for God, the creator, when He creates each human, male and female, not a plural as in Genesis 1:26–28, when it says the man and woman were created in God's image.

Those seem to be pretty significant, and irreversible, differences. So our interpretive question is this: what was the author trying to communicate by including Genesis 2?

Try to imagine how differently the text would read if the woman had been created first, if the woman had named the animals, if God had said it was not good for the women to be alone and so created the man as a helpmate to the woman, if the man had been created out of the woman, if the woman had recognized the man as flesh of her flesh and had named the man, if the man had sinned first, but then God questioned the woman first about what had happened. Would those differences be significant? I think it would make a profound difference in how we understand Genesis two, and so the gender question. Clearly, Genesis two is significantly, shall we say, "male oriented," and *all of that* is because the male was formed first. The chapter, as it stands, is very different in emphasis from chapter one. I am not comfortable with saying Genesis two clearly teaches "male superiority" or even "male headship." Maybe, but not clearly. But there is something there that differentiates it from chapter one. We have to wait for the New Testament to help us understand what is going on here.

I do not assume the differences between chapter one and chapter two to be irrelevant. I believe they are there by God's design and so they mean *something*, but what they mean is not clear. At least not yet. In fact, *none* of these observations are negative about the female gender and *none* of them imply male superiority. But it seems to me inescapable that the genders in Genesis two are *different* and there is something—how can I say it?—primary about the male. Not smarter. Not superior. Not necessarily even leader. But *something*. The difference is not like the positive and negative poles of a battery: sort of identical but opposite. Dr. Giles refers to the "polarity" of the sexes, and I think that is misleading. I'm not sure of the author's intention in using that particular analogy, but it brings to mind an analogy to electricity or batteries. Alike but opposite, as in mirror images. However, that does not fit the narrative of Genesis two as we have it. There is something about the creation of the genders in chapter two that "polarity" just does not describe.[183]

---

[183] The Trinity & Subordinationism, by Kevin Giles, IVP. PO Box 1400, Downers Grove, IL, 60515, c. 2002, pp. 203, 204.

At this point, I want to make four observations.

1. There has been much debate about the significance of the
    word that refers to the woman: a help-mate or "helper-fit." It
    is a unique compound word—two words plastered together,
    occurring only twice in the Bible, both of them in this
    chapter: in verses 18 and 20. One part of the compound
    word means "corresponding to" or "exact correspondence"—
    that is the part usually translated "partner" or "mate." The
    other part means "helper." It does not carry any sense
    of inferiority. In fact, it is often used (over one hundred
    times) in the Old Testament of God who is our "helper,"
    and clearly God is not our inferior. One lesson we need to
    understand is that being a helper does *not* imply inferiority,
    at least in a non-fallen world. The word carries no sense of
    "second place." Yet in this chapter the two genders are not
    presented as being interchangeable. It is our problem that,
    in a fallen world, we understand a helper, and often treat a
    helper, as inferior.[184] It is significant, I think, that when the
    man recognized and named the woman, his response was
    not a utilitarian "Wow, I've finally got some help!" That is
    decidedly *not* his response. His response was, "Wow, here, at
    last, is someone *just like me.*" She was valued and recognized
    as his equal, the same stuff.[185]

---

[184] I had the profound experience of being a "door guard" for the speaker room at the Urbana
Missionary convention. This is a convention for college students over Christmas break intended
to challenge them to consider responding to God's call to the mission field. My job was to guard
the door so that the room was a quiet, safe, and private place for the speakers to meditate, pray,
and relax before speaking to the large crowd of students. So I was privileged to open and close
the door for a number of nationally known speakers, some of whom would be recognized by
anybody on the street. All but one did not even acknowledge that I existed, opening and closing
the door for them. Only one, a woman, stopped, and not only thanked me, but asked how I was
and how the week was going for me. I was blown away by her care for me, a lowly doorman,
especially in contrast to the others. We all need to follow her example of not judging a person's
value by the role he or she fulfills.

[185] The fact that the first half of the term "helper" refers to God in the Old Testament indicates
the word does not imply inferiority. So Elizabeth Elliott's definition—"a helper, to meet,

2. There have been comments and cute wooden plaques made that go something like this: "The woman was not made out of the man's feet, as she would then be below him and inferior; nor was she made out of his head, and so above and superior to him, but out of his side, and so she is equal to him." That may be nice, but it is not necessary to prove the equality of the female gender. The Bible nowhere contains reasoning along those lines. Equality is more profoundly proven from other texts, especially Genesis 1.

3. The text makes no comment on the significance of gender differences. It does not even record that God saw it and said it was good. It does conclude that *the two become one.* The Apostle Paul many, many years later calls this a "mystery" (Ephesians 5:32ff). No, not a mystery, a *great* mystery. And he takes it to be an appetizer of something enormously bigger—Christ and the church. In our text here in Genesis, the one became two: God took the rib from Adam, whatever that means, and made it into the woman, so there were now two where there was previously one. God did not repeat Adam's creation by using another handful of dust to make a woman. The creation of the woman was *out of* the man, not out of dust.[186] Then, when the man recognizes that she is of the same stuff as he is, bone of his bones, flesh of his flesh,

respond to, surrender to, and complement"—does not *quite* fit the word, since it is used mostly of God to us. That from Recovering Biblical Manhood and Womanhood, p. 397, in her article, "The Essence of Femininity: A Personal Perspective." Would her definition apply to God in relation to us? God does not surrender to us. The same word is used of God in relation to us. However, she is right on the mark a couple sentences later when she says, "These two people together represent the image of God.... Neither the one nor the other was adequate alone to bear the divine image." (From Recovering Biblical Manhood and Womanhood, ed. by John Piper and Wayne Grudem, Crossway Books, Wheaton, IL, c. 1991, p. 397.

[186] It is significant, I think, that the man and the woman were *not* created out of the same stuff. The man was created out of dust; the woman was created out of the man. Their *source* was significantly different. That is very important in understanding 1 Corinthians 11, what headship means and does not mean. There it is stated that Christ is the head of the man, but the man is the head of the woman. Some people define "headship" as meaning "source." In that text, if we take "headship" as meaning "source," it would be saying that Christ is the source of the man and the man is the source of the woman. But in this account in Genesis, the "source"

the two become one again. This *is* a great mystery! They did not just come *together*. They became *one*.

And they were naked and not ashamed.

4. The fact is, God could have left Genesis 2, with all its differences, out entirely. He did not. I assume purpose in that and in the gender differences present in chapter two.

Michelle Lee-Barnewall puts it this way: "Genesis 2-3 consistently and strikingly portrays Adam and Eve's relationship in an asymmetrical way. Adam provides the source for Eve's creation and he is the only one told to bring unity to the relationship. He is the one who discovers that he needs Eve, not the other way around.... Adam's naming of Eve falls in line with the trend.... It is part of a pattern of representing Adam as the one from whom the relationship consistently begins.... Eve does not name Adam, nor do they name each other."[187]

So, what have we seen so far? Chapter one highlights the immense truth that man and woman are *equally* created in the image of God. It teaches that gender reflects something of the nature of the Godhead, something of the plurality, equality, and unity of the Godhead. And the man and the woman, both created in God's image, are co-regents over God's creation. Both the man and the woman are able to handle authority. Chapter two highlights the differences between the genders. They are not interchangeable. They are not polar opposites. In fact, the text seems to be quite male-oriented. The male is created first; the female is created out of him

of the man is dirt, and the "source" of the woman is the man. Their "source" is different. More on that profound difference in the chapter on 1 Corinthians 11.

[187] Neither Complementarian nor Egalitarian, by Michelle Lee-Barnewall, Baker Academic, Grand Rapids, MI, c. 2016, pp. 143, 144. This is a very good book and the only one I have read that acknowledges that we cannot ignore the value system of the Kingdom of God as we examine the gender issue. I benefited very much from her insights.

and *for* him. The male names the animals and names the female. The male recognizes the female, not the other way around. There is something very different about chapter two as compared to chapter one, and, my theology of Scripture says, that is intentional.

In the chapter on Hermeneutics, I mentioned the interpretive principle called the creation hermeneutic versus the redemption hermeneutic, and that the redemption hermeneutic overrides the creation hermeneutic. That is most often observed by those who cannot escape, but do not seem to like, the gender differentiation and possible hierarchy in Genesis two. My response to that understanding was that I thought it was creating an artificial dichotomy where none exists. Genesis two, after all, is before the fall, in a perfect world, and so what is there to be redeemed from it?

We cannot just ignore the differences between chapter one and chapter two. In the book <u>Man and Woman, One in Christ</u> by Dr. Philip B. Payne,[188] which is quite helpful in a number of areas, the author points out eleven ways in which complementarians have, in his thinking, misused chapter two to teach the headship of men and the subordination of women. And in some respects, I agree with his analysis. But even though he adequately pointed out what the significance of chapter two was *not*, he neglected to say what the purpose of chapter two *was*. There is some reason for the existence of chapter two, with all its gender differentiation, and, let's admit it, the centrality of the male. My theology of Scripture says that chapter two, with the contrasting gender differences, is there for a reason, so we cannot stop with just saying what it does *not* mean.[189]

---

[188] Philip B. Payne, <u>Man and Woman, One in Christ,</u> Zondervan Books, Grand Rapids, MI, c. 2009, pp. 43–53.

[189] He does say on page 43 that "the dominant focus of the text [that is, Genesis 2] is on the equal status and mutual responsibility of man and woman." I suppose one can say that a text means whatever he wants, but I fail to see how he gets that as the main theme of Genesis two. Chapter one is all about mutuality. In contrast, chapter two is strikingly different, and, as we have discovered, male-oriented. We must explain the purpose of that difference. I don't see how he gets "equal status and mutual responsibility of man and woman" out of chapter two when it is so different from chapter one.

I am not the only one to observe that Genesis 2 is different from chapter one and is male-oriented. Here are several egalitarian authors who admit there is *something* suggestive of hierarchy of the genders in Genesis 2.

I referred to Dr. Kevin Giles above when he describes the "polarity" of the genders in Genesis 2: "It is not conceded that anything in Genesis 2–3 teaches that a woman is subordinated to man before the Fall. Yet even if a hint of this can be found in some mute detail in the story, it would not be of any theological consequence. The whole Bible is determined by a forward-looking eschatology that sees perfection in the future."[190]

Dr. William Webb uses this phrase: "First, the whispers of patriarchy in the garden may have been placed there in order to anticipate the curse."[191]

Dr. Paul Jewett puts it this way: "While the first creation narrative, which includes the fundamental affirmation that Man in the divine image is male and female (Gen.1:27), contains no hint of such a hierarchical view, the second narrative (Gen. 2:18–23), which we have treated as supplementing the first, allows, if it does not actually imply, that the woman is subordinate to the man."[192]

I agree that this chapter does not *explicitly* teach female subordination to the male. In fact, I do not like the term subordination, because it implies inferiority, which I think is mistaken. But I wonder what Dr. Giles was referring to when he says, "even if a *hint* of this can be found in some *mute detail* in the story," if "it is not conceded that *anything* in Genesis 2-3 teaches that a woman is subordinated to man before the Fall"? Why would he mention "*even a hint*" of female subordination being present in chapter 2? There must have been some *hint* of the hierarchy of the genders for him to mention the

[190] The Trinity & Subordinationism, by Kevin Giles, IVP, PO Box 1400, Downers Grove, IL 60515, c. 2002, pp. 203, 204.

[191] Slaves, Women, & Homosexuals, by William J. Webb, IVP, PO Box 1400, Downers Grove, IL, 60515, c. 2001, p. 143.

[192] Man as Male and Female, by Paul K Jewett, Wm B. Eerdmans Publishing Company, c. 1975, Grand Rapids, MI, p. 50.

possibility of *even a hint* being present in the text. But then he says it's irrelevant. Or what was Dr. Webb referring to when he referred to the "whispers of patriarchy"? And what did Dr. Jewett mean when he said that Genesis two not only allows but actually implies the woman is subordinate to the man? It seems all three authors are acknowledging *something* of a gender hierarchy in Genesis two before the Fall even though they don't like it. The presence of a hint or a whisper of gender hierarchy before the Fall is significant. They interpret it as "forward-looking" or that it might "anticipate the curse." They are at least honest enough to admit there is *something* in Genesis two that hints at or whispers about hierarchy. It must be there or we wouldn't have egalitarians such as these three noticing it and calling it a "forward-looking eschatology that sees perfection in the future." The troubling aspect of that description is that it sees perfection "in the future." No, perfection was already there because the man and the woman had not yet disobeyed God. God himself has already described the creation as "good."

That brings up again the question of why God included chapter two of Genesis with its—how can we say it?—male orientation. What would be left out of God's revelation if Genesis two were left out? Wouldn't there be something very significant missing in our understanding of the gender issue if Genesis two were left out? Think back on my hypothetical re-writing of Genesis two where everything said about the man was replaced by the woman. It would radically change what the chapter presents. That, I believe, is what Paul is referring to when he refers to the central events of Genesis two—Adam's creation *prior to* Eve and Eve's creation *out of* Adam—in prescribing gender roles for the church in 1 Timothy 2:13–14 and 1 Corinthians 11. I believe that the purpose of chapter two is to augment the equality of the genders shown in Genesis One with the strange (to us) hierarchy of *equal* beings. And, in fact, as we follow the Scriptures on through the New Testament, we find that same dual truth repeated in every passage that teaches on gender—hierarchy with equality.

In reality, though, there is one word that is "forward looking" and anticipates the results of the Fall. It is the word "ashamed," the very last word in Genesis two, and it is immediately followed by the beginning of the narrative of the Fall. There is no place for shame in Eden, but the presence of that word is a bridge to the unfortunate story that immediately follows.

The Fall

Chapter two ends, as we just noted, with a very strange word: "ashamed." What was there to be ashamed of? It does not seem strange to us because we inhabit a fallen world and understand all too well the meaning of the word. We deal with it every day—unless our consciences have been completely seared. But there are remnants of Eden in us. We were not designed for the world we currently live in. We were designed for Eden. So shame is present in all of us at some point. The fact that we do not scratch our heads in puzzlement at the word "ashamed" indicates that we are citizens of a world far, far away from Eden, which was our real home.

And so we are. The chapter that follows chapter two is chronological; we are not treated to a third account of creation. But it is a Tragedy in the biggest sense of the word. I said in the partial list of beginnings at the start of this chapter that there was the beginning of life in chapter one and in stark contrast, in chapter 50, there was a coffin filled with a human body. Joseph is buried at the end of his life. If those two chapters were all we had, we would conclude something had gone terribly wrong somewhere in between.

And so it did. Chapter three is that story, and it is sad beyond comprehension.

"Now the serpent was more subtle than any other wild creature that the Lord God had made. He said to the woman, 'Did God say,

"You shall not eat of any tree of the garden?'" And the woman said to the serpent, 'We may eat of the fruit of the trees of the garden; but God said, "You shall not eat of the fruit of the tree which is in the midst of the garden, neither shall you touch it, lest you die."' But the serpent said to the woman, 'You will not die. For God knows that when you eat of it your eyes will be opened, and you will be like God, knowing good and evil.' So, when the woman saw that the tree was good for food, and that it was a delight to the eyes, and that the tree was to be desired to make one wise, she took of its fruit and ate; and she also gave some to her husband, and he ate."

Out of nowhere came this creature called a serpent. It is described as "subtle" or "crafty." That is not primarily a negative term. It is used eight times in Proverbs in a positive sense. But he begins to ask questions of the woman that call into question the character of God, and that becomes the central issue in the disobedience of the man and the woman. It was not that they were looking for a way to disobey and test God—to test their wings—to see if God were strong enough to deal with their disobedience. It was not a power struggle.

Yet.

The root cause was doubt instilled by the loaded questions asked by the serpent, doubt that God really did have their best interests at heart and that God really was enough for them.

God had told the man that they may freely eat of every tree of the garden except one. The serpent's question was backwards: "Did God say you shall not eat of *any* tree of the garden?" That, of course, would cause them to starve. How subtle the serpent was—and still is. No, God said they may *freely* eat of *every* tree of the garden—except one. God's offer was overwhelmingly generous, but the serpent phrased the question in such a way as to make God look cheap and to cause the woman to focus on the one thing that was off limits. That is a technique still employed today by the Tempter.

Most people today view a holy life as very boring, unfortunately. The woman, apparently, did not know well enough what God had said, and so she began to get it confused. Perhaps Adam had not communicated with her or had not communicated clearly the exact nature of the command. Perhaps she had forgotten. Perhaps the serpent just got her mixed up.

Regardless of the reason, the woman states the command quite incorrectly, making it *more* negative and *more* restrictive than originally given and even *more* restrictive than the serpent's deliberate misquotation of it. For some reason, she thought, God now did not want them even to touch the tree. That was not part of the original prohibition.

The serpent now jumps on this admission and calls God a liar: "You will not die."

But God said they would die in 2:17. There are now two beings—one uncreated and the other created—who are submitting to the woman exactly opposite propositions. The reason God does not want them to eat of the tree, says the serpent, is that they would become like God himself, knowing good and evil, implying that God wants to protect His turf and keep the man and the woman *small.*

Suddenly the tree had three new attractive characteristics:

a) It was *good* for food. Did they not have the whole garden? Previous to this interaction with the serpent, the garden was sufficient. Now it was not.

b) It was a *delight* to the eyes. It was pretty. The rest of the garden wasn't? Remember in Genesis 2:9 when God gave Adam all the trees of the Garden, they were described as "pleasant to the sight and good for food."

c) It was to be *desired* to make one wise. They *needed* it. Who says there is anything wrong with a little wisdom?

So she took of the fruit and gave it to her husband *who was there with her.* The last five words are apparently not in the original Hebrew text, but seem very clear from the context. The NIV includes them in its translation. When the snake addresses whomever he is talking to in verse 4, interestingly, it says, "the serpent said to the woman, 'you will not die.'" The word for "you" is plural, indicating that Adam was right there, but the serpent was specifically talking to the woman. And Adam was listening.

Since he was right there with her, why did he not speak up when the serpent tempted Eve and when she, under the influence of the serpent, became confused about what had really been said? The man, after all, had been given the commandment by God. He did not have it second-hand, as the woman did. He had no excuse for confusion. Were they not in this together? There is nothing recorded that he said. He was silent. He said nothing. He did nothing. Nothing.

The New Testament seems unclear as to exactly who is at fault. Paul writes to Timothy that it was Eve who was deceived, not Adam. "Adam was not deceived, but the woman was deceived and was the transgressor."[193] But the same author also writes, "Therefore as sin came into the world through one man and death through sin, and so death spread to all men because all men sinned… yet death reigned from Adam to Moses, even over those whose sins were not like the *transgression of Adam,* who was a type of the one who was to come."[194]

Those are not mutually exclusive statements, of course. And it would seem from the actual text of what happened that both descriptions in 1 Timothy and Romans are, in fact, true. From what we have in the text, it looks as though Eve was deceived and Adam wasn't. Adam apparently knowingly and willfully disobeyed.

---

[193] 1 Timothy 2:14. It is important that Paul is just stating a fact of what happened. I don't think he is making a general statement about women being more gullible. There is no Scriptural evidence for that generalization.

[194] Romans 5:12

Eve was tricked into it. Which is worse? I cannot make that call. Scripture does not make that call. Many have been selective about which they emphasize, however. But both lead to consequences, and so both are punishable and neither is excusable. That is the clear position both of the narrative in Genesis and of the New Testament writers also. But it is interesting that, in the Romans text, even though it was Eve who sinned first, Adam seems to be blamed for the sin. To be honest, I am not sure I understand that, and I understand completely that view is open to disagreement, legitimately so. But it does seem to be the view presented in the Scriptures that Adam gets blamed for Eve's sin. However, that is not the end of the story.

Jump ahead for just a minute to the New Testament, to a well known passage in 1 Timothy. It is admittedly a difficult passage to understand: "I permit no woman to teach or to have authority over men; she is to keep silent. For Adam was formed first, then Eve, and Adam was not deceived, but the woman was deceived and became a transgressor."[195] It is not real clear what Paul is prohibiting. We will tackle that issue when we look at the passage itself in its context. But whatever is prohibited, it is prohibited for two reasons: First, it is prohibited because Adam was formed before Eve. What does that have to do with anything? But it must be significant or it would not be recorded in Genesis or referred to in 1 Timothy. The actual text in Genesis two gives no hint that the serial creation of the man and woman is significant, let alone significant of what. But it is also true that if Adam were not formed first, there are many very significant differences in what happened. For some reason, Paul takes it as being significant of *something*. Second, it is prohibited because Adam was not deceived but the woman was. That seems to follow from the text in Genesis. As we said above, Adam seems to be present, but absent. Bodily there but silent. It seems from the text itself, from the New Testament teaching, and from the consequences delivered by God that Adam was hardly innocent. He also sinned. In fact, God said

---

[195] 1 Timothy 2:12–14

the sin was that "he listened to the voice of his wife." (I think we should not push that *too* far. Surely the issue was that he listened to the voice of his wife *instead* of the clear commandment of God. I would hope that it is no sin for a husband to listen to the voice of his wife!) In fact, what Adam is held accountable for is listening to the voice of his wife and eating of the tree of which "*I commanded you, You shall not eat of it.*" So the issue really was disobedience to God rather than listening to the voice of his wife. Since the text itself, since the consequences that follow immediately from God, and since the New Testament teaching see *both* the man and the woman as guilty, it is difficult to see why "being deceived" would prohibit a woman from teaching or having authority over men, while conscious disobedience to the clear command of God (which Adam did) does *not* prohibit the man from anything. Does "being deceived" make one more culpable in God's eyes than blatant disobedience? Tough question. More on that in 1 Timothy.

Back to the text in Genesis: what follows the sin of the man and the woman is a series of because's. That is an important word. It means cause and effect.

When I was in first grade, I had a really mean teacher. Her name was Miss Steeb and she was not pleasant. She seemed constantly bugged at how incompetent we were. We had those big fat black pencils (only the older readers will remember those), one for each student, with our name written on a piece of paper and taped on the end. It had to last the whole year. They did not have erasers on them. If your pencil fell on the floor, you got in trouble. I remember well having conversations with my classmates on the playground as to why she was so mean. Sometimes she would wear an elastic wrap on one of her calves, and we decided that was it. If we came into the classroom and she was wearing the elastic wrap on her leg—watch out: it was going to be a bad day.

As I look back on that from a considerable distance (this took place in the mid '50s), a couple of things stand out to me. First, we had a sense of how a teacher should act. She should *enjoy* teaching.

Why else would one be a teacher? She should enjoy watching her students learn, rather than constantly being bugged at us because we acted like first graders. We *were* first graders. Second, we had an inborn sense of cause and effect. We believed in a cause and effect world, and we were trying to make sense of it. That's really pretty profound for first graders on the playground! So we decided that if she had her leg wrap on, her leg was sore. That was the cause. The effect was that we would suffer.

It is no small thing that we live in a cause-and-effect world. If there were no cause and effect, life would be chaotic and meaningless. The Old Testament book of Ecclesiastes identifies it as a good thing that there exists cause and effect in our world. After the author experiments with just about every possible activity to achieve happiness, apart from God, and he does not find it, but instead decides that everything is futile, *then* he comes to a very profound conclusion. That conclusion is the point of the whole book. And it is good news. The author's conclusion is that God will bring *every* deed into judgment. How can that be good news? Because instead of nothing being significant, *everything* is significant.[196] How is that? God will judge *everything*. If there is no judge, then we have no accountability, no responsibility, and so nothing we do means anything. Life is futile. Lack of consequences for our actions is essentially dehumanizing.[197]

So the list of consequences that follows the act of disobedience in Genesis 3 is not necessarily bad news. It shows that the man and the woman were really free. They *could* disobey God. And now they were doing verbs just like God did in Genesis one, and the verb they did was not allowed by God. Their actions were really significant. We know that because there were consequences for what they did.

In the judgment discourse here in Genesis 3, as in Genesis 1,

---

[196] This is an example of how important it is to study the Bible by whole books—to interpret verses in their context rather than picking out verses out of context, like flowers in a flower bed. You have to read the book of Ecclesiastes to the end.

[197] That is an important principle in child-raising, even though it can be over-utilized.

it is God who is the subject of the verbs. He is the judge. Just as he judged his creation as "good" in the first creation account, now it is God who judges certain actions of His humans as "bad" and hands out the consequences.

"Then the eyes of both were opened, and they knew that they were naked; and they sewed fig leaves together and made themselves aprons.

And they heard the sound of the Lord God walking in the garden in the cool of the day, and the man and his wife hid themselves from the presence of the Lord God among the trees of the garden. But the Lord God called to the man, and said to him, 'Where are you?' And he said, 'I heard the sound of thee in the garden, and I was afraid, because I was naked; and I hid myself.' He said, 'Who told you that you were naked? Have you eaten of the tree of which I commanded you not to eat?' The man said, 'The woman whom thou gavest to be with me, she gave me fruit of the tree, and I ate.' Then the Lord God said to the woman, 'What is this that you have done?' The woman said, 'The serpent beguiled me, and I ate.'

"The Lord God said to the serpent,

"'Because you have done this, cursed are you above all cattle, and above all wild animals; upon your belly you shall go, and dust you shall eat all the days of your life. I will put enmity between you and the woman, and between your seed and her seed; he shall bruise your head, and you shall bruise his heel.'

"To the woman he said,

"'I will greatly multiply your pain in childbearing; in pain you shall bring forth children, yet your desire shall be for your husband, and he shall rule over you.'

"And to Adam he said,

"'Because you have listened to the voice of your wife, and have eaten of the tree of which I commanded you, "You shall not eat of it," cursed is the ground because of you; in toil you shall eat of it all the days of your life; thorns and thistles it shall bring forth to you; and you shall eat the plants of the field. In the sweat of your face you shall eat bread till you return to the ground, for out of it you were taken; you are dust, and to dust you shall return.'

"The man called his wife's name Eve, because she was the mother of all living. And the Lord God made for Adam and for his wife garments of skins, and clothed them.

"Then the Lord God said,[198] 'Behold, the man has become like one of us, knowing good and evil; and now, lest he put forth his hand and take also of the tree of life, and eat, and live for ever'—therefore the Lord God sent him forth from the garden of Eden, to till the ground from which he was taken. He drove out the man; and at the east of the garden of Eden he placed the cherubim, and a flaming sword which turned every way, to guard the way to the tree of life.'"

In this account, do you feel the pain and anger of God? The trees that had originally been given as food now became a place of hiding from God. God's gift became a means of escape from God. (That still happens today. One could write a whole book on that, I think.) The man and the wife hid themselves from each other. They hid themselves from God. Neither accepted responsibility for their actions: The man blamed "the woman thou gavest to be with me." Not only does he blame the woman, but he also blames God who gave him the woman. Imagine how the woman felt upon hearing those words. The woman blames the serpent. The serpent blames no one, but really doesn't even get a chance to talk. And God "drives" them out of the garden, the garden specifically made for them, as one drives an animal, which they had now become.

There are a number of observations to make.

1. First, and very importantly first: The text pointedly does not say, "The woman took and ate of the tree *and she was satisfied.*" That last phrase is missing because the satisfaction was missing. Believing that God is cheap and not out for

---

[198] Again, notice the plural. His creation had become "like one of *us.*"

172

our good, and so taking things into our own hands and disobeying His clear direction for our life, will *never* bring satisfaction. Instead, it brings sadness.

2. God seeks out and asks questions of the man and the woman. He does not ask anything of the snake. He does not require a confession of that animal, but he does of the man and the woman and very pointedly leads them into it. He obviously knew what had happened but asked the man and the woman to verbalize it. After the man responds to God's questions and tells him what happened, He asks the woman a somewhat different question: "What have you done?" And she tells Him. God is not after information. God always knows exactly what has happened when we sin. What God desires is confession. That is still true and a good pattern for us to follow.

3. Even though it was the woman who sinned first, God approaches the man first, then the woman, then the snake. He did not go to the person who sinned first. God went first to the man.

4. Even though God went to the man first, then to the woman, then to the snake, in dealing out consequences God goes first to the snake, then the woman, then the man, *maybe* indicating, I think, that everything is now turned upside-down. The world we now live in is an upside-down world, and we mistakenly take it as normal. When we look at some of the values of the Kingdom of God later on, they will seem exceedingly strange and abnormal, even ridiculous, to us, but that is because we have lived all our lives in an upside-down world. So the word of the Cross is *foolishness* to mankind. And I think some of the aspects of a Biblical understanding of gender will also appear as foolishness to residents of this world. As I understand the Biblical teaching on gender, it seems strange to our ears because the concepts belong to the world before the Fall—a perfect world. But we

are to live them out here in an imperfect fallen world. We Christians are to live by the values of the Kingdom of God in this fallen world, and that puts us into conflict with the world and makes us weird. Or it should.

5. God speaks mysteriously to the snake in v. 15: "I will put enmity between you and the woman and between your seed and her seed; he shall bruise your head, and you shall bruise his heel." Most people understand that to be a "proto-gospel"—that is, a first promise of deliverance from the consequences of this horrible act of disobedience. It would come through the death of Jesus Christ on the cross for us. In one case, the head is injured; in the other, the heel is injured. Clearly the head injury is the more significant. The seed of the serpent would be more seriously injured. So even at this very beginning of the history of the human race, God is not flummoxed. He already has a plan and knows what will come of it. Redemption will come, and it will come through the seed of the woman *alone*. No help of a man will be needed. We will look at this more when we look at the very difficult verse in 1 Timothy 2:15: "Yet woman will be saved through bearing children, if she continues in faith and love and holiness, with modesty." That is an extremely difficult verse, which everybody stumbles on, but for now notice very carefully that it is the *seed of the woman* who will bruise the head of the snake. Not the seed (or offspring) and the man *and* the woman. It is the seed of the woman *alone*. In this profound upcoming event, the man seems to be strangely left out of it.

6. God confronts the man, and the man only, with disobeying the commandment—the very commandment that had been given directly by God to the man. "Have you eaten of the tree which I commanded you not to eat?" To the woman He says, "What is this that you have done?" No mention of disobedience to the command of God that was given only

174

to Adam. That makes us wonder what went wrong? Did Adam not tell her at all? Was his communication with her ambiguous? Did he tell her and she forgot? Did he tell her and she got confused when confronted by the snake? No explanation is given, so we need to be content with that. I think it is significant that when God gave consequences to the woman, He did not confront her with disobeying the commandment. But in talking to Adam, God blamed him specifically for disobeying the commandment given to *him*. In talking with the serpent, God said, referring to the verse immediately preceding, "Because you have done this…"— that is, beguiled the woman—the serpent ends up going on its belly the rest of its life. In talking with the man He said, "Because you have listened to the voice of your wife, and have eaten of the tree of which I commanded you, 'You shall not eat of it...'"—for that reason dust, the dust from which he came, would be his home.

But God says nothing to the woman. That cannot indicate lack of culpability, because God does give her consequences.

7. The consequences for the man and the woman are not the same. Two very significant areas of existence are singled out: for the woman it is childbirth; for the man, it is his work. The word, interestingly, is the same word—labor. For both of them, their "labor" would now be negatively affected. Interestingly, it is through childbirth that woman is "saved" in 1 Timothy 2:15, but again we will visit that difficult verse later.

8. There is another way in which the consequences are not the same. Only to Adam is death prescribed, not to Eve, even though she, of course, sinned just as seriously as Adam did. Of course, she also would die. But Adam's punishment is uniquely tied to his disobedience to the direct command of God.

9. God went first to the man and, apparently, the man alone. Why not to the man and the woman together, since they both disobeyed God? Especially if mutuality is the pattern for gender relationships? Again, it is not clear, and I may be reading more into the text than is clearly there. But, in line with the strange orientation toward the male in chapter two, God seems to be continuing the same pattern in going to the male first and not to both the male and the female for a "team" confession.

10. At this point, I want to point out one very important interpretive issue: it seems there is nothing new introduced in the consequences of the fall. It is all old stuff, something that was around before the fall, in the Perfect Eden, but now is there in an injured form.

   a. The snake presumably got around somehow. But now either his means of motility was radically changed, or at least it was now symbolic of what he had done to the woman and the man.

   b. The woman presumably would have given birth, eventually, but now it was excruciating painful. How sad that the only thing the woman is described as doing in this perfect world, childbearing, is now infected with terrible pain. Any woman who has given birth knows this.

   c. The man was put in the garden to till it and take care of it. After the fall, he had to deal with weeds, and that would involve sweat. And so, the only thing the man is described as doing in this perfect world, also called labor, is also painful and frustrating.

   Incidentally, I have no problem with pain killers in childbirth or weedkillers in the field. I do not think either is unBiblical.

   So the snake's mobility, the woman's childbirth, and the man's work, were all present before the fall, but now were "bent." There is nothing new introduced; we are just presented with old pre-fall concepts, but now damaged so as to make their pre-fall condition most unrecognizable to us.

11. The perceptive reader will have noticed that I have not yet included the last part of verse 16. "Yet your desire shall be for your husband, and he shall rule over you." The word "desire" is the same word as in Genesis 4:7—describing Cain's battle with sin: "And if you do not do well, sin is crouching at the door; its *desire* is for you, but you must master it." The word "desire" that describes Eve's desire for her husband in 3:16 and sin's desire for Cain is the same identical word. The word "master" in 4:7, which describes how Cain must overpower the sin that was "desiring" him, and the word "rule" in 3:16, which describes how Adam would relate to Eve, are the same identical word. And so Cain must "rule" over the sin that is "desiring" him. And Adam will now "rule" over or master Eve, who is now "desiring" him.

Remember that Adam was given the task of naming the animals and did not find one "fit for him," a help-mate. When God made Eve and brought her to Adam, his response was to exult: "This, *at last*, is bone of my bones and flesh of my flesh...." He could say that because of his experience with the animals! He could see the difference! "She shall be called Woman." Woh, man! Do you feel his ecstasy at finding a mate?

But now the relationship between the man and the woman, over whom the man rejoiced after naming all the animals and not finding one "fit for him," is badly damaged. The relationship will still exist but now will be damaged and painful. Do you feel the pain? Anyone who has experienced or watched a divorce will know what I am talking about. As we said at the beginning of this chapter, Genesis is a book about beginnings, and not all of them are good.

I want to go a bit more into the word "master" or "rule"

(depending on the translation), because it will help us understand what the New Testament says about "headship" by contrast. The word describes how Adam related to Eve *after* the fall. But it is not necessarily a negative word. It just means "to be in charge" or "to exercise authority or dominion." "It does not imply bad rule." So says Dr. Philip Payne in his book, <u>Man and Woman, One in Christ</u>.[199] Since all the other consequences of the fall are negative, this one, in this context, must also be negative. But the concept of ruling, in and of itself, is not negative in the Bible. So what is going on here?

There is a great deal of debate right now in the discussion of gender as to what exactly "headship" means. As we'll see when we get to the New Testament passages, "headship" is how the relationship of the husband to the wife is described, as well as of Christ to the church and Christ to God. Those who take the complementarian perspective nearly always describe "headship" as synonymous with "authority." Sometimes "authority" is softened by describing it as "servant-style leadership"—authority that acts as a servant. That is getting closer to the New Testament definition of "headship." More on that later. But the problem with merely defining "headship" as "authority" is that makes "headship" basically the same as "ruling." That must be negative, at least in the context of gender relationships, as it is a result of the fall of man. So what many complementarians are promoting for gender relationships is what God assigned as a punishment for the fall. That is important. We use weed-killer in our gardens and pain suppressants in the birth process, so it really is not consistent to promote husbands as merely the ruler in gender relationships if we define "headship" as merely "authority."

So the role of the husband after the fall, ruling, has deteriorated into the role of the one who is in charge of the wife. That invites the question of what "rule" looked like before the Fall. Was it a perfect hierarchy that did not involve selfish "ruling" and a selfish

[199] Philip Payne, <u>Man and Woman, One in Christ</u>. Zondervan, Grand Rapids, MI. c. 2009, p. 51.

need to fight the "ruling" partner? Or was it a complete lack of hierarchy—complete mutuality? Dr. Payne thinks it was the latter. "Since man's ruling over woman is a result of the fall, man must not have ruled over woman before the fall."[200] Maybe, but I think not, because that answers the question of what was there before the Fall, which "ruling" replaced with "nothing" as the answer. But in the case of the woman's labor and the man's labor there was *something* pre-fall that was then "bent." If Genesis two were missing, with its clear emphasis on the male, "nothing" might be a possible answer. But then the man's ruling would be something *new,* something there where nothing was before. That is very important.

Instead, I think the man's "ruling" is a perversion of and injury to a perfect, completely unselfish but still authoritative role that existed before the fall and that is described by the word "head" in the New Testament. But admittedly there is not enough evidence here to see that clearly—and that is true both for those who say there really is no detailed description of Adam and Eve's relationship before the fall and for those who say a perfect, completely unselfish hierarchy, what the New Testament calls "headship," was what was there pre-fall.

My conviction is that, even in a fallen world, the Scriptures still call us to live correctly and do not allow us to submit to the natural[201] inclinations of our fallen nature. My desire is that, as we go we go through the Scriptures, we will see what it means to live correctly (that is, Biblically) in a fallen world. From what we have seen so far, I suspect that we will either see a perfect hierarchy, one uninfected by selfishness and rebellion, as is present in the Trinity, or the lack of a hierarchy, a complete and unauthoritative mutuality, described for gender relationships. The interpretive problem with the latter is

---

[200] Philip Payne, Man and Woman, One in Christ. Zondervan, Grand Rapids, MI, c. 2009, p. 51
[201] Actually, they are not natural. It is not the way we were designed.

that it means something new is introduced as a consequence of the Fall, whereas none of the other consequences were something new, but instead the consequences were something that was there pre-Fall but now were something *injured*.

But back to the narrative. It is an enormously sad story. I hope that, as we read of God giving the man and the woman everything they wanted and needed for true happiness, and then watching them refuse that, and refusing God and refusing God's goodness and provision, and taking things into their own hands, and then reaping unthinkably negative consequences, we all feel the pain.

We are now only three chapters into the Bible, and we see the man and the woman driven, like animals, away from Home. The door is locked behind them and they cannot return. I said earlier that, if we only had the first chapter and the last chapter of Genesis to read, we would conclude that something had gone terribly wrong. The book begins with lifeforms blossoming in increasing complexity, and now the book ends with the highest and most significant created lifeform being buried in a coffin.

Dead.

Now we have seen what happened.

And so we enter a new era of Biblical history where things are Not Right, where we are away from where we were meant to be, where our memory of Home is only a distant warmth, often deadened by activities and acquisitions to substitute for God. But they never really do and they never really will. So we try new and more activities and new acquisitions and repeatedly face the disappointment of being away from Home.

Deep in our soul, dissatisfaction is part of our lot in life. It is profoundly Sad. And often hidden so deeply we are not aware of it.

But there is hope. God gives us a taste of Joy here in this sad place, and he also tells us that we will again be Home, but not for awhile. It is not until the last chapters of Revelation that we are again At Home. So we do have hope and we have God to thank for that, not ourselves. And hope is what keeps us going until Then.

But until Then, we are strangers in a strange land, away from Home and living, hopefully, by looking forward to getting back Home again where we belong. That is what the Bible calls living by faith, and it is really the only sensible, though not the easiest, way to live.

5

THE CITY ON AN ISTHMUS

"God's judgment on this sex lives on in our age; the guilt
necessarily lives on as well. You are the Devil's gateway; you
are the unsealer of that tree; you are the first forsaker of
the divine law; you are the one who persuaded him whom
the Devil was not brave enough to approach; you so lightly
crushed the image of God, the man Adam; because of your
punishment, that is, death, even the Son of God had to die."[202]

When I resigned from full-time Christian work and went back
to work as a pharmacist, I was, in a sad way, encouraged to see
all the outwardly successful and happy people who needed extra
pills to maintain that happy mood throughout the day, or to get to
sleep at night, or to get going in the morning. That may seem very
judgmental and negative on my part and, if so, I apologize. But it was
freeing to see other people who had the same problems I did. (I don't
use pills to solve those problems, however.) I am uncomfortable with
successful Christians who seem to have no problems. Not only is that
not my life, it does not seem to be the life of people in the Bible, save
one. There is a pattern in the Bible that all the saints had significant

[202] Tertullian, *On the Dress of Women*, 1.1.1. Quoted in an article by Dr. David M. Scholer
entitled, "Dealing with Abuse," on a web site entitled "God's Word to Women." He was quoting
Rita-Lou Clarke in *Pastoral Care of Battered Women*, Philadelphia: Westiminster, 1986, p. 39.

problems. As I observed before, I think the writers of the Bible did not embellish the story to make themselves appear as spiritual giants. One of the overriding themes of the Bible is that God is Good and we humans are sinners. The fact that sinners such as we are form an integral part of God's Story ought to give us hope. Here's why:

1. It proves the reliability of Scriptures. The authors did not make up a story that would make them look better than they were.
2. It gives us confidence in God. He does not need superstars as His instruments. That should give us confidence in His ability to use anybody.
3. It gives us reason for worship. One of the clear themes of Scripture is the consistent fallen condition of man, even spiritual leaders, and the overwhelmingly consistent good character and faithfulness of God. God is always the same, and not only is He always good, He is also always out for our good.
4. It should give us confidence to fulfill the task God has called us to. "God carves the rotten wood and rides the lame horse."[203]

This observation of the human condition from the Biblical narratives is also true on a corporate level. All the New Testament churches had significant issues. They had problems that would give any pastoral candidate pause in considering a call to serve. They had problems that would make many American Christians who want to be "successful" and be part of a "successful" church leave in a minute and go to a more attractive fellowship. Consider some of the problems.

One set of churches had turned their backs on the very central truth of Christianity: that faith in the substitutionary atonement of Jesus Christ on the cross is the only means of salvation.

---

[203] Supposedly from Martin Luther.

One church had incest going on among its fellowship, and they joked about it.

One church had members who believed the return of Christ was so imminent that they quit their jobs and went out to wait.

One church had two women who argued openly, and Paul even addressed them by name, thereby making them famous for all history as being argumentative.

One church was ashamed of Paul because he was in jail.

One church (several probably) were caught up in the beginning of a heresy that denied the divinity of Christ and both allowed rampant sin in the fellowship (because the flesh was irrelevant) and espoused asceticism for the same reason.

It is not a pretty picture, this composite of the New Testament churches. Yet Paul never doubted the salvation of those souls or looked elsewhere for other congregations to serve who were less problematic. He considered the members of these churches to be *saints*.

Of all the churches we know of in the New Testament, Corinth probably had the most significant problems.

The city was located on an isthmus between the Aegean Sea and the greater Mediterranean Sea. Since the route around the tip of the isthmus was dangerous, ships would often be hauled across the isthmus on a primitive road called a diolkos to the other side where they continued their journey. So there was a constant population of sailors passing through, spending a short time on land as their cargo was transported across the isthmus. One does not have to think long and hard to surmise what kind of place this town was and what its main industry was.

There was a temple dedicated to the worship of the Greek goddess of love, Aphrodite, and part of the religious ceremonies involved sexual intercourse with the priestesses of this temple, but in reality they were prostitutes. With all the sailor traffic present, their business must have been quite good. Evidence that this assumption is correct was the presence of more than one thousand such "priestesses"! After all, what better is there to do for a sailor when you have a couple of days on land while your boat rounds the point? It was a seller's market and business was booming.

Religious prostitution was not the only characteristic of Corinth. The sheer quantity of sexual perversion in this city (and in Geek culture of the time) would stun most modern people. Homosexual practice was not only common, but accepted, even honored. Young boys were purchased as slaves and castrated to preserve their youthful appearance. It was not looked down upon for a man to have casual sex with a male prostitute. However, it was looked down upon to be the weaker, passive, "receptive" partner. The word describing the passive, effeminate, homosexual was "soft." In fact, in 1 Corinthians 6:9–10, Paul uses two words to describe the homosexual activity in Corinth: *malakos* (translated as "effeminate" in the NASB, referring to the passive partner) and *arsenokoites* (referring to the "penetrator"). Both would have been sitting next to you in the pew as you worshiped in this church at Corinth.

It's been said that you can recognize the values of a culture by how many words it has for a particular concept, each one expressing some slightly different shade of meaning. So the Eskimos have some 18 different words for "snow." The following quotation describes some of the words the Greek language has for sexual perversion: "In fact, the Greek language has an extensive vocabulary devoted to perverted sex. There's the word *porne*. *Porne* basically means the purchasable one, the one you can buy, the harlot, the whore, the prostitute. *Porneuo* is the filthy business of prostitution. *Porneia* is fornication, sexual sin outside marriage. There's the word *malake*. A *malake* was a sex slave. There is the word *moichos*, that is the adulterer, the one who has sex outside the covenant of marriage. And there are the *heteri*, they functioned as a mistress for no purpose but sex. They had their *heteri*. There is the word *arsenokoites*, homosexual. The *malakos* here translated effeminate but is actually a word meaning "soft" and it was the Greek word for the passive partner in a homosexual relationship. There are more. No sense in talking about any more because this was life in Corinth. And when you went to church, you wound up with a group of these kinds of people who had been washed."[204]

Additionally, there was the cult of Dionysus, a male god, although his gender became somewhat questionable as time went on. The Roman historian Livy describes what worship services dedicated to Dionysus looked like: "From the time when the rites were held promiscuously, with men and women mixed together, and when the license offered by darkness had been added, no sort of crime, no kind of immortality, was left unattempted. There were more obscenities practiced between men than between men and women. Anyone refusing to submit to outrage or reluctant to commit crimes was slaughtered as a sacrificial victim. To regard nothing as forbidden was among these people the summit of religious achievement. Men, apparently out of their wits, would utter prophesies with frenzied bodily convulsions.... Men were said to have been carried off by the gods, because they had been attached to a machine and whisked way out of sight to hidden caves; or to submit to violation."[205]

Corinth itself was known so widely for licentiousness or worldliness that the name of the city actually became a verb, "to Corinthianize," which meant to become a person who takes part in sexual debauchery. A "Corinthian businessman" meant to be a whoremonger. To "play the Corinthian" meant to go to a house of prostitution, and a "Corinthian girl" was a prostitute.

To such a city the apostle Paul came and preached repentance and forgiveness through Jesus. Some believed, and a young church sprang up. In some ways it was fertile ground—any ground can be fertile ground for the Spirit of God to work—but in some ways it

[204] From the web site Grace to You, a talk entitled "Sexual Purity, part 1," delivered in 2005 by John MacArthur. See www.gty.org/library/sermons-library/GTY92/sexual-purity-part-1
[205] Titus Livy, *History of Rome*, Book 39.13

seems extremely unlikely that a healthy church would spring up from such soil, and, sure enough, the church had its share of problems. But then all churches have problems, so that does not indicate an inauthentic conversion experience. But of all the churches, the church at Corinth probably had the most overwhelming issues. Consider:

1. They were caught up in a personality cult, claiming to follow various early leaders among Christianity. Some claimed to follow Paul, some Apollos, and some Jesus. Probably each had an attitude of superiority toward the others, depending on which group you belonged to, looking down on those who weren't as spiritual as your group. In fact, Paul said that there was jealousy and strife as they developed party loyalties depending on whom they followed (1 Corinthians 3:1–23).[206]

2. This was the church that had incest occurring among the fellowship, and they did nothing. In fact, they were arrogant about it (1 Corinthians 5:1–13).

3. Some members were suing other members in secular courts, unable to solve their arguments (1 Corinthians 6:1–8).

4. Judging by Paul's quoting of their slogans back to them, they were a very slogan-oriented church, and their slogans indicated a hedonistic view of life. "All things are lawful for me" was one of them. Another was "Food is meant for the stomach and the stomach for food." Both are illustrative of the hedonism present in the church and the use of slogans to justify it. The habitual use of slogans for a church may

---

[206] Lewis illustrates this issue in *The Screwtape Letters*, which are letters to an apprentice tempter from the "mentor" tempter about his "patient"—a new believer whom the apprentice is trying to lure away from God. "If your patient can't be kept out of the Church, he ought at least to be violently attached to some party within it. I don't mean on really doctrinal issues: about those, the more lukewarm he is, the better. The real fun is working up hatred between those who say 'mass' and those who say 'holy communion' when neither party could possible state the difference…. All the purely indifferent things—candles and clothes and what not—are an admirable ground for our activities." (From *The Screwtape Letters*, Macmillan Company, New York, NY, c. 1961, p. 75.)

be indicative of a shallow-thinking, simplistic approach to the Christian life.

5. There were apparently some who were ascetic and said that sexual intercourse, even with your spouse, was sinful (1 Corinthians 7:1–5).

6. There were many who possessed the charismatic gifts and were misusing them, thinking that the more showy gifts made you more spiritual (1 Corinthians 12:1–30).

7. Their worship services were disorderly and chaotic, with several speaking at once (1 Corinthians 11:2–34 and 14:2–40).

8. Their communion services were ugly, with some not having enough food to eat at the fellowship meal, while others ate like gluttons. The rich were not sharing with the poor. Some were even drunk. (1 Corinthians 11:17–34)

9. There were arguments about whether or not to eat food that had been offered to idols.

10. Apparently there were some church members who were only going through the motions of being a Christian but not manifesting Christian character in relationships. First Corinthians 13 states conclusively that manifesting outwardly religious ecstasy while not loving your neighbor is hypocrisy.

And there were still other issues this church had. If you were a pastoral candidate considering a call to this church, would you give it serious consideration? Yet the apostle never gave up on them. He never doubted the reality of their salvation. Why not? Because he understood the depth of depravity of the soul and also the unrelenting power of God to redeem such souls.[207] He was not paralyzed by the

---

[207] In Galatians chapter one, when Paul says that the gospel he was preaching was not man's gospel, nor was he taught it by men, but it came through a revelation of Jesus Christ, I suspect he was referring to what happened in his mind during his three days of helpless blindness. He was on his way to Damascus to murder Christians, and Jesus knocked him off his rocker (horse, really) and blinded him for three days. The powerful "Jew of Jews" was now utterly powerless.

presence of sin, deep sin, in everybody's soul. It was no contradiction to him that even though the church was full of saved people, even though the Apostle calls them saints in the introduction to the letter, they were still sinners. He understood that they were "in process," still on their way to becoming Godly people but not there yet.

One of the problems in the church at Corinth was the state of their worship services. The whole section from 11:2 through 14:40 deals with the problem of their exceptionally disorderly worship services. It is surely no coincidence that in a city where worship of Dionysus was so chaotic and frazzled, and included clashing gongs and cymbals, that the worship of the God of the Bible would, unfortunately, mimic some of that disorder. The apostle begins this section by explaining, and wanting them to understand, something about order in the Godhead[208] and how that should be exhibited in the life of the church. He ends this section by reminding them that all things should be done decently and in order.[209] So the section begins with order and ends with order. It is critical to interpret what he says about gender in the context of his concern about order in worship.

I am writing this at a delightful Christian family camp that our family attends every summer in northern Michigan. There is a small sign in each sleeping room that asks the family please not to hang wet towels on the woodwork. Why is such a sign necessary?

He describes himself as "advanced in Judaism beyond many of my own age" (Galatians 1:14), and now, as he sat there for three days with nothing to do but think about it, he must have come to the conclusion that he had been an enemy of God in what he had been doing. Instead of serving God, he was actually opposing God. Paul was a zealous Jew. He knew what the penalty for opposing God was. In fact, he was trying to carry out that penalty in killing Christians: it was death. Suddenly the tables were turned—he was the one *deserving* death. Here he was, suddenly knowledgeable of the fact that he had been Wrong his whole life and he was still alive. During those three days of helpless blindness, surely the one question he asked over and over again was, "God, why am I still alive?" So he learned the gospel not by being taught by men but by experiencing it very directly. He must have concluded that he deserved death but was, instead, still alive. Therefore, he could be patient with others. A profound example for us to follow.

[208] 1 Corinthians 11:3

[209] 1 Corinthians 14:40

Because families *do* hang wet towels on the woodwork and so ruin the varnish. In the same way, we can get a sense of the issues in the Corinthian church by what Paul feels the need to correct them on. When he writes to the church at Corinth, "If any speak in a tongue, let there be only two or at most three, and each in turn; and let one interpret,"[210] that indicates that there probably *were* more than two or three people speaking in a tongue, that probably they were doing it all at once, not "in turn," and there was no interpretation going on. Otherwise, why would the apostle have said such? The fact that he has to say, "If a revelation is made to another sitting by, let the first be silent," indicates that some were *not* being "silent" while a revelation was being made. So we have the statement that "all things should be done decently and in order." No such statement would have been necessary if all things *were* being done decently and in order. Obviously they were not, and you can tell that by the directions given to them by Paul. Apparently, in the mind of the apostle, the lack of order in the worship services of this church was no small concern. For him, everything about the church, including the orderliness of its worship, ought to reflect something of the nature of God.

Of all the texts in the Bible's teaching about gender, 1 Corinthians 11:2–16 may be the most muddy. It has been called a minefield of interpretive problems. As I have tried to figure out what it says, I have become convinced that the traditional interpretation about women wearing veils may not have been what Paul was writing about. There are three different words that have been loosely translated as "veil." However, only in verse 15 is there a word that refers to a garment, translated variously as "veil" or "covering." There Paul is actually making the point that a woman's hair is given her as a "veil," seemingly indicating that no extra covering or "veil" is even required of a woman. Her hair is adequate. Actually, the text talks as much about men's appearance as women's, so it is a bit mysterious

---

[210] I Corinthians 14:27

to me that this text has been interpreted as being about the necessity of women wearing a veil in church and saying nothing about men.

Just as in Genesis one and many other texts, here, structure is critical in figuring out what the author is trying to communicate. The skeleton in this text, on which much of the flesh is attached—and, frankly, much of the flesh is a cultural expression of the principles that I call the skeleton—consists of verses 3, 8, 9, 11, and 12. Here is what those verses say: verse 3: "But I want you to understand that the head of every man is Christ, the head of a woman is her husband, and the head of Christ is God." That seems to be foundational. Verses 8 & 9: "For man was not made from woman, but woman from man. Neither was man created for woman, but woman for man." Verses 11 & 12: "Nevertheless, in the Lord woman is not independent of man nor man of woman, for as woman was made from man, so man is now born of woman."

Headship of the male, of which there are some cultural expressions encouraged in this chapter that we have yet to figure out, comes from the fact that the man was not made *from* the woman, or *for* the woman, but the other way around.

There is an *equally* important balancing principle that man now is *not* "independent" of woman and now comes *from* woman (in birth). If we are Biblical Christians, we need to hold both those principles with equal strength, as Paul does.

There are two primary points to be understood, and these are important to keep in mind as we work our way through the chapter:

1. In this chapter, male headship is based upon the fact that the female was created out of the male—and that was a *result* of the male being created first. We will return to that issue in 1 Timothy, where, again, I must go against church tradition, which has seen primogeniture as the issue. I don't

think that is true. It was Adam's primary creation that led to Eve's being created *from* Adam, which is where male headship finds its origin.

2. Headship does not eliminate equality. Verses 11 and 12 (which teach the mutual dependence of the genders) do not trump verses 8 and 9 (which teach the primacy of the male). Nor do verses 8 and 9 trump 11 and 12. Both are equally true and carry equal weight.

I am going to start in the middle of the text before attempting to figure out the text as a whole. I wade in with a great deal of trepidation, since I am going to end up at a place different from where Biblical scholars have for hundreds of years. I'm a pharmacist, not a theologian. I may be wrong. As always, I encourage the reader to do his own homework and think for himself.

There is a strange expression at the end of verse 10, the verse right in the middle of our two theme verses for the chapter. That verse says that a woman ought to have *something* on her head, either authority, or control over her hair style, or a sign of authority, which could have been a veil, *because of the angels.* The word translated as "angels" could just as well have been translated as "messengers." "Angels" seems difficult to understand: how or why would whatever women had on their heads affect *angels?* The word "messengers" makes the most sense for the following reason: most associations or clubs in Corinth were only allowed to meet monthly by the Roman government because of concern about sedition. The Jews, however, were granted special permission to meet weekly in their synagogues. The weekly Christian meetings, which fell under the umbrella of Jewish meetings, were surely a puzzle to the authorities, since there was no statue for their "god" and they did not meet in synagogues but in houses. The vestibules of Roman houses were open to the public, and this is where the church at Corinth would have met. This way, an outsider or messenger could come in and observe what was going on, which, apparently, was not unusual.

Dr. Bruce Winter offers this insight: "The word 'messenger' in the first century did not necessarily imply that he was only the bearer of messages. It was also used of the conveyor of information about those he visited to the person on whose behalf he had been sent.... The role of information-gatherer who reports back to the sender appears to be what Paul is concerned about...." "For this reason," Paul states, the wife is under obligation to wear the sign of her marriage as she prays and prophesies because of what its absence signaled to the inquisitive outsiders—she portrayed herself as the promiscuous Roman wife, i.e., an unashamed adulteress."[211] In practice, the government would send a "messenger" to check on a particularly questionable assembly to see if they were a threat to the government or not and then report back what was going on. This idea of a messenger "checking out" what the young church was up to makes much more sense than the mysterious idea of angels watching the church meeting from heaven.

The presence of "outsiders" or "unbelievers" or "messengers" was apparently not unusual or unexpected. In chapter 14, verse 16, Paul talks about "blessing in the Spirit" and then asks, "how can anyone in the position of an *outsider* say the 'Amen'?" In verse 23, he asks, "If, therefore, the whole church assembles and all speak in tongues, and *outsiders* or *unbelievers* enter, will they not say that you are mad?" (italics mine). Surely, part of Paul's concern in this long section on order in worship was what outsiders from this very mixed-up, disorderly community would think of this church. He wanted the church to be *different*, and his reason for that was the orderliness of its Triune God. So whatever he is saying, whether it is about veils, head coverings, or hair styles, it seems to be rooted in his concern for how the church appears to outsiders. It's about being different from the town where this church was located, which

---

[211] <u>After Paul Left Corinth,</u> by Bruce W. Winter. William B. Eerdmans Publishing Company, Grand Rapids, MI, c. 2001, pp. 134–138. The whole idea of suspicion by the Roman government of Christian meetings, and thus, messengers reporting back to the Roman government comes from this book.

had more than its share of chaotic services. It's about reputation. Head coverings, whatever Paul meant by that term, somehow communicated something to that particular culture, as evidenced by Paul's concern for the church's reputation. And apparently the church's reputation among outsiders was a very important concern for the Apostle. At the end of the discussion, Paul says, "If any one is disposed to be contentious, we recognize no other practice, nor to the churches of God."[212] Discussion over.

Now back up to the beginning of the chapter, verse two, as we try to figure out what the author is saying to this church, in that context, and then we can figure out how to apply that in our culture.

Paul, as is his pattern, starts with the theory and then moves on to the application. The starting point is something he wants this church to understand. The word is interesting. We have all said at some point, when we finally come to understand a difficult problem, "Oh, now I see." Interesting that we would use a word for vision that really means to understand. Such is the word used here. It is *eidon*, a word that can be used to mean both "to see" and "to know." It implies that there is a picture following that helps us to understand something. And he wants the Corinthians (and us, I assume) to see and to understand, as well.

What Paul wants this church to understand, *to see*, first of all is the nature of three different relationships. "But I want you to understand that the head of every man is Christ, the head of a woman is her husband, and the head of Christ is God."[213] So the three relationships are Christ to man, man to woman (or more likely husband to wife), and Christ to God. The word for "man" is *aner*, meaning "male." It is not the word *anthropos*, which would just indicate a human being. Probably he had husbands and wives in mind. He is saying Christ is the head of the males (or husbands), and they are the head of the females (or wives). And the Godhead, or possibly the Father, is the head of Christ. The reason I think this

---

[212] 1 Corinthians 11:17
[213] 1 Corinthians 11:3

is about husbands and wives instead of men and women in general is that Paul, when using the word for head, *kephale*, in the context of human relationships, he is nearly always talking about marriage relationships. There is one word that describes all three relationships: "head." Don't miss the significance that the same word is used by Paul to describe the relationship of Christ to males, or husbands, of men to women (or probably husbands to wives), and Christ to God. As I observed in Genesis 1, there is something about gender relationships that is an image of relationships among the persons of the Trinity. The human creature, existing as male and female, is a plural creation made in the image of a plural God. Here we find the same word, "head," describing *both* gender relationships in marriage and relationships in the Trinity. The Greek word for head is *kephale*, and there has probably been more written and more argument about the exact meaning of this word than about any other single issue in the gender discussion. It is an important issue, and we'll look at it at the end of the chapter. Before we look at what the apostle wants us to understand, let's first look at the order in which the relationships are listed.

That order is not God to Christ, Christ to the male, and the male to the female, in some sort of "descending" order, implying a chain of command. It is Christ to the male (or husband), the male to the female (or the husband to the wife), and Christ to God, which is not in a chain-of-command type of ordering. Is it significant that it is *not* that type of order? Dr. Bilezikian definitely thinks so:

"Had Paul wanted to establish a hierarchy in verse 3, he would have typically arranged the headship sequence in a downward order of authority as God/Christ/man/woman. He could even have included the Spirit in between Christ and man. It is inconceivable that Paul would have so grievously jumbled the sequence in a matter involving God, Christ, and humans when he kept his hierarchy straight as he dealt with a lesser subject in 12:28"[214] In that text in

---

[214] Beyond Sex Roles, Bilezikian, 3rd edition, pp. 105, 106.

195

chapter 12 of the same book, he is referring to lists of various roles in the church appointed by God: first apostle, second prophets, third teachers, and so on. But notice that, in that text, the words first, second, third, and so on make it explicit that order was important to the author in that context. Those words are missing here. In another place, the same author writes to the same church, "The grace of the Lord Jesus and the love of God and the fellowship of the Holy Spirit be with you all."[215] Notice that the order here is different. Without the presence of order-indicating words like first, second, third, and so on, it seems that order may not have been in the author's mind at all. He may have listed the God/Christ relationship last as a summary. It does not seem that in this case the order was important to Paul. I definitely do not think it is structured as a "descending" order, with the women on the bottom. And if *kephale includes,* but does not solely consist of, authority, then there still is the possibility of hierarchy in all three relationships.

The text we are looking at is about headship: Christ to the male, the male to the female, and God to Christ. In reality, there are four different "heads" listed in this chapter, and that is part of what makes it difficult to interpret. There is the head of the male, which is Christ. There is the head of the female, which is the male. There is the head of Christ, which is God. And there is the thing on top of our necks which is also called a head. Since the head of the male and the head of the female are *different,* and since each gender may do something that dishonors his or her respective head, it makes sense that the male and female are each doing something *different* that dishonors his or her respective head. Christ is never mentioned as doing something which dishonors His head. Of course.

"Any man who prays or prophesies with his head covered dishonors his head, but any woman who prays or prophesies with her head unveiled dishonors her head—it is the same as if her head

---

[215] 2 Corinthians 14:14

were shaven."[216] "Does not nature itself itself teach you that for a man to wear long hair is degrading to him, but if a woman has long hair, it is her pride? For her hair is given to her for a covering."[217]

The word "covered" in verse four, describing the condition of the man, is *kata*. It means "down from" or "moving from upper to lower," and Paul says that this condition for a male "dishonors his head." We know the head of the male is Christ, the creator of the male. The word "unveiled" in verse five, describing the condition of the woman, is *akatakylptos*, which means "not covered or unveiled," and that condition "dishonors her head." We know that her head is the male, so whatever the woman is doing, it shows dishonor for her head, the male, probably referring to her husband. The word "degrading" in verse 14, describing the male with something "down from," is the same word as the one used in Romans 1:26, *atimia*, describing homosexual relations. So Paul describes homosexual relations and a male with something "hanging down" with the same negative adjective.

In verse 14, we are asked, "Does not nature itself teach you that for a man to wear long hair is degrading to him but if a woman has long hair, it is her pride? For her hair is given to her for a covering." As I said before, this is the only time in the whole chapter that an actual covering is mentioned, and we are told that a woman's "long" hair actually makes that covering unnecessary. Her hair functions as a covering. The word for "long hair" is *komao* and it means to have long hair, just as it is translated. Notice that, for the male, it is to his shame but for the female, it is her pride. The Greek word *komao* is exactly the same for each gender. That is important: the same condition is shameful for one gender but honorable for the other. So the *different* genders must display their hair in a *different* manner. It makes the most sense that what Paul is talking about is hair rather than a covering, because he says that long hair makes the covering unnecessary—for the female.

---

[216] 1 Corinthians 11:4, 5
[217] 1 Corinthians 11:14, 15

Verse 14 says that long hair on a male is "degrading." If a woman will not cover (*katakalypto*) herself, then she should shave her head, which was punishment for an accused adulteress, but which was also present in Dionystic worship when women shaved their heads in possibly sex inversion to make her look like a male. Did you hear that—to make her look like a male. Males apparently wore short hair. Either way, it was quite a negative symbol. What makes the most sense with the words and with all the sexual perversion, confusion, and inversion present in that culture, is that long, effeminate hair, hanging "down from," on males, is what Paul is talking about, which, in that culture, signified homosexual practice and availability.

For the women, on the other hand, to wear hair "down" in public was inappropriate. Women in public normally wore their hair "up," that is, curled about on top of her head. Loose hair flowing "down" *in public*, since it was normally worn that way only at home, signified sexual availability, which, of course, was a slap in the face of, or to use the Biblical phrase, dishonoring, to her husband, who was her head.

In both cases, both the males and the females were praying and prophesying—that is, talking to God and listening to God for a word to share from Him to others. The God they were talking and listening to was their creator, the one who made them male and female. But their physical appearance sent a clear message to their culture that they were in rebellion to how God had made them. Or did not care. Or were communicating messages about availability for activities that were dishonoring to their Creator. Who was God to deny them any sort of sexual pleasure? (What a contemporary question that is!) So they were both dishonoring their "head." The male was dishonoring his head, his creator, by wearing his hair "hanging down," which was associated with homosexual behavior and availability. The female was dishonoring her head, her husband, by wearing her hair loose and flowing instead of done up on top of her head, thus publicly flaunting her sexual availability, which was dishonoring to her head, her husband. In fact, Paul tells us that if a woman will not wear her hair in an appropriate style, then she should shave her head, which was what an accused adulteress would do. So such a woman was acting like an adulteress, showing to everybody her sexual availability.

"For a man ought not to cover his head, since he is the image and glory of God; but woman is the glory of man. For man was not made from woman, but woman from man. Neither was man created for woman, but woman for man. That is why a woman ought to have a veil on her head, because of the angels."[218]

The word which describes what a man *ought not* to do, to cover his head, is *katakalypto*, which Paul has just used to say what women *should* do. "If it is disgraceful for a woman to be shorn or shaven, let her wear a veil."[219] That is the word that is translated as "let her wear a veil." It is a compound word from *kata*, which means "down from" and *kalypto*, which means to cover or hide. The women *ought* to do this and the men should not. "That is why a woman ought to have a veil on her head." Or long hair, which serves as a veil.

Dr. Winter makes a point about the word "ought," which is the English word for *opheilo*. "The first-century concept of obligation, especially Paul's use of it in ethical discussion, has not been taken into account sufficiently by New Testament scholars. The invoking of the term in 11:2–16 [he is referring to the term *opheilo*] provides the most powerful argument that could be used in correcting conduct in the first century."[220] This strong sense of obligation coincides with the way Paul ends the discussion in verse 16: "If any one is disposed to be contentious, we recognize no other practice." So this chapter is egalitarian in that it describes something that both males and females were under equal obligation to do regarding head

[218] 1 Corinthians 11:7–10
[219] 1 Corinthians 11:8
[220] Winter, ibid., p. 131

coverings or, as I believe it is talking about, hair styles, which affirm sexuality and marital relationships the way God designed them, not exhibiting the incredible sexual confusion, inversion, and perversion of the city where this church was located.

Verse 10 is a difficult verse. Some translations begin the verse with "For this reason," indicating that it is a conclusion based on what went before. The preceding verses are all about the designed different-ness of males and females and how their hairstyles need to reflect that. What went before was the reference to Genesis, where the female was created from the male and for the male. There really is no word for "veil" in the original. The RSV has a footnote to the effect that the word in Greek is "authority" and the translators added "veil" as being a "sign of authority." All the verse says is that for this reason a female ought to have *authority* on her head. It does say "on" her head, meaning physically on her head, which makes it hard to understand exactly what he is talking about. The word is *exousia* and means the power of choice, liberty, authority, or the power to make a decision. It is the word used three times in 1 Corinthians 9:4–6: "Do we not have the *right* to our food and drink? Do we not have the *right* to be accompanied by a wife, as the other apostles and the brothers of the Lord and Cephas? Or is it only Barnabas and I who have no *right* to refrain from working for a living?" The words "right" in italics are our word *exousia*. I confess I do not understand the point Paul is making in verse ten. I think what makes the most sense is the most simple understanding of the verse, in light of the context: that women should take charge of or be responsible for how they style their hair and do it in such a way that, in their culture, does not communicate dishonor or disrespect for her husband, who is her head. Long, flowing hair in public, rather than hair done up, would communicate that. In other words, she has the right or authority or responsibility to style her hair in such as way as not to dishonor her husband. That is *her* responsibility. An inappropriate hair style would do just that.

Verse eleven begins with a significant word: "Nevertheless"

(RSV) or "however" (NIV). That indicates that the following verses will be going in a significantly different direction than the verses preceding. And so they do.

"Nevertheless, in the Lord woman is not independent of man nor man of woman; for as woman was made from man, so man is now born of woman. And all things are from God."[221]

Many have observed the completely egalitarian tone of these verses, which is a legitimate observation. In contrast to the fact that woman was made *from* man and *for* man, as Genesis 2:20–23 and 1 Corinthians 11:8–9 tell us, now we are told an equivalent and differing truth: Man comes out of woman (in birth), and man is not independent of woman. The egalitarian flavor of these verses appears to contradict the complementarian flavor of verses 3–10. For many, it's an "either/or" proposition. We must accept the complementarian teaching of the first part of the chapter and ignore the egalitarian tone of verses 8 and 9 as "difficult" verses. Or we must accept the egalitarian tone of the second part of the chapter and ignore the complementarian tone of the first part of the chapter as "difficult" verses. That certainly was the case in the long list of quotations in the chapter on the Trinity, Hierarchy, and Equality.

One way of accommodating the seemingly contradictory teaching is to label the first part of chapter eleven as a "Creation Hermeneutic" grounded in the creation story in Genesis and the latter part as a "Redemption Hermeneutic" grounded in the redemption of Jesus. As I asked in the chapter on Hermeneutics, what needs to be redeemed from the perfect creation in Genesis two? However, having said that, I must again acknowledge the ugly way men have dominated and abused women in the fallen world where we live, both in the church and outside of the church.

I don't think that verses eleven and twelve *contradict* verses four through ten. It's a both/and rather than an either/or proposition. The

---

[221] 1 Corinthians 11:11–12

only way I can make sense out of that is to back up and look at verse seven and then at the crucial verses before that.

"For a man ought not to cover his head, since he is the image and glory of God; but the woman is the glory of man."[222]

The woman is the glory of the man, not another woman, just as the woman was the glory of the man in Genesis two. She was made from *him* and for *him*. That is a distinctly Christian perspective and one in contrast to the sexually mixed up city where the church was. One of the many difficulties in this chapter is found in these verses: the suggestion that the man, and the man alone, was created in the image of God. That, of course, cannot be completely true, since Genesis 1:26–28 says that both the male and the female were created in God's image. In fact, one of the main points of this book is that the male-female (or really husband-wife) relationship mirrors the relationships among the persons of the Trinity—a hierarchy of equals. It is the male-female relationship, not a male-male relationship or a female-female relationship, that mirrors the relationships among the *different* members of the Trinity. So in what sense is the male and the male alone in God's image? It must be in the sense that the male, and the male alone, is the head of the female. It is in the male-female relationship that the male demonstrates headship. As God is the head of Christ, so the male is the head of the female, or rather the husband of the wife. Only the male, *in that sense*, is in the image of God, since the male is the head of the female. I want to remind us again that, even though God is the head of Christ, they are both equals, just as the male and the female are equals. Headship does not eliminate equality.

For a long time I wondered why the chapter does not begin with the statement that Christ is the head of the man, the man is the head of the woman, and the *Father* is the head of Christ. But it says that *God* is the head of Christ. So the male is the head of the female just

---

[222] 1 Corinthians 11:7

as God is the head of Christ. But God is made up of three persons, I believe, in hierarchy, who are equal and *one*—that is, inseparable. So it is a different use of "image" from Genesis one. And so the hierarchy of equals in the Trinity is mirrored in the hierarchy of equals in the male-female (or husband-wife) relationship. It does not imply the female's inequality any more than Christ is inferior to God, which, of course, He is not. But it does imply a different and, dare I say it, submissive *but equal* role.

That backs us up to the definition of headship at the beginning of the chapter. It needs to be said at this point that it would seem an egalitarian view of marriage would necessitate the position that the husband and wife are the head of each other, which seems to be a bit hard to comprehend—at least, if headship means anything.

Paul began this section of the book by wanting his readers to *understand* three concepts: that the head of the male is Christ, that the head of the female is the male, and that the head of Christ is God. Again, I am assuming that he is talking mainly about husbands and wives here. The common characteristic in all three relationships is *headship*. Since that word describes both the relationship of the husband to the wife and that of Christ to God, then again it must be true that gender relationships mirror Trinity relationships. The Greek word is *kephale*, and its precise meaning is the subject of a tremendous about of debate. So let's dig into that. At the risk of oversimplifying, the camps seem to be divided as follows:

1. One camp looks at the secular usage of the word in Bible times and adopts the definition of "authority" for headship. Following are several examples.

   "In this verse [the author is referring to 1 Corinthians 11:3 which says, "the head of every man is Christ, the head of the wife is her husband, etc."] 'head' refers to one who is in a position of authority over the other, as this Greek word (*kephale*) uniformly does whenever it is used in ancient literature to say one person is 'head of' another person or group."[223]

"Paul uses the word head with the meaning 'authority' in Ephesians 1:22."[224]

"But we have already seen that the clear meaning of head is 'authority' and thus a hierarchy is established."[225]

"Christians throughout history usually have understood the word head in these verses [referring to 1 Corinthians 11:3] to mean 'authority over.'"[226]

"All the major lexicons for the New Testament period list a meaning such as 'authority over' or 'ruler-leader' as a meaning for *kephale* when applied to persons"[227]

2. A second camp looks at the secular usage of the word in Biblical times and claims that *kephale* cannot mean authority but instead means "source" or "origin."

"The lexicographers (with various editions spanning more than 100 years—from 1836 to 1940) apparently found no example in their study of Greek literature where *kephale* could have only the meaning 'one having authority,' 'supreme over' or anything similar."[228]

---

[223] Wayne Grudem, <u>Evangelical Feminism and Biblical Truth</u>. Crossway Books, Wheaton, IL, c. 2004, p. 45.

[224] <u>Recovering Biblical Manhood and Womanhood</u>, edited by John Piper and Wayne Grudem, Crossway Books, Wheaton, IL, c. 1991, chapter five, "Headcoverings, Prophecy and the Trinity," by Thomas Schreiner, p. 127.

[225] Ibid., p. 130

[226] Ibid., p. 425, in Appendix 1, "The Meaning of *Kephale* (head)," by Wayne Grudem.

[227] Ibid., p. 458

[228] <u>Women, Authority and the Bible</u>. InterVarsity Press, 1986, p. 99, in an article entitled, "What Does *kephale* Mean in the New Testament?" by Berkeley & Alvera Mickelsen.

"Heinrich Schlier, describing *kephale* in the TDNT [*Theological Dictionary of the New Testament*], lists twenty-seven possible English translations of metaphorical meaning of *kephale* outside the new Testament, none of which conveys the idea of 'authority.'"[229]

"The New Testament contains no text where Christ's headship to the church connotes a relationship of authority. Likewise, the New Testament contains no text where a husband's headship to his wife connotes a relationship of authority."[230]

"That leaves us with Cyril's view—the first member as the source/ground of the other's being—as the most likely meaning here."[231] The context of this comment is the text we are studying: 1 Corinthians 11:3.

"'Source' fits better than 'authority' as the meaning of *kephale* in 'the man [with the article] is the *kephale* of a woman'…. [I]t is most natural to understand 'the man' as in 11:12 as a reference to 'the man,' Adam, from whom woman came. This fits perfectly with the established meaning of *kephale* (head) as source since Adam was the source from whom the woman was taken and since both verse 8 and 12 refer to this event."[232]

"This strongly suggests that Paul was using 'head' in verse 3 with the Greek meaning of 'source, origin, base, or

[229] Ibid., in a response to the the Mickelsens' article, written by Phillip Baron Payne.
[230] "A Critical Examination of Wayne Grudem's Treatment of *Kephale* in Ancient Greek Texts," an appendix in Beyond Sex Roles by Gilbert Bilezikian, 2nd ed. (Grand Rapids, MI: Baker Book House, 1990), p. 248–49.
[231] Discovering Biblical Equality. IVP Academic, edited by Ronald W. Pierce and Rebecca Merrill Groothuis, c. 2005, p. 155, from the article, "Praying and Prophesying in the Assemblies," by Gordon D. Fee.
[232] Phillip Payne, Man and Woman, One in Christ, Zondervan, c. 2009, p. 130.

derivation.' Man was the 'source of..,' God is the source of Christ, as taught in John 8:42, 'I proceeded and came forth from God.'"[233]

"All these examples show that 'source' is a well-established meaning of *kephale*.... It would still make good sense to understand *kephale* to mean 'source' referring to the incarnation. This is how Jesus himself expressed that he came from the Father in John 8:42, 16:27–28 and 17:8.... In contrast to interpretations of *kephale* as 'authority over,' the meaning 'source' implies no inherent subordination of Christ. It simply affirms that Christ came from the Godhead in the incarnation."[234]

A couple of observations are in order:

1. It would seem that how the word was used in secular Greek would be a matter of fact. What do the lexicons say? Yet, as we have seen, people are all over the place on that issue and at completely opposite ends of the spectrum. Did you notice how one of the authors who thinks *kephale* means "authority" states that all the lexicons list "authority" as a *possible* meaning, while one of the authors who thinks *kephale* means "source" said that there is no lexicon that says "authority" is the *only possible* meaning of *kephale*. Those statements could very well both be true, and probably are. It is very easy just to quote sources that agree with your premise and ignore sources that don't. And then those on the other side of the debate do the same and both sides sound as if they are right! That certainly calls into question our ability to approach an issue, even an issue of historical

[233] Women, Authority, and the Bible, p. 107, from the article titled, "What Does *kephale* Mean in the New Testament?" by Berkeley & Alvera Mickelsen.
[234] Phillip Payne, Man and Woman, One in Christ, pp. 128, 134, 135.

fact, with objectivity. How else can we have such strongly opposite views about what a word meant? That should give us pause about ourselves. All of us. I remember a small wooden plaque hanging in a bait shop that read, "All fishermen are liars except me and thee. And frankly, I have my doubts about thee." It is too simple to say (or assume), "All others are biased in what they bring to the facts in this debate except you and me. And frankly, I have my doubts about you." As I said in the chapter on hermeneutics, where we observed different well educated scholars who differed on which text was the "window text," we probably all bring a bias to the content. This is cause for humility and self-examination rather than a fighting spirit. This is about finding Truth, not about me winning an argument.

2. In Scripture, Kingdom of God content is often added to the commonly accepted secular definition of a word. To limit the meaning of a word in Scripture to only the secular meaning of the word will severely limit the revelation of God in His Word. It should not surprise us that God uses secular words to reveal Spiritual Truths. What other words can He use? C. S. Lewis gave us a hypothetical example of a group of people called the Flat-Earthers. They lived in only two dimensions and could not comprehend three dimensions. So their understanding of the reality of a sphere passing through a plane of existence was that of a dot which became a circle and then became a dot again, and then disappeared. They did not have enough dimensions to comprehend a sphere passing through a plane. In the same way, we must not limit the definitions of the words in the Bible to the definitions spoken by secular people who lived in Bible times. Those definitions do not have the dimensions to explain heavenly things. But we start there since those are the only words we have to use.

So the reasoning of the Mickelsens is flawed when they say, "To understand what the apostle Paul really meant when he wrote about man or husband being the head of the woman or the wife in Corinthians and Ephesians 5, we must carefully examine the meaning of the word *kephale* ("head") in the Greek of Paul's day."[235] Now, it would be unfair to put words in their mouths: they might have meant that is the place to *start*, which it obviously is. But what the word meant in secular Greek usage in Paul's day is only the place to *start*. Then we go on to see how the Apostle uses the word, how the Apostle changes or adds content to the word in the Scriptures. That is how God reveals spiritual truth through the vehicle of secular words. As people who study the Bible, we must go all the way in determining the meaning of words, especially how they are used in the Scriptures, which may well be, and probably will be, different from how it is used in secular culture.

Most significantly, using the meaning of 'source' for *kephale* hardly eliminates authority from the definition. In the last two quotations in the list above, by the Mickelsens and by Dr. Phillip Payne, the authors refer to John 8:42 as proof that the 'source' definition refers to Jesus' coming from the Father to the earth—the Incarnation. "Jesus said to them, 'If God were your Father, you would love me, for I proceeded and came forth from God.'" That, they say, proves the meaning is "source" and eliminates the meaning "authority." I find that very perplexing because they pointedly ignore the very next phrase, which is also part of Jesus' words: "I did not come of my own accord, but He sent me." Those words were said in the same breath by Jesus and carry the same weight as evidence in figuring out the definition of headship. Doesn't the fact that Jesus describes

---

[235] <u>Women, Authority, and the Bible</u>, in the article, "What Does *Kephale* Mean?" by Berkeley and Alvera Mickelsen, InterVarsity Press, c. 1986, p. 97.

His coming to earth as not being of his own accord, but as being *sent*, imply some sort of authority to which Jesus is submissive? Now I want to be very clear that this is not adversarial authority. It was not Jesus coming to earth against His will, submitting but not wanting to, with His eyes rolling like an angry teenager. That is most definitely *not* the picture. If that's the way we see it, it's because we are putting baggage from living in a Fallen World onto the miracle of the Incarnation. But it clearly seems to be Jesus coming as a result of submission to the Father. Look again at all the quotations describing Jesus' submission to the Father in the chapter on the Trinity, Hierarchy, and Equality on page 90 in this book. Do they not indicate that this phrase is not an isolated instance but is a summary of the Incarnation? Jesus came as a result of being *sent*. I therefore cannot agree with Dr. Payne, who says that "the meaning 'source' implies no inherent subordination of Christ. It simply affirms that Christ came from the Godhead in the incarnation."[236] No, Jesus did not just "simply" decide to come from the Father on His own accord. That is just not true. He came because He was *sent*.

Here are two paraphrases of verse three, each one using one of the two most common definitions of "head":

Now, I want you to understand that the authority of every man is Christ, the authority of a woman is her husband, and the authority of Christ is God.

Now, I want you to understand the source of every man is Christ, the source of a woman is her husband, and the source of Christ is God.

[236] Ibid., <u>Man and Woman: One in Christ</u>, p. 135.

There are a couple of problems with the first paraphrase in which "head" means "authority."

1. It seems thin. If the only Biblical content to the word "head" is authority, then we are left with a boss-employee relationship or a chain of command. Egalitarians and complementarians both are uncomfortable with that.

> "Bilezikian... says that there is not the slightest evidence in the Bible for a 'chain of command within the Trinity.'"[237]

> "I would not use the phrase 'chain of command'...."[238]

A boss-employee relationship hardly describes the relationship of the Son to the Father. Nor should it characterize a husband-wife relationship, though very unfortunately it has in both Christian and non-Christian marriages. Whether or not the term "head" *includes* authority as part of the definition remains to be seen. But if *kephale* means *only* authority, then all we're left with is a chain of command—something nobody is comfortable with.

2. If "authority" is all headship means, then it seems we are left with the consequences of living after the Fall. The husband rules over the wife. What is the difference between the husband being the head, the "authority" over the wife, and the husband "ruling" over the wife? The status of the husband ruling (or having authority) over the wife was a result of the fall, and therefore a negative one. Apparently

---

[237] Gilbert Bilezikian, <u>Beyond Sex Roles</u>, 3rd edition, pp. 105, 106, 229.

[238] <u>Recovering Biblical Manhood and Womanhood</u>, Crossway Books, Wheaton, IL, c. 1991, p. 129. "Headcoverings, Prophesies, and the Trinity," by Thomas Schreiner. The author, Dr. Schreiner, a complementarian, is qoting Dr. <u>Belezikian</u>, an egalitarian. One thing they agree upon is they both do not think the phrase "chain of command" describes the relationships among the persons of the Trinity or gender relationships. He says he would not use the phrase "chain of command" in either case.

what happened after the Fall was that the position of headship deteriorated into just being the one in authority, the boss. So it follows that "authority" cannot be the *total* definition of *kephale*. That is too small. If we're going to be Biblical, we need to be thoroughly Biblical.

However, the use of the definition of "source" as the meaning of "head" also raises a number of problems.

1. In what way is God the source of Christ? It is interesting to me that those who reject any notion of order in the Trinity and so define it as the heresy of subordinationism tend to be those who define headship as "source." That is really necessary, though, for if headship includes authority, then there is authority in the Trinity, and that, for them, is subordinationism. But if they deny the meaning "authority" for head, they are left with the meaning of "source," and they are then faced with the issue of how God is the source of Jesus Christ and find themselves dangerously close to the heresy of Arianism, which saw Jesus as a created being. Why? Because they see Christ as the head (source) of the male because God *created* Adam. And the husband is the head (source) of the woman because the woman was *created* out of the man. But in both cases they were *created*. Don't miss the serious problem here—one of several very significant problems. The man had a beginning: dirt. The woman had a beginning: the rib of the man. But Jesus had no beginning. To use the definition of "source" for "head" to describe two beings who were created and one who was uncreated seems to me to lack consistency for the word and to be a problem so serious as to disqualify that meaning for "*kephale*." It would lead us dangerously close to the Arian heresy, which said Jesus was created—just like the man and the woman were created, and so not an eternal being.

211

2. The word used for man is *aner*. It means specifically males, rather than humankind in general. If humankind in general were what the apostle meant, the word would have been *anthropos*. So the apostle is talking about males when he says that Christ is the head of every man—meaning that Christ is the head of every male. That is important because whatever the word *kephale* means, it is something Christ is to males but not to females.[239] It is males who are *kephale* to females. Christ is *kephale* to males and males are *kephale* to females. That is simply what the text says. If *kephale* means "source," then in what way are males the source of females? The first answer that comes to mind is the account in Genesis where the woman was made "out of" the man. God took the rib from the man and formed it into the woman. And so the male is the "source" of the female. That seems clear enough. The problem with that understanding is that if we take that part of the narrative in Genesis 2 as supplying the meaning of source, then we are left with the dust as being the "source" of the man, since the man was formed from the dust, by God, just as the woman was formed from the male, by God. But this verse has just said that the "source" of the man is Christ, not dust—if we are consistent in applying the Genesis text. Surely the apostle did not change definitions of a word in the same verse? Well, no, obviously what is meant is Christ *through* the dust. But then is Christ not the source of the female *through* the rib of the male? The text says that the male is the source of the female—not Christ or God, who made the woman out of the man. It would seem to me that to say the male is the source of the female in the same way that Christ is the source of the man, which the parallelism of the passage requires, is to come dangerously close to saying females are

[239] For this reason, I have to assume he is talking about the marriage relationship of men and women.

212

not created in the image of God. She would *only* be the image of the man. That cannot be a viable understanding, because the Scriptures say clearly that females are created, together with males, in the image of God in Genesis 1:26. Hopefully we have already dealt with that problem.

3. One explanation of how God could be the source of Christ is merely that Christ "came from" God in coming to earth, in the Incarnation. And then the man is the source of the woman because she "came from" the man.[240] And Christ is the source of the man in that Christ (or God, really) made the man out of the dust. But this also raises a number of problems, some of them similar to those in number two above.

   a. In God being the source of Christ, an uncreated eternal being "left" an uncreated eternal being in taking on the form of a human body and coming to earth. b) In Christ (or God) being the source of the man, Christ (or God) *fashioned* the man out of the dust. He *fashioned* a previously non-existent, non-living (and therefore a non-eternal) being out of dust. c) In man being the source of the woman, God fashioned a living being out of a previously existing living being. Again, the parallelism of the passage crumbles.

   So if *kephale* means "source," then there are three quite different meanings of "source," all in the same verse. It would seem that the author would use the word in similar ways to illustrate the similarity of the three relationships. But if *kephale* means "source," he is not doing that—not even close.

4. There is similarity between the woman's source being the man and Christ's source being God. But the text also says that

---

[240] So says Phillip Payne in <u>Man and Woman, One in Christ</u>, pp. 138 and 139. "God is the *kephale* of Christ anchors Paul's concern in the Godhead. This most naturally refers to Christ's source as from God in the incarnation."

Christ is the "source" of the man (if *kephale* means source), and there the similarity breaks down. While the woman came "out of" the man, and Christ came "out of" God (in the incarnation), the man did not come "out of" Christ. The man came "out of" the dust. In the case of the woman, a human is the 'source" of a human. In the case of Christ, Christ came "out of" God, eternal from eternal. But in the case of the man, a living being came "out of" non-living dust—a result of the handiwork of God. That act is just not similar to the woman coming out of the man or Christ coming out of God in the Incarnation. It is very different.

The problems with the meaning of "source" for *kephale* seem to me to be insurmountable. As noted above, this particular text does not significantly define headship. Actually, we will have to wait until we look at Ephesians 5 to find much content about what *kephale* means in the Kingdom of God, and that is what we are searching for. We are not searching for what it meant in the secular culture of the time. But of the two options batted around today (both of which, I think, miss the mark), the one that *includes* some sort of completely *unselfish* authority seems to be closer to the mark. But the Biblical definition includes more, as we will see in Ephesians 5.

Here is how one person summarized the issue. Jen Pollock Michel quotes a commentary by Richard B. Hays, who, she says, is a strong egalitarian on this issue, and she is impressed with his hermeneutical candor: "Any honest appraisal of 1 Corinthians 11:2–16 will require both teacher and students to confront the patriarchal implications of verses 3 and 7–9. Such implications cannot be explained away by some technical move, such as translating *kephale* as 'source' rather than 'head' because the patriarchal assumptions[241] are embedded

---

[241] As I have defined the terms "patriarchal" and "complementarian," I would not describe these verses as "patriarchal" but instead "complementarian."

in the structure of Paul's argument."[242] What are the "patriarchal implications" in verses 7 through 9? Those are the verses that say that man is the glory of God and woman is the glory of man. Also that man was not made from woman but woman from man. Also that woman was created for man and not man for woman. Those verses are uncomfortably complementarian. He is honest, as an egalitarian, about what the words say, and all of us who profess to maintain a high view of Scripture need to follow his example.

As we said above, verse 10 is a conclusion based upon what went immediately before. We know that because it begins with the words, "That is why" in the RSV, or "It is for this reason" in the NIV, or "Therefore" in the NASB. Those words all indicate that what is coming is a conclusion based on what went before—in verses 7 through 9. There are two statements immediately preceding verse 10. One says that the man was not made from woman but woman from man. The other says neither was man created for woman for woman for man. Those statements reflect the complementarian position, and honesty requires us to admit that. They are balanced, but not eliminated, by verses eleven and twelve, which talk about the equality and mutual dependence of both genders. Our ability to maintain that Biblical balance is central to understanding what I believe is the Biblical position on gender.

Before we move on to the 1 Corinthians 14:33–40 text, how can we summarize the teaching of chapter 11? As I said at the beginning, this text presents a minefield of problems. Virtually everybody who tries to understand what the passage teaches makes assumptions and takes liberties with the language. So have I. I want to be honest about that. My point is that I am not alone in doing so. Given the context of the city where the church was located and the sheer amount of sexual perversion and inversion present and Paul's concern for the

[242] *Christianity Today*, in the column, "her.meneutics," p. 23, March 2014, by Jen Pollock Michel.

reputation of the church in that town, and given the ambiguity of the words themselves, the following is what makes the most sense to me.

Paul is concerned about hair styles and what is communicated by those hair styles displayed by church members, Christian believers, living in that mixed-up community. A man wearing his hair long, in an effeminate style, hanging down, *in that culture* communicated a homosexual lifestyle and *availability*. Thus he was dishonoring his head, Christ, his creator, who made him a male and made a female for him, not another male. A female who wore her hair flowing down in public, rather than done up on top of her head, was advertising her sexual *availability*, like a prostitute, and so she was dishonoring her head, her husband, if she refused to change. It was appropriate, then, to shave her head, as that was punishment for prostitutes and that was how she was acting. Both were inappropriate in the context of church service or in the Christian life, and both brought dishonor to their respective heads.

There really is no clear definition presented here for the concept of headship. There certainly is some "source" language in the passage. "For as woman was made from man, so man is now born of woman." But the attempt to define headship as source falls short, as we have already seen. The consistent avoidance of the submission issue in the Incarnation of Jesus by those who define headship only as source is a mystery to me. Since God is the head of Christ, just as Christ is the head of the male and the male is the head of the female, we should ask the question how does God relate to Christ as Christ takes on human flesh in the Incarnation. Actually, there is not a lot to look at in Scripture to answer that question. But we do know how Christ Himself described His coming: He was *sent*. He says consistently that He did not come of is own authority. God describes His Son as being one with whom He is well pleased. How does Christ function as head to the male? He is merciful, gracious, and *not* self-serving, even though He is in authority over the male. Those statements give us hints as to what the Biblical definition of headship is, which we will wait on until we look at Ephesians 5.

That brings us to another difficult passage in 1 Corinthians 14:33b through 40. Though some have said this passage does not belong in the Scripture, that seems to me to be an extraordinarily dangerous place to begin. True, there are some texts that are doubtful such as John 8:1 through 11 or Mark 16:9 through 20. In both cases, there is good textual evidence that probably these texts were not in the original. There is no such evidence regarding 1 Corinthians 14:33b through 36. In all the oldest manuscripts, those verses are present—though in a few, they are present after verse 40. Having said that, even if we accept this passage as a genuine part of the Pauline text (and I do), it remains a difficult passage.

There are some who say that verses 34 and 35 about women being *silent* do not fit in with the flow of thought in the previous verses.[243] However, I think this section about women being *silent* fits in quite well with what has gone on before: in verse 28, a tongue-speaker is to keep *silent* when there is not an interpreter. In verse 30, if a revelation is made to another sitting by, let the first be *silent*. The same Greek word is used in all three instances. This section seems to be about order and just plain courtesy in the worship services. It really does follow quite well.

"As in all the churches of the saints, the women should keep silence in the churches. For they are not permitted to speak, but should be subordinate, as even the law says. If there is anything they desire to know, let them ask their husbands at home. For it is shameful for a woman to speak in church. What! Did the word of God originate with you, or are you the only ones it has reached?"

---

[243] Phillip Payne, Man and Woman, One in Christ, Zondervan, Grand Rapids, MI, 49530, c. 2009, pp. 254–55.

What are some of the problems which jump out at us?

1. It appears that this text directly contradicts 1 Corinthians 11. Why would there be instructions given for women on how to wear their hair when they prophesy and pray if they were to "keep silence" in church, as this text might imply? Aren't praying and prophesying done "out loud"?
2. There is nothing in the "law" anywhere that talks about women being silent as evidence of their being subordinate.
3. Could it really be true that women were not allowed to say *anything*—that it really was "shameful" to say anything in church? The word "shameful" is the same word as "disgraceful" in chapter 11, when it says, "it is disgraceful for a woman to be shorn or shaven."[50]
4. It is definitely not an "ad hoc" prescription that the women keep silence. This is prescribed "as in all the churches of the saints."[51]

In trying to figure these verses out, I want to be up-front about the assumptions I make regarding both passages (1 Corinthians 11 and 14:34–35), and others as well.

1. The praying and prophesying were done out loud. They could be heard.
2. I assume this was really happening. I think they really were praying to the God of the universe and receiving words from the God of the universe. And the women were speaking out loud.
3. I assume sense, not contradiction, in the Scriptures, as they are God-written (especially in this case, where the context is the same—same author and same church).
4. I also recognize that I am at an enormous cultural distance from the hearers of this text, and so something may seem

ridiculous to me, but to them it might have been very easy to understand or even incredibly progressive.

Also, let me be honest with a couple of interpretations that I cannot accept.

1. I cannot accept that this is a later scribal addition to the original letter. Following are some of the reasons that some do believe this is not an authentic Pauline phrase.
   a. It is somewhat unusual for Paul to appeal to the practice of "other churches." Actually, the phrase, "As in all the churches of the saints," occurs only here in the New Testament. But it must be noted that in 1 Corinthians 7:17, 4:17, and 11:16, something very similar occurs. "Only, let every one lead the life which the Lord has assigned to him, and in which God has called him. This is my rule in all the churches." "Therefore I sent to you Timothy, my beloved and faithful child in the Lord, to remind you of my ways in Christ, as I teach them everywhere in every church." "If any one is disposed to be contentious, we recognize no other practice, nor do the churches of God."
   b. The author makes a general appeal to "the law." However, there is nothing in the Old Testament that comes anywhere close to supporting what the author is saying here. But that is an interpretive issue rather than reason for deleting the text from Scripture.
   c. It seems harsh compared to other texts in Scripture. But before we start deleting parts of Scripture that seem harsh, we need some evidence, other than harshness, to support our pushing the delete button. There is not a lot. Paul must be given the privilege of saying something only one time without our concluding it must not be Pauline because it seems unusually harsh and because

we cannot find anything else like it in his other letters. I think we must not dismiss this text as not being part of the original text.

2. A second interpretation that I cannot accept is that this verse is the "controlling verse" and so all the instructions in chapter 11 were addressing a hypothetical situation. By that, I am referring to the suggestion that the women were really not speaking at all when they prayed and prophesied. Chapter 11 gives instructions for the possible situation where women were praying and prophesying, but they, of course, were not, since it is prohibited by this verse. I cannot accept that. I believe women were really speaking, not silent, in the Corinthian worship services.

3. Some have interpreted this verse as prohibiting women from "weighing" or "judging" prophesy because of verse 29: "Let two or three prophets speak, and let the others weigh what is said." Women, it is said, are prohibited from judging the prophesies of others because they are subordinate, and that would involve exercising authority over men, which is prohibited in 1 Timothy 2. And so that is what is being referred to when it says that women are told to keep silence.[244]

I cannot accept that understanding of this text, because it seems unreasonable that women could prophesy but not judge prophecy. It seems unreasonable that women could not weigh the prophesies of their sisters. And it seems unreasonable because it is stated as a universal prohibition, not just a prohibition of weighing prophesies. Women are, after all, encouraged to teach or train younger women in Titus 2:4, so it does not seem to fit that they would be prohibited from judging the prophesies of, at least, other women. But it is stated as universal. So if a male or female gives a false prophecy and there are men present, the women

---

[244] James Hurley, <u>Men and Women in Biblical Perspective</u>, Zondervan, Grand Rapids, MI 49506, c. 1981, pp. 191ff.

are to keep silence. And if the men do not speak up? Then what? What if only women are present and a false prophecy is given? Can women in that instance judge the prophecy? Not if we take the prohibition of women speaking as universal. Yet that is how it is presented: that is the practice "in all the churches." In fact, the clear pattern in the text is the inclusion of everybody: "*each one* has a hymn, a lesson.... If *any* speak in a tongue.... Let *two or three* prophets speak, and let the *others* weigh what is said.... You can *all* prophesy one by one, so that *all* may learn and *all* be encouraged...." The clear atmosphere in the text is inclusive of everybody. It would be too jarring then to say, "Oh, but even though women can prophesy and learn and be encouraged, give a hymn or a *lesson*, they cannot weigh the prophesies. That is for the men alone." That's especially true because he says, "Let the others weigh what is said," and at that point there is no exclusion of women stated. No, there are just too many problems with that understanding of this verse.

4. So, I do not take this verse literally. However, lest I be condemned as a heretic, it must be recognized that currently very few take this verse literally.

So, how do we solve this puzzle? If I were a member of the First Church of Corinth, how would I have heard this? What would it mean to me? There are several issues that may help us.

1. The first is the issue of context. As we noted at the beginning of our study of 1 Corinthians, this whole section is about maintaining order in the services of the church. In the opening of this section, chapter 11, Paul appeals to the order in the Trinity and teaches that this church should have a specific reflection of that orderliness in its services. The section directly before our text is clearly about maintaining

order in this very charismatic (and apparently chaotic) church:

"If any speak in a tongue, let there be only two or at most three, and each in turn; and let one interpret. But if there is no one to interpret, let each of them keep silence in church and speak to himself and to God. Let two or three prophets speak and let the others weigh what is said. If a revelation is made to another sitting by, let the first be silent. For you can all prophesy one by one, so that all may learn and all be encouraged; and the spirits of prophets are subject to prophets. For God is not a God of confusion but of peace. As in all the churches of the saints, the women should keep silence in the churches. For they are not permitted to speak, but should be subordinate, as even the law says. If there is anything they desire to know, let them ask their husbands at home. For it is a shameful thing for a woman to speak in church. What! Did the word of God originate with you, or are you the only ones it has reached? If any one thinks that he is a prophet, or spiritual, he should acknowledge that what I am writing to you is a command of the Lord. If any one does not recognize this, he is not recognized. So, my brethren, earnestly desire to prophesy, and do not forbid speaking in tongues; but all things should be done decently and in order."[53]

Notice that two times before silence is enjoined on the women, silence is *also* enjoined on others: when there is no interpreter for a tongue or a prophecy and when a revelation is made to another, the first should keep silent. In both cases, the reason is to maintain an orderly service. So there are really three instances in this text where Paul enjoins silence—only once upon women, and that is apparently to maintain an orderly service.

We have a pretty clear hint as to what the women were talking about in the verse that follows the command for them to be silent. It says if they want to learn something, they should ask their husbands

222

at home. Their disruption was rooted in their desire to learn. Paul does not condemn their desire to learn or imply it is inappropriate. He only condemns the disruption.

The text says, "If there is anything they (the women) want to know, let them ask their husbands at home." Women were, after all, newcomers to the worship services. They were largely excluded from Jewish services and were considered incapable of learning. D. A. Carson notes "that in a Greek *ekklesia*, a public meeting, women were not allowed to speak at all. By contrast, women in the Christian ekklesia… were encouraged to do so. In that sense, Paul was not trapped by the social customs of Corinth: the gospel, in his view, truly freed women from certain cultural restrictions."[245] It makes sense that they were talking and so disrupting the order of the service because they were wanting to know what was going on. They were newcomers. The fact that Paul's injunction for them to "be silent" after two other injunctions to "be silent," both given in the context of maintaining orderliness, implies that what Paul was after was orderliness rather than chaos in the service. Such chaos mimicked the chaotic services of Dionysus and did not reflect the orderliness appropriate to the worship of the Triune God. And Paul wants the worship of the Triune God of the Bible to be *different*.

Before moving on, it must be noted that Paul *encourages* women to learn. He does not say or imply that their cooperation in the service was in any way inappropriate. The common, culturally held assumption that women were incapable of learning was not held by the apostle. And he was not hesitant to encourage a practice that was culturally offensive.

That leaves us with the problem of Paul's statement that the women are not permitted to speak, but should be subordinate, as even the law says.[246]

---

[245] John Piper and Wayne Grudem, Recovering Biblical Manhood and Womanhood, Wheaton, IL, Crossway Books, 1991, p. 153.

[246] Many complementarians say that Paul is referring to Genesis 3:15, where God says that one of the consequences of the Fall is that the man would rule over the female. The problem with that is that they are then taking the listing of the results of the fall by God as prescriptive rather

This is quite difficult, mainly because nowhere does the Old Testament say that women should be silent because they are subordinate. Nor is there a text that equates silence with subordination. There is a progressively developed theme throughout Scripture of the headship of the male, and, among other issues, it includes authority as well as service. But there is no statement to the effect that the women should keep silence in the services because the law says so. Anywhere.

I think it is possible that Paul is repeating a practice he has used previously in his letter—that of quoting back to them some of the slogans that were commonly used in this fellowship. It seems that this was a very slogan-oriented church. If you've ever been around a slogan-oriented fellowship, you will know what I mean. Knowing the slogans and quoting them puts you in the "in" group. We've already seen that being in the "correct" group was important in this divided church. It's a way of appearing to have "knowledge," to appear "mature," and both of those qualities were important issues for this church. Paul had two sources of information about this church. In 1:11, he says, "It has been reported to me by Chloe's people that there is quarreling among you." And in 7:1, he says, "Now, concerning the matters about which you wrote...." So there was the report he had heard and the letter they had sent to him. Therefore, he could quote back to them some of their slogans. Here is a partial listing:

"I belong to Paul." (1:12)
"I belong to Apollos." (1:12)
"I belong to Cephas." (1:12)
"I belong to Christ." (1:12—that was for the REALLY spiritual ones!)
"All things are lawful for me." (6:12, 10:23)

---

than descriptive. Weeds and pain in labor are also God-ordained results of the fall. So we should not give pain medication to women in labor nor use weed killer in our fields or even hoe our gardens if we are consistent. No, I think the results of the fall are descriptive, not prescriptive.

"Food is meant for the stomach and the stomach for food."
(6:13)

"It is well for a man not to touch a woman." (7:1)

"All of us possess knowledge." (8:1—there's our word "knowledge")

"An idol has no real existence." (8:4)

"There is no God but one." (8:4)

"We are no better off if we do not eat, and no better off if we do." (8:8)

"Let us eat and drink, for tomorrow we die." (15:31)

"Bad company ruins good morals." (15:32)

Now, sometimes it is not clear that the apostle is quoting a slogan of theirs. Sometimes it is. In 1:12, Paul says, "each one of you says…," and then quotes their slogans. So there it is clear. Other times it is not. The quotation marks are sometimes a translator's judgment. Some translations will have the above statements in quotation marks and some will not.

As I said before, this is a difficult text and nobody interprets it literally. Here is what makes the most sense to me of this tough text. I think what Paul is doing in 14:34 is quoting a slogan of theirs: "They are not permitted to speak, but should be subordinate, as even the law says." That slogan would fit with the tenor and tone of this problem—an infected, legalistic, and somewhat arrogant church. It would solve the problem of the vague appeal to the law where there is no such statement in the Old Testament. It would be the same type of hyper-legalistic application of what, in certain circumstances, would be a legitimate Biblical principle. For instance, in chapter 7 verse 1, we find the phrase, "It is better not to touch a woman." Most translators take that phrase as a slogan of theirs, a euphemism for sexual intercourse. Sexual intercourse is not bad—in marriage. But they defined it as evil, even though Scripture does not, and so came up with their slogan. "It is better not to touch a woman." I think verse 34 is another slogan of theirs—a slogan to the effect that women should not be permitted to speak, as the law says.

But that also is a hyper-legalistic application of the patriarchalism of the Old Testament. Now the women were trying to learn in this new experience of corporate worship. And they were upsetting the decorum of the service by their questions.

So the line of thinking for the author runs something like this: He is making a strong case for an orderly worship service and three times enjoins silence on certain people with that end in view. One of them is women, who, from the context, are asking questions during the service in the desire to learn—and so they are told to wait to ask their husbands at home. Why, *even you say*, Paul says to this disorderly church, "They are not permitted to speak, but should be subordinate, as even the law says." So, when he enjoins silence on the women, for the purpose of order, he is quoting back to them one of their slogans, something they already believe, but in the wrong sense. The reason they should ask their husbands at home is most likely because the husbands knew what was going on, since this was not new for them.

Taking the text this way, that he is quoting a slogan of theirs, makes more sense with verse 36: "What! Did the word of God originate with *you*, or are *you* the only ones it has reached?" Do you catch the sarcasm? They had created a slogan that they were using with the authority of God's word.

The word translated "what!" is an interesting word. It is used to express strong disapproval of a preceding statement. It could be translated as "nonsense!" or our common phrase today, "You gotta be kidding." It appears in 6:9, 6:16, 6:19, 11:22 (same sense but different word), as well as here in verse 36.

His strong, sarcastic negative response to them, when he says, "What! Did the word of God originate with you?" then makes sense if he is quoting one of *their* slogans. He wants to make the point that their slogans do not carry the authority of God's word.

In the concluding verses to the section on order in the church, verses 37 to 40, the author makes the strong statement to the effect that there really is no other option available. "If any one thinks that he is a prophet, or spiritual, he should acknowledge that what I am writing to you is a command of the Lord. If any one does not recognize this, he is not recognized." That sounds harsh, if not dictatorial. But it must be read as a summary of the whole section on order in the church, which it is. The fact is, chaotic, disorderly worship services do *not* represent God who was the object of their worship. In this instance, they seemed uncomfortably close to the chaotic, disorderly, and even sexually promiscuous celebrations of the false gods and goddesses of the city. From what is written in this section, it seems that people were talking all at once. People were prophesying all at once. The women were bugging their husbands, trying to find out what was going on. The dress, and especially the hair styles, did not reflect the way God created the different genders. Women were wearing their hair as a prostitute would. And there was blatant homosexual dress obvious enough that it was easily recognized. Surely it is perfectly appropriate for the apostle to say that this does not represent God well to outsiders, to non-believers, and needs to be corrected. End of discussion.

So in summary, here are the points gleaned from the first letter to the Corinthians from the two passages we have examined:

The whole section of 1 Corinthians 11:3 through 14:40 is about order in public worship services. That is the conclusion in verse 40: "But all things should be done decently and in order." Also verse 33: "For God is not a God of confusion, but of peace." The foundation for that order is the profound orderly relationship among the persons of the Trinity in chapter 11 verse 3 and its reflection in gender. That is what Paul wants us to understand or to see. "I want you to understand (see) that the head of every man is Christ, the head of a woman is her husband, and the head of Christ is God." This concept is central to my understanding of gender relationships— that one set of relationships, gender relationships, reflects the other set of relationships—that is, relationships among the persons of the Trinity. This verse and its corresponding Old Testament text, Genesis 1:26 & 27, are my "window texts," the central thought through which other texts are to be understood, not discarded.

The earthly working-out of that quality of relationship in the Corinthian church, and by extension in our modern church, is two-fold:

a) There should be some visible evidence of both the headship of the male and the non-interchangeability of the sexes. For males, that meant a hair style that did not communicate homosexual availability. For females, it meant a head covering or probably longer hair appropriately "done up," not in the loose flowing down that communicated sexual availability. In both cases, it was about avoidance of insult to the person's head—for the male, it was his creator and for the female, it was her husband, her head. Verse 10 in chapter 11, which says that the woman ought to have a sign of authority on her head, or more likely, authority or responsibility, to style her hair in such a way that communicated fidelity to her husband, her head, is a conclusion to three statements that went direction before:

1. The man is the image and glory of God, but the woman is the glory of man.
2. Man was not made from woman, but woman from man.
3. Neither was man created for woman, but woman for man.
   Verse 10 then begins with the words, "That is why...."
   So the head covering, or hair appropriately styled, in that culture, was an outward symbol of those statements.

b) The second, but by no means secondary, issue is that there is complete equality between males and females, even as there is between the persons of the Trinity. Verse 11 begins with the word "Nevertheless." The NIV uses the word "however." Those words indicate a change in thought, an opposite understanding, from the hierarchical understanding that went before. The change is stated as:

1. Woman is not independent of man, nor man of woman. (verse 11)
2. As woman was made from man, so man is now born of woman. (verse 12)

   There is a mutuality, a mutual dependence, an equality of the genders, as there is among the persons of the Trinity. If hierarchy is not taught in the beginning section of the chapter, as some believe, then they have to explain the use of the word "nevertheless" or "however" used to begin the egalitarian section in verse 11. If there is no hierarchy in verses 4 through 9, what is the change that "nevertheless" introduces?

The apostle Paul could hold both concepts at the same time, even though we, as citizens of a fallen world, have a difficult time with that. Paul could hold both. One does not trump the other. It is crucial for those of us who believe in the authority of the Bible to hold both aspects of this Biblical balance as Paul did. This is very important, because historically women have been perceived as inferior to males. That should be evident from the quotations at the beginning of some of the chapters in this book. And even today among some complementarians, there is a subtle sense in which women are still considered as inferior. For example, consider this sentence in the preface to the book Recovering Biblical Manhood and Womanhood on page xiii: "Manhood and womanhood as such are now often seen as irrelevant factors in determining fitness for leadership."[247] The author clearly sees it as negative that manhood and womanhood are *irrelevant* in choosing leaders. He apparently thinks manhood and womanhood *should be* relevant in determining fitness for leadership. In other words, women are not

---

[247] Recovering Biblical Manhood and Womanhood, ed. John Piper, p. xiii.

fit for leadership. Maybe "fitness" is a technical term here. Maybe the author of that sentence did not mean to imply that women were "unfit" for leadership, spiritually, emotionally, or intellectually. Yet that seems to be what he is implying. When the Bible talks about the headship of the male, I do not find any teaching anywhere that a female is "unfit" to lead. The reason that is so important is that if women are "unfit" to be the head, then Christ is also "unfit" to be part of the Godhead. Clearly that is unacceptable.

So my thesis is that gender is a reflection of both the mutuality and the hierarchy in the Trinity. Gender, then, is a form of general revelation. We should not be surprised that we find Scripture teaches both. We must hold both at the same time and not discard one at the expense of the other. It is because we are on this side of the Fall, where the male "rules," which is a description of what happens rather than a prescription for what God wants, that we struggle with this concept.

Before we leave this book of the New Testament, I want to make four observations.

The first is that there is no teaching about female submission to the male, or more likely, wives to husbands, in this text. It's about hair styles that communicate rebellion against respective heads. One is a hair style on males that communicates availability for homosexual relations, which would be an insult to the male's creator, his head, who made him a male for whom sexual relations are to be with a female. The other is a hair style on a woman, or wife more likely, which communicates sexual availability, which would be an insult to her head, her husband. Headship is not really defined, and there does not seem to be any teaching on the necessity of wives to submit to their husbands.

The second observation is the beautiful mutuality in the sexual relationship in a different section of 1 Corinthians, in the opening verses of chapter 7, verses 1 through 7. The phrase, "It is well for a man not to touch a woman," follows the introduction, "now concerning the matters about which you wrote," in verse one. At this point in the structure of the letter, he is responding to some questions the church had apparently written him about, and so he is quoting back to them one of their slogans when he says, "It is well for a man not to touch a woman." "To touch a woman" is most probably a euphemism for sexual intercourse. Apparently part of the super-spiritual atmosphere in the church (and I might add, a fake spirituality) was to avoid intercourse.

Paul's answer to their question was:

a) Each man should have his own wife, which is probably another euphemism for intercourse. (verse 2)
b) The husband should give to his wife her conjugal rights. (verse 3)
c) The wife should do likewise to her husband. (verse 3)
d) The wife does not rule over her own body, but the husband does. (verse 4)
e) Likewise, the husband does not rule over his own body, but the wife does. (verse 4)

We probably miss the radical meaning of those words because of our cultural distance from the text. In that culture, the wife had duties to the husband, but not him to her. The wife was the property of her husband. The idea of conjugal rights that applied equally to both was radically counter to the cultural norms. In this text, Paul lifts women out of the culture of subjection, in which they lived, to equal personhood with their husbands, even though the husband still functioned as the head.

The third observation is Paul's willingness to be counter-cultural and his willingness to call the early churches to be the same. There are those who say the reason we find any texts at all in the Bible teaching about women being submissive to men is out of a desire not to offend the culture of the time. That seems to me to be untenable:

Paul and Jesus both did not hesitate to offend the culture of the time for the sake of truth. That is what, from a worldly perspective, led to Jesus' crucifixion: they wanted to get rid of him because He was upsetting their system. Paul's teaching caused riots and landed him in jail. They were both fearless in their proclamation of the truth despite opposition. Paul taught his churches that they were to be *different*, like aliens in a foreign country, and that they should expect persecution as a result. To subjugate one gender to another, merely out of fear of offending the culture of the time, seems both very lame and sexist.

The fourth observation is that, even though the husband functions as the head, we are told that he should give to his wife her conjugal rights in chapter 7 verse 3. Or in verse 4 we are told that the husband does not rule over his own body, but the wife does. So headship can still leave one under obligation to the other person, the person over whom one functions as the head. The role of headship is not fully defined in this passage, but it clearly does not constitute absolute authority. Headship is not the same as "ruling," which is a result of the fall. Headship does not mean ordering the relationship to the advantage of the person functioning as the head. In the chapter on Ephesians 5:21–32, where Paul provides us with a definition of headship, I will relate several true stories where headship was practiced—by Bible believing Christians, I might add—as meaning the husband was the boss with the privilege of ordering his wife around to his pleasure. That is *not* the Biblical picture.

There is a mutuality in Biblical teaching on gender relationships, but one gender, and only one, still functions as the head. There is authority, as we'll see more clearly as we move on through the New Testament, but not an absolute, self-serving authority. It is not the privilege to do what you want and expect everybody else to do what you want. It is *not* that. It is not even what we would call "leadership." This is a big mystery—the relationship of equality and hierarchy in

232

the Trinity as reflected between man and woman. For us of small minds and, even more, the prejudice of living in and experiencing only a fallen world, we scratch our heads. (By that, I mean the thing on top of our necks.) We are trying to understand, to see (to use Paul's words) a concept we don't have enough dimensions for. We are like flat-earthers, trying to understand a three-dimensional picture. It is hard. It is hard to remember Home when you've never been there. But that is the purpose of revelation, and that is why revelation (by that I mean Scripture) is *necessary* for us to live while we are away from where we were designed to live. We need God to tell us about Home. And by comprehending the somewhat opaque truths of the Bible and trying to apply them, we may experience a taste of Home.

May God help us to do just that.

6

THE CITY WHERE
DIANA WAS KING

Part A
Ephesians 5:21 to 33

"Women are evil, my children, and by reason of their lacking authority or power over man, they scheme treacherously how they might entice him to themselves by means of their looks..."[248]

"The dynamic of my parents' marriage never fit with the paradigm commonly associated with conservative Christianity: that of an authoritative father dictating to a mealy-mouthed mother who just needed to stay in her place and recognize that her husband always knew better."[249]

---

[248] *The Testaments of the Twelve Patriarchs,* Reuben 5, quoted in <u>Biblical Manhood and Womanhood</u>, p. 182.

[249] Megan Phelps-Roper, <u>Unfollow: A Journey from Hatred to Hope—Leaving the Westboro Baptist Church</u>, c. 2019, p. 10, published by Farrar, Straus, and Giroux, imprint of Quercus Editions, Ltd. 50 Victoria Embankment, London EC4Y ODZ.

I have heard many sermons in my lifetime, but only two on Ephesians 5:21–33. I remember both of them. One was pretty straightforward and stuck rigorously to the text. The other was not and did not.

I was a first-year staff worker with a college campus Christian organization and was "checking out" the churches close to the campus to which I was assigned. One inhabited a very old brick building with high ceilings and globe lamps that hung down three or four feet from the ceiling, and the whole building contained lots of beautiful old oak woodwork. It was a church that had had a significant student ministry in the past, but the people had grown old, their pastor had moved to another city, and so their interest in student work had waned. This particular morning I noticed that nearly everyone in the congregation had white hair. I felt very out of place. But their pastor was a newly hired young blade just out of seminary who brought a lot of energy and enthusiasm. I could tell that quickly. He was preaching on the last part of Ephesians 5. He started out mildly enough, but as the sermon went on, he became more and more agitated. As he approached his conclusion, his voice raised in a gradual crescendo until at the end of the sermon he boomed out his final conclusion that what this country needed was more men who were willing to be lord of the home and less weak-willed males who were unwilling lead as they were supposed to.

I was uncomfortable with his conclusion but could not really articulate a reason why. His summary just did not seem to represent the passage fairly. But I had never been to seminary and felt very hesitant to critique a pastor, particularly one who had more theological education than I. I was a pharmacy major. I might know more about drugs than he did, but I assumed that my lack of training disqualified me from criticizing his exegesis of the passage.

The pastor invited me to his house for Sunday dinner, and, as a single guy, I jumped at the chance for a home-cooked meal.

It met all my highest expectations. His wife was totally amazing. He, unfortunately, was not.

They had 3 kids—one infant, one toddler still in diapers, and one about four years old who was able to sit at the table and feed himself. All three children were her responsibility—completely. She struggled to feed three mouths at once: the baby's, the middle child's, and lastly hers. She did not get much. As the meal went on, she became more and more distracted trying to take care of all three kids in addition to her husband and the guest—me. At one point, I was out of mashed potatoes and gravy (a common occurrence for me), and the husband, the preacher, told her she needed to get up and get me some more potatoes, in order to "take care of the guest at the table." She gave him a stressed-out look, as the youngest kid in her lap was crying, and he was doing nothing to help but instead was talking to me. He looked at her and told her it was her job to get me more food, so she put the kid in one arm and got up and got more mashed potatoes and gravy for me while the husband watched her. Then she sat down and continued to try and feed her crying child while the husband talked on with me.

I was embarrassed. I felt guilty of being the cause of her stress, since it was I who was out of mashed potatoes and gravy. I did not have the Biblical knowledge or the understanding of the passage we had just studied in church, or more likely just the courage, to offer to help this woman and so to disagree with her husband who had invited me to dinner. Now I can say, from a later perspective, that he was wrong in his sermon and in his understanding of what the passage said, as well in how he treated his wife. He had not taught what the passage said. He had done what is often done in attempting to teach a text: he had taught what he wanted and conveniently ignored sections of the text that did not meet his agenda. His definition of headship was skewed. This is no minor issue. We must let the Bible give us definitions and not impose our own definitions on Scripture. We submit to Scripture rather than use it to further our agenda.

The city of Ephesus was an enormously significant city, the most important city in the Roman province of Asia. In it was a magnificent road, seventy feet wide and lined with columns, that ran through the center of the city to the fine harbor. Because of this harbor, the city was both a great export center at the end of the caravan route from Asia and a natural landing point from Rome. Its population was perhaps one third of a million. The city was famous for the presence of the temple to Diana, or Artemis, a goddess who was depicted as having many breasts. Or there is some thought that her chest was decorated with bull testicles. Whichever was true, she was a fertility goddess, and her temple was ranked as one of the wonders of the world until AD 260, when it was destroyed by the Goths. It was four times the size of the Parthenon at Athens. With this city being the center of the worship of Artemis, and the constant coming and going of sailors, it was a very cosmopolitan place.

In this less-than-safe environment, a small church sprang up as a result of a visit by the Apostle Paul to the city. The church in Ephesus warrants more words in the New Testament than any other church. The birth of the church is recorded in the book of Acts, chapters 19 and 20, and it was a tumultuous birth, with loud crowds and riots, as Paul upset the status quo of the city. The book of Ephesians, though there is some doubt, was probably written to this church. The books of 1 and 2 Timothy were written to its young pastor. Lastly, the church is mentioned as one of the seven churches in the book of Revelation. That particular text contains a somber warning. The writer mentions that the believers there had shown perseverance through difficult times. They could not tolerate wicked men. They had remained theologically pure. They had not grown weary in the battle for truth.

But they had grown cold.

"I have this against you: You have forsaken your first love....
Repent and do the things you did at first. If you do not repent, I
will come to you and remove your lamp stand from its place."[250]

---

[250] Revelation 2:4, 5

Apparently they did not repent. The city declined in importance due to the loss of the harbor, which was necessary for the city to exist. It gradually filled up with silt and so became unusable as a harbor. The area around Ephesus became a swamp, and mosquitoes were rampant. A series of malaria epidemics decimated the population, and consequently the citizens of Ephesus abandoned the city in the short period of about a hundred years. After that, a series of earthquakes destroyed some parts of the remaining city. But some of the structures were preserved because nobody wanted to come to haul off the stones due to the unhealthful conditions and disease. Archaeological excavations at the site of the ancient city are now six miles from the current shoreline due to the harbor silting in and eventually disappearing. So not only did the church disappear, as warned might happen, but the city also. A sobering warning for us.

Given that the city was home to the temple of Artemis, a goddess of fertility, it is not surprising that the church struggled with gender issues, and, in fact, probably the two best known and most significant passages dealing with the issue of gender are found in letters that this church would have received: the letter to the Ephesians and the book of First Timothy. Timothy was the pastor of the church at Ephesus, and the two letters designated as 1 and 2 Timothy are the Apostle Paul's letters of advice to this young pastor. Ephesians 5:21–33 is probably the best known teaching on marriage in the New Testament. It is not without controversy, but that is hardly surprising. In my dealings with the public, I have concluded that one can probably find somebody who will disagree with any proposition, even whether the earth is round or whether men have ever walked on the moon. The presence of controversy about a passage says more about the nature of the human condition than the essential truth or clarity of a text.

When one mentions the last part of Ephesians 5 about marriage, many of us already have heard of the passage. I suspect that what comes to mind for most of us is that this is a passage about how wives need to submit to their husbands. That is what the passage is about—right? If that's what you think, I'd like to change forever your perception of this text. Not that the issue isn't there—it is. But there is an enormously bigger issue in the text than that. For some reason, that bigger issue is not what seems to come to mind first when we think of the text.

Submission of wives is mentioned three times:

a) "Wives, be subject to your husbands" (verse 22). The command form of the verb is actually not there but is taken from verse 21. More on that below.
b) "As the church is subject to Christ, so let wives also be subject in everything to their husbands" (verse 24).
c) "Let the wife see that she respects her husband" (verse 33). Note that the verb here is not to be subject or to submit, but to respect, which is different.

There is also a three-fold calling to husbands, and it is consistent:

a) "Husbands, love your wives as Christ loved the church and gave himself up for her" (verse 25).
b) "Even so, husbands should love their wives" (verse 28).
c) "However, let each one of you love his wife as himself" (verse 33).

Actually, the whole middle section of the passage is not about the submission of wives, but the calling of the husband to love his wife *unconditionally* as Christ loved the church. At the very least, when we hear of this passage, the calling of the husband to love his wife sacrificially *ought* to come to mind as often as wifely submission does.

But more importantly than that, both callings, that of the husband to the wife and that of the wife to the husband, are applications of what is the real theme of the text which is the analogy of human marriage to the church's relationship to Jesus Christ. That is the central issue and should not be clouded by our prejudices that we bring to the text. Notice the *five* repeated comparisons of the marriage of a husband and wife to the relationship of Christ with His church:

a) "For the husband is the head of the wife *as* Christ is the head of the church" (verse 23).

b) "*As* the church is subject to Christ, *so* let wives also be subject in everything" (verse 24).

c) "Husbands, love your wives *as* Christ loved the church and gave himself up for her" (verse 25).

d) "For no man ever hates his own flesh, but nourishes and cherishes it, *as* Christ does the church" (verse 29).

e) "This is a great mystery, and I take it to mean Christ and the church" (verse 32).

So how husbands and wives are to relate to each other is an appetizer of something much bigger, the relationship of Jesus Christ to His church. That is the Reality that marriage relationships should reflect. Even at the absolute best, they will pale compared to what we will experience in heaven when we all relate to our perfect Groom. That's why, when the Bible talks about heaven, it talks about a wedding feast, the Marriage of the Lamb, the wedding garments and other wedding talk.[251] That is the theme of the passage, and if we emphasize only one aspect of the application of that theme, we mis-use the Scripture and mis-apply it. We must not do that. As we dig into this text, let's remember that we are studying an appetizer, an analogy. In order to do justice to the analogy, and so honor to

---

[251] Again, I quote Jonathan Leeman: "God gave us sex to give us the faintest whiff of what our union with Christ will be like." <u>How the Nations Rage: Rethinking Faith and Politics in a Divided Age</u>. Thomas Nelson in association with Wolgemuth and Associates, Nashville, TN, c. 2018, p. 45.

Christ, we must apply the teaching on the roles with the definitions and weight that the Scriptures do. If we emphasize one as opposed to the other in a manner that Scripture does not, we are not submitting to Scripture.

As we said in the chapter on interpretation, understanding Scripture is not always a simple task. And none of us comes to the text as completely unbiased hungry learners. The fact is we are all sinners and so have the temptation to skew an interpretation to our advantage. It is certainly attractive for men to over-emphasize the duty of wives to submit. That can be very useful. It can also be attractive for wives to over-emphasize the duty of husbands to love their wives and sacrifice themselves for them. That, also, can be very useful. We, as humans, can be amazingly blind to our own sin. Or each one of us can attempt to fulfill our respective role to submit or to love and then view ourselves as martyrs, proud of how spiritual we are and how much better we are than others who do not follow the text so carefully as we do. We can be very clever in our sin! I know that too well from first-hand experience.

One important help in interpretation is to figure out how a proposition in a text relates to what comes right before it and right after it. Especially in the letters, there is a train of thought that needs to be followed. We seem to be habitual cross-referencers, attempting to see how a particular word or phrase or thought relates to a similar word or phrase or thought in another part of the Bible. We study the Bible sometimes like a person walking through a flower garden, picking individual flowers that are particularly attractive out of the whole garden. Topical studies are not without value, but it is far more valuable, even more necessary, in understanding a text to discern how the word or thought or proposition relates to what went right before it and to what comes right after, rather than to some other book in the Bible in a completely different context. That way, we, the readers, read the letter in the manner in which it was written, rather than as a bunch of unconnected thoughts.

The problem with Paul is that it is sometimes hard to know where to stop in following his train of thought backwards. His thinking is complex. The passage we are looking at does not stand by itself but is connected to what went before. That is particularly significant in the passage we are looking at because verse 22 ("Wives, be subject to your husbands, as to the Lord") does not even have the command "be subject" in the original language. Virtually all translations add the verb in its command form, taking it from verse 21. It is a general term describing how we relate to one another, or *should* relate to one another, if we are really filled with the Spirit.

If we back up to where Paul's thought begins, we really end up backing up to the beginning of the book. In chapter one, we have the lofty passage about the eternal purposes of God for us, that we who had first hoped in Christ have been destined and appointed to live for the praise of his glory. The apostle's desire for us is that we might know what is the hope to which we have been called, what are the riches of his glorious inheritance in the saints, and what is the immeasurable greatness of his power *in us* who believe,[252] and so on. The section ends with the apostle's acknowledgment of His power at work *in us* and His ability to do far more abundantly than all we ask or think.[253]

How does one follow that up? What do people look like who live out that vision? One would expect a people with such a lofty vision of life and life's purpose to be a wonderfully victorious and successful people, with smiles and joy and success in whatever they do. They would understand the "immeasurable greatness of his power *in us* who believe" and would be basking in the glorious inheritance from God the Father.

The beginning of the application that follows immediately from that text is jarring. "I therefore, a prisoner for the Lord...."[254] At first glance, one might think he is talking about being a "spiritual"

---

[252] Ephesians 1:11, 12, 18
[253] Ephesians 3:20
[254] Ephesians 4:1

prisoner for the Lord, someone who *really* belongs to Jesus. But no, the apostle is in the clinker, behind bars. With all the lofty purposes of God for us in eternity, how could the apostle—the author of those words—end up in jail? Even more so, in jail "for the Lord"? It seems to be God's will that the apostle is languishing behind bars. Jail is not a pleasant, comfortable place. How could God, who has blessed us with every spiritual blessing,[255] cause his main spokesman to be in jail?

What follows this is even more jarring, as it is a statement of what kind of people we *should* be as a result of God's work in our life. It is not a statement of victory, success, prosperity, ease of life, and smiles and joy and good parking places in the mall parking lot: "I… beg you to live a life worthy of the calling to which you have been called, with all lowliness and meekness, with patience, forbearing one another in love…."[256] The juxtaposition is significant. The picture of glory and unimaginable blessing followed by a lowly life in this world must be intentional and real. That is the tension we live with. Lowliness and meekness are Godly characteristics of all people, men and women alike. Those are marks of a spiritual person. Those are marks of a godly person. Those are marks of a mature person who knows who he is and who God is. That tension is forever present in us who are citizens of the glorious world to come but have to go to work Monday in this present fallen world. We may be victors in Christ, but this world is tough. We might even end up in prison "for the Lord." As time moves on and history grinds onward toward the End, that situation will become probably worse. In order to live a life in this world, with lowliness, meekness, and patience, we *must* keep in mind the blessing *awaiting* us in heaven. That is where our hope lies, and *waiting* for that hope is what will enable us to live life in this fallen world. This world is not our home.

Chapter 5, verses 1 and 2, begin a section of principles of the Christian life, with the specifics spelled out in the verses following.

[255] Ephesians 1:3
[256] Ephesians 4:1, 2

"Therefore, be imitators of God, as beloved children. And walk in love, as Christ loved us and gave himself up for us, a fragrant offering and sacrifice to God."[257] Following that statement are a number of specific examples of what that looks like, ending up with verse 18 and following: "And do not get drunk with wine, for that is debauchery; but be filled with the Spirit, addressing one another in psalms and hymns and spiritual songs, singing and making melody to the Lord with all your heart, always and for everything giving thanks in the name of our Lord Jesus Christ to God the Father. Be subject to one another out of reverence for Christ. Wives be subject to your husbands, as to the Lord. For the husband is the head of the wife as Christ is the head of the church, his body, and is himself its Savior. As the church is subject to Christ, so let wives also be subject in everything to their husbands. Husbands, love your wives, as Christ loved the church and gave himself up for her, that he might sanctify her, having cleansed her by the washing of water with the word, that he might present the church to himself in splendor, without spot or wrinkle or any such thing, that she might be holy and without blemish. Even so husbands should love their wives as their own bodies. He who loves his wife loves himself. For no man ever hates his own flesh, but nourishes and cherishes it, as Christ does the church, because we are members of his body. 'For this reason a man shall leave his father and mother and be joined to his wife, and the two shall become one.' This is a great mystery, and I take it to mean Christ and the church; however let each one of you love his wife as himself, and let the wife see that she respects her husband."[258]

Now, I always grimace when I hear a speaker say something like, "What the text *really* says…" and then refers to a Greek or Hebrew word or construction about which the hearers, like me, are totally clueless. I grimace because I have no idea of what the text *really* says

---

[257] Ephesians 5:1, 2
[258] Ephesians 5:17–33

and have little hope of discovering what the text *really* says because I do not know Greek or Hebrew. I commend the readers of this book to do your own homework and use the commentaries and the plethora of other Bible study aids to determine if what I am saying is correct. That's what I did.

The word "but" usually indicates a contrast. The command in verse 18 that is given in contrast to avoiding being drunk with wine is this: *"But* be filled with the Spirit," and it is followed by four present participles. They are:

1. Addressing one another in psalms and hymns and spiritual songs.
2. Singing and making melody to the Lord with all your heart.
3. Always and for everything giving thanks in the name of our Lord Jesus Christ.
4. Submitting to one another out of reverence for Christ.

The way the text reads, it seems as if these four present participles tell us what it looks like to be filled with the Spirit. A. Skevington Wood puts it this way: "The four participial clauses derive a certain imperative force from *plerousthe en pneumati,* 'be filled with the Spirit,' on which they depend. They are to be treated as coordinate rather than subordinate. They modify the subject and thus describe the condition of those who are continually being filled in the sphere of the Spirit.... [The] fourth participial clause *hypotassomenoi,* "submitting yourselves," is appended to *plerousthe,* "be filled," in verse 18. It supports the contention that syntactically this verse should be attached to what precedes. If he had meant to make a complete break, Paul would have employed an imperative. There is a close link with what follows, however, since "wives" is annexed without a verb of its own."[259]

---

[259] The Expositor's Bible Commentary, Frank E. Gaebelein, general editor, Zondervan Publishing House, Grand Rapids, MI, c. 1978, volume II, *Ephesians,* by A. Skevington Wood, pp. 74 and 79.

Now that may sound like Greek (some of it is), but what he is saying is what we said before—that the four present participles describe what behavioral qualities will be exhibited by someone who is filled with the Spirit. The first three are hardly controversial. The last one might be. One of the signs of a Spirit-filled person is a willingness to submit. That is a gender-neutral statement in the same way the other qualities of a Spirit-filled person are gender-neutral. That applies equally to men as it does to women. A person who needs to be in control or is "disposed to be contentious"[260] is not demonstrating qualities that the Spirit produces, no matter how gifted he or she might be. As we said in the chapter on "The Trinity, Hierarchy, and Equality," where we looked at the theme of submission in 1 Peter, submission *is* a Christian word, and one that should characterize all believers, both men and women.[261] That is not to say there is no authority structure in the Kingdom of God. Just the opposite is true. How could you have submission without authority? It is to say, however, that even authority is wielded with a submissive attitude. What that looks like may require a whole second book, but for now the best thing to do is to look at Jesus. He clearly functioned as an authority figure with His disciples, with everybody and everything, even the winds and the seas.

But He also functioned as a servant.

Submission, then, is not a concept that we, as followers of Jesus, as believers in the Bible, can dismiss. Men and women, both. Like it or not. Even those who trumpet the phrase "mutual submission" as the overriding description of the marriage relationship have to admit the presence of submission. Mutual submission does not mean you never have to submit to the wishes of your spouse against your own wishes. Submission is a mark of being filled with the Spirit. If you reject the idea of being submissive, then don't call yourself

[260] 1 Corinthians 11:16
[261] The Apostle Paul uses the word some 23 times in the New Testament.

a follower of Jesus or consider yourself filled with the Spirit. That applies equally to both genders.

The significance of the grammar, the present participles and their dependence on the command to be filled with the Spirit, indicates that what many translators have done with this text is really a translator's decision: to make a command out of a participle and to make it the topic sentence for what follows. "Submit to one another out of reverence for Christ" is not the topic sentence for the paragraph on the relationship of husbands and wives. Nor is it a command.[262] The grammar supports those assertions. However, the lack of a verb in verse 22 ties that verse to what goes before, so we cannot make a complete break from verse 21, "submitting to one another out of reverence to Christ," as if that concept does not apply to marriage. It does. In the Biblical model for marriage, there will be mutual submission, since a marriage of two Christians is a subset of the body of Christ and the text just said that "submitting to one another out of reverence to Christ" ought to characterize believers in the Body of Christ. There will be mutual submission in a healthy Christian marriage, just as there is mutual submission in the Body of Christ.[263]

---

[262] Some have made much of the fact that it is not a command, implying that that lessens its force, maybe to the point of denying any hierarchy at all. Like fruits of the Spirit, a submissive attitude is an outgrowth of the presence and activity of the Holy Spirit in a person. But the author does make a special application to wives. Why did the author insert "wives to husbands" instead of "spouses to each other"? If mutual submission summarizes the gender relationship in marriage, what is the point of saying, "wives to husbands" and not "husbands also to wives" or "spouses to each other"? It seems to me to be a required interpretive question to ask what Paul meant by inserting the phrase "wives to husbands" if the observation that there is no command indicates there is no hierarchy. Incidentally, in a parallel passage—Colossians 3:18—with much of the same content, the call of wives to submit to husbands *is* in the command form, and includes the phrase "in the Lord." That would seem to indicate that it is not just a temporary accommodation to the culture of the time.

[263] The present participle, "submitting to one another out of reverence to Christ," describes, along with the other three present participles, an action that should characterize the Body of Christ. Mutual submission *should be present*. Yet in the Body of Christ, which is characterized by mutual submission, there is still a hierarchy. There are still "elders who rule." Mutual submission does not eliminate a hierarchical structure. That is so important, let me say it again: Mutual submission does not eliminate a hierarchical structure. The Body of Christ is not entirely "mutually submissive", with hierarchy absent. But in our fallen world, that seems

But having said that, there are unique applications to wives and husbands, and they are gender-specific. Verse 22, as we have said, has no verb in the original. "Wives, be subject to your husbands, as to the Lord." The command, "be subject," is not there in the original, but as we said above, it really is a subset of the general characteristic of "being subject to one another." It is notable that the author applies that concept *only* to wives: "Wives to your husbands." Just as the Father is *never* revealed as submitting to the Son in the relationships in the Trinity, as those who most dislike that concept unconsciously revealed in their definitions of subordinationism,[264] so there are certain callings that are unique to the wife and to the husband. In a parallel passage in Colossians, Paul says that it is to their "own" husbands to which wives are to submit. So it seems this is about marriage, not secular culture at large. We need to notice that the whole point of this discussion is that marriage is not just another relationship between two humans. It is enormously bigger than that. It is a "great mystery," as the apostle said. If it was a mystery to him, how much more so to us! The mystery is that marriage is a reflection of Christ's relationship with His church.

Remember in the chapter on fingerprints and appetizers, I quoted from the Narnia Chronicles where the children are trying to convince the witch, who lives in the Underworld, about life in the Overworld? They find that they have to resort to *analogy* to try to describe to her what they think she has never seen. She, however, makes fun of them and accuses them of creating concepts that are nothing more than their small concepts, but enlarged. The term that was used to describe that supposed error was anthropomorphic projection. However, the opposite was, and is, true; because there is

incomprehensible to us. As I observed in the chapter on "The Trinity, Hierarchy, and Equality," for a group of humans to function, hierarchy is required. That is just reality. The reason it is reality, I believe, is that it is also a fingerprint of our creator who consists of a hierarchy of complete equals. We are created in His image. See footnote 103 on page 86 and pages 145-147 in chapter 5 on Genesis.

[264] See page 100 in this book in the chapter titled, "The Trinity, Hierarchy, and Equality," where I dealt with this.

248

an intelligent Creator, with a Design in His creation. And so there are fingerprints left in His creation that really point to the Bigger Reality in heaven that we are waiting for. That is the case rather than anthropomorphic projection, as some would accuse.

What we have in the "great mystery" here is probably the greatest fingerprint God has left on His creation. It is why I nearly always cry at weddings. There is something unimaginably profound and eternal about marriage. It is far bigger than what it appears—a signed piece of paper, exchanged rings, and the hope it will work out. It is nothing less than a picture of Jesus Christ's relationship with His people. In fact, the Greek word for church, *ekklesia*, is feminine. And so when the same author, Paul, prays for the churches with which he is acquainted, he prays that they might "know" God. He was not talking theology there (maybe partially) but relationship. It is the word used of Adam when it was said that "Adam knew Eve his wife and she conceived and bore Cain." It is the word for sexual intercourse. That God would stoop so low and lift us so high as to have such an intimate relationship with Him is beyond imagination.[265] So as we examine the relationship between and a man and a woman, a relationship which is described by Paul as analogous the relationship between Christ and His church, we are again on holy ground. Off with the shoes. It is the same ground as in Genesis 1:26 and 27 where the human creature, created as male and female, are three times described as being made in the image of God. *Three* times—one wonders if that number is significant.

Because it is such a lofty concept, we want to get it *right*. It might be an interesting study to see how many pages written about this topic have been historically devoted to the calling of wives to

---

[265] It is also in stark contrast to most Middle Eastern gods and goddesses, who viewed human beings as nasty little things who were to be avoided if possible. And, significantly, Middle Eastern deities were both male and female. So when the Bible reveals one God, it usually, but not always, speaks of that one God in masculine terms. That is very different from the cultures around Israel. I believe the Bible was not just revealed in a culture that we have now outgrown. One cannot blame the patriarchy of the Old Testament on the surrounding patriarchal culture. The Bible, then as now, is very counter-cultural.

submit versus the equally important calling of husbands to love their wives sacrificially *as Christ loved the church.* In my exceedingly brief experience, which probably is not representative, the balance seems to be heavily weighted toward wifely submission, with the husband's call to sacrificial love glossed over, apparently as if that is secondary. Maybe we think we've got that pretty well covered? I think not. In this passage, they each have corresponding roles, and we need to maintain a Biblical balance in discussing those roles. As we said before, this book is not about the "women's issue," as if the men have no problem here. No, it is about gender relationships. It's about how we relate, husband and wife, in marriage and in the church, and how that quality of relationship mysteriously reflects something much, much larger to the watching world.

Three things need to be said about these roles as we delve into them.

1. They are independent of one another. Both the role of the wife and the role of the husband are callings that each fulfills regardless of how the partner performs. The husband's call to love his wife and sacrifice himself for her is not conditional on her being a good wife to him. He is just called to do that. Period. The wife's calling to submit to the husband does not depend on his sacrificing himself for her. Period. These two roles are really sub-sets of the larger role that we are all called to, and that is to love our neighbor. It doesn't matter if our neighbor is mean and rude. In a sense, the love to which we are called, which is like God's love for us, is *blind.* There is nothing in the person being loved that earns our love. It's about us, not them. *While we were yet sinners,* God loved us.

There are, of course, common-sense issues and, frankly, personal safety issues, that come into play in certain instances that may be very complicated, and I leave those individual issues and their resolution to pastors as they care for their congregations. But we start with the principle and then look at the exceptions. And exceptions do exist.

2. The two roles are completely about callings to serve the other person. There is no mention of rights. This is not about conjugal rights, but conjugal duties to serve. Both partners are called to that. Both roles are completely about service, not about "legitimate" demands one might make of the partner.

3. They are counter-cultural. They were when Paul wrote them, and they still are. In Greco-Roman society, it was well recognized that wives had responsibilities to their husbands, but husbands had no responsibilities to their wives. It was a man's world. The wife was a servant and a mistress. That is definitely not the way Paul describes the Christian marriage, and so he was counter-cultural when he wrote this letter. Let's be done with this fear of offending our culture or worrying about hindering our evangelistic outreach by being so different. Paul did not worry about that, and we must not, either. Let's just live the way the Scriptures tell us, and we will be attractive by contrast.

Now, as we approach the teaching on marriage in Ephesians, I want to begin with the end. It is a mystery. That does not mean it is totally incomprehensible. But it is difficult. It is spiritually understood. By that I mean that it belongs to the Other World, the Kingdom of God, and so it will seem weird and strange. It *is* weird and strange. One of the liabilities of the current modern age in which we live is that if something is hard to understand, we tend to give up at the beginning. We don't like hard things. I ask you, the reader, to not be conformed to the world in this area. Rarely will I ask a person to be like me, but let's be attracted to the puzzle, instead of wearied by it at the start.

The main theme of the text, as we have already said, is that the relationship between a husband and wife is to reflect the relationship of Christ with the church. That crucial little word "as" appears four times, and Paul himself summarizes the issue by saying the whole thing is a mystery and refers to Christ and the church. So five times in 16 verses this concept is mentioned. Since there are two people involved, and since it is the very nature of their relationship to mirror the relationship of Jesus to the church, there are corresponding issues addressed to each of them—three of them, to be exact.[266]

Let's look at the different roles in the order the text does, which, I think, does not indicate any relative importance. As we noted, verse 21 ("being subject to one another out of reverence to Christ") is a present participle, one of four, clarifying what it looks like to be filled with the Spirit. Verse 22 ("Wives, to your husbands, as to the Lord") has no verb but takes its verb from the participle in verse 21, "being subject to one another." Verse 21 applies to everyone in the body of Christ. Verse 22 is intended for wives. From verse 21 we can say that men, of whom husbands are a subset, if they are filled with the Spirit, will be characterized as "being subject to one another" and, at times, one of the "one anothers" will be their wives. That would seem unquestionably to follow from verse 21. In the same manner, women, of whom wives are a subset, if they are filled with the Spirit, will be characterized as being "subject to one another," and, presumably, one of the "one anothers" will be their husbands. That would also seem to follow necessarily from verse 21. Therefore, both genders, in marriage, will at times be submissive to each other. Neither gender has the privilege of being what we would normally call the "boss," which, in our fallen world, means that submission goes one way and not the other. If you don't like the concept of being submissive to another person, you are probably not alone in that, but let's recognize it for what it is—sin, independence, and selfishness— and not mislabel it as "Biblical feminism" or "male leadership."

---

[266] For egalitarians who do not differentiate male/female roles, this is a problem. There is a difference between Christ and His Bride, the church. The difference is profound. To say there is no difference between the husband/wife role would then imply there is no difference between the Christ/church role, which is, of course, ludicrous.

However, only wives are specifically called to submit to the other party in the marriage, to their husbands. Husbands are never explicitly called to submit to their wives.[267] If mutual submission were the summary of the marriage relationship, which as I noted is not supported by the grammar, we should see *somewhere* specifically husbands called to submit to their wives. Those words are not found anywhere in the Bible.[268] And if mutual submission were the summary of the marriage relationship, then what is the purpose of verse 22, where wives alone are called to submit to their husbands and not the other way around? Why did the author even write that verse, especially since it would be contradictory to verse 21 if verse 21 were the summary of marriage? I suppose one could say that he is accommodating his culture at this point, but that is speculative, with nothing in the text to suggest that. And in fact, as I said before, what he is writing is already counter-cultural. No, while mutual submission does describe something in the marriage relationship, as it describes *all* relationships in the Body of Christ, if the members in the Body of Christ are Spirit-filled, there are still roles unique to each gender, and those roles reflect the different roles of Christ in relationship to His church. *That* picture is the summary of the marriage relationship, not mutual submission. It seems clear that the relationship of Christ and his church is not one of mutual submission. But, as we saw (and I beg your forgiveness

---

[267] Again, we should not be surprised at this. It is not new. In the chapter on the Trinity, Hierarchy, and Equality, I noted that the Father is never revealed as submitting to the Son. Having said that, in the Trinity, as in marriage, the relationship cannot be described as a boss-employee relationship, with authority going one way. Instead they serve one another. Our ability or inability to comprehend this other-worldly concept is central to this whole issue. If we see "headship" as merely authority, then we are left with the husband "ruling," which was a result of the fall and which is not a prescription of how God wants Godly husbands to treat their wives but is a description of life after the fall.

[268] So I find myself perplexed with Dr. David Scholer's comment in his article, "Dealing with Abuse," on the web site *God's Word to Women*. "I am fully convinced that the Bible does not institute, undergird, or teach male headship in either the traditionalist or complementarian forms of evangelical thought." Please see https://godswordtowomen.org/scholer.htm. Now I can see how one could avoid the submission of women by re-defining what headship is, but when the Bible *always, without exception* describes the male as the head in a relationship and calls on the wife to submit, I don't understand how he can say it doesn't teach male headship.

for belaboring this point, but it is so important to understand), Christ certainly *serves* the church, even as He headed toward the Cross, and the disciples were at their unbelievable height (or depth) of unworthiness. At that point in the narrative, they asked Him to serve them, and He readily agreed. That is our model. *He* is our model. The Biblical idea of headship includes servanthood as much as authority. It includes both.

Two times the wife is called to submit to her husband. One time, at the end of the text, she is called to "respect" her husband. In verse 23, we are told *why* the wife is to submit to her husband. That verse begins with the word "for," used in the sense of "because." "For the husband is the head of the wife *as* Christ is the head of the church." The wife is to submit not because the husband is bigger or more spiritual or less vulnerable to deception or smarter or more mechanical or more anything, but because he *represents* something—the headship of Christ to His church. I want to say that again: it's not about his being superior in any way; it's about who he is representative of. The grammar is crucial. The wife is to submit herself to her husband *because* he is the head in the relationship. And let me say this again: it is not because he is superior in any way.

There have been many pages written about what headship in the New Testament means. There have been many studies of how the word *kephale* is used in its secular context, the thinking being that that information will help us to understand the Bible. Here, we need to let the Bible define what "headship" looks like in the Kingdom of God and not import secular definitions into the Kingdom. As I said before, it is a common practice for the Biblical writers to take a secular word and then add to or change the definition as they apply it to the Kingdom of God. Whether or not *kephale* included authority in secular usage may be helpful, or it may not. But here it is clear that the reason the wife is to submit to the husband is *because* he is the head. That's just what the words say. "Wives, be subject to your husbands [or 'wives, to your husbands' taking the 'being subject" from verse 21] as to the Lord. *For* the husband is the head

254

of the wife as Christ is the head of the church."[269] I see no other way to understand that verse. The reason why the wife is to submit to her husband is *because* he is the head of the relationship.[270] There is something about the position of being the head in a relationship that calls the other person to be submissive. And that understanding certainly fits with the analogy of Christ and the church. How can we say that Christ does not have authority over His church?[271] If we say that *kephale* does not include authority, then we by necessity remove Jesus from having authority over His church, which he bought with His own shed blood. If we say the wife is not called to submit herself to the husband, we have to explain away the effect-to-cause relationship indicated by the word "for" in verse 23. The relationship of the husband to the wife is analogous to the relationship of Christ and His Church.[272]

When my wife and I got married, we were intentional about using the traditional vows that included the now anachronistic phrase "promise to obey" on the part of the wife. Don't think I didn't hear about that when I went back to work at my secular job in a pharmacy after we got back from our honeymoon. A number of my co-workers attended, and they let me know very quickly their opinion of that word. Frankly, in retrospect, I wish we had not used that word, despite its long tradition in the wedding vows. The reason has nothing to do with what other people thought of it, but the fact that it is not a Biblical word. In the passage we are looking

---

[269] Ephesians 5:22, 23

[270] I have not read one egalitarian author who deals with this effect-to-cause relationship.

[271] That is the problem with taking verse 21, "be subject to one another out of reverence to Christ," as the topic sentence for the paragraph following on marriage and so describing the marriage relationship as one of complete mutuality. If there is no authority in the understanding of position of "head" and so mutuality describes the marriage relationship, then by necessity it also describes the relationship of Christ with the Church. That is hardly a relationship of mutuality.

[272] So I find myself scratching my head at Gilbert Bilezikian's statement, "The New Testament contains no text where Christ's headship to the church connotes a relationship of authority. Likewise, the New Testament contains no text where a husband's headship to his wife connotes a relationship of authority." From the appendix to <u>Beyond Sex Roles</u>, 2nd edition. (Grand Rapids, MI: Baker Book House, 1990, pp. 215–252.)

at, farther on, children are told to obey their parents. But that is not the word used to describe how wives are to relate to their husbands. The author's choice of a different word is, I think, significant and intentional. Wives are told to submit themselves. They are not told to obey. There is a difference.

There is also another very significant difference between "submit" and "obey," as they are used in this passage. There is a difference in "voice" of the verb.

I remember learning about the "voice" of a verb both in studying English grammar and in taking a foreign language. There is an active voice where the subject acts upon the direct object. For example, "I throw the ball." And there is the passive voice where the subject is acted upon. For example, "The ball is thrown by me." In Greek, there is another voice—one that we do not have in English—called the middle voice. In that construction, the subject acts upon itself. For example, "The ball throws itself." The way it is translated in our text in verse 24 in the RSV is this way: "As the church is subject to Christ, *so let wives also be subject* in everything to their husbands." What the author really is saying is that wives should subject themselves to their husbands. It is in the middle voice. It is the wife's calling. The command is not given to husbands to act upon their wives, an active voice verb. "Husbands make your wives submissive to yourself." That's *not* it. Nor is it given in the passive voice: "Wives, be ruled by your husbands." That's not it, either. The command is actually given to wives in the middle voice: they are to submit themselves to their husbands. There is a significant difference. The action belongs to the wife, not the husband. The husband's calling is not to make his wife submissive, but to love his wife as Christ loves the church and also as he loves himself. The fact that the role of submission is something she does herself and not something imposed on her by a "superior" husband implies equality of personhood. It implies that the role is one she chooses to shoulder rather than one forced upon her by a "higher" authority. Do I mean to imply that she therefore may disregard that calling if she doesn't like it? No. That directive comes with apostolic authority. But I do mean to imply that this role is one she chooses out of loyalty to a Biblical worldview, rather than out of submission to a superior, more knowledgeable husband. It is done out of a willingness to be part of God's revelation to the world, a revelation of the church's same loving submission to Christ. It is not the same as a child's obedience to its parents.

So what does Biblical headship look like? Is it synonymous with "authority," as many have said? Is it the same as "boss"? Is it the same as "leader"? Is it the same as "lord"? That was the word that the young pastor used in the sermon I heard as a young man just out of college.

Very often the husband has been described as the leader, the one held accountable for the household, the spiritual leader of the marriage and the family. And so "leader" has come to mean the same thing and to be substituted for "head." "In the home, Biblical headship is the husband's divine calling to take primary responsibility for Christ-like *leadership*, protection, and provision." "Submission refers to a wife's divine calling to honor and affirm her husband's *leadership* and help carry it through according to her gifts.... We speak of her disposition to yield to her husband's guidance and her inclination to follow his *leadership*."[273]

However, the husband is never called "the leader" in the Bible. We have tended to use the two words, "leader" and "head," as synonymous. They are not. In our world, the leader is the decision-maker, the one who really understands, he who gives guidance, the one with vision who determines the direction the "followers" will go in. And so the wife, by default, becomes the follower, the one who does not have the vision and understanding to be the leader. And, frankly, the inferior one in the partnership of marriage. Rarely has it been described that crudely, but that, unfortunately, is some of

---

[273] Recovering Biblical Manhood and Womanhood, Crossway Books, a division of Good News Publishers, Wheaton, IL 60187, c. 1991, both quotations from page 61 in an article entitled, "An Overview of Central Concerns: Questions and Answers," by John Piper and Wayne Grudem.

the baggage of using the word "leader' for the husband instead of "head."[274]

On page 50 of the book <u>Recovering Biblical Manhood and Womanhood</u>, a hypothetical situation is presented. "A housewife in her backyard may be asked by a man how to get to the freeway. At that point, she is giving a kind of leadership. She has superior knowledge that the man needs, and he submits himself to her guidance. But we all know that there is a way for that housewife to direct the man that neither of them feels their mature femininity or masculinity compromised. It is not a contradiction to speak of certain kinds of influence coming from women to men in ways that affirm the responsibility of men to provide a pattern of strength and initiative." What is interesting about this comment is that giving directions to the freeway is giving a "kind of leadership" because of her "superior knowledge." Now, to the credit of the author of that statement, his point is that it is perfectly appropriate for her to do that, in a way that does not compromise her "femininity" or his "masculinity." But my point is that leadership, here defined as "superior knowledge," a better understanding of the situation—how to get to the freeway—is the word used of the male's role in relation to females, and that, I think, is not synonymous with the Biblical view of headship. Nor do I think the issue is "to not compromise femininity or masculinity," but merely to be courteously helpful and not arrogant. Since the male is the "leader" and since leadership is portrayed as having superior understanding, it is difficult not to conclude that wives have an inferior understanding and so are not fit for "leadership." The fact is, "leader" is not a neutral word; it implies

---

[274] So I must respectfully part company from the thinking in <u>Recovering Biblical Manhood and Womanhood</u> on page 63: "When the headship of the husband is given as the *ground* for the submission of the wife, the most natural understanding is that headship signifies some kind of leadership." The italics are not mine but the author's. No, rather than jumping from the statement that, since the wife is called to submit, therefore the husband is called to lead, we must instead let the Bible define the role of the head rather than assume it to be a position of leadership. Biblical thinking is that, if the wife is called to submit, so the husband is called to function as the head—with the Bible defining what head means.

superior competence. It also implies inferior competence for those condemned to be followers—women.

So there are at least three problems with referring to the husband's role as one of leadership and claiming Biblical support for that view:

1. The Bible never uses that term to refer to the husband.

2. Being the leader implies superior knowledge and understanding. That is who we look to as leaders in our culture. In any group, the leader should be superior in understanding and in vision. To say that the natural role and the Biblical role of the male is that of leadership and that that role is denied to women implies inferiority of women. It implies inferiority of knowledge, vision, and understanding for females. That's why "leader" is not the appropriate term for the husband in a marriage relationship. Women are not inferior to men. I remind you of all the statements at the beginning of the chapter on "The Trinity, Hierarchy, and Equality" when various people said that one cannot be both submissive and equal. In their minds, hierarchy eliminates equality. If we describe the male role as one of *leadership*, then I would have to agree with them. If the husband is always the leader, it is difficult not to view the wife as unfit for leadership, not as mature, as knowledgeable, or insightful, not capable of leading, since her calling is only to follow.

3. There is an even more serious problem, however. In 1 Corinthians 11:3, which we have already studied, God is the head of Christ. If we define headship as being the leader, then it would follow that Jesus, who is the "follower," would be inferior to the Father, which, of course, is heretical. Headship describes the role of God to Jesus, Jesus to the church, and the husband to the wife. If "leadership" is synonymous with "headship," then that implies that Jesus is only fit to follow. That cannot be true.

Gender relationships are fingerprints of two specific relationships in the Kingdom of God. One is the relationship between the three persons of the Trinity. That is taught in 1 Corinthians 11. "But I want you to understand that the head of every man is Christ, the head of a woman is her husband, and the head of Christ is God."[275] So headship describes both the relationship of the Godhead to Christ and the relationship of a husband to his wife. God is not described as being the leader of Christ. That just doesn't "feel" right, does it? It doesn't feel right because that word is inadequate to describe the relationship of the Father with the Son. Yet that's exactly what Dr. Wayne Grudem says: "Here, Paul says [referring to 1 Corinthians 11:3] that, just as in the Trinity the Father is the *leader* and has authority over the Son, so in marriage the husband is the *leader* and has authority over his wife."[276] (The italics are mine, not the author's.) The reason that doesn't *feel* right is because it's *not* right. Headship is a more nurturing, servanthood-oriented, self-denying role than one that is synonymous with authority—the one who decides which way to go. Now some may say that, when we talk about Biblical leadership, that is what is involved, and hopefully, that is true. However, when we use the word "leader" as synonymous with "head," there are several issues raised:

1. It, rightfully, needs to be qualified as a servant-like, unselfish style of leadership. It also needs to be defined as a *nurturing* role rather than just a role of authority, the "boss."
2. We are using a word that non-believers, or those who are Biblically uneducated, just will not understand correctly.
3. We are using a word that, really, is synonymous with the curse where the man is described as being the "ruler" over the woman. As we have said before, that is not a negative

---

[275] 1 Corinthians 11:3. That verse actually, I think, explains and unfolds what is hinted at in Genesis 1:26 & 27 where the man and woman, uniquely, are described as being created in the image of a plural God. See pages 144 to 145 in the chapter titled "Beginnings" in this book.
[276] Wayne Grudem, Evangelical Feminism: A New Path to Liberalism?, Crossway Books, Wheaton, IL, c. 2006, pp. 116, 208. Both pages say exactly the same thing.

word meaning dictator or despot. It just means the man is "in charge" or, really, the "leader."

4. We are using a word the Bible does not use.

There is a second relationship of which gender relationships are a fingerprint, and that is the relationship of Christ to his Bride, the church. That is precisely what the current passage we are studying teaches. In both texts, this text and the one in 1 Corinthians 11, the husband is called the "head," never the "leader." Jesus also is never described merely as the "leader" of the church, only the head. The words are just not interchangeable.

I admit the possibility of my misunderstanding the nature of the roles traditionally taught by Bible believing Christians. It is difficult for me to pin down where I have absorbed what the role of the husband looks like. But my sense is that, among Christians who presume to take the Bible "literally," the role of the husband, the "head," the "leader," is best summarized by the phrase, "A man's home is his castle," and, by implication, he is the king. He is the leader, the decision-maker, the "spiritual leader." He makes the decisions, and the wife, and everyone else, follows.

Susan Sumner in her book describes a situation[277] where a Christian wife and husband were disagreeing on the weighty subject of whether or not to get a dog. He wanted one. She didn't. The duty of caring for the dog would be almost exclusively hers. The husband decisively told her that as the head in the relationship he wanted the dog and felt they should get it, and, despite her protestations, they did. And she took care of it.

There is another story in the same book that tells a story of the age-old "hot water controversy" that plagues many households in modern America. The hot water tank was not adequate to supply hot showers for everybody in the household at the same time—in this case, the husband and the wife. If the husband is the head of

---

[277] Susan Sumner, Men and Women in the Church, InterVarsity Press, PO Box 1400, Downers Grove, IL 60515, c. 2003, pp. 200ff.

the wife, who gets the hot water? In this case (this was a Christian marriage, and they both believed in the authority of the Bible in their lives), they *both* agreed that the husband, as the "head," got the hot shower. The wife got the lukewarm shower. Or worse.

I was talking with a young associate pastor who had been recently married. He said that his senior pastor had given him the advice that, early on in their marriage relationship, he needed to establish that he, the husband, was the head, that is, the authority. Pick something, he said, pick anything, and make that an issue. Even if it is something like whether you roll the toilet paper from the top or the bottom of the roll. Make an issue of that and demand obedience on that issue in order to make a point. That would establish him as the head.

The book How I Changed My Mind about Women in Leadership is very helpful in understanding the pain and, frankly, oppression, perpetrated onto women in the Christian church. It ought to be required reading for anybody who desires to work this issue through. In one of the articles, authored by Stuart and Jill Briscoe, the marriage of one of the author's parents is described: "Like most young people I spent little—if any—time studying my parents' marriage, but I was aware on occasion that my mother would express her opinion, but usually my father would get what he wanted. I learned somewhere along the line it had something to do with 'submission.'"[278]

Now, I have said before, we all have an amazing ability to misinterpret Scripture. I don't give these examples with an arrogant air to show how wrong other people can be. I offer these true examples to show how Bible-believing Christians have swallowed as Biblical doctrine what, I believe, is not Biblical doctrine. Does the husband getting the hot shower while the wife gets the cold one sound like something Jesus would do? Does getting a dog, which the husband wanted over the wife's protestations, and then her taking the responsibility for the care of the adopted animal sound

---

[278] How I Changed my Mind About Women in Leadership, from the article entitled, "Buried Talents," by Stuart and Jill Briscoe. Zondervan, Grand Rapids, MI, c. 2010, p. 61.

God, Gender, and a Fallen World

like something Jesus would do? Does making an issue of how one unrolls the toilet paper to make the point of who is the authority sound like something Jesus would do?

I hope we all see these real-life examples as mistaken applications of the concept of the headship of the husband. These were all Bible-believing Christians. But note that, in all the examples, the concept of the head was the boss. The decision-maker. He called the shots. And, conveniently, he called the shots in a way that would serve him best. If *he* wanted a dog, then *they* got a dog. If there was not enough hot water for a shower for *both* of them, then *he* got the hot shower. Being the head meant that the husband had the authority or needed to establish that authority by such a non-essential as how you unroll the toilet paper when you're sitting on the throne (pardon the pun).

I think that both the complementarians and the egalitarians have it wrong to some degree. The egalitarians think it is wrong for one gender to be called the head and not the other—even though that's exactly what the Bible does. It is unjust to call wives to submit to their husbands. It is demeaning to be called a helpmate to the husband. I think they miss the fact that in the Kingdom of God the servant is the highest role, and the most common use of the word "helper" in the Old Testament is to refer to God Almighty as He relates to us humans. To be a servant is to follow in the footsteps of Jesus himself. We should not struggle with being called to serve another.

The complementarians have it wrong in two ways. One is thinking that headship means the one making the rules. He is the boss. The other is in thinking that submission only applies to females and not to males. Even though headship uniquely describes the husband, that does not mean he is exempt from serving his wife. The husband is to the wife as Christ is to the church. Jesus was a servant to the church. He died for her. So the husband, as the head, does not have the role of choosing the best for himself and letting

263

the wife do with what is left. That is wrong and unBiblical. And far too common.

So what is the role of the husband to the wife, this role that is defined as "headship," this role to which the wife is to submit herself "as to the Lord"?

a) "Husbands, love your wives as Christ loved the church and gave Himself up for her" (verse 25).
b) "Husbands should love their wives as their own bodies" (verse 28).
c) "Let each of you love his wife as himself" (verse 33).

The calling of the husband is to love his wife, to sacrifice himself for her unconditionally, in the same way that Christ did for the church. Well, of course. Is that not obvious? But then why all the argument about the meaning of *kephale* as "authority"? Why is there so little discussion about how the husband is to love his wife? I very much appreciated Dan Allender's answer to the question posed to him about what it means to be the "head" in the marriage relationship.[279] He said the "head" is the first to die. The first to sacrifice himself for the good of others, especially those to whom he is fulfilling the role of "head." Biblically, the one who fulfills the role of "head" is a servant who has authority, but not authority to call the shots to benefit *him*. Traditionally, that is not the way headship or, especially, leadership has been understood. Here is what one person observed: "The irony is that within the Christian community it is wives who are told to sacrifice themselves for their husbands. Not the husband, but the wife is repeatedly told to give up her agenda and adjust her life to his."[280]

Headship is not a calling to be a "boss" or even to be the "leader."

---

[279] From "Marriage: Life after I do (Conversations with Donald Miller and Dr. Dan Allender and Dr. Tremper Longman) Convergence DVD series by Creative Trust Media, 5141 Virginia Way, Brentwood, TN
[280] Sarah Sumner, <u>Men and Women in the Church</u>, InterVarsity Press, Downers Grove, IL, c. 2003, p. 170.

That word is never used of the husband, though there will be times when his role will certainly contain aspects of what we define as leadership. The wife is called to submit. In belaboring this point, I do not want to be misunderstood as denying the wife's calling to submit to her husband. That is her clear calling.

But the calling of the husband is much larger than merely being the leader, the decision-maker, the *authority*. As believers in the authority of Scripture, we must let the Scriptures define the roles and not the fallen world we live in.[281] That is not easy, as there is a constant tendency to confuse what Scripture says with the values of where we live, the kingdom of this world. So we must sear into our thinking the three-fold calling of the husband as the head— and that word *does include* authority. In that position of authority, of headship, he is to love his wife as Christ loved the church and sacrificed Himself for Her. That's what it means to be the head. And so the senior pastor who advised his newly married associate that he needed to establish himself as the head of the relationship by making an issue of something as irrelevant as how you unroll the toilet paper was *really* missing the point. Why not establish yourself as the head by loving your wife as well as you possibly can? Is that not how the Scripture defines headship—a servant with authority? Then her calling is to figure out how to submit to the husband God gave her. But the loving aspect of the definition was conveniently left out. And this was a pastor who would argue vehemently, and did argue vehemently, about the importance of Scripture and would deny people the term "evangelical" if they did not hold the same view of Scripture he did.

The calling of the wife is to submit to her husband, in the same way as the church does (or should) submit to Christ. Two times she is called to submit to her husband, and lastly she is called to respect

---

[281] That is the limitation of all the word studies of what *kephale* meant in common usage in Paul's time. They are helpful, but not definitive. Paul uses the word with a very different definition. Translation is rarely, if ever, merely substituting one word in one language for a word in another language that has an identical meaning.

him. That is her job. She is not the head. That's the mystery and the high calling of both the husband and wife. It's a team calling, of two equals. And it's a calling that will model to the unbelieving world something so bizarre and unworldly and *beautiful* that it will be attractive by its peculiarity and quality. And in the long run, it will, or should, point people to something much bigger—a plural Godhead who is the Real Thing of which marriage is only an appetizer, and to a quality of relationship with His people that is amazing, to say the least.[282]

I know this will raise questions in all our minds. Does that mean a wife needs to be submissive to a husband who is a selfish, smelly creep? I'm afraid the answer is yes. However, it is not unsubmissive to ask a husband to change his habits. But there is a flip-side to that: does it mean a husband needs to love and serve a wife who is a drama queen, has 52 pairs of shoes, and is constantly unsatisfied? I'm afraid the answer is yes. As Christians, we are called to do what is *right*, and the result will not always be a rose garden. Look at our Savior. Where did it get him? Were His disciples always easy to love? Were the people around him easy to love? As He went to the cross, sacrificing Himself so we could escape the penalty for our sins, and as in the process people called Him names, spat on Him, mocked Him, stripped him of his clothes, and then gambled for his robe, how did He act?

---

[282] As mentioned in the Introduction, this is not about the "women's" issue. It's about gender— God's purpose in it. An example of what I want to avoid is the book titled Women, Authority, and the Bible, which I have quoted several times. It is a collection of articles and responses by twenty very well known Christian scholars of today. I would say it is, on the whole, on the egalitarian side of the spectrum. What intrigues me is the title—as if it were only a women's issue. "*Women*, Authority, and the Bible." On the back cover, the book is described as "Essential reading for all concerned about women in the church." Even Gilbert Bilezikian's book, Beyond Sex Roles, an intensely anti-complementarian book, has the subtitle, "What the Bible says about a Woman's place in Church and Family." I fail to see how you can talk about one gender without talking about the other. I do not say that as a male out of a sense of being "left out," but out of an understanding that you cannot talk about one gender without talking about the other. Do the men have no need to grow here? Ironically, it seems these egalitarians display the unconscious patriarchialism which they so indignantly critique.

We've all experienced *mystery*. For me it often happened in my college classes. Sometimes things are just hard to comprehend, particularly when it is a concept belonging to a foreign system like the Kingdom of God. So Nicodemus struggled and apparently did not get what Jesus was talking about. It's like looking at a picture puzzle, knowing that, in the picture, there is something hidden and you look at it and look at it, and suddenly you see it plain as day and you wonder how you could have failed to see it before.

Paul ends this passage on marriage by saying that it is a *mystery*[283] and that it has to do with oneness. We have already talked about "Oneness" earlier. That word applies to the Trinity, to the body of Christ, and to marriage. It's something that is difficult to understand. The text does not say that husbands should love their wives *as if* they were their own bodies.[284] In fact, says the apostle, the husband who does love his wife really loves himself. "He who loves his wife loves himself." There is a very profound and easily missed difference between "a husband should love his wife *as if* she were his own body" and "he who loves his wife loves himself." Why he says what he says only makes sense in light of the verse directly following, which Paul quotes from Genesis. "For this reason a man shall leave his father and mother and be joined to his wife, and the *two* shall be come *one*."[285] As we said in the chapter on Beginnings, it's not that the two come together; they actually become *one*. They are no longer *two* but *one*. Because of that, a man is really loving himself when he loves his wife—because they are *one*. He should nourish and cherish his wife "*as* Christ does the church, *because* we are members of his body."[286] Christ does not love the church *as if* we were members of His body. He loves the church *because* we are members of His body.

---

[283] This mystery, the mystery of the image of Christ and His Bride, the church, which is mirrored in this world as the relationship between a husband and a bride, would need to be deleted from Scripture by those egalitarians who would promote complete mutuality between a husband and wife. There is definitely not mutuality between Christ and His church.

[284] Ephesians 4:28

[285] Genesis 2:24

[286] Ephesians 4:30

So husbands are not called to love their wives *as if* they were loving their own bodies, but in loving their wives, they *are*, in fact, loving their own bodies. They really are one, even though there are two people in the oneness. The concept is the same as the "oneness" of God. "Hear, O Israel. The Lord our God is One Lord."[287] Yet God is still plural, a Trinity, even though God is One. In the same way, in marriage, two become one. So the idea of a being who is somehow plural yet still one describes both the Triune God and a husband and wife in marriage.[288] And that is not surprising, since one was created in the image of the other, according to Genesis 1. Marriage, then, is not just a union, but a Re-union. Just as God made Two out of One when He created the woman out of the man, so in marriage, the two are re-united to become one again. Not just together, but One. This is a profound mystery, a great mystery, a sacred mystery.

So the church is the Bride of Christ. The marriage between a husband and a wife is to reflect the relationship of Christ to His church. Unity in plurality. Two working together as one, as in Genesis 1, where a plural noun takes a singular verb. After the fall, all marriages fall short of the Design, but the Design is still there and, even though we all fall short, we will function best when we attempt to follow the Design. That's a high calling because we are all sinners, and so such a calling is beyond our ability. But it is still our calling and, perhaps, with God's help and our own determination to live for His kingdom *instead of ourselves*, we can grow together and closer to God.

With God's help.
Definitely with God's help.

---

[287] Deuteronomy 6:4
[288] It also describes, or should describe, the Body of Christ.

7

THE CITY WHERE DIANA WAS KING

Part B
1 Timothy 2:1 to 15

"The woman taught once, and ruined all. On this account therefore he saith, let her not teach. But what is it to other women, that she suffered this? It certainly concerns them; for the sex is weak and fickle, and he is speaking of the sex collectively."[289]

"And [Satan] first tried his deceit upon the woman making his assault upon the weaker part of that human alliance, that he might gradually gain the whole, and not supposing that the man would readily give ear to him or be deceived, but that he might yield to the error of the woman. For not without significance did the apostle say, 'And Adam was not deceived, but the woman being deceived was in the transgression.'"[290]

---

[289] John Chrysostom, "Homilies on Timothy" (Homilies 8-9) in *A Select Library of the Nicene and Post-Nicene Fathers of the Christian Church,* 1ˢᵗ series, ed. Phillip Schaff (1886-1890; reprint, Grand Rapids, MI: Eerdmans, 1976) 13:435 (source: Slaves, Women & Homosexuals, William Webb, p. 262).

[290] Augustine, City of God, ibid. 2:272 (source: William Webb, p. 263).

"That a man endowed with a spiritual mind could have believed this [the lie of the serpent] is astonishing. And just because it is impossible to believe it, woman was given to man, woman who was of small intelligence and who perhaps still lives more in accordance with the promptings of the inferior flesh than by the superior reason."[291]

Churches change. Like athletic teams, the personnel are constantly moving on and new people are joining. So a church may change its character over the passage of time as pastors change, elders change, and members move on. I've been a member of my church for about 45 years. Many people have changed; some have died and gone to heaven; some have moved away; some have left in disappointment or disgust; leadership has changed; our constitution has changed; our building has changed. Our statement of faith has not. I hope it is all for the better; history will tell.

As I observed in the last chapter, the church at Ephesus warrants more text than any other church in the New Testament. Both its birth (Acts 19:1 through 20) and its impending death (Revelation 2:1 through 7) are recorded. In between we have three letters from Paul to the middle-aged church: the letter intended for the church at Ephesus and the two letters to its young pastor, Timothy. So we have an opportunity to watch this New Testament church change and to see how it responds.

The birth of the church as recorded in Acts 19 was tumultuous. It is recorded that many people became believers, also that fear fell upon both the Jews and the Greeks, and "the name of the Lord Jesus was extolled. Many of those who were now believers came confessing sin and divulging their practices. And a number of those who practiced magic arts brought their books and burned them in the sight of all.

---

[291] Augustine, *Literary Commentary on Genesis 11.42*. Quoted in the article, "Dealing with Abuse," by Dr. David M. Schuler, found on the website God's Word to Women. See https://godswordtowomen.org/scholer.htm. He is quoting Rita-Lou Clark in *Pastoral Care of Battered Women*, Philadelphia: Westminster, 1986, pp. 61–85.

They counted the value of them and found it came to fifty thousand pieces of silver."²⁹² That is no small bonfire! There must have been an enormous practice of witchcraft present in Ephesus, and as a result of the many conversions there was a huge bonfire of books. There also came a man named Demetrius, a silversmith, one of many who made their living by making silver shrines of Artemis. Unfortunately for him, the number of conversions to Jesus, and away from Artemis, was so large that the silversmiths were afraid of going out of business. In an amazing display of illogical reasoning, they decided to have a riot. Paul wished to talk to the crowd, but his disciples refused to let him. It is recorded that for two hours the crowd shouted, "Great is Artemis of the Ephesians!" Eventually the town clerk quieted them down and they dispersed.

Paul exhorted the disciples and then left.

Some time later, we don't know for sure how long, from Miletus he called the elders of the church (significantly, they had already formed some sort of rudimentary government) to speak with them one last time. In a very emotional address, he warned them, "Take heed to yourselves and to all the flock, in which the Holy Spirit has made you guardians, to feed the church of the Lord, which he obtained with his own blood. I know that after my departure fierce wolves will come in among you, not sparing the flock; and from them among your own selves will arise men speaking perverse things, to draw away the disciples after them."²⁹³

That is a significant prophecy. In fact, the very thing he predicted came to pass. In the book of Revelation, in the Risen Lord's evaluation of the church, it is recorded of this church that they "cannot bear

---

²⁹² Acts 19:17–20
²⁹³ Acts 20:28–30. The word translated as "men" in the phrase, "and from them among your own selves will arise *men* speaking perverse things...," is the word *aner*, meaning males. So the prophecy is that heresy would come through males. In fact, Paul names six males in this letter who have strayed doctrinally, but he names no women. Apparently women are not more theologically inept than men, as the quotations at the beginning of this chapter indicate. If it is men who are straying theologically, that raises a question why Paul would prohibit women from teaching men. Maybe there is something different going on than avoiding being culturally offensive or women being more susceptible to theological error.

evil men but have tested those who call themselves apostles but are not and found them to be false."[294] There were, apparently, over the lifespan of this church, some who called themselves apostles but were not. Actually, the books of 1 and 2 Timothy were written to counteract the false teaching of these false apostles whom Paul had predicted. The church was smart enough to recognize their scam, tested them, and disqualified them as teachers. That was good! They were right in doing that. In fact, a little farther down in the last words of Jesus to the church at Ephesus, in Revelation 2:6, Jesus compliments them for hate! "Yet this you have, you hate the works of the Nicolaitans, which I also hate." It is not known for sure who this group was, although there is considerable speculation that it was a group of followers of one of the first deacons chosen in Acts 6:5 named Nicolaus. Tradition has it that he fell into the temptation of an early heresy called antinomianism, which taught that God's grace was infinite and so we may go ahead and sin flagrantly. It doesn't matter because God will forgive. That clearly is not a doctrine found in the Scriptures, and so it was appropriate to stand firm against it. The presence of that heresy is largely tradition and may or may not be true. However, it is true is that, even though the church stood firm against the flood of wrong doctrine, the cost was enormous. Not a cost in lost lives or physical suffering. Not that. There was a different cost to the church. Jesus says to them at the end of the story, "I have this against you, that you abandoned the love that you had at first."[295] In the midst of the battle for doctrine, they became loveless and cold. It's an extremely sad ending to the story of the church at Ephesus.

As we open to 1 Timothy, we find the church in the midst of the battle against heresy that Paul had predicted in the book of Acts, and from which we find the wreckage in the book of Revelation. The conflict first shows up as a strange charge given by Paul to the pastor, a young man named Timothy. It shows up immediately after

---

[294] Revelation 2:2
[295] Revelation 2:4

the normal introduction. He was to shut some people up. In verse three, Paul says that when he left he urged Timothy to charge certain people not to teach any different doctrine, nor to occupy themselves with endless myths and speculations.[296] There were persons present in the church at Ephesus who "have wandered away into vain discussion, desiring to be teachers of the law, without understanding either what they are saying or the things about which they make assertions."[297] Those are strong words! Paul named a couple of them: "Certain persons have made a shipwreck of their faith, among them Hymenaeus and Alexander, whom I have delivered to Satan that they may learn not to blaspheme."[298] At the time of writing to Timothy, this was a church in the midst of a bloody spiritual battle. The wolves, as predicted, had arrived and were already at work.

The exact nature of the battle is not really clear, but we can draw some hints from what Paul writes to Timothy:

1. Some were teaching a different doctrine. That is a big deal. (1:3)
2. Some were occupied with myths and endless genealogies. They were not productive discussions. They promoted speculations and division rather than the divine training that is in the faith. (1:4) This is also seen in chapter four verse seven where Timothy is enjoined to have nothing to do with godless and silly myths. This book bristles with accusations of persons who have strayed doctrinally and are teaching others to do the same. Six males are actually named.
3. The men were apparently not praying, or, if they were, they were doing so against a backdrop of anger and quarreling. For some reason, unfortunately, praying often seems to be the activity of women more than men. The word used by Paul is *aner*, meaning males.

---

[296] 2 Timothy 1:3, 4
[297] 1 Timothy 1:6, 7
[298] 1 Timothy 1:19, 20

4. The women were not dressing themselves modestly and sensibly, but with braided hair or gold or pearls or costly attire. We may roll our eyes in disbelief as we read about extravagant dress, but we make a big mistake if we assume that we, of course, have no problem in this area.

5. Some were despising Pastor Timothy's youth.

6. At the conclusion of the letter, Paul talks about those who were puffed up with conceit; they knew nothing and had a morbid craving for controversy. They were present in that church.[299] It would not have been necessary to say something like that if that problem were not present.

7. There were apparently some present, characterized as "being lovers of self, lovers of money, proud, arrogant, abusive, disobedient to parents, ungrateful, unholy, inhuman, implacable slanderers, profligates, fierce, haters of good, treacherous, reckless, swollen with conceit, lovers of pleasure rather than lovers of God, holding the form of religion but denying the power of it."[300] They were infecting others with their sin, apparently with women specifically as their target. The text says that some of these people made their way into households and captured weak women who would listen to anybody and could never arrive at a knowledge of the truth. In saying that, I don't think he is saying women can never arrive at a knowledge of the truth, as if as women they were unable to do that. Some have, unfortunately, believed that. I think he is saying because they will listen to *anybody*, they will never be able to make a decision about what is true and so to discern some proposals as false. That is a disease many are afflicted with today, both men and women.

8. There were some in the church who were well off financially. (1 Timothy 6:17) That may have been part of the reason some of the women were dressing in an ostensibly stylish

---

[299] 1 Timothy 6:3-5
[300] 2 Timothy 3:2–5

manner. Paul's commandment to them, through Timothy, is to not be "haughty." As we've said before, the fact that he says something like that indicates the problem was present. There were some rich people who, as a result of their wealth, felt themselves "better" than the rest and so they were "haughty."

So the picture of this church was not an encouraging one. They were in the midst of devastating doctrinal and relational battles. It was not an easy place for a young, timid pastor such as Timothy!

I've been around people who love to argue. I've been around people who love to be exactly right and to condemn others who are not as "right" as they are, and, as a result, they feel spiritually superior. I've been around people who love to talk and speculate and then argue about meaningless minute issues in the Scripture, which they bring up and which get you nowhere. But they, of course, are on the correct side of that irrelevant issue and want you to know it. Around that kind of person I have always felt a sense of competition. I have felt like they were trying to crawl on top of me. I have felt smothered. Perhaps you know exactly what I am talking about. Perhaps you've experienced such people. I am not talking about a healthy desire to understand, dialogue, and search for correct doctrine together and then submit to it. That is a good thing. "We know that the law is good, if any one uses it lawfully."[301] I'm talking about a desire to be on the *other* side of a line, on the *better* side of a line, that separates the really spiritual from the normal, run-of-the-mill believers. It separates those "in the know" from everybody else. That may well be what Paul is referring to in 1 Timothy 6:4, where he describes certain people who have a morbid craving "for disputes about words, which produce envy, dissension, slander, and base suspicions... imagining that godliness is a means of *gain*." Godliness, in this case, believing the right position about some

---

[301] 1 Timothy 1:8

minor, meaningless issue, was a way to prove yourself to be a superior Christian, a means of *gain*. So, as a result, you could feel doctrinally superior and look down on those who did not agree.

C. S. Lewis described this game in a small article, which was really an address to young people, entitled "The Inner Ring." It, unfortunately, is not read very much today. Lewis was, at the time of the address, by his own confession, a middle-aged moralist. He acknowledged that he could talk to them about the lust of the flesh or about the lust of the eyes. But he chose another lust to warn them about: the lust of being in the inner circle, the ones *in the know*. "It is the sacred little attic or studio, the heads bent together, the fog of tobacco smoke, and the delicious knowledge that we—we four or five huddled beside this stove—are the people who *know*."[302] It is a deadly lust, he says. "I wonder whether, in ages of promiscuity, many a virginity has not been lost less in obedience to Venus than in obedience to the lure of the caucus. For of course, when promiscuity is the fashion, the chaste are outsiders. They are ignorant of something that other people know. They are uninitiated."[303]

This church seems to be infected with this disease: a burning desire to be in the inner ring, the spiritually elite, to be among those who have arrived, those who "know." So the men were involved in *meaningless* arguing about endless genealogies and myths and— judging from the directions given to Timothy in 2:8—not praying. The women were dressing fit to kill, intent, as so many are today, on being *more* stylish than so-and-so and on the cutting edge of fashion trends. It is not surprising that there was such a paucity of prayer among the men and an equivalent lack of modesty and simplicity among the women. Both were symptoms of a desire to be better, more trendy, to be the upper crust rather than manifesting a humble awareness of sin and helplessness before God. It was a competitive Christianity, but the competition was not about Christian things.

---

[302] C. S. Lewis, <u>The Weight of Glory</u>, Wm. B. Eerdmans Publishing Company, Grand Rapids, MI, c. 1949, p. 59, from an article entitled "The Inner Ring."
[303] Ibid., pg 59

It was an ugly intrusion of This World into the Household of God. And so this book contains (in my opinion) the second strongest condemnation of Paul in the whole New Testament when he says he has turned two members (both men) over to Satan so they could learn something.[304]

The harshness of his action against these men invites a question caused by a common interpretation of our text. Many people say that the reason women are prohibited from teaching or exercising authority over men is that they were largely uneducated and, as a result, were teaching erroneous doctrine. Therefore, they should not be allowed to teach—at least temporarily—until they became better educated. This interpretation, which is probably the most common interpretation among those who see the prohibition as temporary, raises all kinds of problems that we will visit later. But for now, one of those problems is the lack of any condemnation of any women who were supposedly teaching erroneous doctrine corresponding to the strong condemnation of the *men* who were actually teaching erroneously. Only men are mentioned. If the men were worthy of such a harsh consequence as deliverance over to Satan, why not also the women *if* there really were women teaching erroneous doctrine? The absence of such a corresponding condemnation is striking.

Now, I realize much of this talk concerning the addiction to trendiness and cultural accommodation to the world is somewhat speculative. It is speculation based on what Paul says to them. Whether or not this speculation legitimately describes the church does not change our interpretation yet to come. But I think it does legitimately give us a flavor of the church situation.[305]

---

[304] 1 Timothy 2:20. "Among them are Hymenaeus and Alexander, whom I have delivered to Satan that they may learn not to blaspheme." For what it's worth, I think the strongest condemnation is reserved for the Galatians where he twice says in the first 10 verses that anyone preaching a different gospel than his should be accursed—which meant stoned to death. Or in chapter 5 verse 12, he says that anyone still preaching circumcision should go ahead and cut the whole thing off! Those are strong words! Check it out for yourself.

[305] The desire to be culturally trendy is still around. It is dangerous and possibly unfair to make an analysis of an author's soul (the author I am about to quote) from what he writes. So I will not name him because I could be very wrong in my judgment of him. But I find it interesting

Such is the context of 1 Timothy 2, which appears to contain some of the clearest and most restrictive teaching on women in the church. It also contains one of the most obtuse verses, in my opinion, in all of scripture, in verse 15. There were present both seriously erroneous doctrines being taught and a lust to be spiritually elite, better than the average believer. That's our situation as we turn to chapter two.

Before going any farther, I would like to observe that there are sections of this text that *everybody* interprets less than literally. Maybe it's the part about the men praying with holy hands raised, or the part about women not wearing their hair in braids (we've all seen braided hair in church, right?), or the part about women being silent, or the part about women being saved by having children. Both the context and the originally intended meaning seem difficult to understand. Few people today with a high view of Scripture take these verses (for example, the ones about women keeping silent in the churches) in the same manner the church has for some 2000 years. That should give us pause. On the other hand, the church can be wrong, as it was in understanding what the Bible taught about the structure of the Solar System. So, as has been true with other texts, we must approach this text with humility and an attitude to learn and possibly adjust our previous understanding. The church historically could have been wrong. *We* can be wrong.

Chapter two begins with the words, "First of all," which hardly seems like a first subject if it begins chapter two. But Paul has gone

---

how he reacts to his observation that "recent scholarship has largely underscored that the dominant Biblical portrait of God is drawn with male imagery. Therefore, what is a culturally and personally sensitive theologian to do with what seems, frankly, to be an embarrassment? Why did God reveal Godself almost all the time as 'himself' and not 'herself' or 'itself' or 'himself/herself'?" This author seems embarrassed by the way God has revealed Himself in masculine terms because it is not culturally acceptable. But he calls his embarrassment "cultural sensitivity." Perhaps our culture has gone wrong and God is right and we are too timid or too afraid of being different from our culture to acknowledge our culture's sickness. Not knowing the person directly, it would be wrong and arrogant of me to accuse, but we need to ask ourselves the hard question if whether or not we are willing to be different, odd, or, worst of all, "outdated" because of our attachment to Jesus. It seems the believers at Ephesus struggled in this area.

off on two tangents as he approached the topic he wanted to deal with first, which is prayer. One of the tangents is the purpose of the law in verses 8 through 11, and the other is the nature of Paul's calling in verses 12 through 17. Then he states the flip-side of the charge he gave to Timothy in verse 3 about shutting some men up. He charges Timothy to wage warfare, holding fast to the faith and conscience.

The first subject in chapter two is prayer, both in verse 1 and verse 8. "First of all, then, I urge that supplications, prayers, intercessions, and thanksgivings be made for all men, for kings and all who are in high positions, that we may lead a quiet and peaceable life, godly and respectful in every way."[306] That's an interesting prayer request. It's interesting in its contrast to what we might pray for. Rarely have I heard prayers for the Christian community today that we might live quiet and peaceable lives, godly and respectful in every way. We seem to be more interested in sick grandparents, jobs, and freedom from hardship. Living godly, quiet, and respectful lives does not rank very high on our agenda. Maybe it did not rank very high on the agenda of the church at Ephesus, or Paul would not have had to remind them of that.

In verse 8, we read, "I desire then that in every place the men should pray, lifting holy hands without anger or quarreling...." I think it is safe to assume that Paul would not have exhorted them to do that *if* the men were already praying, lifting holy hands without anger or quarreling. Or if, in fact, they were already doing it, he would have urged them to continue; but he does not say that. Prayer, with lifted holy hands, without anger and quarreling, was apparently not happening at this church—by the men.

The article "the" before the word "men" seems strange at first. It surely cannot mean that only the men were to pray, not the women. That would go against many examples in Scripture of women praying and also cannot be supported by teaching anywhere else in

---

[306] 1 Timothy 2:1, 2

Scripture.[307] The significance of the article before the word "men" must mean either that "the men" specifically were *not* praying, or, maybe, that "the men" were praying and at the same time quarreling and were angry with each other. This was a man's problem. The word Paul uses is *aner*, meaning males, not people in general.

Do men find it harder to pray than women? Does it come more easily to women because they are supposedly "weaker" and so more easily go to God from a position of need?[308] I don't know, and to make any conclusive statement would be speculative. Men seem to be by nature competitive and combative, whether on the battlefield or the athletic field or *talking* about the athletic field or even, I'm afraid, when talking about theology. Men need to be the victors, to be more right than the others in the conversation. They need to win. It's all about competition. Prayer does not come easily to them. We are more comfortable arguing about theology than praying about theology. That definitely seems to be true at the Ephesian church.

My experience at church prayer meetings is that it is usually the women who pray more than the men, at least out loud. We have a delightful single woman in our church who has some form of mental disability. She is quite simple—and I in no way intend that as derogatory. She has difficulty expressing herself and spelling and appears to be at about a grade school level intellectually, even though she is 56. But you should hear her pray. She seems to switch into a different mode of being and her mouth overflows with articulate praise and thanksgiving to God. Even her words are more clear and she expresses herself much more clearly when she prays. In our prayer meetings, she is *always* the first to pray, as if she were anxious to jump in and praise her God and hold up her friends in prayer before the King. The men, myself included, seem to hold back. I'm not sure why. The other women, on the other hand, seem to jump in, led by Rebecca, gladly running into the presence of the King. I fully

---

[307] 1 Corinthians 11:5, which exhorts a woman, *when* she prays, to do so with an appropriate head covering, for instance.

[308] We'll look more at the supposed "weakness" of the female gender in the chapter on 1 Peter 3.

realize much of this is speculative; but my limited observations seem consistent that women find it easier to pray, and if my speculation that the cult of competitive trendiness really did infect this church at Ephesus, it makes sense that it would be hard for the men to show their vulnerability and helplessness in prayer. The need to be trendy squelches vulnerability. It's about competition and being strong.

Verse nine begins in the RSV with "also," or in the King James with "in like manner also," indicating that what follows is in a similar vein. "Also that women should adorn themselves modestly and sensibly in seemly apparel, not with braided hair or gold or pearls or costly attire, but by good deeds, as befits women who profess religion."[309] If Paul had to exhort the women *not* to do that, they probably *were doing* that very thing. The presence of the word "also" indicates that these issues are connected, possibly flip-sides of the same issue—competitive prayer by the men and competitive dressing by the women. They are mirror images of each gender's need to prove its superiority, to be more spiritual, legitimate members of the "inner ring," either through stylish clothes or theological superiority coupled with prayer-less self-confidence. Each is a desire to be *better*.

It is an interesting question: what is the purpose of stylish dress? It is not the purpose of this book to answer that question, but it is invited by the text we are studying. It is interesting to me that before the Fall, the man and woman wore no clothes. And they were not ashamed. If I could make a jump from that to heaven, it may well be that we will not wear clothes in heaven. I know, I know, for those of us living this side of the fall and before heaven, we blush and turn our heads. We are *ashamed*. That is natural for us to react this way. The other possibility, implied by the Bible, is that we might all wear white robes, indicative of our sins being washed away by the blood of Jesus. Either way, we will all be the *same*. No more looking in the mirror and carefully pruning ourselves. No more dressing to impress

---

[309] 1 Timothy 2:9, 10

and waiting for compliments on our attire. Either way, the playing field will be level. The need to be "in style" will be gone. I apologize for the speculation about which I know nothing, but *if* it's true that there will be no stylish clothes in heaven, then it makes sense that the apostle would challenge Christians in his churches to start living heaven's value system out in this world by starting to de-emphasize stylish dress and jewelry.[310]

There is another possible interpretation of the apostle's call to the women in the church at Ephesus. David Scholer, in his article, "Women's Adornment,"[311] quotes a number of Jewish and Graeco-Roman passages that give us insight into what "style" communicated or achieved in the cultures from about 200 BC to AD 100. Here is a quotation from another source, one nearest to the time of Christ: "In this way [a woman] will avoid being overly dressed or luxurious or made-up.... She should not wear gold or emeralds at all—materialism and extravagance are characteristics of prostitutes."[312] This quotation sounds amazingly similar to our text here and the one in 1 Peter 3 about avoiding external extravagance.

Dr. Scholer's conclusion is that "there is no question that in the cultural context of the early church the rejection of external adornment was part and parcel of a woman's submission to her husband and a recognition of her place among men in general. External adornment was clearly seen as indicative of two most undesirable characteristics: 1) sexual infidelity; and 2) materialistic extravagance.... The adornment injunctions were one piece with the role and rule of wifely submission and public silence. To the degree and manner in which the adornment instructions are culturally conditioned, so are the submission and silence injunctions."[313]

---

[310] I recently taught a Sunday School class at my church on 1 Timothy. I challenged the attendees there not to compliment people on how they looked on a Sunday morning but instead just to say how good it was to see them there or some other form of encouragement instead of how they were dressed.

[311] "Women's Adornment," from the magazine, <u>Daughters of Sarah</u>, Jan-Feb 1980, pp. 3–6.

[312] A translation from M. R Lefkowitz and M. B. Fant, *Women in Greece and Rome*, pp. 84 to 86.

[313] Daughters of Sarah; ibid. p. 6.

He seems to be saying that since external adornment no longer signifies sexual infidelity, then wifely submission is also therefore no longer required. But submission is not *caused* by the external adornment of women. Lack of external adornment was a *sign* in that culture of wifely submission. The fact that it does not necessarily represent the same thing in our culture does not logically mean that wifely submission is also no longer required. Nor does it necessarily mean that we can ignore Paul's exhortation to dress modestly.

Frankly, I think it is a mistake to thoughtlessly dismiss the apostle's call to the men to pray without quarreling and to the women to dress more modestly as outdated and therefore irrelevant.[314] I think it is a mistake to assume our modern western churches have no application to make from these verses. Our culture is enamored with power, not dependence on God, with style, not modesty; with being trendy, not with being servants of one another as we should and with winning arguments rather than finding truth. What is it that causes us to have an almost knee-jerk reaction to write these verses off as not applicable? *If* you were to apply these in our modern culture, what kinds of attitudes would arise in your soul? Would you women be ashamed to go out in public without make-up and jewelry? Would you men be ashamed to pour your heart out to God in public and to raise your hands like an infant raises its hands to its mother? Is that too feminine for us modern men? Right now, are you ashamed to publicly thank God for the privilege of food at a restaurant? Or when you have company over for a meal? It seems to me that prayer-less self-confidence and a need to put on a "false face" by using make-up may very well go hand-in-hand, as both seem to involve a cover-up. I think that instead of quickly dismissing

---

[314] In my reading I came across at least two well educated authors who reasoned that since we do not apply the first section of chapter two of 1 Timothy about the men praying and the women dressing more modestly, then why apply the second part about gender roles in the church? I fail to understand that reasoning. First, we need to ask why we fail to apply the first section: is there good reason for that? Secondly, we need to ask, if we fail to apply the first section—even legitimately—does it necessarily follow that we can fail to apply the second? What is the connection between the two?

these verses, those of us who profess to have our soul set on heavenly things, not on earthly things, should do some soul searching to see if perhaps we are also caught up in the trendy culture of our time and so read the Scriptures through lenses that filter out what is not palatable to the world we live in.

The situation at Ephesus was quite negative and not fitting for the church of Jesus Christ. This church at Ephesus, and all of our churches, need to be reminded of our calling. They (and we) have been "blessed in Christ with every spiritual blessing in the heavenly places, even as he chose us in him before the foundation of the world, that we should be holy and blameless before Him.... In Him we have redemption through his blood, the forgiveness of our trespasses, according to the riches of his grace, which he *lavished* upon us.... We who first hoped in Christ have been destined and appointed to live for the praise of his glory."[315] Those words were written to this very church at an earlier time. How unfitting that they should be caught up in endless, meaningless quarreling, stylish competitions, and not praying! Clearly, they were already on the downward slide, which continues eventually to the death of the church.

Verse 11 continues, "Let a woman learn in silence with all submissiveness. I permit no woman to teach or to have authority over men; she is to keep silent. For Adam was formed first, then Eve; and Adam was not deceived, but the woman was deceived and became a transgressor. Yet woman will be saved through bearing children if she continues in faith and love and holiness, with modesty."[316]

We are quickly overwhelmed with the statement that Paul does not permit a woman to teach or to have authority over men. Because of our cultural distance, we miss the stunning statement that Paul considered women capable of learning. Just like men. Did you catch what he is saying? "Let a woman *learn*." In that culture, women, or young girls, were not taught the Torah. "Every man who teaches

---

[315] Ephesians 1:3–4, 7, 12
[316] 1 Timothy 2:11–15

his daughter the Torah is as if he taught her promiscuity."[317] "Let the words of Torah be burned up, but let them not be delivered to women."[318] Such theological learning was reserved for males only. Now, let's come to grips with this: the Apostle Paul described himself (before he was a believer in Jesus), "as to the law a Pharisee" and "as to righteousness under the law—blameless."[319] Yet he is now is encouraging the young pastor Timothy to do something that he, as a Rabbi, was prohibited from doing: encouraging women to learn spiritual truth. How does one explain the change? It must be his new understanding of Scripture brought about by his conversion to Jesus. Before we come to grips with his statement of prohibition of women teaching, we must come to grips with his radical position that they could and even *should* be taught. That is a very positive statement about the female gender, a very egalitarian statement about the female gender, and a Biblical one though it was culturally unacceptable.[320]

The word translated "silence" or "silent" is an interesting word: *hesychia* in Greek. It only appears four times in the whole New Testament—two of them here in these verses. A form of the word appears in verse 2 where Paul exhorts the church to pray that they could live a "quiet and peaceable life." It is the word translated as "peaceable." That should give us a hint that he is not necessarily talking about avoidance of sound but instead is talking about an attitude or demeanor. Surely the ideal Christian life we are to pray for is not one where we go around in silence in this world. It occurs one time also in the Acts passage quoted below, and once in 2 Thessalonians 3:12, where Paul is exhorting certain persons who were "living in idleness, being busybodies, not doing work. Now such persons we command and exhort in the Lord Jesus Christ to do

---

[317] Mish Sotah 3:4, quoted in <u>Women, Authority and the Bible</u>, p. 70.
[318] Jer Sotah 19a, quoted in <u>Women, Authority and the Bible</u>, p. 70.
[319] Philippians 3:5, 6
[320] This encouragement of women to learn, as well as other teachings of Paul that treat women as equal with men, were culturally very unacceptable. So the often-heard comment that Paul was afraid of offending his culture and that, in proscribing certain roles as only for men, his desire is to not offend the culture, is mistaken.

their work in *quietness* and to earn their own living."[321] It does not seem from the 2 Thessalonians passage that it means complete lack of sound, and, notably, it is applicable to both genders.

There is another word, *sigao*, which comes closer to the meaning of our English word "silence." It is the word used in 1 Corinthians 14:28 and 34, which we've already studied: "But if there is no one to interpret let each of them keep *silence* in church and speak to himself and to God," and "As in all the churches of the saints, the women should keep *silence* in the churches. For they are not permitted to speak...." The word itself and the context also indicate that what is meant in 1 Corinthians 14:28 and 34 is really silence—no talking. Quiet. As we saw, it was related to the need for order rather than chaos in worship services and also applied to the situation where a person spoke in tongues and there was no interpreter present. The speaker was to be *quiet*.

However, the first word *hesychia* does not necessarily indicate lack of sound. It is more a quality of spirit than complete silence. The passage from Acts below includes *both* words. The actual word used is *sige*, which is the noun form of *sigao*. The reader can see how they are used differently. It is also the other remaining usage of our word *hesychia* in the New Testament.

Acts 21:37 through 22:2 is a section recording Paul's speaking in Jerusalem to a large gathering of Jews who, of course, hated him because he was teaching against the law (they thought) and had brought Greeks into the temple. The mob became violent-they seized Paul dragged him out of the temple and began to beat him. Some Roman soldiers came and arrested him and bound him with two chains and brought him into the barracks. At that point, Paul begged to be allowed to speak to the mob, which he was allowed to do. Here is how the event is recorded:

"Paul, standing on the steps, motioned with his hand to the people; and when there was a great hush, [*sige*, which means "silence".]

---

[321] 2 Thessalonians 3:11, 12

he spoke to them in the Hebrew language, saying, 'Brethren and fathers, hear the defense which I now make before you.' And when they heard that he addressed them in the Hebrew language, they were more quiet.[*hesychia*]."[322]

   The first "quietness" in the account, described as "a great hush," is the word *sige*, which means lack of sound. The NIV translates it as "silent" instead of "a great hush." So when Paul began to address the crowd and motioned to the people, "there was a *great hush*." They stopped making noise—they quieted down. Then when he spoke to the crowd in their own language, they became "more quiet" (RSV) or just "quiet" (NIV). This is our word *hesychia*, which describes a change in *attitude* from merely "quiet," meaning lack of sound. They were already silent, as evidenced by the word *sige*. Then they became *more quiet*. Please see what is going on here and what it indicates about how these words are used. The crowd quickly became silent (meaning lack of sound), but they were not "quiet." So it must be possible to be silent—that is, to not make any noise—yet also to be not "quiet." They became "quiet" when he spoke to them in their own language. What happened was their demeanor changed. They became open to being taught.

   Hesychia is the word translated as "quiet" here in 1 Timothy, and it indicates an attitude. When Paul exhorts the women to be quiet as they learn, he is talking about an *attitude* that should be present in learners, meaning to be teachable. He is not necessarily saying they cannot talk or make any sound. If he wanted to say that women should not make any sound, he would have used the word *sigao* or *sige*. He did not use either of those words.

   My wife is an elementary school teacher. That is not a calling I am attracted to! But she loves to teach. One of the struggles, if not the biggest struggle, in teaching is getting the students to have an attitude of quietness. I do not mean by that silence—most school

---

[322] Revised Standard Version, Thomas Nelson, Inc. New York, NY c.1972 p.132

rooms are not nearly as silent as mine was when I was a student in the '50s and '60s. Silence, or lack of sound, is not the issue. The issue is an attitude of teachability and submission to the teacher.

Any of us who have been parents have had the experience of trying to "teach" one of our kids and experiencing the lack of "quietness" that Paul is referring to here—even though the child might be silent. You can see it in the rolling of the eyes, the body language, the attitude of "you can't tell me what to do." In the very positive transition from the unBiblical position of women being perceived as not competent to learn to the Biblical position of being co-bearers of the image of God, there is the temporary position of *learning*, and an attitude that is conducive to learning is what is required to make progress. That is described by the word "quiet." And so the statement that the women should learn "in silence with all submissiveness" is not a statement about women being silent in church, making no sound— even though at first glance it looks like that. It is a statement about what kind of attitude is necessary for learning.[323] It is a statement about the kind of demeanor a learner should have. In Ephesus at this point in history, this principle was very applicable to the new set of students called women. Paul considered women capable of learning just like men. Don't miss the fact that he considered women as being teachable and was actually *encouraging* them to learn, a practice that the rabbis of his time looked at with disdain. It is also a very counter-cultural statement that women were not only capable of learning just like men, but that they *should* learn, just like men.

Now at the risk of belaboring the point, I remind us all of three facts:

1. The word translated as "silence" in the RSV is more a quiet, teachable spirit than absolute silence. It describes an attitude of *learning* rather than lack of sound. It is not a statement to the effect that women could not speak in church.

---

[323] See Job's attitude: "Teach me and I will be silent. Make me understand how I have erred" (Job 6:24) or "Men listened to me, and waited, and kept silence for my counsel" (Job 29:21).

2. The very fact that women were encouraged to learn was counter to the current practices of the time. That was a strong positive statement about women: they were considered capable and equal with men in the area of learning.
3. The apostle did not shy away from encouraging pastor Timothy and the church at Ephesus to a practice that was different from the cultural norms. He did not avoid a practice because it might offend people or "hinder the evangelistic outreach" of the church.

That brings us to verses 12 through 15, which do not seem to follow logically from verse 11.

"I permit no woman to teach or to have authority over men; she is to keep silent. For Adam was formed first, then Eve; and Adam was not deceived, but the woman was deceived and became a transgressor. Yet woman will be saved through bearing children, if she continues in faith and love and holiness, with modesty.[324]

Before wading into this difficult verse, I want to remind us that the word translated as "silent" is our word *hesychia*, which means that she is to manifest an openness to being taught, not necessarily keeping the mouth shut.

The very first issue that should jump out at us is the prohibition of teaching by a group of people (women) who were just encouraged to learn. What sense does that make? Why would women be encouraged to learn but prohibited from passing on that learning to others?

Another issue that jumps out in our very egalitarian culture is that it seems unfair and sexist to prohibit one gender and not the other from *anything*. If the genders are equal, how can one be

---

[324] 1 Timothy 2:12–15

prohibited from an activity of which it is presumably capable, and why on earth would that be commanded?

There are a number of interpretations of this prohibition. Following is a list of the most common ones, and I will explain their strengths and weaknesses one by one.

1. Some say the present tense ("I *do not permit*") indicates a limited applicability, limited only to the time of the contemporary persons involved.

2. Some say the first person singular ("*I* do not permit") indicates that Paul is giving his opinion about the present situation, but again it is not a universal principle to be followed.

3. Some say that women were prohibited from teaching because they were (unfairly) uneducated and therefore not qualified to teach. Once women were properly educated, which Paul here promotes, the prohibition would not longer be in effect.

4. Some say that women were actually already involved in teaching and they were teaching unorthodox doctrine and therefore were not allowed to teach. This really is very close to situation number three. After all, that was Paul's first command to Timothy in 1:3, so this seems to follow in the same vein.

5. Some say that women were prohibited from teaching because it was culturally unacceptable and would have brought discredit to the gospel of Jesus Christ. Since that is no longer true, the prohibition is not longer applicable.

6. Some say this does not apply to church structures at all but instead to husband-wife relationships. Those who say this call the church a "redemptive institution," and therefore the restrictions on women "teaching," whatever that means, don't apply.

1. Possibly the present tense of the verb ("I do not permit," meaning "I do not currently permit") indicates applicability only to the situation current at Ephesus. To expand or apply it to current modern Western church structures is not legitimate.

   The use of the present tense does not necessarily indicate lack of universal application. There may be other indicators of limited applicability, and there are certainly instances in other texts where an application is not universal, but the verb tense alone does not necessarily indicate that. Romans 12:1 exhorts us, "I *appeal* to you therefore, brethren, by the mercies of God, to present your bodies as a living sacrifice, holy and acceptable to God, which is your spiritual worship." We do not take the present tense of *appeal* to indicate lack of universal application. Actually, Scripture bristles with present tenses that we unquestionably take as applicable to our time, two thousand years removed from the writing. The verb tense is really not very helpful for that argument.

2. Some say that Paul's use of the first person singular ("*I* do not permit) indicates that Paul was just stating his opinion, but that he did not intend it to have universal applicability. That is a low view of apostolic authority. We do not take other statements of Paul as merely opinion. For example:

   "First of all, then, I urge that supplications, prayers, intercessions, and thanksgivings be made for all men...."[325]
   "I desire then that in every place the men should pray...."[326]

---

[325] 1 Timothy 2:1
[326] 1 Timothy 2:8

We do not read those similar statements from the immediate context as merely Paul's unauthoritative opinion, which we are free to disagree with. This is an apostle speaking, and when he says that he urges, or desires, or does not permit, we really do not have the privilege of assuming autonomy from his direction, unless there are other indications of limited applicability. The first person singular pronoun by itself does not indicate that. On the other hand, it must be noted that many Christians do not follow the apostle's directive to pray with hands raised. We assume that to be a cultural manifestation of reaching towards God, which is what prayer is. That, I think, is unfortunate, but I'm not arguing that point; that is not the purpose of this book.[327]

3. Some say women were prohibited from teaching because they were (unfairly) uneducated and therefore not qualified to teach. Once they were properly educated, a goal that Paul here promotes, the prohibition would be lifted. That would mean that the prohibition was temporary and was limited to the contemporary circumstances. However, this understanding of the text raises more problems than it solves. At first there might seem to be some reasonableness to this understanding because in the next two verses, Paul refers to Eve as the one who was deceived (because of being "uneducated") and became a transgressor. The thinking goes something like this: In the Genesis account, to which Paul appeals, Adam was formed first and the commandment not to eat of the Tree of the Knowledge of Good and Evil was given to him and to him alone. Eve was not around yet.

---

[327] Even Dr. David Scholer, a staunch egalitarian, agrees with this. "I reject the suggestion that Paul's 'I do not permit' is a basis for limiting 2:11–12 because it is only opinion. Paul often expresses his apostolic authority in personal terms (e.g., I Cor. 7:40, 7:12)." From <u>Women, Authority, and the Bible</u>, p. 203.

So when the Devil, in the form of a snake, came to tempt Eve with the trick question, "Did God say you may not eat of any tree of the garden?"[328] she blew it. She gave a garbled account of what God had said. That lack of understanding or "education" opened the door for the Devil to mess with her mind on the subject of whether or not God was Good, and so she fell to the temptation. Then she *taught* Adam, and he fell, too. Therefore, Paul is saying, the situation at Ephesus is similar in that the women, because of unfortunate and unfair cultural practices, had been prohibited from hearing God's word and were uneducated just as Eve was. So the women should be prohibited from teaching lest they lead the church into sin just as Eve did Adam.

That explanation is not without problems, legitimate though it may seem at first.

a. Why did Paul not say that? That reference to Eve is admittedly difficult because Paul does not explain why he refers to the Genesis account or what the analogy is to Ephesus. That is part of the complexity of this text. But the fact is there are not any words in the text that indicate that Paul intended the prohibition to be temporary due to women's lack of education. That understanding must be an inference, and some do infer it from the present tense of the verb. The fact is that Paul does not blame Eve for false teaching and so leading Adam to sin. He uses her as an example of a person who was *tricked* rather than of a person who taught false doctrine because of lack of training. That is an important distinction.

b. If the prohibition is due to ignorance, and so lack of qualification to teach, why does Paul say the women

---

[328] Genesis 3:1. Remember: what God actually said to Adam was that he may freely eat of *every* tree of the garden, save one.

are not to teach *men*? It seems that uneducated women should be prohibited from all teaching until they became educated, rather than just from teaching men. What does the gender of the supposed learners have to do with it?[329] That is a question that *requires* answering if we are to accept the prohibition as being temporary due to cultural influences that kept women uneducated. In addition, it is not a valid assumption that all women were uneducated and that all men were educated. We know that is not true.[330] Additionally, Priscilla was in this church. She was educated. See point d. below. In addition to all that, we know there were men leading the disciples away from the truth. Paul names six males. This was his original prophecy to the elders at Miletus. If there were already men leading disciples away from the truth, what sense does it make for Paul to prohibit women from teaching men because they might lead the men astray?

c. If the prohibition is due to lack of education, why does Paul not prohibit *all uneducated people* from teaching rather than just women? Surely not all males were automatically qualified to teach, nor were all females uneducated. Paul lists six males who have left the faith and turns one of them over to Satan.

---

[329] One possible reason is given by Dr. Phillip Payne: "Paul does not establish a rule that would be impossible for Timothy to monitor, namely, teaching by women when no men were present." P. 394, in <u>Man and Woman, One in Christ</u>. It seems his reasoning is that women must not teach men because it is the men's role (perhaps because they were the more educated) to monitor the doctrinal correctness of the women's teaching and Paul does not make a rule about a potential situation where there were no men to monitor the teaching. But then that raises the question why, since men were "necessary" to monitor doctrinal correctness, does Paul not prohibit women from teaching in any situation instead of only teaching men? That would seem to be an exceptionally dangerous situation—uneducated women teaching freely with no men to correct them! (Pardon my sarcasm.) I find Dr. Payne's interpretation wanting.

[330] Acts 4:13

d. If the prohibition was temporary until the female gender gained the necessary education, why does he not make some reference to the fact that this is temporary and once women become educated they will be allowed, even encouraged to assume a teaching role just as he has encouraged women to be learners?

The lack of reference to any other uneducated people being also prohibited from teaching is really quite sexist on Paul's part. There were probably uneducated males present in the church, who, if being in a teaching position required education, should *also* have been prohibited from teaching. So why only mention women? No, the fact that women are prohibited from teaching men indicates that there is something more here than just lack of preparedness. Given the fact that Paul has listed several people who have left the faith, some of whom were teaching unorthodox doctrine, *all of whom were men*, makes his prohibition of women teaching men confusing, if not clearly sexist.

Some[331] have said that we must interpret this injunction against women teaching in the historical and social context of the letter. It is a mystery to me why Paul would use the term "women" as synonymous with "uneducated" or "perpetrators of error," especially in

---

[331] "They argue that if Paul had intended 2:11–12 to mean that the women who were involved in the false teaching should be prohibited from teaching or exercising authority in the church, he could easily have said so at this very point.... Such an objection does not take seriously the character of I and II Timothy as an occasional letter.... Paul is not obligated to give a full account of the whole social context shared by him and his original readers.... The complete literary context and the shared experience and knowledge of author and first readers made such discussion unnecessary." From <u>Women, Authority, and the Bible,</u> pp. 203, 204, in an article entitled, "I Timothy 2:9–15 & The Place of Women in the Church's Ministry," by David Scholer. If I understand what he is saying, it seems that since this letter was written to deal with doctrinal issues, then the prohibition also must also be about doctrinal issues. Maybe so or maybe not. More evidence needs to be provided. Additionally, that ignores the fact that the word Paul uses in prohibiting women from teaching is *didasko*, which means orthodox teaching instead of *heterodidaskaleo*, which refers to unorthodox teaching. That is important.

this situation where he has already named six men who have gone doctrinally astray. That would make Paul a sexist because not all women were uneducated. Priscilla is a member of this church and she was well educated, so not all women in that church were uneducated.[332] To use the term "women" as a substitute for "uneducated" not only is sexist, but just is not true. Not all the women were uneducated.

e. This letter is a letter from Paul to Pastor Timothy, who is a pastor of the church at Ephesus. One of the church members there, we can deduce from the history written in the book of Acts, as well as the greetings at the end of 2 Timothy, was Priscilla. She is the poster-child for those who interpret Paul's prohibition of women teaching as limited and local. She was probably one of the best educated women in the early church. Paul had stayed with her and her husband for 18 months in Corinth, as they were both tent-makers. Surely she would have gained much theological insight and understanding by working with Paul. Imagine what they talked about as they stitched their tents together. Probably she and her husband Aquila attended the meetings in the synagogue where Paul argued *every week* about Jesus and persuaded many Jews and Greeks. Then they went with Paul to Ephesus, probably around AD 51, and there they came upon a Jew named Apollos, who was described as being "eloquent" and "well versed in the Scriptures." "He had been instructed in the way of the Lord: and being fervent in spirit, he spoke and taught accurately the things concerning Jesus, though he know only the baptism of John."[333] But Priscilla and Aquila, when they heard him, we are told by Luke, felt it necessary to

---

[332] In fact, the church probably met in her and her husband's house. See 1 Corinthians 15:8, 19.
[333] Acts 18:25 and 26

correct something in his theology and so "took him and expounded to him the way of God more accurately."[334] The result of their "teaching" was that when he wished to cross to Achaia, the brethren encouraged him and wrote to the disciples to receive him. And when he arrived, he "greatly helped those who through grace had believed, for he powerfully confuted the Jews in public, showing by the scriptures that the Christ was Jesus."[335] He apparently benefited from the teaching of Priscilla and Aquila. The actual word, however, is not the common word used for teaching in 1 and 2 Timothy, but a different word. It is translated as "expounded" or "explained." This happened in Paul's absence, as Paul had left for Caesarea. It is worth noting that the text does not say that Priscilla taught Apollos but that "they took him and explained to him the way of God more accurately."[336] The activity was not something Priscilla did alone to a man; it was something they both did. And it was not "teaching"; it was a different Greek word— explaining or expositing.

It was to the church where Priscilla was a member that Paul was writing this prohibition about not permitting a woman to teach or exercise authority over men. Why did he not excuse Priscilla from that prohibition if he was really concerned about uneducated persons fulfilling a role of teacher? Or why not set her up as an example to mimic? It seems quite mistaken to say that the prohibition was because of lack of education of

---

[334] Acts 18:26. The text tells us that Apollos "knew only the baptism of John," so it may well be that what Priscilla and Aquila did for Apollos could be better categorized as evangelism. Even though he was well versed in the Scriptures and taught accurately the factual things concerning Jesus, he may not have actually *experienced* forgiveness through a personal commitment. That, however, is speculation.

[335] Acts 18:27, 28

[336] Acts 18:26

women when one of the most educated women around was in the congregation and she was not excepted.

f. Eve did not actually *teach* Adam anything. All she did was give him the fruit and he also ate of it. To disqualify women from teaching men seems a bit of an over-response to this action and does not even seem to follow.

So the objection that Paul was really prohibiting women from assuming a teaching role because they were uneducated and so were not qualified to teach seems difficult to support. It certainly is true that women had been discriminated against and so were uneducated, but that was not the ground for the prohibition here.

4. Some say that women were actually already involved in teaching and they were teaching unorthodox doctrine and therefore were not allowed to teach. This really is very close to situation number three. It is a well known fact that the letters 1 and 2 Timothy and Titus were written to combat false doctrine. Maintaining an orthodox doctrinal stance is very important in these letters. And still is. However:

a. There is no evidence anywhere in 1 or 2 Timothy that women specifically were teaching error. Some have referred to 1 Timothy 5:13 as describing women: "Besides that, they learn to be idlers, gadding about from house to house, and not only idlers, but gossips and busybodies, saying what they should not." While the passage is not complimentary towards women, the content of their "message" does not seem to be erroneous doctrine from the words "gossips" and "busybodies." In fact, if one looks at the context, the apostle is talking about younger widows staying busy, not being idlers, because they "learn to be idlers, gadding about from house to house, and not only idlers but gossips and busybodies, saying what they should not."[337] That is hardly the picture of women *teaching* false doctrine. If anything, instead of women being the *source* of erroneous doctrine, they are pictured as the *victims* of it. "They *learn...* to be gossips and busybodies, saying what they should not."

In 2 Timothy 3, Paul is talking of the last days when men will be lovers of self, lovers of money, proud, etc., holding to the form of religion but denying the power of it. For among them, says Paul, "are those who make their way into households *and capture weak women*, burdened with sins and swayed by various impulses, who will listen to anybody and can never arrive at a knowledge of the truth. As Jannes and Jambres opposed Moses, so these men also oppose the truth, men of corrupt mind and counterfeit faith; but they will not get very far, for their folly will be plain to all, as was that of those two men."[338]

The picture that the Pastoral epistles present is that women were the victims of the erroneous doctrine, not the perpetrators. Notice that the example given from the Old Testament is of males, and they are specifically named—Jannes and Jambres. In the books of 1 and 2 Timothy, no fewer than six people are specifically named who have drifted doctrinally, and they are all men. Phygelus and Hermogenes in 2 Timothy 1:15, Hymenaeus in 1 Timothy 1:20 and 2 Timothy 2:16, Philetus in 2 Timothy 2:16, Demas in 2 Timothy 4:10, and Alexander in 1 Timothy 1:20 and 2 Timothy 4:14. It seems to me difficult to accept the proposition that

---

[337] 1 Timothy 5:13. Lest we use this verse as an example of women teaching error when it accuses women of "saying what they should not," it must be noted that the word for "saying" is *laleo*, which just means to talk or tell using the mouth and tongue. It is not *didasko*, which means to teach, or *heterodidaskaleo*, which means to teach erroneous doctrine.
[338] 2 Timothy 3:2–9

women were teaching false doctrine when none are named but six men are named. Remember, also, that Paul's prophecy at Miletus was that certain men—and he used the word for males—would arise from among them, desiring to lead people away from the truth. And all the people he names are males. Women are absent.

b. The word for teaching error is *heterodidaskaleo*, which is used in 1 Timothy 1:3 ("I urged you... to remain at Ephesus that you may charge certain persons not to teach any different doctrine...") and in 1 Timothy 6:3 ("If anyone teaches otherwise and does not agree with the sound words of our Lord Jesus Christ..."). That is the word used of teaching error. That is *not* the word used here in 2:12 when Paul says, "I permit no woman to teach or have authority over men...." The word used there is *didasko*, which is the word used by Paul for correct teaching, especially in contrast to erroneous teaching. It seems difficult to say the problem was women teaching error when that is not the word Paul used and should have if they were really teaching error.

c. Interestingly, in those two verses, 1:3 and 6:3, Paul uses indefinite pronouns rather than pronouns referring only to males or to females. So *anyone* teaching unorthodox doctrine is to be prohibited, not just females. It seems clear that prohibiting females from teaching unorthodox doctrine is not what this verse is about. Men would have been and should have been prohibited, also.

5. Some say that women were prohibited from teaching because it was culturally unacceptable and would have brought discredit to the gospel of Jesus Christ. Since that is no longer true, the prohibition is no longer applicable. That is the point of Dr. John Stackhouse's book, Finally Feminist. His starting point was that he wanted to be a feminist but he struggled with what he understood the

Bible to teach: "Let's consider just two more methodological points that helped me move beyond my tense position of wanting to be a feminist but not seeing how I could justify such a move given the Biblical texts that seemed to forbid it."[339] "May I invite you to consider the Bible in the way I am suggesting, which does, I think, make better sense of the elements of both patriarchy and equality that many egalitarians and complementarians agree are present. My fundamental practical question therefore is this: What are Christians supposed to do when society itself shifts to egalitarianism?"[340]

Or Dr. Philip Payne puts it this way: "For women to assume to themselves authority to teach *if it had never affected men* would not have caused particular social notoriety in Paul's day. But in Paul's day, for women to teach with self-assumed authority *over men* could bring *shame* to the church, especially if they teach nonsense associated with false teaching."[341] Notice that he says, "*could* bring shame." In other words, he is talking about a hypothetical situation. He also says this hypothetical situation could bring shame if the women were teaching nonsense associated with false doctrine. As we saw above, there is no evidence that women were teaching nonsense or false doctrine.

The possibility that the prohibition was due to the apostle's desire not to offend the culture of his time is a real possibility but requires more evidence to be convincing:

a. Jesus and Paul did not hesitate to be counter-cultural. And it is true that Paul was already flouting cultural norms by encouraging women to learn, just like men.

---

[339] Dr. John Stackhouse, <u>Finally Feminist</u>, Baker Academic, Grand Rapids, MI, c. 2005, p. 28.

[340] Ibid., p. 72

[341] Philip Payne, <u>One in Christ</u>, p. 395. Notice that part of the problem for Dr. Payne is that he assumed the women "self-assumed" the authority to teach.

    b. In Titus 2:5, he encouraged the older women to teach the younger women to "be sensible chaste, domestic, kind, and submissive to their husbands that the word of God may not be discredited." There are no words here in 1 Timothy similar to "in order that the word of God not be discredited," which indicate concern for cultural acceptability.

    c. It would seem sexist to continue a discriminatory practice against women merely in order not to offend outsiders.

    d. If not offending the culture was really Paul's reason for the prohibition, why does he appeal to Genesis? If the church's reputation is his reason, he does not hesitate to say that. In chapter six verse one, the church's reputation is (partially, I believe) his concern, and he states that very thing: "Let all who are under the yoke of slavery regard their masters as worthy of all honor, so that the name of God and the teaching may not be defamed." I have to point out that in Ephesians 6:9, which would have gone to the same church, he also says that "Masters should do the same to them." Masters need to treat their slaves *fairly.* That is counter-cultural! He pointedly does not say something to the effect that they should do this so the name of God not be defamed. Treating slaves unfairly probably would *not* defame the name of God in that culture, but treating them fairly was the morally *right* thing to do. We must not miss that: cultural acceptability is not primary in terms of ethics; moral correctness is. I also need to point out that slavery in that culture was not based on race, as here in our sorry history. So for Paul to appeal to Genesis when his real reason is the reputation of the church makes him dishonest and deceptive, something I cannot accept.

    e. This church was located in Ephesus, the city where, as the chapter title suggests, Diana was "king." The city had a female goddess. In that cultural context, why would it be culturally unacceptable to allow women to teach? I think the evidence suggests that a need to avoid offending the culture was not at the root of the prohibition.

6. Some say that the prohibition does not apply to church structures but instead to husband-wife relationships. That seems difficult to accept because Paul says explicitly that the purpose of the whole book of 1 Timothy is that one might "know how one ought to behave in the household of God which is the church of the living God."[342] There is no mention of his switching applications from the church to husband-wife relationships leading up to the prohibition, and immediately afterward he continues talking about church applications by listing qualifications for elders—which significantly include the ability to teach, something he has just prohibited women from doing. And if this did apply only to husband-wife relationships in the home, would it really mean that the wife could not teach the husband anything? In my marriage, that would not be a pretty picture—or workable.

Before we move on, we must look at the profound passage in John 17, the well known high priestly prayer of Jesus as He prays for His disciples' lifestyles after He leaves this earth. "I do not pray for these only [meaning the twelve who were with Him] but also for those who believe in me through their word [those who would believe because of the disciples' words, that is Scripture, so those people would be the church] that they may all be one; even as thou,

---

[342] 1 Timothy 4:15

Father, art in me and I in thee, that they also may be in us so that the world may believe that thou hast sent me."[343]

Please notice a couple of things: 1) Jesus prays that the church that would be a result of the disciples' witness would be "one" as the Trinity is "one." We have already observed that "oneness" in the Scriptures is a kind of plural "oneness," a "oneness" made up of parts, like a cluster of grapes. See page 110 in the chapter "The Trinity, Hierarchy, and Equality" and page 437 in the Conclusion. That concept comes from the word "echad" in Deuteronomy 6:4. "Hear, O Israel: The LORD our God is one LORD." It could also be translated: "Hear, O Israel: the LORD our God, is one." Jesus desires and prays that the church, his body, would reflect the quality of relationship present in the Trinity: "that they may all be one; even as thou, Father, art in me and I in thee." 2) As we observed in the chapter on the Trinity, that relationship is a hierarchy of equals. And so that same quality of relationship should be present *in the church*. So these verses *do* apply to the church. He even states that clearly. He prays that they would be *one* as the Trinity is *one*, "that the world may believe thou hast *sent* me." So what Jesus prays for is that the world would see that Jesus came to the earth because He was under the authority of the Father. But—I hasten to add—also that He was equal with the Father. Jesus wants the world to see that in how we relate in the church. So the quality of relationships in the *church*—that is, a hierarchy of complete equals—is a means of revelation about God who is, namely, a hierarchy of complete equals.

One last issue before we move on to figuring out what the text does teach is to ask why, if women were prohibited from teaching men due to a lack of training or to teaching erroneous doctrine, were they not only allowed but even encouraged to teach other women?[344]

---

[343] John 17:20, 21

[344] "They [the women] are to teach what is good, and so train the younger women to love their husbands and children" (Titus 2:3, 4). There are really two words used here. One is translated "to teach what is good," and the other is "train." The word for "teach what is good" is the word *kalodidaskalos*. It is a compound word consisting of the word *didaskalos*, which means a teacher

Would that not perpetuate the doctrinal errors along gender lines? This also seems very sexist.

I find the arguments limiting the prohibition in verses 11 and 12 to be less than convincing. Dr. David Scholer and many others support the view that the prohibition is temporary and that Paul assumed that the original hearers would have clearly understood that. "Those who see 2:11-12 as excluding or limiting women in ministry usually object to such a historical construction. They argue that if Paul had intended 2:11-12 to mean that women who were involved in the false teachings [notice his *assumption* that the problem was false teaching by women, when, as we noted above, that cannot be supported from the text] should be prohibited from teaching or exercising authority in the church, he could easily have said so at this very point.... [But] such an objection does not take seriously the character of I Timothy as an occasional letter or the full context of I and II Timothy. ...To assert that Paul did or could have easily written for the sake of twentieth-century interpreters begs the whole question of the contextual and historical situation addressed in I Timothy."[345] With all respect to Dr. Scholer (and I have had the privilege of hearing his exposition of the book of 1 Corinthians and it was excellent, even though, obviously, I did not agree with him on everything), I think this is a straw man. Of course, Paul was not writing with twentieth-century readers in mind, nor were *any* of the other Biblical writers. However, I think it is safe to assume that he did write with *some* readers in mind, namely, the members of the church

---

of the things of God—it is the noun form of *didaskaleo*, which is what Paul is prohibiting women from doing to men in this text. Here in Titus, it seems that this teaching is to be done by women to women, and the result is that they would train the young women to love their husbands and children, etc. The other part of the word is *kalos*, which means what is good, approved, genuine. So women were considered capable of exhorting others to live rightly, of training, and also of *teaching*. This prohibition we are struggling to understand in 1 Timothy, then, is not about competence. Otherwise, why would Paul say the women are to "teach what is good" and use the word *kalodidaskalos*?

[345] Women, Authority, and the Bible, pp. 203, 204, from an article entitled, "I Timothy 2:9-15 & the Place of Women in the Church's Ministry," by Dr. David Scholer.

at Ephesus. So the question for us as "twentieth-century interpreters" is why, if what he was intending to say was that "women who were involved in the false teachings should be prohibited from teaching or exercising authority in the church"—did he write, "I permit no woman to teach or to have authority over men"? They are decidedly not the same. Such a statement seems to imply that *all* women were infected by unorthodox doctrine and that therefore *no* woman was allowed to teach, and, for some reason, they were prohibited from teaching such false doctrine to *men* and only to men. What does gender even have to do with it? Evidence that women *were* teaching false doctrine is lacking. And why not just prohibit the women from teaching at all, rather than just from teaching *men*? Or why not just prohibit those who are teaching *erroneous* doctrine from being allowed to teach and encourage those who are teaching correct doctrine? Why did Paul use the word *didasko* for orthodox teaching instead of *heterdidaskaleo* for unorthodox teaching when he says that he does not permit a woman to teach—that is, if they really were teaching erroneously. If women were teaching unorthodox doctrine, Paul should have used the word for unorthodox doctrine, which was *heterodidaskaleo*. He did use that word in this book, referring to men who really were teaching unorthodox doctrine. I fail to see how reading the prohibition of women teaching or having authority over men can be really a prohibition of women from teaching error until they were properly educated and theologically astute. The words are just not synonymous, not only for us as "twentieth-century readers," but also for the original first-century readers.

Sometimes the easy part of the work of interpretation is determining what a text does not say, which is what I have tried to do. Before moving on to the harder part, determining what the text *does* say, I want to compare two different texts from the book of 1 Timothy. They are from the same author, the same book, the same context. I find this comparison helpful as a final step in determining that the issue in 1 Timothy 2 is not about prohibiting women from promulgating false teaching but something else. For those who say that Paul was just using words that first-century readers would have understood as prohibiting false teaching by women, we can look at a text where Paul says that very thing, although *not* limited to either gender. The book of 1 Timothy is definitely about preventing false teaching. That does not mean that everything in the book is about that. Paul begins the book with a charge to Timothy to shut the mouths of those who were teaching incorrect doctrine: "As I urged you when I was going to Macedonia, remain at Ephesus that you may charge certain persons not to teach any different doctrine (*heterodidaskaleo*), nor to occupy themselves with myths and endless genealogies which promote speculations...."[346] He concludes the book with the same issue, which is the passage quoted below, and I want to compare it to 1 Timothy 2:12–14. Please read and compare the two passages carefully and thoughtfully—out loud, if that helps. Again, they are from the same author, same book, same context, same audience. The question is: are these two texts about the same topic? In comparing them, ask yourself if the vocabulary is the same, if the tone is the same, if the intensity is the same, as those are hints as to whether the subjects are the same. Also remember that the word for teaching orthodox doctrine, as Paul uses it in this book, is the word *didasko*, while the word for teaching unorthodox doctrine, as it is used in 1 Timothy, is *heterodidaskaleo*. The quotation below, from 1 Timothy 6, begins with a command to Timothy.

"Teach (*didasko*) and urge these duties. If any one (a generic term that includes *both* genders) teaches otherwise (*heterodidaskaleo*) and does not agree with the sound words of our Lord Jesus Christ and the teaching which accords with godliness, he is puffed up with conceit, he knows nothing; he has a morbid craving for controversy and for disputes about words, which produce envy, dissension, slander, base suspicions and wrangling among men who are depraved in mind and bereft of the truth...."[347]

---

[346] 1 Timothy 1:3
[347] 1 Timothy 6:2b–5b

Now read the text we are trying to understand from 1 Timothy 2, quoted below.

"I permit no woman to teach (*didasko*) or to have authority over men; she is to keep silent. For Adam was formed first, then Eve; and Adam was not deceived, but the woman was deceived and became a transgressor."[348]

If the reason behind the prohibition of women teaching is that they were teaching unorthodox doctrine, then the subject of those two passages is basically the same. However, the tone, the vocabulary, particularly the word used for "teach," and the intensity *feel* quite different. He seems far more intense when talking about prohibiting false teaching than about whether or not women should be allowed to teach (whatever that means) men. Therefore, I think the subject is different.

Now for the hard part! It is often easier to say what the text does not mean than what it does mean. And this is a notoriously difficult text to interpret. And, as I said before, virtually everybody, in the effort to understand this text, ends up with something less than a literal understanding of the words. So we proceed with caution and humility and prayer.

The first step is to get at the meaning of the word "teach." I'm not sure I can think of any other single word (in this context, at least) that has been so uncritically *assumed* to mean the same to us as it did to the original writers and readers as this word. In one sense, Dr. Scholer is correct as I quoted him above: we need always to ask the interpretive question, "How would the *original* readers of the letter have understood what he was saying?" Automatically when we read the word "teach," what comes to mind is a very 20th-century definition similar to the one with which I began this book. I was a

[348] 1 Timothy 2:12–14

student in my Inorganic Chemistry class in the fall of 1967. There was a teacher present, but in college they are called professors. The activity that occurs in a classroom is "teaching." And (hopefully) learning, too, though not always! What does the activity of teaching consist of for us as modern westerners? A person gives a public lecture. He (or she) is the teacher. There are students who madly take notes (though some sleep) and then take those notes home and study or memorize them. The final step in "teaching" is when the test is given to "test" the students to see if they have learned what the teacher has taught. If a certain percentage of correct answers is obtained, the student is deemed to have "learned" the material.

Since that has tended to be our visual definition of what teaching is, we have applied this text to mean that women should be prohibited from giving a lecture to a mixed audience where men are present. But it is permissible, according to this interpretation, for a woman to give a lecture to an audience where only women are listening.

That understanding has raised all kinds of inconsistencies and questions from people who are sincerely trying to understand and apply Scripture. Why is only a public lecture considered "teaching"? Why is a book or video not considered teaching? To some it is. In both instances, there is a passage of content just as in a public lecture. Why can a woman who believes very strongly that women should not teach men write a book about why women should not teach men? Is there not the slightest possibility that such a book might fall into the wrong hands? Like the hands of a male? Or should males not read books written by women? What if a male were to ask a woman for advice? Could a woman never teach a man in any circumstance? Could there never be a female seminary professor, since she would be teaching men about Kingdom-of-God concepts, not just multiplication tables?

We once had a young female staff worker with one of the campus ministries live with us for several years in a downstairs bedroom. In the course of her working with the Christian group on campus, she had often had occasion to speak, and to speak to a group of students containing males. One particular night, she came home very distraught and angry because when she got up to speak, half the group left—all the males. Maybe their motives were pure. Maybe they did not want to take part in an activity they considered unBiblical. Maybe they were male chauvinists. Maybe they were just arrogant. That is an issue God will have to judge, not I, even though I strongly disagree with what they did. But they certainly felt that what she was doing was obviously so wrong that they could not remain in the same room and, in the process, deeply hurt a child of God.

To make "teaching" synonymous with giving a public lecture is, I think, a mistake. Jesus was called a "teacher." He was called "teacher and Lord." What He did by gathering a small group of disciples, traveling around, and in the context of living together, giving "life lessons" which, it assumed, He had the authority to do, was called "teaching." And there were other "teachers" around. The Pharisees asked Jesus, "Why do John's disciples and the disciples of the Pharisees fast, but your disciples do not fast?"[349] Notice that Jesus' practice of having disciples and being a "teacher" to them was not odd. John had some and the Pharisees had some as well. Following are some differences between how "teaching" happened in New Testament times and how it happens in our times, and so why, I believe, we may misinterpret this text:[350]

1. The teaching that happened between a teacher and his disciples does not fit our modern scheme of a public lecture with note-takers at desks, followed by test taking as a litmus test of whether the student has learned the content.
2. While there was certainly some content passed on, the majority of what Jesus taught was about life, righteousness,

---

[349] Mark 2:18
[350] For more on the Jewish understanding of "teaching" and how it differs from our understanding of the word, see Robert Saucy, JETS, March 1994, pp. 79–97.

character, and the kingdom of God. Certainly an increase in knowledge and understanding was part of the goal, but that was not the complete goal, unlike modern teaching in the school system where increase of knowledge and appropriate skills are the only goals. Jesus did not just teach academic theology. Think, for example, of the directions that were given the older women in the book of Titus: they were to "*teach* what is good and so train the young women to love their husbands and children, to be sensible, chase, domestic, kind, and submissive to their husbands."[351] The measure of success in their teaching would be how they would live and treat people, not how much content they had absorbed. That is a very different measure of success than getting 85% of the questions correct on a test over the most recent chapter in the textbook.

3. In our educational system, the only authority the teacher has is authority over content and classroom decorum. Imagine a situation where the teacher requires for a passing grade in the class that students respect their parents, avoid sexual promiscuity, avoid gluttony, and be kind to everyone. I am not talking about in the classroom only, but in all of life, outside the classroom, 24 hours a day. Such a teacher would not last in our school system, and that is appropriate. But that is the kind of teaching that took place in New Testament culture. It is not the same as teaching in our culture. Therefore, I think it is a mistaken application merely to prohibit women from giving a lecture to an audience consisting of both men and women, whether that be in a church, para-church organization, or Sunday School. The content as well as the level of authority is different. The way the word seems to be used in the New Testament is closer to soul-care, or discipleship, or spiritual mentoring.

---

[351] Titus 2:3, 4—but to be honest, the word translated as "teach" is a different word—*sophronizo*—which means more to admonish or exhort or to discipline.

Or eldering. That is an important observation, as that is the topic that follows *immediately*. The chapter division between chapter two and chapter three is a much later addition to the text. It was not in the original letter to Timothy. It is important to observe that in the author's mind the issue of "teaching" leads naturally into the topic of eldering. What Paul is talking about does not fit our concept of teaching, which usually involves giving a public lecture. "The teacher-disciple relationship required both learning the content and *living out the teaching* [italics mine], in other words, a total personal demand."[352]

Interestingly, in 1 Corinthians 14:26, where Paul is addressing the problem of chaotic fellowship services in the church at Corinth, he uses the noun form of the verb *didasko*, "to teach," meaning "a lesson." He says in that verse, "When you come together, each one has a hymn, a lesson, a revelation, a tongue, or an interpretation. Let all things be done for edification."[353] The word that is translated as "lesson" in the RSV is translated as "doctrine" in the KJV and NIV. It is the word *didache*, which is the noun form of *didasko*, which is what Paul is prohibiting women from doing in the church at Ephesus when done with authority. It is the word used in 2 Timothy 4:2, when Paul exhorts Timothy to be "unfailing in patience and in *teaching*." Clearly in the 1 Corinthians passage, *anyone* can do it. The word "each one" or "every one" is in the original. It is not a translator's choice. It is gender-neutral. A woman can bring a lesson, a *didache*, a doctrine, apparently to a mixed group. So giving "a lesson," which would fit our concept of "teaching," is not prohibited to women. In Titus 2: 2, the older women are to be "teachers of what is good." The word used there is *kalodidaskalos*, again, a compound

---

[352] Neither Complementarian nor Egalitarian, by Michele Lee-Barnewall, Baker Academic, Grand Rapids, MI, c. 2016, p. 93. But she is quoting Robert Meye in Jesus and the Twelve: Discipleship and Revelation in Mark's Gospel, Grand Rapids: Eerdmans, 1968, p. 97.
[353] 1 Corinthians 14:26 (RSV)

word containing the word *didaskalos*, which is the noun form of our word *didasko*, one who teaches. So in that instance, women were actually commanded to teach. Not all "teaching" by women is prohibited. But some apparently is prohibited. It would seem that a public lecture is not prohibited. It would seem that it is *not* true that women could not be trusted to teach as if they were incompetent. But there is something here in 1 Timothy that is prohibited, and I think it has to do with the word *authority*.

In our culture, authority is a dirty word. And there is very good reason for that; we have all heard ugly news stories about how leaders have abused their authority or how parents have abused their children and how church leaders have abused their authority. I have no cure for that, only embarrassment and apology. We live in a fallen world where all are sinners, including church leaders. Rightly or wrongly, the church has responded by largely eliminating the authority of pastors and elder boards in the lives of people. Elder boards have largely become boards of trustees, making policy decisions rather than being personally involved in the lives of church members and actually "teaching" in that context. It seems in the New Testament that those who were designated as elders really did have the responsibility to be gently and positively *involved* in people's lives for good and for righteousness and not for evil gain. They were to feed the flock. The qualifications required of such people were steep, and they should have been.

So we are extremely uncomfortable with the subject of authority, and rightly so. Notice that it is difficult to talk about teaching without bringing up the issue of authority, even if all that is mentioned is the lack of authority of the teacher over anything but classroom behavior or content in our culture. In New Testament times, the teacher had an enormous amount of authority over the life of the student, or really the disciple; it was not just about content; it was about life and godliness. That, I think, is why Paul mentions the issue of authority in verse 12: "I permit no woman to teach or have authority over men." You could not separate them in that culture as we do in ours.

The word "authority" (*authentein*) is a rare word, and there is considerable ambiguity over what it meant to the original hearers. In fact, this is the only time it appears in the Bible. Paul did use a different word for authority (*exousiazo*) in some other contexts, but even that word was used only three times. Some have noticed that, in some lexicons, the word he used here may have had a negative sense, such as to usurp authority (the King James version even translates it that way), but that sense did not appear until some two hundred years after the letters to Timothy were written. Still, there are many who think the word *authenteo* should be translated as "usurp authority" or "domineer" or "act in an overbearing manner" or "assume authority inappropriately."[354]

A key word that helps us to understand what is going on here is the word *oude*, which is translated as "or" and which connects the two verbs "have authority" and "teach." It is used somewhat in the sense of "neither, nor" in our language. It connects two words that are either *both* negative or *both* positive, but it is not used to connect a positive word and a negative word. Or it connects words that are similar, as in "neither of the night *nor* of the dark" in 1 Thessalonians 5:5. Or it can connect antonyms, as in Galatians 3:28: "neither Jew *nor* Greek, neither slave *nor* free."

Because Paul uses that particular word, it follows that he is prohibiting either teaching (in a positive sense) and having authority (in a positive sense) over men, or teaching (in a negative sense— teaching error) and having authority (in a negative sense, that is, domineering authority) over men. If the circumstance is negative (by that I mean teaching error and exercising a domineering authority)

---

[354] Actually, the meaning "assume authority" or "usurp authority" *may* be what Paul meant here. He could be saying that for women to take a position of authority over men, especially a position that involves teaching and discipling, *would be* inappropriate and therefore would fit the definition of assuming or usurping the authority that is not hers to assume. However, since that would be a negative situation, it would also mean that "to teach" would also need to be negative, and that is not a possibility given the word Paul uses for it. Also, it must be noted that there is zero evidence in the Scriptures or outside the Scriptures that women actually were teaching false doctrine.

if men did it, presumably, that would be prohibited also. It would be bad whichever gender did it. The sense of the prohibition is either teaching erroneously and usurping authority over men or just teaching and exercising authority over men. They are either both negative or both positive. But if they are both positive, it is prohibited for women to do both to men. What hints are there in the text as to which understanding is intended by the author?

1. As we said above, there is no evidence that women were teaching error.
2. The word for "teaching" (*didasko*) is used positively in every instance in the pastoral epistles of 1 & 2 Timothy and Titus, except in Titus 1:11, where it says, "They are upsetting whole families by *teaching* for base gain what they have no right to teach." It is difficult to know exactly what Paul means, but the issue seems to be not teaching incorrect doctrine but doing it for the purpose of personal gain. Teaching correct doctrine is very important. To use *didasko* negatively, meaning to teach incorrect doctrine, would stand out as a very unusual use of the word.
3. There is a different word that is used to describe erroneous teaching by the false teachers in 1 Timothy 1:3 and 6:3. "As I urged you when I was going to Macedonia, remain at Ephesus that you may charge certain persons not to *teach* (*heterodidaskaleo*) any different doctrine...," or in 6:3—"If any one *teaches otherwise* (*heterodidaskaleo*) and does not agree with the sound words of our Lord Jesus Christ and the teaching (*didaskalia*) which accords with Godliness, he is puffed up with conceit...." The word *didasko* is used of orthodox doctrine and, significantly, it is the word used here in 2:12. The word *heterodidaskaleo* is used of unorthodox doctrine. It is not the word used in 2:12. So what Paul is prohibiting women from doing is teaching correct doctrine, not incorrect doctrine. It is not a negative word.

4. If both the activities were negative, that is, what he was talking about was teaching error and usurping authority, again the question needs to be answered why only the women were prohibited from this activity and why only from doing so to *men*? It is really not a very profound statement to say that teaching error and usurping authority is not allowed. But why prohibit only women from doing that? And only to men? Surely it was not permissible for men to do those activities. We know that some men were teaching unorthodox doctrine at Ephesus and Paul condemned them by name, but there is no evidence presented that women were. So why would Paul only prohibit the women from teaching unorthodox doctrine? And, very significantly, the word for men, over which women are not to assume authority, is for males, not people in general. The word is *aner* not *anthropos*. For those who say the whole prohibition is cultural, limited to a certain issue at Ephesus where women, who were assumed to be uneducated, were being prohibited from teaching men—for those of that conviction—they must explain the use of *aner*, males, instead of *anthropos*, human beings. The prohibition is about women teaching males, not the unprepared avoiding teaching others until they are prepared.

5. Philip Payne and others propose that since (in their opinion) *authenteo* is a negative word, what Paul is really prohibiting here is teaching in such a manner as to assume or usurp authority inappropriately. So the situation would be a person doing good and orthodox teaching (required by the word *didasko*) but doing it with self-assumed authority.[355] But that invites two questions: why is gender even brought into it? Is it the practice itself that Paul is prohibiting—that

[355] See Philip Payne, Man and Woman, One in Christ, p. 359. Or Discovering Biblical Equality, p. 219, where Dr. Linda Belleville says that a better translation is, "I do not permit a woman to teach so as to gain mastery over man."

316

is, teaching orthodox doctrine—but with a view towards usurping some sort of authority that is inappropriate? Or is the issue women doing it to men? That is what the words say. And secondly that is a positive concept and a negative concept being connected by the word *oude*, which would be highly unusual.

Since the meaning of the word *authenteo* is debatable, we have to look at the problems that would be raised by taking the negative meaning of the word, to usurp authority, and the above five points are indicative of the problems raised. Those problems need to be answered if we are to take the meaning as something like "usurp authority" or be dictatorial. The reader will have to decide, of course, but I find that the above problems indicate that the positive meaning of "exercise authority" fits far better with the context.

So it seems that the two activities women were prohibited from exercising were good activities, not bad ones. Since *"oude"* must connect either two negative words or two positive words, and since the word for "teach" is always used positively in the Pastorals, and since the word for unorthodox teaching is not used here, then the word for "exercise authority" must also be a positive word. So the word *"oude"* is connecting two good activities, not a positive word (teach) and a negative word (usurp authority).

So what is going on? Why would the apostle encourage women to learn (against cultural norms) but prohibit them from teaching?

"For Adam was formed first, then Eve; and Adam was not deceived, but the woman was deceived and became a transgressor. Yet woman will be saved through bearing children, if she continues in faith and love and holiness, with modesty."[356]

---

[356] 1 Timothy 2:13–15

317

There are, I think, two words that are crucial to understanding what the apostle meant in these difficult verses. They are "for" at the beginning of verse 13 and "yet" at the beginning of verse 15.

The "for" at the beginning of verse 13 is in the sense of "because." There are some who say the word itself (*gar*) does not require the sense of "because" but could be just introducing an explanation. Frankly I fail to see the difference between the two; either way, Paul is giving a reason or explanation for what he just said. And there are two reasons given:

1. Adam was formed first, then Eve.
2. Adam was not deceived, but the woman was deceived and became a transgressor.

First, let's tackle a simpler issue: The fact that the woman is described as becoming a transgressor does not mean that Adam was not also a transgressor. Clearly, both were. Paul blames Adam for the entry of sin into the world and compares the opposite results of Adam's action to the results of Christ's action in Romans 5:18 & 19. "Then as one man's trespass led to condemnation for all men, so one man's act of righteousness leads to acquittal and life for all men. For as by one man's disobedience many were made sinners, so by one man's obedience many will be made righteous." The man, Adam, was also a transgressor, clearly. Our text here in 1 Timothy only says that he was not deceived, which, if you read the Genesis account, is true. He ate of the tree undeceived by Satan, with his eyes wide open. Eve was tricked into it. Adam just disobeyed.

Second, the type of their transgressions was different. As I said before, Eve was deceived. For whatever reason (we are not given the reason), Satan attacked her, attacked her first, and attacked her from the blind side, by tricking her. For whatever reason, she blew it. She was tricked, and when she tried to answer by appealing to God's word, she messed it up. It was downhill from there.

Adam, however, who was there with her, made no effort to resist and calmly disobeyed the clear words given him by God. The silence of his fall was thundering. The woman at least made some attempt to appeal to what God said and to resist. Adam did not.

"She also gave some to her husband, and he ate."[357]

That was it.

Which is more worthy of condemnation? I make no judgment. Like Saul and Jonathan, they were together in life and together in death.[358]

It is possible that the prohibition of women teaching or exercising authority over men is due to their inherent gullibility. In fact, on the surface, that is what the text seems to be saying.

However, that does not seem to hold up under examination:

1. There is *nothing* else in the rest of Scripture that says anything like that. If this verse is saying that women are inherently more gullible than men and so are not to be trusted in teaching or exercising authority—if that's what this verse is saying, it stands alone in all of Scripture.

2. That has not been my experience, which, of course, is not final. But I think it is hardly a universal experience to say the female gender is inherently more simple and gullible.

3. *If* that proposition is true, it invites the question of why Adam's blatant disobedience does not disqualify men as teachers the same way Eve's being deceived disqualifies women as teachers. Does that indicate that blatant

---

[357] Genesis 3:6b

[358] "Saul and Jonathan, beloved and lovely! In life and in death they were not divided." (2 Samuel 1:23)

disobedience to the *known* will of God is not as serious a trespass as being tricked into it? Surely not.

4. *If* that is true, then why are women encouraged to teach other women in Titus? That would be the uneducated leading the uneducated, the blind leading the blind.

5. *If* that is true, it makes Jesus' willingness to entrust to women the most significant news in all history, the fact of His resurrection an incredibly dangerous move.

6. *If* that is true, it makes Paul's reference to women as co-laborers in the gospel confusing.

As I have said before, this is a difficult passage. And it is true that *everyone*, from the most strident conservative to the most free-thinking liberal, at some point does not take this passage as literally true. What follows is what makes the most sense to me.

Verse 14, about only the woman being deceived, really is connected with verse 15. We will come to that later. Verse 13, about Adam being formed first, is really the cause for the prohibition or, more clearly, an explanation of Paul's line of reasoning in making the prohibition. That verse is the one joined to the prohibition in verse 12 by the Greek word "gar" in the sense of "for." Verse 14 is not part of the cause but introduces verse 15.

The question before us is, what does being formed second, which Eve had no part in, have to do with being prohibited from teaching and exercising authority over men? Or why does being formed first, which Adam had no part in, qualify him for teaching and exercising authority? It does not seem reasonable.

Most who believe that the prohibition is not temporary think that what Paul is referring to is the Old Testament practice of primogeniture: "If one ventures into the dusty archives of the church's past, there awaits an interesting discovery: by far the clearest explanation throughout church history for the logic of 1 Timothy 2:13 is primogeniture. Much of the time no explanation is given. There is an assumption that readers understand the logic. When an explanation was given, however, primogeniture is the clearest elaboration of the logic. Modern proponents of patriarchy, then, are joined by numerous ancient voices within church history to support the primogeniture thesis."[359]

Primogeniture is the practice in which the firstborn is granted prominence within the family unit and was viewed as devoted to God. It was a common practice among contemporary cultures with Old Testament Israel where the firstborn was often sacrificed to the pagan deity. In contrast, in Israel, the firstborn was viewed as especially set apart for God, not sacrificed. Now, as I said, the church has traditionally seen the appeal to Adam's creation prior to Eve as the first example of primogeniture and because of that understood Paul's reasoning to be based on primogeniture.

At the risk of disagreeing with a long history of church tradition, I think there are a couple of problems with this interpretation, even though it is what the church has historically believed.

1. Even though Scripture refers to the primogeniture system, God himself did not originate the practice and hardly follows it consistently. Because of that pattern, it does not seem to be an absolute principle. In the foremost example of God's sovereign choice, His choice of Jacob over Esau, God chose the second-born, not the first-born. If primogeniture really were a principle of the Kingdom, it would seem that God would support his own principle by sovereignly choosing the first-born as an example of God's sovereign ability to choose. There are numerous other examples of God's ignoring the principle of primogeniture.[360]

2. There really is not a clear Biblical text that supports the principle that primogeniture is ordained by God. It was a

[359] Slaves, Women & Homosexuals, by William Webb, InterVarsity Press, Downers Grove, IL, c. 2001, p. 135.

[360] Slaves, Women & Homosexuals, pp. 135 ff. God curses firstborn Cain but accepts Abel's offering. God chose Jacob over Esau. Samuel thought he should anoint Jesse's eldest son as the king of Israel, but instead God chose his youngest.

common practice in the cultures contemporary with Old Testament Israel, however.

3. Primogeniture really seems like an inappropriate concept to use to prohibit women from teaching or exercising authority over men. The practice of primogeniture comes up *after* the fall; it was not part of the creation. Why, in the New Testament church, would God make such a prohibition applicable to one gender merely as a reminder of an institution that appears after the Fall? Especially when God Himself does not follow the principle? The practice of primogeniture really does not seem a significant principle to use to understand gender relationships in the New Testament church.

The problem is that Paul really does not say what his reasoning is in relating the prohibition of women from teaching and having authority over men to Adam being formed first. We are left to speculate on that. At the enormous risk of going against much of church history, I think that primogeniture is not the issue. Primogeniture is not the endpoint in going back from the prohibition in 1 Timothy 2. I think it points to something larger. I think the fact that Eve is blamed and Adam is not is a hint that there is something going on in Paul's mind other than basing the prohibition of women teaching on Eve's being tricked. That would make a mockery of Adam's blatant and conscious disobedience by allowing males to assume the role of teacher and prohibiting females because of Eve's disobedience. I think Paul's thinking is based on something else.

Genesis 1:26 and 27 teach (I believe) that gender relationships reflect something of the relationships among the persons of the Trinity. When a plural God created human beings, He created them male and female, specifically and uniquely in His image. Then we have the twin chapters of Genesis 1 and 2 with the introduction of the twin truths of complete equality (from chapter one) and gender differentiation (from chapter two). Those two chapters form the whole foundation for my understanding of gender as revealed in the Bible. The creation of Adam and Eve, with Adam being *created first* and Eve being created *out of* Adam, are *the* central events of Genesis 2. Everything seems to be secondary to that. Those two events are also the central events on which Paul bases his argument for gender differentiation in 1 Corinthians 11, as well as here in 1 Timothy 2. Remember the list of some ten differences between Genesis 1 and Genesis 2? And how those differences make Genesis 2 strangely "male-oriented"? I observed that there were several egalitarian authors who acknowledged some sort of a "hint" of hierarchy in Genesis 2. It is significant, I think, that those egalitarian authors, who are uncomfortable with hierarchy, could not avoid seeing it in Genesis 2, in the perfect creation of God. The reason they couldn't avoid seeing it is simply because it is there.

But we could not draw any conclusions as to what the significance of those differences was. At least not yet. But now, Paul here in 1 Timothy 2 makes an application from that *central* event of chapter two. Since it is that chapter, which introduces the aspect of a hierarchy of equals in gender relationships (not clearly, not completely, but still inescapably) and not in Genesis 1, that would be missing in our understanding of gender were Genesis 2 not in the Bible. As we saw in the chapter on Genesis, chapter two in that book presents the genders very *asymmetrically*. They are not like positive and negative poles on a battery. Remember all the events that *hinted* at the headship of the male—that he was created first and Eve was created out of Adam, that he named her just as God named the parts of creation and just as he named the animals, that he recognized her and not she him for what reality was—"bone of my bones and flesh of my flesh"—not just a helper for his work but *somebody just like him*. Whatever would be missing from our understanding of gender in the Bible if Genesis 2 were left out is what Paul is reminding us of here by referring to the central event of that chapter—Adam's creation prior to Eve. Ultimately, since gender relationships reflect something of Trinity relationships (as a result of humans being created in the image of a plural God), Paul is referring to the perfect hierarchy of equals in the Trinity, of which gender relationships are an *image*. So when Paul prohibits women from teaching or having authority over men, he is saying that it is a reflection of the perfect hierarchy of equals in the Trinity.

Additionally, since Adam was created first, it follows necessarily that Eve was created second. And *out of* Adam. As we learned on pages 214 and 228 in the chapter on 1 Corinthians 11, in Paul's mind the fact that Eve was created out of Adam makes Adam the head of Eve. "*For* [in the sense of 'because of this'] man was not made from woman, but woman from man. Neither was man created for woman, but woman for man." That is his conclusion to everything he has said before in that chapter about males and females, including the headship of the male to the female. As I said at that point, headship is not defined. It is defined elsewhere. But Adam's being formed first and Eve's being formed second and, a result, *out* of Adam, introduces the concept of headship, but that concept is not connected to Adam's primary creation until the New Testament. Now, to be sure, Paul says a couple of verses later that "Nevertheless, in the Lord, woman is not independent of man nor man of woman; for as woman was made from man, so man is now born of woman." So, as we said then, headship of the man does *not* erase equality. That is the tension we need to hold in this fallen world. That sentence, right there, may be the most important sentence in this whole book. But both in 1 Corinthians 11 and here in 1 Timothy, Adam's prior creation means something—namely headship. But that—and this is consistently the picture we find in the New Testament—his headship does not mean inequality or male dictatorship.

There is one application Paul makes of this principle, and that has to do with elders. The chapter division between chapter two and chapter three does not exist in the original, and so what Paul has been talking about leads, naturally, into the subject of elders in the church. We will deal with that in the section on miscellaneous texts in chapter 10 when we deal with 1 Tim 3:1 and following.

324

That leaves us with verse 15 yet to interpret. The second crucial word "yet" in this text is found in the beginning of verse 15. It is the translation of the Greek word *de*. The King James version translates the word as "Notwithstanding," and the NIV translates it as "But." The word indicates that a proposition is coming that does not follow from went before. It is the word Jesus used over and over again in the part of the Sermon on the Mount where he presumed to interpret the verbal traditions of the Pharisees and enlarge upon them and complete them: "You have heard that it was said to the men of old, 'You shall not kill and whoever kills shall be liable to judgment.' *But* I say to you that everyone who is angry with his brother shall be liable to judgment and whoever insults his brother shall be liable to the council."[361] "You have heard that it was said, 'You shall not commit adultery.' *But* I say to you that every one who looks at a woman lustfully has already committed adultery with her in his heart."[362] "It was also said, 'whoever divorces his wife, let him give her a certificate of divorce.' *But* I say to you that every one who divorces his wife, except on the ground of unchastity, makes her an adulteress; and whoever marries a divorced woman commits adultery."[363]

That structure occurs some six times in that section of the Sermon on the Mount. "You have heard it was said… *But* I say." It is a profound contrast and one that begs interpretation. Especially it raises the question of who on earth is this Man? Who does He think he is to go *beyond* their traditions? And that is exactly what He did. He did not negate them, but He internalized them to the thought-life, to the soul-life, to the life of motives.

But… interpreting the Sermon on the Mount is not the purpose of this book. The word "but" that Jesus used to contrast his extension of the Pharisaic traditions to the issue of the heart and soul is a

[361] Matthew 5:21, 22
[362] Matthew 5:27, 28
[363] Matthew 5:31, 32

translation of the Greek word *de*. It introduces a contrast, a direction not expected from the previous statement.

The home basketball team averaged six inches shorter on the front line. *But* they out-rebounded the visiting team by a margin of ten rebounds.

Do you see how the second statement is not what would normally be expected from the first statement? The word "but" gives the reader the hint that there is a proposition coming down the pike at us that does not follow from the previous statement.

Since this word is the word that Paul used to begin verse 15, it indicates that, whatever verse 15 is proposing, it is not an expected result from verse 14 about Eve being deceived. Let's wrestle with this most difficult verse. I believe it is one of the most exciting and encouraging verses in the whole Bible on women. It is, more importantly, about the complete sovereignty of God. But it is also the most difficult to figure out. Our starting point is that, whatever it says, it is not what one would expect to follow verse 14 because of the first word in the verse, *de*, translated as "yet."

"And Adam was not deceived, but the woman was deceived and became a transgressor. *Yet* woman will be saved through bearing children, if she continues in faith and love and holiness, with modesty."[364]

Here are the issues that make this verse so tough to understand that *nobody* takes it literally:

1. The word translated "woman" in the first part of the verse is singular and appears to refer back to the woman in the previous verse, to Eve.
2. The first verb *sosthesetai*, translated "will be saved," is singular, but the second verb, *meinosin*, translated as "remain" or

---

[364] 1 Timothy 2:14 & 15. The RSV footnotes "bearing children" with the note, "*or by the birth of the child*, and "continues" with *they continue*.

"continue," is plural. Look at the verse again: "Yet woman will be saved (singular) through bearing children if she (really "they") continues in faith and love and holiness, with modesty."

3. There is an article in front of the phrase "bearing children," the word "the." The RSV has an alternate translation as a footnote: "or by the birth of *the* child."

4. The word *sosthesetai* is a form of the infinitive *sozein*, which means "to save." It is the very common word used to describe salvation in the New Testament, as well as an escape from a negative situation such as a shipwreck.

That's what we have to work with. What sense can we make of this verse, which says in effect, "Yet woman will be saved through the birth of the child as long as they remain holy and modest?"

First, our word *sosthesetai* does not always mean "to save" in the sense of what we mean by becoming a Christian, being born again. As observed in chapter two on hermeneutics, the New Testament writers, by necessity, took secular words and gave them Kingdom-of-God definitions. Paul could use the same word, and did use the same word, to describe both his escape from a shipwreck and his eternal justification before God. So it may be describing something very mundane or profoundly eternal. We use the word "redeem" to talk of a situation when a negative situation is turned around. So when a basketball team unexpectedly loses to an inferior team and then defeats a superior opponent in its next game, we say the team "redeemed" itself. We also use the word to describe what has happened to us when we became Christians, when we came to accept that we were bought back with the price paid by the death of Jesus on the Cross. So we say we were "redeemed." The word "redeem" can be used to describe a very profound event brought about by the death of Christ or a very mundane act by a basketball team.

I think what the apostle is talking about here is the "salvation" or redemption of the reputation of the female gender, not in the "becoming believers in Christ" sense but in the sense of the basketball team that showed what it really could do.

When the author begins with the singular word for "woman," I think he is referring to the female gender as a whole, and so it is singular. He is referring back to the most recently named woman in this letter, to Eve, who stands as a federal head for all women. So he is using Eve as a figure for all women and in so doing is saying "womanhood," the female gender, as represented by Eve, is "saved" or redeemed.

When the author says that womanhood is "saved," he is saying that the female gender is redeemed—that is, redeemed in the sense of showing what *good* the female gender is capable of and so is redeemed from the historic blame of being the cause of the fall of the human race.

When the author says "through bearing children" or, in an alternate translation, in the footnote of the RSV, including the article that is present in the original, "by the birth of *the* child," he is referring to the most important birth of any child, the birth of our Savior, Jesus Christ. The "the" indicates that the author had in mind a very specific birth.

Throughout church history, as evidenced by the quotations of church fathers in this book, Eve has been described as a pretty despicable character, less worthy than a man, easily deceived, weak, even the source of sin for the man. Those descriptions have been written by males.

In contrast to the historically negative view of women, and in contrast to verse 14, which tells us (correctly) that Eve was deceived and became a transgressor, now verse 15 tells us that the female gender, of which Eve is representative, is "saved" or redeemed through the birth of our Lord and Savior. Not saved in the sense of justification, but redeemed in the sense of reputation. Lest we think that women are inherently less worthy than and inferior to men, which is what the quotations at the beginning of some of the chapters in this book have said, we must remember that it was through a *woman* that Jesus came. It was through the *obedience* of a woman that Jesus came. She was not unworthy.

And so the mysterious hint in Genesis 3:15 that some sort of "fix" would come through the "seed of the woman" is finally resolved. It is through the "seed of the woman" and *hers alone,* since she was a virgin, that Satan is defeated. And the feminine gender has been redeemed. Mary, mother of Jesus, needed no help from a man and received no help from a man, in bearing the Savior of the World. This was her task and hers *alone.* And she quietly accomplished it. And so sin entered the world because a woman was tricked into disobedience, but the Savior entered the world because a woman obeyed and so "redeemed" the feminine gender. There was no man involved.[365]

I think many protestants have unfortunately missed the wonder of Mary, Mother of Jesus, and her amazing, quiet obedience. Picture her situation: she had done nothing wrong and she found herself pregnant outside of wedlock. I know, many teenage girls today have told angry fathers that they did not understand how they could be pregnant since they had not had sex with anyone. Yeah, right. Sorry, but that happened once and only once. With Mary, it was really true. And her future husband was ready to divorce her, though he was determined to do it quietly.[366] She had no say in that. What a position to be in! To be pregnant out of wedlock qualified the young woman for stoning to death. If Joseph did divorce her—a very reasonable action to take—she would have been a single, poor, pregnant young woman—a perfect candidate for an abortion.[367] Her

---

[365] Interestingly, Diana, or Artemis, the goddess whose enormous temple was in Ephesus, the home of the church to whose pastor this letter is addressed, was also supposedly a virgin and was known as "the mother without spouse, the Original mother." (From The Golden Bough by Frazier.)

[366] Matthew 1:20. Joseph is described as "a just man and unwilling to put her to shame," and so he "resolved to divorce her quietly." It is very significant that "a just man" does not receive pleasure out of someone else's sin or feel the need to demean the person publicly. It is easy to miss what a bad situation this was for Mary. Her being pregnant outside of marriage would have made her a slut in the eyes of many in that culture.

[367] Abortions were accomplished by physical trauma to the belly, abortifacient herbs, bloodletting, physical dismemberment of the unborn fetus, vigorous jumping, fasting, or carrying extremely heavy loads.

only defense was that the child was conceived by the Holy Spirit. Again, yeah, right—try to explain that to somebody. Yet she does not rail and shout at God for her extremely unfair situation, one that really and truly was not her fault, one that she did not choose. Her response when it was explained to her? "Behold, I am the handmaid of the Lord."[368] Or again: "Mary kept all these things, pondering them in her heart."[369] If only the world were populated with men and women who followed *her* example of inconvenient submission to the will of God.

I do not think that quiet submission to the inconvenient authority of God is only a feminine characteristic. The same characteristic is obviously a characteristic of Jesus, who was a male. It is a characteristic that should be present in all children of our Heavenly Father. But here is a *woman* who displays it clearly for us all and is an example for us all, men included, to follow. Because of her willingness to accept quietly the incredibly confusing road God had mapped out for her, because of her willingness to be a servant, our Savior came into this fallen world.

So in this text, as in the other New Testament texts we have studied so far, and as in Genesis 1 and 2, there is teaching about both hierarchy and equality. But this text, I think, more than any other, elevates the feminine gender to its proper place in the Story of God. It was through a woman that sin entered the world, and then to the man, and it was through a woman that the Savior entered the world, with no help from a man.

We do live in a fallen world where things are profoundly not right. Unfortunately, we are so comfortable with being away from home that it seems normal to us. It is difficult to comprehend the Design because we are so used to the Mess. But the pattern is still there and it would be to our advantage to try to emulate it. I wish that we could see the astounding beauty and sacredness of the Design. Clark Pinnock puts it this way: "Due to polemics, it

---

[368] Luke 1:38
[369] Luke 2:19

often sounds as if their [meaning those who believe in some sort of significant role differentiation between the genders] delight is to keep women in their subordinate place,[370] whereas in reality there is great beauty in the relationship between women and men that they describe. The delicate interplay, the give and the take between man and woman—a mirror of the redemptive relationship between Christ and the church—speaks nothing of superiority and inferiority, but only of a vastly fulfilling love that welcomes the differentiations God as assigned."[371]

If only we could digest that and live it out, even partially, in this world. As I have said, I think the Bible-believing church needs to repent of an unBiblically low view of the female gender. But the egalitarians do not have the answer in trying to avoid the Design of gender roles. In heaven, we will finally get it right. We will not only see but partake of that beautiful relationship, unhindered and unadulterated by sin. And we will be partakers of the Real Thing, of which gender relationships are an image, the relationship of Jesus with His Bride, the church, the members of which are those of us who have trusted in Christ.

And it will be beautiful beyond comprehension.

---

[370] Let's be honest. For many, perhaps, there has been a wicked tendency to do just this.

[371] Women, Authority, and the Bible, edited by Alvera Mickelsen, InterVarsity Press, Downers Grove, IL, c. 1986, p. 58, from an article entitled, "Biblical Authority & the Issues in Question," by Clark Pinnock.

8

LIVING AWAY FROM HOME

1 Peter 3:1 through 7

"All the same, the New Testament, without going into details,
gives us a pretty clear hint of what a fully Christian society
would be like. Perhaps it gives us more than we can take…
there will be no manufacturing of silly luxuries and then
of sillier advertisements to persuade us to buy them. And
there is to be no "swank" or "side," no putting on airs…. It
is always insisting on obedience—obedience (and outward
marks of respect) from all of us to properly appointed
magistrates, from children to parents, and (I am afraid this
is going to be very unpopular) from wives to husbands."[372]

I think that probably there is no other book in the Bible that makes
me squirm more or is more culturally unacceptable or politically
incorrect or just plain challenging to my personal comfort level than
1 Peter. (It would be a tight race with the Old Testament prophets
though.) It is so politically incorrect and so opposite from the current
modern western worldview that its teaching may whiz right by us as
we read it. Even as I read through it just before sitting down to type,

---

[372] C. S. Lewis, Mere Christianity, Macmillan Publishing Co., Inc., New York, NY, c. 1943,
1946, 1952, p. 80.

I was again challenged with new observations—not new content, as it has always been there—but seeing again what the words say. I live in a society where personal peace and comfort is the primary goal of life. We have tended to believe Satan's lie that real life comes from outward beauty and accumulation of things. Creativity is not Satan's strong suit; he still is about the same game of getting us to believe that God really is not sufficient and not out for our good, and so we have to supplement life with the cultural equivalent of eating from the "tree in the midst of the garden." I want to remind us of the striking absence of the words "and they were satisfied" when Adam and Eve ate from the tree from which they were forbidden to eat. The author of Ecclesiastes puts it this way: "He who loves money will *not be satisfied* with money; nor he who loves wealth, with gain: this also is vanity."[373] It is futile. Yet we easily fall into the same error. When we obtain something, we expect it to bring deep satisfaction, and when it doesn't we tend to assume that the problem is that we just don't have enough and so need more to be satisfied. But the problem is not that we don't have enough; the problem is that we are expecting life from something that cannot give life.

The book of 1 Peter was written to a very specific audience. The opening lines of an epistle are usually skipped over as not being very important. Author. Audience. Grace and Peace, etc., etc. Peter begins his letter in this way: "To the Dispersion in Pontus, Galatia, Cappadocia, Asia, and Bithynia, chosen and tested by God the Father and sanctified by the Spirit for obedience to Jesus Christ and for sprinkling with his blood." I don't know how any times I read those words before I realized I was clueless about what the dispersion was or why Christians were addressed as "exiles." So I did some research into the background of those terms.

After the dismissal of Adam and Eve from the Garden, which we read about in chapter five, the rest of the Old Testament is the story

---

[373] Ecclesiastes 5:10

of God reaching out for His people in hopes of relationship with them. It really is pretty amazing that God would want relationship with His continually disobedient people, with the descendants of the people He kicked out of the Garden. But despite His advances they continued to run away from God.

It is significant that the fingerprint God chose to communicate this rejection of His steadfast kindness toward His people with was *adultery*. Not a scorned friend, not a lost brother, but a jilted husband. The more intimate the relationship, the greater potential for pain. God chose *marriage*, not acquaintance, or friendship, or even familial relationship to describe His relationship with His people. Marriage is the most intimate relationship we humans experience. Their rejection of Him continued for over hundreds of years despite God's faithful sending of His prophets to plead for His people to return to Him. But they did not. So God sent the pagan Assyrians to invade Northern Israel, and in 722 BC Israel fell to them. The foreign, Godless troops deported the northern ten tribes of God's people off into captivity. The southern two tribes, called Judah and Benjamin, did not learn from their sister Israel but instead followed her example of apostasy and in 587 BC fell to the invading Babylonian army. Jerusalem was leveled. God's temple, the temple built by Solomon at God's direction, was destroyed by foreigners. This was done *at God's direction*, and the best of Israeli culture was carted off to captivity in Babylon. Unlike the deportation of the northern tribes, who intermarried and eventually lost their identity, the exile of the southern two tribes was temporary, and, as predicted, after seventy years they miraculously returned to Jerusalem to rebuild a wall around the city and God's temple. Not all returned, however; some stayed "in a foreign land" but maintained their Jewishness and built little temples called synagogues in the foreign lands where they were currently living. Some 450 years later, when the Apostle Paul was traveling through the area sharing the Good News of Jesus the Messiah wherever he went, he found these little communities of Jews with their own synagogues ready and prepared to hear the Gospel of the Messiah. And he always went to them first.

This scattering of the Jewish people from their homeland has always been part of the cultural identity of the Jews. For nearly two thousand years, they did not even have a homeland officially, even though that small bit of geography at the east of the Mediterranean was, in their minds, still theirs.

We used to have a delightful Jewish family who lived several houses from us, and they were always ready to talk about religion very freely and even attended a Seder that our church sponsored as part of our Easter celebration. Whenever I listened to the father, Jordan, talk about his time in Israel, I would sense tears coming to his eyes as he talked about what was, to him, very much Home even though he was born in America and was an American citizen. That sense of "being away from home" is, unfortunately, not very much a part of our Christian identity, particularly our North American Christian identity. That is why I am belaboring the point so much. It is very much part of the Jewish identity. In fact, the Father of the Jewish people, Abraham, at the time of his being chosen by God to be the founder of the Jewish people, was told first of all to "leave home." And later on when his wife Sarah died in the land of Hebron and Abraham was looking for a plot to bury her in, he described himself and requested the plot in this way: "I am a stranger and a sojourner among you; give me property among you for a burying place, that I may bury my dead out of my sight." If you've ever seen the movie *Fiddler on the Roof,* you get a sense of their national, cultural sense of being away from home. They were a culture within a culture. They looked different, they dressed differently; they talked differently. They knew they were not at home. This scattering of the Jewish people is called the Diaspora, the dispersed ones, those away from home. The Dispersion.

Now this is what faces us as we look at the opening of the book of 1 Peter. The author was a Jew who had come to understand that Jesus was the promised Messiah. He was writing to Christians, those "chosen and destined by God the Father and sanctified by the Spirit for obedience to Jesus Christ and for sprinkling with his blood." That describes what a Christian is. But he called them (and he uses a Jewish term here) the "exiles of the Dispersion." In what sense were they "exiles" or members of the "Dispersion"? They were almost surely not all Jews.

The reason they were addressed as exiles is answered immediately in verse 3: "By His great mercy we have been born anew to a living hope through the resurrection of Jesus Christ from the dead, to an inheritance which is imperishable, undefiled, and unfading, kept *in heaven* for you." Our hope is not here. Our home is not here. We are foreigners in a foreign land. We *really* need to comprehend that truth. Peter, a Jew who understood Jewish history, saw that the historical fact of the Jewish Dispersion was an appetizer of the Christian life. We also are dispersed, exiles in this world, away from our Home. The whole New Testament in reality is written to a people away from Home; but the book of 1 Peter, more than any other, has that as an underlying theme. "Peter, an apostle of Jesus Christ to the exiles of the Dispersion...." "Conduct yourselves with fear throughout the time of your exile...." "Beloved, I beseech you as aliens and exiles to abstain from the passions of the flesh.... Maintain good conduct among the Gentiles...." "Let the time that is past suffice for doing what the Gentiles like to do...."

If anybody needs to be convinced that living away from Home is our situation, surely the book of 1 Peter provides one of the greatest reasons: one *suffers* for doing what is *right*. Think about that. Should one not be rewarded for doing right? What kind of messed up system are we living under? The world we live in is such that one does what is right and, instead of receiving accolades, he suffers for it. As we have seen, one of the results of the fall was that the world is upside-down. Let's get this straight: it certainly appears as if riding the golden crest, enjoying a life of ease and prosperity, is not guaranteed as the result of Godly living, at least in the New Testament. How can one explain that, unless we are in a world that is upside-down? "For one is approved if, mindful of God, he endures pain while suffering *unjustly*. For what credit is it, if when you do wrong and are beaten for it you take it patiently? But if when you do *right* and *suffer* for it you take it patiently, you have God's approval. For to this you have been called, because Christ also suffered for you, leaving you an example, that you should follow in his steps." "But even if you do suffer for righteousness' sake, you will be blessed." "When you are abused, those who revile your good behavior in Christ may be put to shame. For it is better to suffer doing right, if that should be God's will than for doing wrong." "Beloved do not be surprised at the fiery ordeal which comes upon you to prove you, as though something strange were happening to you." "Yet if one suffers as a Christian, let him not be ashamed." "Therefore, let those who suffer according to God's will do right and entrust their souls to a faithful Creator."[374]

In Old Testament language, Gentiles were non-Jews; they were not God's people. So Peter is writing to an audience who are God's people but are living among people who are not God's people. I commend to all of us that that is *exactly* where we are supposed to be. Jesus prayed specifically for his disciples not to be taken out of the world: "I do not pray that thou shouldst take them out of the world, but that thou shouldst keep them from the evil one.... As thou didst send me *into the world,* so I have sent them *into the world.*"[375] That is where we are to live. But this world is not our Home. Heaven is our home.

So this book of 1 Peter is about how to live a Christian life in a non-Christian world, and that is our current reality. The challenge is to not accept the cultural values of the place where we are living, but to be different. Radically different. Uncomfortably different. We must be comfortable with being odd. As the King James Bible puts it, to be *peculiar.*

The result, by necessity, will be conflict. The Bible calls that suffering. It happened to Jesus. It will happen to us, and we should

---

[374] 1 Peter 2:19–21, 3:14, 3:16 & 17, 4:12, 4:19
[375] John 17:15,18

not be stunned by that turn of events. "Do not be surprised at the fiery ordeal which comes upon you to prove you, as though something *strange* were happening to you...."[376] As I said before, what more clear evidence is there that we live in a fallen world than the common and normal experience of doing what is right and *suffering* for it? That happened to our Leader, and we should not be surprised if the same happens to us, his followers.[377]

One of the themes of the book of 1 Peter, referred to by C. S. Lewis in the quotation at the start of this chapter, is that of being submissive. I'm not sure we can come up with a more foreign and culturally unacceptable theme than that. It applies to both genders.

"Be subject for the Lord's sake to every human institution, whether it be to the emperor as supreme, or to governors as sent by him to punish those who do wrong and to praise those who do right."[378]

"Servants, be submissive to your masters with all respect, not only to the kind and gentle but also to the overbearing."[379]

"Likewise you wives, be submissive to your husbands, so that some, though they do not obey the word, may be won without a word by the behavior of their wives."[380]

"Likewise you husbands, live considerately with your wives, bestowing honor on the woman as the weaker sex, since your are joint heirs of the grace of life."

---

[376] 1 Peter 3:12

[377] That raises the uncomfortable question of our lack of suffering. Perhaps we are living a life more conformed to this world than a life conformed to the value system of the Kingdom of God.

[378] 1 Peter 2:13,14

[379] 1 Peter 2:18 I do not think this verse condones injustice or the horrid condition of forced slavery, but does acknowledge the presence hierarchy infected with injustice in a fallen world.

[380] 1 Peter 3:1

Hierarchy, or order, I believe, is part of the created world and not a result of the Fall. First Peter bristles with hierarchy. Servants are to be submissive; wives are to be submissive; we are all to be submissive; even Jesus was submissive. But hierarchy was badly mangled in the Fall, and that is what we live with. Rulers can be and are incredibly corrupt. Governments can be agents of unthinkable amounts of suffering. Husbands can be very mean and insensitive. Life is not fair. That is our situation. This is the result of living in a fallen world where the perfect design was horribly injured. The hierarchy that God designed was one where we were all created in the image of a plural God who consists of a hierarchy of equals. For those of us on this side of the Fall, which is everybody, it is difficult to comprehend a hierarchy of *equals,* uninfected with selfishness and sin. Most people think that to be in hierarchy means, be definition, to be unequal. That is a summation of all the quotations at the beginning of the chapter on the Trinity, Hierarchy, and Equality. That's what it looks like in *our fallen world.* The original perfect hierarchy, that of husband and wife, was injured as a result of the fall, so that the husband became the ruler, and the wife became the lowly follower whose job is to encourage her husband in his leadership. However, there is still a Reality there, somewhere underneath the broken image we deal with in this world, which is Good. The reality of our being created in the image of a plural, hierarchical God is why we, the only beings created in God's image according to Genesis 1, *require* hierarchy to function in a group. And we feel very much out of place unless we are in some sort of group.

I believe that we should make every effort to correct the injustice of the fallen world in which we live and the enormous damage that evil hierarchy inflicts upon people, even though we will probably never get it completely right. We should do that even at our own cost. The fact that we will never solve the problem does not allow us to do nothing. It is significant that Moses acknowledged the same issue in his initial instructions to God's people after their deliverance from Egypt: "For the poor will never cease out of the land: therefore

I command you, You shall open wide your hand to your brother, to the needy and to the poor, in the land."[381] The fact that they would not eliminate poverty was not an excuse to do nothing. Instead, it was reason to open *wide* the hand of generosity. The same is true with attempting to eliminate the evils and oppression of unjust hierarchies. It is the unjust aspects of a fallen hierarchy that we need to eliminate, even though we never will completely do that this side of heaven. But since (I believe) a just hierarchy is designed into the Creation, it would be a wrong-headed exercise to try to eliminate hierarchy altogether. It needs to be corrected.

We need to let the Bible give us direction in how to work out the fallen hierarchy where we live. In every didactic passage we have studied so far on the issue of gender, there is present teaching on both the hierarchy of the genders and the mutuality or equality of the genders. The same is true in this passage in 1 Peter 3. The equality and mutuality of the genders is not merely an afterthought to the real meat of the issue, which is the submission of women to men. They are both equally central. That was true in the very beginning in Genesis 1 and 2, and that theme continues throughout the whole Bible.

"Likewise you wives, be submissive to your husband, so that some, though they do not obey the word, may be won without a word by the behavior of their wives, when they see your reverent and chaste behavior. Let not yours be the outward adorning with braiding of hair, decoration of gold, and wearing of robes, but let it be the hidden person of the heart with the imperishable jewel of a gentle and quiet spirit, which in God's sight is very precious. So once the holy women who hoped in God used to adorn themselves and were submissive to their husbands, as Sarah obeyed Abraham, calling him lord. And you are now her children if you do right and let nothing terrify you. Likewise, you husbands, live considerately

---

[381] Deuteronomy 15:11

with your wives, bestowing honor on the woman as the weaker sex, since you are joint heirs of the grace of life, in order that your prayers may not be hindered."[382]

In looking at our passage here in 1 Peter 3, we are greeted with the opening word "likewise" or "in the same way" in some other versions. That indicates that two concepts are going to be compared, one preceding and one following. As careful readers, that should make us look backward before going forward to see what is compared.

So what has come before in the passage? The immediately preceding context is the example of Jesus who suffered unjustly in dying for our sins, the just for the unjust. "When he was reviled, he did not revile in return; when he suffered, he did not threaten"[383] Even though some marriages are terrible and some wives are treated wrongly as uneducated subordinates, the example of Jesus' suffering seems a bit overly negative as an example of how wives are to be submissive to their husbands who may well be mean and insensitive!

The text immediately preceding the example of Jesus is the call of servants to be submissive to masters.[384] This also seems a bit negative as an example of wives being submissive to their husbands, though, sadly, in some marriages, one spouse treats the other as a virtual slave.

The text preceding the example of servants submitting to their masters is the call to all believers to be subject for the Lord's sake to every human institution (or every institution ordained for men).[385]

The text immediately preceding that is the call by the Apostle Peter to those who received his letter to "maintain good conduct among the Gentiles, so that in case they speak against you as

---

[382] 1 Peter 3:1–7
[383] 1 Peter 2:23
[384] 1 Peter 2:18
[385] 1 Peter 2:13

wrongdoers, they may see your good deeds and glorify God"[386] That seems to be the theme sentence for what follows.

So the whole context preceding the calling to wives and husbands alike in chapter three is the gender-neutral call for us as believers to maintain good conduct in this fallen world where we live as oddities. That is defined in a general way as being submissive to the institutions ordained by God instead of being demanding and refusing to serve others.[387] It means living in hierarchy.

We live in a world where this kind of thinking is foreign. But that seems to be what Peter is calling the readers of this book to. Even though the world scoffs at this view, with good reason because of the evils that have been perpetrated by the hierarchies in this world as a result of living after the Fall, it is what we are called to. I do not want to be misunderstood. I'm not talking about a weak-willed avoidance of responsibility or an avoidance of conflict. And I am especially not talking about refusing to stand up for what is morally right. I in no way believe the Bible supports slavery[388] or evil dictator-like hierarchy. Even though we live in a fallen world where hierarchy is often evil, we still should attempt to live in it and also attempt to correct the evil. No doubt, living in such a hierarchy will sometimes involve inconvenience, if not evil and suffering. Where it is evil we should resist it. However, I think we are being naive if we think our unwillingness to submit (I'm talking about both men and

---

[386] 1 Peter 2:12

[387] I do not think this or any other passage in the Bible condones the evils of slavery. However, it is true in the Kingdom of God that *voluntarily* giving up one's life to serve another is virtuous. To demand that of somebody is not. I realize that is viewed as pathological in our current world system. I'm glad that Jesus did not think that way.

[388] I do not think the Bible supports the American institution of slavery or any institution of slavery, as I have already said. American slavery was a double evil—treating human beings as property and ugly racism. It was only people of one skin color who were slaves in America. While the Bible does call slaves to submit to their masters, it also calls masters to "do the same to them." We must not miss that. That part of Biblical teaching seems to have been ignored. Ephesians 6:5, 9. Slavery is evidence of hierarchy gone terribly and inhumanly wrong, and the fact that Christians used the Bible to support this institution is inexcusable. But, as I have said, hierarchy—not inhuman hierarchy, but good hierarchy—is part of the creation. I have tried to make it clear what "good hierarchy" is. It is most definitely not slavery.

women here) or our unwillingness to serve another is not sometimes a result of personal selfishness and independence.

So that is the general principle and the context preceding the "likewise" that introduces the calling of both wives to husbands and husbands to wives. It is one of maintaining a submissive attitude and lifestyle in general rather than demanding to be served or refusing to serve others. Remember Jesus: He specifically said that He did not come to be served but to serve.[389] We all, both men and women, are followers of Him and so need to follow His example.

In our passage, there are twin commands, one to wives and one to husbands. The command to wives is to "be submissive to your husbands, so that some, though they do not obey the word, may be won without a word by the behavior of their wives."[390] The command to husbands is to "live considerately with your wives, bestowing honor on the woman as the weaker sex, since you are joint heirs of the grace of life."[391]

As noted before, the word that introduces the respective callings of both the wife and the husband is "likewise," and it is the identical word in the Greek—both for husbands and wives. Both genders are called to follow the general pattern of submissiveness and servanthood of Jesus that precedes this section. It applies to men and women equally. That is plain by the introductory "likewise" introducing the calling for each gender.

However, the callings are not the same. The wife is to "be submissive" to her husband. The husband is to "live considerately" with his wife. As I have noted before, the husband is never explicitly called to be submissive to his wife, and that pattern continues here. In the Scriptures, the Father is never revealed as being submissive to the Son. That, I think, is a significant pattern and not coincidental. And just as the Father is never revealed as an arbitrary, self-serving boss, so the husband is never allowed to use his position as the

[389] Mark 10:45
[390] 1 Peter 3:2
[391] 1 Peter 3:7

head in a self-serving manner. Dr. James Hurley coined the term "self-sacrificing headship."[392] But that is redundant. The Biblical definition of "headship" includes being a self-sacrificing servant, and the fact that we have to put "self-sacrificing" as a modifier in front of "headship" shows how we don't understand the Biblical concept of headship very well. It also introduces a major problem that I have with the complementarian view of this subject. The word "leader" is usually substituted for the word "head." There is an aspect of headship that includes authority. What I want us to understand is that unselfish servanthood is *just as much a part* of the definition of "head" as is authority. That is evident from our study on Ephesians 5. It is evidence of our residence in a fallen world that we so often misunderstand that concept.

It is at this point that I must part company with many of my brothers and sisters who also hold a high view of Scripture as I do. Words are important, both words in Scripture and the words we use to try to communicate the words of Scripture. There has been much written on the meaning of the term head and the Greek word it translates, *kephale*. At the center of the debate is whether or not the word includes, or is synonymous with, authority. I have found Dr. Wayne Grudem's research very helpful in this area.[393] But with all due respect to Dr. Grudem, he follows the pattern of most Christians who acknowledge the authority of Scripture in calling the husband the leader. He uses the English word "leader" as synonymous for the Biblical word "head." I disagree.

In his article in Recovering Biblical Manhood and Womanhood entitled "Wives Like Sarah, and the Husbands who Honor Them,"[394] which deals with the passage we are looking at in 1 Peter, he structures it along the general lines Peter does: first dealing with wives and

---

[392] James B. Hurley, Man and Woman in Biblical Perspective, Zondervan Publishing House, Grand Rapids, MI, 1981, p. 244.

[393] See "Appendix 1: The Meaning of Kephale" in Recovering Biblical Manhood and Womanhood, pp. 425–467. The reader is encouraged to read this to get a sense of the debate in this area.

[394] Ibid., pp. 194–208.

then with husbands. The first point in his outline is "Directions to Wives," with subpoints a) What Submission Does not Mean (with 7 points under that), b) What Submission Does Mean (with 3 points under that), c) The Old Testament Examples of Submission (which looks at the example of Sarah), d) The Rewards of Submission, e) The Universal Rightness of a Wife's Submission to Her Husband, and f) The Beauty of Submission.

He then moves to the section dealing with husbands. For clarity, I want to remind us what the passage actually says: "Likewise, you husbands live considerately with your wives, bestowing honor on the woman as the weaker sex, since you are joint heirs of the grace of life, in order that your prayers may not be hindered."[395]

His outline of this passage is entitled "Directions to Husbands," with four main subsections: a) What Considerate Leadership is Not (with 5 sub-points), b) What Considerate Leadership is, c) The Reasons for Considerate Leadership, and d) The Rewards of Considerate Leadership.

Yet in the Biblical text, there is no mention of the word "leader," nor is the husband anywhere in Scripture called the leader. But he sees the whole text as being about male leadership, even though that word is never mentioned. Now, to be fair, the word "head" is never mentioned either in this passage. The husband is called the "head" in other passages in the New Testament, however, but never the "leader."

I remember well as a young single Christian guy having debates with other guys about how the male had to be the spiritual leader in a relationship with a girl and whether or not that meant, by necessity, you could only date, or marry, someone less spiritually mature than you. Otherwise, how could the husband be the spiritual leader? So in addition to all the other qualities we were looking for in a potential wife, the infamous "checklist," we had to determine if she was our spiritual inferior to be marrying material![396]

---

[395] 1 Peter 3:7

[396] I remember with crystal clarity talking with a pastor about finding a mate and he asked if I had my list of what I was looking for, and I, of course, did. Then he asked if I had my list of

Sometimes the shades of meanings of words can be extremely subtle and yet extremely significant. In speaking to the college group at our church once, I tried an experiment on them. I have referred to this language issue earlier in this book. I had heard somewhere that one can recognize the values of a culture by how many different words with shades of meaning it has for a particular concept. For example, I had heard Eskimos have some eighteen different words for "snow." So, as a measure of the values of the secular culture we were living in, I asked these students how many different words they could come up with for the concept of "getting drunk." Coincidentally, they came up with 18. Each had its own shade of meaning. There is a difference between being soused and being snockered. Between merely being drunk and "tossing your cookies." Between being "high" and "blitzed." The difference between being so drunk you "ralph" or "Buick."

As I have struggled with the various pieces of this puzzle over the years, trying to try to figure out what the Biblical view of gender is, one of the surprising pieces to me was the subtle but significant difference between the word "leader" and the Biblical word "head." I challenge us to use the Biblical word as we talk about gender. Not that being the head does not involve at times some aspects of being a leader. It is more that the English definition of leader falls short of the Biblical definition of "head." And so we have to coin the term "self-sacrificing leadership." But if we think Biblically, "headship" means that you put the needs of the person over whom you function as a head *before you*. Servanthood is part of the definition. But that is not true for our English word "leader."

The problem is that "headship" is a concept that belongs to the Kingdom of God, and in our fallen world we have no exact equivalent. So we end up redefining it with something we are familiar with in our world and calling it "leader" or "male governance." It is critical

what kind of person I wanted to be in order to be a good husband. I was embarrassed. I had nothing. I had not even thought of that issue. How easy it is to be blind to our own issues and see with crystal clarity issues in other people!

that we understand the difference between the Biblical concept of "headship" and what we often mistake it for, which is "leadership." They are not the same.

Look at the texts we have studied. The position of the husband is not a position of personal superiority. It is not a position of boss in relation to employee or commander to soldier, as some have caricatured it. The word "leader" conjures up the vision of one who has superior knowledge and vision and understanding. The decision-maker. The one whom people follow. But the way the position of "headship" is presented in the Scriptures, it is a position of equality, just as the position of the Father with the Son is a position of equality—but still with authority. Yet the very titles for those two persons of the Trinity also indicate hierarchy. The title of "leader" does not seem synonymous for the term Father, does it? Does it "feel" right to say the Father is the "leader" of the Son? I think not, even though there is authority and hierarchy in the terms Father and Son, as well as equality of substance.

The picture on the front of Dr. James Hurley's book[397] shows a peasant woman bowing before a peasant man in an obvious position of servile submission. I would assume from the title of his book that this pictures what man and woman should be in Biblical perspective, since that is the title of the book. It would be an interesting experiment to see what other people see in that picture. It may well be my problem that I see that piece of artwork as demeaning to women. I don't see the female gender as being inferior in any way in the Scripture. That picture looks like an inferior person acknowledging a superior person. Biblically, the male is not superior to the female.

In the book Recovering Biblical Manhood and Womanhood, the authors point to an instance where a man has to ask a female for advice: "To illustrate: it is simply impossible that from time to time a woman not be put in a position of influencing or guiding

---

[397] Man and Woman in Biblical Perspective, op. cit.

men. For example, a housewife in her backyard may be asked by a man how to get to the freeway. At that point she is giving a kind of leadership. She has superior knowledge that the man needs and he submits himself to her guidance."[398] The author goes on to say that her "guidance" or "leadership" should be exercised in a way so that "mature femininity or masculinity" is not compromised.

Do you catch the subtle bias involved in that quotation? Apparently, to have "superior knowledge" is not normally a feminine quality. And so the woman needs to be careful in giving advice to a man so that she does not compromise her femininity or his masculinity. If one gender has a monopoly on "superior knowledge" and so needs to be careful not to compromise her gender's femininity, it seems to me that that gender must really be inferior.

Now let's look at the text itself. There are parallel instructions given to wives and husbands, both introduced by the word "likewise." As observed earlier, both genders are treated equally and both are called to continue the patterns of submissive behavior outlined in the verses preceding.

The calling for wives is:

1. Be submissive to your husbands.
2. Avoid the outward adorning with braiding of hair, decoration of gold, wearing of robes.
3. Display the hidden qualities, those of an imperishable jewel, of gold, which are a gentle and quiet spirit.

The calling for husbands is:

1. Live considerately with your wives.
2. Bestow honor on the woman as the weaker sex.

___

[398] John Piper and Wayne Grudem, <u>Recovering Biblical Manhood and Womanhood</u>, Wheaton, IL, Crossway Books, a division of Good News Publishers, c. 1991, p. 50.

There are three reasons given for these commands: 1) They are joint-heirs of the grace of life; 2) in order that your prayers may not be hindered; and 3) so that some unbelieving husbands may become believers by the behavior of their wives.

This text differs a little from the passage in Ephesians 5 where the command to wives to be submissive to their husbands is really not a command but takes the verb from the preceding verse. By contrast, in this text, the verb form really is sort of a command. It is the same structure as the command for wives to be submissive to their husbands in Colossians 3:18.[399] It is a verb form foreign to English speakers: the middle voice. In English we have two "voices": active and passive. The active voice is when the subject acts on the direct object: "I throw the ball." The passive voice is when the subject is acted upon by someone or something else—named or unnamed. "The ball is thrown," or "The ball is thrown by me." The middle voice, not used in English, is a construction where the subject acts upon itself. It is not acted upon by an outsider. Wives are to submit themselves to their husbands—that is the middle voice. The husbands are not to make their wives to be submissive, as if the husband were the subject and the wife were the direct object. The grammar does not support that. And that is why the translators chose to translate the words as "be submissive" to catch this flavor of the middle voice. That is the calling for the wife in this text. It is the wife's calling to be submissive, not the husband's to make her submissive. She needs to do her part; he needs to do his. His job is not to force her to do hers, and her job is not to force him to do his.

As I said in the introduction to this chapter, this letter is written to Christians living among non-Christians. And that is where we are supposed to be. Here we find Christian wives married to non-believing husbands. That probably was a condition that was a result of the wife becoming a Christian after marriage to her husband.

[399] "Wives, be subject to your husbands, as is fitting in the Lord."

Apparently a non-believing husband can be so stunned by the submissive behavior of his wife that he converts to her faith as a result! What is it about a submissive wife that is so convincing? The behavior, not the words, of a submissive wife can cause a man to come into the Kingdom of God.

The result here of an unbelieving husband being "won without a word by the behavior of their wives" is Profoundly Good and surely cannot be the result of a "thug" attitude being satisfied in the husband. The fact that such a behavior in a wife can bring about such a good change in a husband must indicate the profound truth and goodness of the wife's behavior. How could a behavior, *which some say is wrong*, that of being submissive to your husband, bring about such a good change of soul in the husband? This is behavior that is commanded to wives by the Apostle. It is not an example of God using an unholy behavior to bring about a good result, something He can and does do.

God is a master at using Broken Tools. He, as we have observed before, can use a pagan king to accomplish His purposes in the person of Cyrus. But here we have the Apostle *commanding* a behavior that many say is wrong and unBiblical and then saying an unbelieving husband may come into the Kingdom as a result of observing this behavior in his wife. How can this be?

God can certainly use evil actions to bring about good results. But He does not command them. Dr. John Stackhouse's book, Finally Feminist, has as its theme that fact that the emphasis on hierarchy in the New Testament times was about not offending the culture and thus inhibiting the spread of the Gospel. But now that egalitarianism is culturally acceptable, we must not inhibit the spread of the Gospel by insisting on hierarchy in the church and family. What he is saying is that women needed to be submissive to their husbands and so follow the cultural norm, even though that was wrong. But as a result their husbands would become Christians.

That interpretation raises a number of problems:

1. As we have said before, it does seem sexist: the freedom (and personhood, if you believe some feminist literature) of women needs to be sacrificed in order to see some men become Christians. If I were a woman, I would feel used and manipulated. And God would be the author of that!
2. If this is not the way Godly women are to behave toward their husbands, then it means that God is using and Paul is commanding women to act in an unBiblical but culturally acceptable manner for some specific evangelistic purposes. Again, it seems sexist.
3. It invites the question of why the submissive attitude of a wife toward her husband would cause that husband to become a Christian. What is it about a submissive wife that would make a husband become a believer? Especially if that is inherently wrong?
4. Perhaps most significantly, when the husband becomes a Christian, is the wife then supposed to change her behavior? Or is she to continue to act (as egalitarians would say) in an unBiblical manner, that of being submissive to her husband after he becomes a Christian?

No, it seems to me that this text lines up well with other texts in the New Testament in two ways:

First, being submissive is not insulting or secondary and does not imply inferiority. At least, not in the Biblical view.

Second, it really is the way the marriage relationship is designed. Or let me say, it is *part* of the way the marriage relationship is designed. The husband has his part as well, and it is not to function as the leader but as the *head*—as the Bible defines head. Each gender has its own role.

Let me note at this point two differences from the other three passages we have studied—Ephesians 5, 1 Corinthians 11, and 1 Timothy 2.

First, in this text in 1 Peter, there is no reference to anything bigger being involved. Remember in Ephesians 5, the marriage relationship was treated as an appetizer of the relationship of Jesus Christ to his bride, the church. In 1 Corinthians 11, the husband-wife relationship was treated as a fingerprint of the relationships within the Trinity. Headship describes both. In 1 Timothy 2, the restrictions put on women were a symbol of what went on in the Garden and the prior creation of Adam, which was a fingerprint also of the relationships in the Trinity. Maybe the lack of reference to anything bigger is because the people Peter is writing to live among a population that does not accept the God of the Christians or the Bible. That is just speculative.

But here in 1 Peter, there is nothing referred to outside of the potential of the husband becoming a believer as a result of the wife's good behavior. If this were the only passage in the Bible teaching on husband and wife relationships, it would be easy to interpret the calling of the wife to be submissive as utilitarian: good for converting the husband, but that is all. Nothing bigger.

However, lest we relativise the teaching of this text away, notice that the behavior encouraged by the Apostle Peter is described as being very "precious" in God's sight. And we are given an example in the person of Sarah of the type of behavior to follow, and she is from another culture 1,800 years removed. So what Peter is calling for here is bigger than a submission to the ego of a non-believing husband. It is good and right in God's eyes and therefore good, not bad. We have seen that in a fallen world good behavior may bring about bad results: suffering. But in a fallen world, bad behavior will not bring about good results, except by the intervention by God.

Second, even though Peter says that the wife is supposed to act in such a manner that her unbelieving husband may be converted to Christ as a result, that does not necessarily mean there is no transcultural component to what he is commanding. Dr. William Webb puts it this way: "The submission lists instruct Christian wives to submit and obey their husbands…. It is important to note that a wife's submission is explicitly linked to purpose statements about evangelism and Christian mission…. Peter tells wives to obey their husbands so that unbelieving husbands 'may be won over without words.'"[400] (1 Peter 3:1) "The one clear purpose statement within the submission lists is that of evangelism and Christian mission.[401]

It is a significant error, I believe, to say "the one clear purpose statement within the submission lists is… evangelism." He seems strikingly selective in only looking at 1 Peter. Just because the potential conversion of husbands is listed as a result of wifely submission does not mean that is the *only* purpose of wifely submission. It could be right in and of itself. It could be right for the purposes listed in the other passages. If the only purpose of wifely submission is the evangelism of ungodly husbands, why is that purpose mysteriously stated *only here?*[402]

So what are the good characteristics of a wife that are so profound that they can cause the whole soul of a husband to be changed?

She is to be submissive to her husband, reverent, chaste, and displaying, or "wearing" (as in clothing) a gentle and quiet spirit. The only other times the word "gentle" is used in the New Testament, two of them—they both refer to Jesus, who was, need I say it, a male. The other characteristic, quietness, is a quality that the whole

---

[400] William Webb, Slaves, Women & Homosexuals, IVP, Downers Grove, IL, c. 2001, p. 107.
[401] Ibid., p. 106
[402] I cannot buy the pervasive assumption by so many that Paul's teaching on hierarchy is meant to avoid offense to the surrounding culture, and therefore, temporary. I just cannot believe the Paul would sacrifice the female gender to evangelism. "In order for Paul's gentile mission to succeed, the behavior of Christian women would need to be consistent with what was practiced by women in the broader first century Greco-Roman world. Therefore, Paul's gender concerns were often missional when he addressed gender roles in the church and the home." So says Cynthia Long Westfall in her book Paul and Gender. Only in I Peter is evangelism tied to women's behavior. I think this understanding of gender roles is really more demeaning to women than the understanding that there is something bigger involved.

church should seek after. The church is encouraged to pray for those in positions of power, "that we may live a quiet and peaceful life, godly and respectful in every way."[403] That is our word *escheat*, which means quiet in attitude but not necessarily absolutely silent. Both these concepts apply to both genders, but there is something uniquely feminine and attractive to males when they are found in a woman. They are both "inner" qualities and are contrasted with "outer" qualities that are to be avoided: outward adorning with braiding of hair, decoration of gold, and wearing of robes.

I remember giving a talk on this passage and glossing over the teaching on outward adornings that were to be avoided as being "obviously cultural." One listener called me on my assumptions. "How do you know they are obviously cultural? And if they are, how do you know that the encouragement to display qualities such as a gentle and quiet spirit are not also cultural? How can one dissect a passage that way, discounting one part of a sentence as cultural but not the other? They are, after all, part of the same sentence."

I was stumped. My ignorance and assumptions were uncovered for all to see.

Not being a woman, I do not completely understand the need to put on make-up and jewelry. But I know in my own soul the need to appear in certain ways that make me more appealing to my culture. Or, at least, I *think* make me more appealing to my culture. Stylish clothes. Being trendy, up on the latest fashions, music. Being a "hunk." Driving a big truck. (Loud is better.) Having a six-pack (which I don't—or if I do, it is well hidden by my two-liter). What is at the root of all that?

While I think the main thrust of this passage is the outward versus the inward qualities, rather than a command against braids and earrings, it does invite the hard question for all of us: Which are we more concerned about? When you get ready for church, do you think more about preparing by concentrating on the condition

---

[403] I Timothy 2:2

of your soul and the God you are about to worship or by getting your make-up on and having your car washed so it looks nice in the parking lot? For you women: could you go to church with no make-up or jewelry? For you men: do you feel the need to show off your new phone or impress others in the narthex with the importance of your job? Or your "importance" in general? Or your muscles gotten by endless hours at the gym by wearing a tight fitting shirt? If our home is really not this world but the world to come, why do we let this world determine how we dress and act? I confess I am confused by the sheer quantity of make-up and jewelry some women wear—women confessing openly the truths of the Bible. Or the need of some men to show off their big truck or muscles. What drives that, particularly in light of this passage? I realize I risk coming across as an arrogant hypercritical legalist, but I ask these questions because of what the passage says, not out of a desire to condemn. At this point, I leave it to the readers, both men and women, to self-evaluate. But one thing that seems crystal clear: the qualities of a quiet and gentle spirit completely eclipse outward beauty as a mark of femininity. So which are we going to cultivate?[404]

The example of a godly woman given to the reader is Sarah, the wife of Abraham. As I pointed out in the introduction to the section on Corinthians, everybody in the Bible is a very mixed bag of good

---

[404] The danger introduced here is huge. I have an enormous amount of respect for the Amish people and am very attracted to their lifestyle. My grandparents' farm in northern Indiana had a small Amish church right across the road, and even as a child I longed to be part of their community. I was entranced by the long line of horse and buggies coming down the road on Wednesday nights for mid-week church, at which the men would play baseball and the women mow the lawn (!?). Two women behind a mower in their long dresses in the hot summer while the men played. But in their desire to be simple, they introduce a new legalism—who can be *more* simple? Buttons are sometimes not allowed—too extravagant. You can't use rubber tires on your tractors. Or you can't have rubber tires on the back, but you can on the front. Or you can't even use tractors. Simplicity is defined by a very rigid style of dress (and other issues), which is required by all. All that does is bear witness to our fallen nature and our ability to twist any principle of Scripture into a new law that is "keep-able" and that allows us to go to God from a naive position of strength, because we have lived rightly—that is, because we have kept the rules. Then we can feel confident before God. That position of feeling confident because one has "kept the rules" is condemned in the New Testament, both by Jesus and by Paul. It is condemned more strongly than sexual promiscuity!

and bad. Sarah fits well into the description: In a misguided effort to help God carry out His promise to give offspring to both her and Abraham, she made the suggestion to Abraham that he go sleep with her maid, Hagar, and get her pregnant, and they would just count that baby as the offspring. Abraham took her advice.

In another instance, when God, much later, returned to have a talk with Abraham and told him that, yes, indeed, they would have a son together in their old age, Sarah laughed at God. And when God confronted her with laughing at His promise, she choked it down and said, "No, I didn't laugh." But God said, "Oh yes, you did." God desires honesty about our faults, not a cover-up.

A year later, she was pregnant.

However, as with the other characters in the Bible, don't let their faults eclipse what they did that was good and right. There were also some examples of amazing submission to Abram, even when his ideas were morally questionable at best and probably downright wrong.

When God called Abram to leave his country and go to a land which He was to give him, Sarai went along.[405]

When Abram went to Egypt because of a famine in the land God had given him, Sarai went along and submitted to Abram's misguided and self-centered plan to lie to the Egyptians that Sarai was his sister, not his wife, and so Abram would be protected because of his beautiful "sister."[406]

When Abraham again lied about Sarai being his sister and not his wife, this time in Gerar, in order to save himself, she again went along with the misguided plan.[407]

So Sarah does show evidence of wearing the kind of jewelry

---

[405] Genesis 12:4, 5 and 13:1

[406] Genesis 12:10–20. I confess I am troubled with that text. I do not think the Biblical pattern of submission of wives to husbands includes submission when the husband wants her to do something wrong.

[407] Genesis 20:2–18

Paul is talking about here: the inner jewel of a submissive heart. At least she did sometimes, and those are the times when we need to follow her example, even though the example she was following was mixed up.

There should be at least two encouragements for us as readers of these events:

1. All characters in the Bible have committed significant sins, even the "heroes" of Biblical history. They were real people with a fallen nature just like ours.
2. Yet God was able to use them profoundly and carry out His plan completely. Even though Abraham and Sarah both fell far short of God's ideal, His plan was accomplished through them. Completely and exactly. Just as He said.

Therefore, Peter says to the women readers of his book, you can live without fear: "let nothing terrify you." Why? Because God accomplished His purpose through such an imperfect husband and wife as Abraham and Sarah, and so we can have confidence. We do not have to help God accomplish His purposes. And if one or both of us make a mistake or commit an intentional act of disobedience, God is not paralyzed. There were bad, selfish, misguided decisions on the part of both partners in that marriage, but God still worked out His will. That is not an excuse for disobedience: "And you are now her children *if you do right.*" It is reason for a quiet confidence: "*let nothing terrify you.*" The assumption, of course, is that what we are really after is God's will in our life, not our agenda.

So if God is really in control and you do not have to manipulate or manage life to make it work, it makes sense for Peter to say that wives should be submissive to their husbands. Sarah's life is a good example of that.

That brings us to the parallel command to husbands, parallel because it begins with the identical word, "likewise." Again, this refers back to the calling in 2:11 to abstain from the passions of the flesh that wage war against your soul and to maintain good conduct among the Gentiles. What follows is a series of callings to fit into the hierarchy of life and not demand personal agendas be accomplished. That, apparently, was what was meant by "maintain good conduct among the Gentiles."

The calling for husbands is for them to live considerately with their wives and to bestow honor on them as the weaker sex.

A couple of things should jump out at us:

The first is that this is not what one would expect from the calling delivered to wives. It would seem to follow from the call of wives to submit to their husbands that Peter would then turn to the husbands and exhort them to lead, to lead strongly, and to lead well. That, after all, is the mirror image of submission. But that is not what Peter calls the husbands to do. He calls them to live considerately with those who are to submit to them. Remember my three (wrongheaded but true) examples of what people thought the role of the "head" was in a Christian marriage in chapter seven? In one case, the husband got the hot shower first and if there was any hot water left, then the wife got what was left. In the second case, if the husband wanted a dog but the wife did not, especially because she would have to take care of it, then the husband got the dog because he was the "head" and the wife took care of it. And thirdly, a senior pastor gave the advice to his newly married younger associate pastor that he needed to establish himself as the "head" in the relationship and so pick something—even something as meaningless as whether you roll the toilet paper from the upside or the downside—and make an issue of it, calling his wife to obey him. That would establish him as the "head." Notice that the definition of "head" is the boss, the one in charge. And it was perfectly appropriate to use that authority for *his* own benefit. But the calling of the husband here in I Peter is to live *considerately* with his wife and bestow honor on her as the weaker sex. As believers in the trustworthiness and authority of the

Scriptures, we need to listen to them carefully, and attempt to weed out our hidden agendas and try to do what it says, not what we read into it.

The second issue that should jump out at us is this: if you know anything about the culture of the time, you know that wives were considered the property of the husband. To exhort the husband to "live considerately" was very counter-cultural. So the argument that Paul is just giving these instructions about gender relationships in marriage in order to avoid offending the culture is not true.

The third issue is that part of the calling of the husband is to bestow honor on the woman as the weaker sex. "Weaker" is one of those words that carries an enormous amount of cultural baggage, baggage from the culture of a fallen world. I well remember the comic books of the '50s that invariably had an advertisement inside the back cover about being a "weakling" on the beach and how one needed to sign up for a muscle-building course from one particular muscleman—I think his name was Charles Atlas—and then you would no longer be a weakling. And the girls would admire you.

It should jump out at us that the husband is to bestow *honor* on the wife as the weaker sex. In other words, *to be weak is worthy of honor.* It must not be negative to be weak. It is surely a result of living in a God-ignoring fallen world where being strong, independent, powerful, and not needing help are virtuous. In fact, one of the most common criticisms of Christianity is that it is a *crutch* for those who are too weak to get on by themselves.

Well, yes, that's exactly what it is, as a matter of fact. The Apostle Paul said that when he was weak, he was strong.[408] That was a man speaking. Weakness is not negative in the Kingdom of God.

Significantly, the comparative form of the adjective is used. The husband is to bestow honor on the woman as the *weaker* sex. It does not say, "as the weak sex"—the only one that is weak. The comparative indicates that they are both weak, and the woman is the

---

[408] 1 Corinthians 12:10

weaker. If it said the husband was to bestow honor on the woman as the weak sex, that would indicate only she was weak. Not the man. But that is not what is says. Both are weak, but the woman is the weaker—and worthy of honor for that.

I'm not completely sure exactly what the author was intending to communicate about the nature of femininity by calling the feminine gender the weaker of the two. But it is clear that it was *not* negative. The word could also be translated as "the more vulnerable," and possibly that is what is intended. There may be something intuitively obvious about the nature of femininity that it is described as weak or vulnerable—easily injured. What is important is that we not see it as negative, which is the command given to husbands.

I recently took one of my daughters to see a stage presentation of the story *Beauty and the Beast*. It is a story with a number of sub-plots and one of them is about how the village "hunk" named Gaston is out to get Belle, a beautiful young woman who enjoys reading, which he doesn't, to marry him. She thinks he is crude. He thinks she is the most beautiful girl in town and that makes her the best. At one point in the play, when Gaston was putting the pressure on Belle to marry him, she raised her hand to hit him in the face. Everybody in the audience chuckled. Then he raised his muscular arm to hit her, and everybody in the audience gasped. Both were only threats; nobody hit anybody. But I was struck by the contrast in the spontaneous reactions among the people in the audience. This was in a Big Ten university town, and the audience of several thousand was largely college-educated. The play was performed by a traveling theater company. This was not a bunch of country bumpkins. Yet the audience, which was in no way Christian, clearly thought it was amusing that a woman would hit a man, but very wrong that a man would hit a woman. Apparently the audience was not troubled by a woman hitting a man, but they were troubled by a man hitting a woman. Are they not the same? I realize that it is politically incorrect, but it seems clear to me that there is something universally and intuitively obvious about the feminine gender being the weaker gender. What we need to understand is that is a quality that is not negative.

Recently in an intense argument with my wife I was struggling to forgive her and show compassion to her. We both had been misunderstood by the other and both had made negative assumptions about the other's actions and words. I was really struggling. I remembered an activity the day before in which her weakness was apparent and, significantly, that aroused compassion in me. It aroused forgiveness in me. I don't know how to explain that, except that it happened. I think that real men show compassion. Jesus did in spades. And so should we. Real men are not thugs.

Fourth, the commands to the wife and husband, as is true in the other passages we have studied, are notably *different*. The command to the wife is to be submissive to her husband. The command to the husband is to live considerately with his wife, a lifestyle that, as we have noted, was culturally not acceptable. If mutual submission were the summary of the marriage relationship, which is what most egalitarians say is true, then this would be the perfect place for it to be taught. The apostle had just said that wives were to be submissive to their husbands. He should also then say, "Likewise, you husbands, be submissive to your wives." But that is not what the text says. It seems to me that that is a stumbling block for the mutual submission view of marriage. It just is not taught.

The fact of their being joint-heirs of the grace of life is the foundation for how the husband is to treat the wife.[409] The words are: "*Since* you are joint heirs of eternal life." It is because they are *joint-heirs, equal heirs*, that the husband needs to treat his wife appropriately—considerately. As we have seen in every New Testament text that teaches on the issue of how the genders are to

---

[409] It seems to me that the fact that both men and women are *joint heirs* of the *grace* of life indicates neither gender is more liable to sin than the other. Grace is the characteristic of God which forgives us our sins. As evidenced by some of the quotes of church fathers at the beginnings of some of the chapters, this has not been the position of the church historically. As a male believer, I apologize to my female sisters for the false belief that women are more likely to sin than men. The New Testament blames Adam as well as Eve for the original sin.

relate to each other, hierarchy and equality are both taught. Both. So here, they are *joint*-heirs of eternal life. They are in it together, as equals. So they must treat each other appropriately.

An heir is someone who is looking forward to an inheritance. There is something good coming, but in the future. It is not here now. It is yet to come. So we are to live looking forward to what is to come. The first part of this letter tells us where our inheritance is kept: undefiled, unfading, *in heaven*. That is where our inheritance awaits us, though there are numerous appetizers we can enjoy here and now. I do not mean to ignore the very present joy and peace lavished on us by God the Father. But it pales compared to the Joy and Peace we will receive when our full inheritance is ours. Then there will be no more longing, no more unfulfilled hopes—and no tears. There will be no more suffering for doing what is right, and no more will those who do wrong prosper. They will be long gone, and only those who have been dressed in the white wedding garment of the Bride of Christ will be present.

But even though our sins have been forgiven, right now we are like a bride—*betrothed*. Waiting. We are promised, but not yet married. Now we live in two worlds, and we have to decide which one we will be out of step with. We cannot be in step with both. That is our current situation. We are not yet home.

And so we wait.

9

MISCELLANEOUS TEXTS

So far, I have looked at the major didactic texts in the Bible that teach on the issue of gender. In all of them, there are the twin themes of hierarchy and equality, two concepts that most people in this fallen world see as contradictory but that the Bible does not see as contradictory.

There are additional texts that shed light on the Biblical understanding of gender. Most are narrative texts. By that I mean they report what happened, often with no comment as to whether what happened was good or not. It is easy to import our prejudice into the text and so conclude that some doctrine is "taught" from a narrative text. As I said in the chapter on hermeneutics, we have the example of Deborah in the book of Judges who clearly fulfilled a position of leadership, as well as the example of Jesus who chose only male disciples. It certainly was unusual for a woman to fulfill the role Deborah did, and it would have been very unusual for Jesus to appoint six men and six women as disciples. Is God willing to be counter-cultural in the situation of Deborah but unwilling in the situation of Jesus? That's a difficult question to answer, and that is the liability of looking to narrative texts for doctrine. But they are helpful, and in order to be thorough we need to look at several of them. Some texts are quite short, as short as one verse. Some may deal only indirectly with the topic of gender but still may help us see the mindset of the Biblical authors on this subject.

Abigail and Nabal
1 Samuel 25:1 through 44

I choose this text first because it exemplifies the difficulties in interpreting and applying a narrative text. I frankly think this passage offers little help in our discussion, but I have included it because others have. I will not quote the text in its entirety but will summarize it.

Nabal was married to Abigail. He was very rich. He was also "churlish and ill-behaved."[410] She, on the other hand, was "of good understanding and beautiful." Abigail is a common name for people who are Biblically literate to name their daughters—with good reason. She clearly is an admirable person. I never have known anyone to name their son Nabal! Every time I have heard someone refer to this passage in the context of the gender issue, it has been Abigail who is referred to. Never Nabal.

David and his men were in the wilderness and they sent to Nabal and politely asked for supplies. As we said, Nabal was very rich. Even though David's men had watched out for Nabal's sheep-shearers in the past, Nabal answered according to his character: "Shall I take my bread and my water and my meat that I have killed for my shearers and give it to men who come from I do not know where?"[411]

This enraged David and he prepared himself and his men for war. Abigail, without Nabal's knowledge, "made haste" and gathered two hundred loaves, two skins of wine, five sheep ready dressed, five measures of grain, a hundred clusters of raisins, and two hundred cakes of figs and told her young men to take them to David. And she followed them. But she did not tell her husband Nabal.

---

[410] 1 Samuel 25:3
[411] 1 Samuel 25:11

When they reached David, she fell at his feet and begged David's mercy.

"Let not my lord regard this ill-natured fellow, Nabal; for as his name is, so is he. But I your handmaid did not see your men of my lord, whom you sent."[412] She went on to manifest great intelligence and diplomacy and discretion, which eventually turned David away from what he admits would have been a great evil. Abigail went back to Nabal, who was in the midst of a great party and was drunk out of his mind. The next morning when he was sober, she told him what happened and "his heart died within him, and he became as stone."[413]

David took this as the Lord avenging the insult toward him and sent his servants to ask Abigail to marry him. Her response: "She rose and bowed with her face to the ground, and said, 'Behold your handmaid is a servant to wash the feet of the servants of my lord.'"[414]

I have read that this event from Old Testament history gives us an example of:

1. a woman who is far more intelligent and diplomatic and worldly-wise than her husband.
2. a wife who makes her own decision, even without telling her husband, and God obviously blesses it.

Those two statements seem true beyond dispute to me. I can see why people would name their daughters Abigail. She is a very exemplary woman!

It is also true when she consents to marry David (she became one of a number of David's wives), she calls him "lord." She also calls herself a "handmaid" and "servant" to David. She does not at this

---

[412] 1 Samuel 25:25
[413] 1 Samuel 25:37. Probably a heart attack or stroke. An appropriate way to die for a heavy eater and drinker who may well have also been diabetic.
[414] 1 Samuel 25:41

point see herself as an independent woman who can do whatever she wants and has no need of keeping her husband informed.

So what do we do with passage? She is an independent, intelligent, and wise woman who makes her own decisions, even without telling her husband. She also views herself as a handmaid and servant to her next husband. Her first husband seems to be an alcoholic and "churlish and ill-behaved," and the other is David, a man after God's own heart, though there are a number of areas in his life that are hardly exemplary. What does this show us about the gender issue?

Frankly, not much, and that is the difficulty of making doctrine from narrative passages. But for those who would say that the female gender is by nature, easily deceived, indecisive, and weak, Abigail would certainly seem to put that argument to rest. She is one intelligent woman.

Galatians 3:25–29

"But now that faith has come, we are no longer under a
custodian; for in Christ Jesus you are all sons of God, through
faith. For as many of you as were baptized into Christ have
put on Christ. There is neither Jew nor Greek, there is neither
slave nor free, there is neither male nor female; for you are
all one in Christ Jesus. And if you are Christ's, then you
are Abraham's offspring, heirs according to promise."

Most readers will be utterly aghast that I would include Galatians 3:28 as a "miscellaneous text" in our discussion of gender. For many, this is *the* determinative text, the "window" text by which we understand all other texts. I respectfully disagree, but first a little background.

The book of Galatians is probably one of the earliest of Paul's writings and one of his most intense. All of his other letters that had specific churches as the intended audience began with an expression of thanks by the Apostle for the church in mind. Not Galatians. In fact, it begins not with not an expression of thanks, but of shock. "I am astonished that you are so quickly deserting him who called you in the grace of Christ and turning to a different gospel...."[415] The Apostle is clearly very agitated at this church, and the issue is this: They initially made a decision to trust the sacrifice of Jesus Christ on the cross as payment for their sins; they were redeemed. But now some have felt the need to add some requirements to what Jesus did on the cross so they could be *really* confident before God, as if the death of Christ on the cross needed some extra help. As I have said before, the strongest condemnation, both by Paul and by Jesus himself is aimed not at the sexually promiscuous, nor at the worldly, nor even at the pagans, but at the strongly religious who felt self-confident because of their quality of religious life and rule-keeping. Because of their *self*-confidence. Remember the story Jesus told of the Pharisee and the sinner. The Pharisee was thankful to God that he was not a sinner like the publican several yards away from him. Yet who went home justified, according to Jesus? The sinner. We must not miss that fact—those of us who might feel proud of our commitment, proud of our correct theology, and very comfortable condemning others for their sin or maybe slightly incorrect views (in our opinion) on a particular subject. If we feel more spiritual than others and especially if, accompanied by that, we feel the need to condemn others because they are not as correct as we are, then we are in grave danger of an enormous self-confident mistake.

This letter was written to a church, or a group of churches, who were making the error of thinking, perhaps unconsciously, that the cross of Christ was inadequate by itself and there needed to be some additional work done by "believers" to be really sure of their salvation. It would be an interesting discussion to see if any of that is present today in the modern Evangelical church! Paul develops in this book a long and complex discussion of the historical place of

---

[415] Galatians 1:6

works and faith in the development of God's people. His argument is that God's people have always had relationship with their Creator by *faith*. It was never by being "good enough." Abraham, the Father of the Jews, was justified by *faith*: "he believed the Lord and he reckoned it to him as righteousness."[416] That's where Paul's argument begins. After a long and involved discussion about the legitimacy and historicity of faith, he arrives at his conclusion, and it is stunning. As non-Jews, it is likely to whiz right over our heads. The astounding conclusion is that not only are we justified by the death of Jesus on the cross as payment for our sins, but something totally unexpected follows: we are *adopted* as children of God! And we find ourselves calling out to God as "Abba! Father!" The jump is enormous, from the legal arena of "merely" being justified to actually becoming children of God and calling God "daddy." The word "abba" (no relation to the singing group) was a crib term—probably something like our term "da-da." Addressing God with such an informal term of endearment would have been unthinkable. Old Testament Jews considered God so Holy and so Other that they did not even say His name out loud. He was too holy. Remember that Jesus was accused of blasphemy because He called God his Father.[417] Now, says Paul, we can call Jehovah God by the name of daddy. Unthinkable.

My wife and I have four children, three of them adopted. I remember well one of the adoption proceedings. They, by necessity, happen in a courtroom, with a judge, just because in our legal system, that is how it is done. It is not adversarial; the birth moms were not there and were probably not even aware it was going on. In one of the proceedings, after the official part was done, which takes about five minutes, the woman judge stood up, stepped down off the bench, and sat down beside us to talk. "You need to understand," she said, "this child you have just adopted is the same as a biological child to you. If you ever have a biological child, it

---

[416] Genesis 15:6

[417] "This was why the Jews sought all the more to kill him, because he not only broke the Sabbath, but also called God his Father, making himself equal with God." John 5:18

will be illegal to discriminate against the adopted children in your will. The birth certificate will have your names as the parents. There is no difference. This is your child and you are the parents." We nodded in agreement that we understood. And we continue to nod in agreement, even though God has given us a biological child, as well; there is no difference. We are one family with four God-given children, and we love each one and get angry at each one without prejudice. And they with us.

So this book teaches that we are adopted into God's family as children of God and we are not second-class children. We are really His. And Jesus is not ashamed to call us brothers and sisters.[418]

The book of Galatians is a book about how one enters the Kingdom of God. Entry is not accomplished by being a member of God's chosen people, the Jews. This letter teaches that Greeks, a term that in that culture meant non-Jews, were not disqualified from entering the Kingdom of God because they were non-Jews. They did not have to convert to Judaism first. That would have been the position of those who received this letter, those who were depending on pedigree or circumcision for acceptance with God. They were demanding that you become a Jew (by being circumcised) before believing, or in addition to believing, in Jesus.

Paul's position was that one does not enter the Kingdom of God by being a Jew or non-Jew. It was not by being a slave or non-slave, that is, a freeman. And it is not by being a male or a female. In the Kingdom of God, those distinctions make no difference. We

---

[418] "That is why He [Jesus] is not ashamed to call them brethren...." Hebrews 2:11. I prefer to use the gender-neutral phrase "brothers and sisters" because I think that is what the author of Hebrews meant. I also use the gender-neutral word "children" when paraphrasing the verse, which tells us that we are adopted into God's family. However, it must be noted, in this supposed *Magna Carta* of the egalitarian position, the Bible uses the phrase "sons of God" rather than "children of God," which, it seems, would have been far more appropriate if Paul were elucidating the egalitarian position in this verse. I admit it is a slippery slope to know how far to go in translating the Bible as gender-neutral. While I think usually when the Bible uses the term "brethren" when referring to members of the Body of Christ, it is perfectly appropriate to take that as "brothers and sisters," I am not ready to refer to God the Father as God the Mother or even as God the Parent.

must see the context of this popular verse: it is about entry into the
kingdom of God, and there are no closed doors to anybody. "For
as many of you as were baptized into Christ have put on Christ."[419]

In the Old Testament temple there were four courts through
which one came closer to God. The outer court was the court of
Gentiles. The next court was the court of women. The next court
was the court of Jews. The innermost court was the court of the
priests. (This describes the temple of Herod.) To allow a Greek to
pass "closer to God" than the court of the Greeks was a trespass
punishable by death. The Roman government allowed the Jewish
people to put a Greek (a non-Jew) to death for going "too far" into
the temple, even if the person was a Roman citizen. This was the
offense for which the Roman mob almost killed Paul on his last visit
to Jerusalem: "The Jews from Asia, who had seen him in the temple,
stirred up all the crowd and laid hands on him crying out, 'Men of
Israel, help! This is the man who is teaching men everywhere against
the people and the law and this place; moreover he also brought
Greeks in to the temple, and he has defiled this holy place.' For they
had previously seen Trophimus the Ephesian with him in the city,
and they supposed that Paul had brought him into the temple."[420]

Maybe that passage gives us moderns some sense of how
unthinkable it was that Greeks could become intimate with God just
as Jews, God's chosen people, could. Now, there was no difference
because of the shed blood of Jesus on the cross.

Do not miss the fact that, second to Greeks, it is women who
were excluded from coming closer to God. The court of the Greeks
was the farthest from the center of the temple. The next farthest
court from the center was the court of women. Women were only
one step from the bottom of the pecking order, one step above the
"dogs." In addition to that, circumcision, the mark of the covenant
between God and his people, could only be performed on males.
The women had no mark of the covenant. We must not miss the

---

[419] Galatians 3:27
[420] Acts 21:27–20

stunning point Paul is making: that Greeks were acceptable in the Kingdom of God *just like Jews*, and that women were acceptable into the kingdom of God *just like men*. They no longer had to remain at a distance from the temple. In Christ, all comers are acceptable. When He died on the cross, the protective curtain in the temple protecting the inner sanctuary of the priests was torn from top to bottom, opening up entry into the Holy of Holies to anybody, including women, Greeks, and slaves. The only requirement is to be baptized into Christ. Women, Greeks, slaves, are all equals in the Kingdom of God and are just as much members of God's Kingdom as Jews, free people, and males. As the judge said to us, "There is no difference." We are all blood brothers or blood sisters, and it is the blood of Jesus which binds us together on an equal footing.

It is by *application* from this principle that some have concluded that the roles of men and women in the church, or husbands and wives in the marriage relationship, are no different, sometimes even interchangeable. However, this text does not *teach* anything about role distinctions in the Church. It is only about the entry requirements into the Kingdom, and they are the same for all—for Greeks, slaves, and women. All are equal before God.

Not everybody agrees that this verse does not apply to roles in the Body of Christ. Dr. Philip Payne puts it this way: "Some have tried to evade the practical consequences of all believers being 'one in Christ'; by interpreting Galatians 3:28 to mean merely that Greeks, slaves, and women can also become sons of God through faith in Christ."[421] Or "Each of these pairs identifies a social division. To say that they do not apply to the social realm is to miss their most apparent application."[422] Dr. David Scholer puts it this way: "Thus, rooted in its exegetical-historical framework and in Paul's hermeneutical intentionality, along with what I consider our legitimate hermeneutical extensions, I understand Galatians 3:28

---

[421] Payne, Phillip B. <u>Man and Woman, One in Christ,</u> Zondervan, Grand Rapids, MI, c. 2009, p. 79.
[422] Ibid., pg 94

to be the fundamental Pauline theological basis for the inclusion of women and men as equal and mutual partners in all of the ministries of the church." "It is sometimes suggested that Galatians 3:28 cannot be used to support the participation of women in ministry because it does not mention any specific function or office of ministry. This represents a very limited perspective on the implications of texts in their own literary and historical contexts."[423] Dr. Cynthia Long Westfall puts it this way when referring to Galatians 3:28: "The priorities and hermeneutics that Paul applied to the Jew-Gentile can and should be extended to the gender issue."[424]

There is an important hermeneutical issue here, and the authors quoted above are honest about it. You can tell by the words they use. They use words such as "application," "hermeneutical extension," "practical consequences," "implications," and "should be extended" in the above quotations. They do not use the words "teaching" or "doctrine." An application of a text, or a "hermeneutical extension" of a text, or an "implication" of a text, are not the same as a doctrine taught in a specific text. We must be very clear on the difference. Admittedly, when trying to interpret a text written two thousand years earlier in a very different culture, it may be a challenge to discern the difference between teaching and implication or application. That is why I have frequently used the word "humility" when we come to a text, meaning that we desire to be taught by the text itself rather than use the text to support our view. I am not accusing these authors of doing that.

But we must recognize that their understanding of the application or implication of a text is not as authoritative as the plain teaching of the text. The teaching carries the authority of God's word. Their "application" or "hermeneutical extension" does not. We can disagree with *them* without disagreeing with Scripture. It certainly is possible

---

[423] Both quotations by Dr. Scholer are from the address delivered at his installation as professor of New Testament, as recorded in "Theology, News and Notes," June 1998, p. 22.

[424] Westfall, Cynthia Long, Paul and Gender: Reclaiming the Apostle's Vision for Men and Women in Christ. Baker Academic, Grand Rapids, MI, c. 2016, p. 185.

to apply the teaching of this text in the area of gender relationships and to conclude that there are no role distinctions based on gender in the church. That would seem to be a very plausible application. If we find other texts teaching something different, then we need to re-examine our application of this text.

Galatians was one of Paul's earliest letters. As we examine other letters, later letters, we actually do find teaching about role expectations of men and women, husbands and wives, in the Kingdom of God. The fact is that the three distinctions mentioned in Galatians 3:28 were probably the three most culturally divisive distinctions of the time. These were not minor divisions of which only the elite of the culture would have been aware.

It is also obvious, or at least should be obvious, that the distinctions are not all of the same origin. Slave and free, Jew and Greek were not there by the design of the creator. However, male and female were there by design of their creator. That is obvious from our reading of Genesis 1:26 and 27. So the nature of the divisions are different. Interestingly, the words connecting slave and free, Jew and Greek, are different from the word connecting male and female. The word connecting Jew with Greek and slave with free is our word from 1 Timothy, "oude." Remember, it is a word that connects two similar terms, either similarly positive or similarly negative. It was the nature of that word that helped us understand "teach" and "exercise authority." Because of the nature of that word, they either needed to be both positive or both negative. But the word connecting male with female is the word "kai," which is just plain "and." While I am not sure of the significance of that observation, it may lend weight to the argument that the male/female contrast is of a different nature than the other two. People are male and female by design, and so becoming a believer in Christ and entering the Kingdom of God does not necessarily erase all differentiations if the differentiations are by design. The verse really reads, "There is neither Jew nor Greek, there is neither slave nor free, there is neither male and female." Notice how the sense of division is removed by using the word "and" instead of "nor", which is what the text really does. It also brings to mind the words of Genesis 1:26 and 27, where God created man as "male *and* female." We are male and female by design. We are not Jew or Greek, slave or free by design.

Additionally, there is the phrase that says, "we are all one in Christ." As we have seen, that phrase is used over the course of Biblical history to describe a unity of different beings with different roles but still having a mysterious unity. Oneness describes the Body of Christ, a grouping with different roles and with authority roles, but all are equal and of the same value. Oneness describes the marriage of two very different people, a man and a woman, two beings of equal value, but with (I believe) different roles with different authority. Oneness describes the Trinity, a grouping of different persons, with different roles and (again, I believe) differing authority, but still equal with each other. "Hear, O Israel, the LORD is one." Jesus prayed that his disciples would all be one. A male and female become one in marriage. Yet all are equal, even though there are different roles and there is an authority structure. It is a concept that only belongs to the Kingdom of God and is foreign to our thinking.

The issue here is similar to, and may be the same as, the issue that I described as the creation/redemption hermeneutic in the chapter on hermeneutics. If there is a differentiation between male and female that is designed by the creator, and if there is evidence for that in Genesis 1 and 2,[425] then there is nothing to be redeemed from a perfect creation, and entry into the Kingdom of God will not erase that differentiation. It is a differentiation by design.

Having said that, let's not miss the shocking contrast with Old Testament history after the Fall. In the New Testament teaching, women are accepted into the church of Jesus Christ as complete

---

[425] I believe, of course, that there is evidence of differentiation in Genesis 2, before the Fall. Remember at least two egalitarians who acknowledged some mysterious hierarchy in Genesis 2: J. I. Packer and Richard Longenecker. See footnote 14 in the chapter on Hermeneutics or footnote 39 in the chapter on Trinity, Hierarchy, and Equality.

equals. The exclusionary Court of Women no longer exists, nor does the Court of the Gentiles. Dr. Payne states the concept well: "'There is no male and female' undermines the law's purity regulations that kept women from full participation in worship; the barriers in the law separating Jews and Greeks, slaves and free, male and female, are done away in Christ, freeing them from the bondage of the law."[426]

If, as some believe, gender differentiation or gender roles are removed by Galatians 3:28, it raises an interpretive problem with Colossians 3:18, which says, "wives, be subject to your husbands, as is fitting *in the Lord*." If being "in Christ" in Galatians 3:28 removes gender roles, why are wives called to be subject to their husbands "in the Lord" in Colossians? Colossians was written *after* Galatians. That verse would seem to contradict the hermeneutical extensions made by Dr. Payne and Dr. Scholer and Dr. Westfall. Additionally, in verses 10 and 11 in the same chapter in Colossians, there are verses very similar to Galatians 3:28 that say, "and have put on the new nature, which is being renewed in knowledge after the image of its creator. Here there cannot be Greek and Jew, circumcised and uncircumcised, barbarian, Scythian, slave, free man, but Christ is all, and in all." There is no mention of male and female. Now it is dangerous to make an argument from silence, but in this verse, male and female are not named as a division that is to be erased in Christ. It would seem that, if Paul were the egalitarian that some think he is, he would have included the male/female division here as worthy of being erased "in Christ." And he would not have called on wives to submit to their husbands "in Christ."

The book of Ephesians was also written later and deals with some of the same subject matter but in more detail. The whole chapter of Ephesians 2, verses 1 through 22, deals with how the death of Jesus Christ on the cross has broken down the dividing wall between Jews and Gentiles. "Therefore remember that at one time you Gentiles in the flesh, called the uncircumcision by what is called

---

[426] Ibid., p. 83

the circumcision, which is made in the flesh by hands[427]—remember that you were at that time separated from Christ, alienated from the commonwealth of Israel, and strangers to the covenants of promise, having no hope and without God in the world.... But now in Christ Jesus you who once were far off have been brought near in the blood of Christ. He has broken down the dividing wall of hostility.... So then, you are no longer strangers and sojourners, but you are fellow citizens with the saints and members of the household of God, built upon the foundation of the apostles and prophets, Christ Jesus himself being the cornerstone, in whom the whole structure is joined together and grows into a holy temple in the Lord, in whom you also are built into it for a dwelling place of God in the Spirit."[428] What happened in the "dots" in the middle of those verses is that the blood of Jesus made them fellow-citizens of the Kingdom of God. Both Jews and Gentiles. The dividing wall he refers to was a literal wall, about five feet high, separating the court of Gentiles from the courts of Jewish women and men. It was inscribed with the words: "Foreigners must not enter.... Whoever is caught will have himself to blame for his ensuing death."[429]

In chapter three, he continues with the same theme: "When you read this you can perceive my insight into the mystery of Christ, which was not made known to the sons of men in other generations as it has now been revealed to his holy apostles and prophets by the Spirit; that is how the Gentiles are fellow heirs, members of the same body, and partakers of the promise in Christ Jesus through the gospel."[430]

---

[427] Why does Paul describe circumcision as something "made in the flesh by hands"? I think he is trying to communicate that this is something that, even though prescribed by God, has happened after the fall. It is not a designed-in distinction, and in fact God has in Christ removed it.

[428] Ephesians 2:11–14, 19–22

[429] Expositor's Bible Commentary, edited by Frank Gaebelein, volume 11, Zondervan Publishing House, Grand Rapids, MI. c. 1978 p.40. See also website larsheukeland website by Wordpress, arshaukeland.com/bits-pieces/archeology/ephesians/the-dividing-wall-of-the-court-of-the-gentiles-in-herods-temple-ephesians-2/ which lists the wall as being 1.4 meters high.

[430] Ephesians 3:4–6

Clearly, the entrance of Gentiles into the Kingdom of God on an equal footing with Jews was a very big deal for Paul. However, we must not miss the fact that, a couple of chapters later, in Ephesians 5:21–33, Paul teaches about gender roles in Christian marriage. It would seem that, if being "in Christ" erased the roles of Jew and Gentile, slave and free, male and female, Paul would not in one book teach on how the dividing wall between Jews and Gentiles has been broken down and yet in the very same book teach on prescribed gender roles for husbands and wives. That brings into question whether Galatians 3:28 can be applied to erase gender roles. It would seem that, if it is a legitimate "hermeneutical extension" from Galatians 3:28 that gender roles are erased, then Paul would not in the book of Ephesians (in the same breath, so to speak) have taught that the dividing wall between Gentiles and Jews is broken down, that we are "fellow citizens with the saints and members of the household of God,"[431] and then teach that there are still gender roles between wives and husbands, which are reflective of the relationship between Christ and His church.

In fact, I do not think it is a "legitimate hermeneutical extension" from Galatians 3:28 that there is no difference in the roles for men and women in marriage and in the church. We have to look elsewhere for that. It is an application or an implication of the text and not a direct teaching found in the text. It seems to me to be a weak hermeneutic to choose as a central text one that only deals with the subject of gender roles by "implication" or "practical extension" rather than by direct teaching, and whose "implication" or "practical extension" is contradicted by other, later texts, namely Colossians 3:18 and Ephesians 5.

---

[431] Ephesians 2:19

Colossians 3:14, 18

Colossians was a letter of Paul probably written to refute the early beginnings of a heresy called Gnosticism. The Gnostic heresy was strange theology that included the concept that the flesh was evil, the "spirit" was good, and there was little or no connection between the two. Since the physical world was evil, or of no account, that raised some problems for the concept of the Incarnation, since the Bible taught that Jesus was God *in the flesh*. So the Gnostics taught that Jesus Christ was an intermediary between God and this physical world, a created being, something less than God. They also taught that what was really important was having an ecstatic experience in the Spirit, a *gnosis*, and then you were a member of the spiritual elite. You were "in the know." Verses 19 and 20 in chapter one would have confronted this heresy. "For in him all the fullness of God was pleased to dwell, and through him to reconcile to himself all things whether on earth or in heaven, making peace by the blood of his cross." These two verses contain two concepts that flatly contradict some basis Gnostic doctrines: A) Jesus was *fully God*. The whole fullness of God was pleased to dwell in Jesus. B) The reconciliation to God was accomplished by something as gross as *blood*. One cannot get more earthy than shed blood, and this was shed by a being in whom the whole fullness of God was pleased to dwell.

That is just a bit of the context of the book of Colossians. In chapter three, we find a couple of verses similar to those we just studied in Galatians 3. "Here there cannot be Greek and Jew, circumcised and uncircumcised, barbarian, Scythian, slave, freeman, but Christ is all in all." Then farther on we find: "Wives, be subject to your husbands, as is fitting in the Lord. Husbands, love your wives, and do not be harsh with them."

Just a couple of observations are in order. First, in the Kingdom of God, and in its manifestation on earth, the church, there should not exist the cultural divisions current in that society, such as slaves and free, barbarian or Scythian, and so on. In fact, there should not even be the division of Jew or non-Jew. In our world where, sadly, the Church of Jesus Christ is known as one of the most segregated sections of society, that should challenge us. Second, it is interesting, especially in comparison to Galatians 3:28, that there is no mention of men or women as a cultural division. Why that particular division is mentioned in Galatians 3:28 and not here is a mystery to me. And third, not only is that division absent, but the author goes on to say that wives should submit themselves (it is a middle-voice construction) to their husbands *as is fitting in the Lord.* So, it would seem, this is a principle that belongs to the kingdom of God. It is not a principle that is a result of the Fall and is so erased by the death of Jesus. This would seem to contradict the "legitimate hermeneutical extension" of Galatians 3:28, where that verse is interpreted to erase gender roles. At the very least, it would make Galatians 3:28 not a wise choice for a central text, since it only applies by "application" to the subject at hand and there is another verse by the same author that contradicts that "application."

1 Corinthians 1:11, 12 and Colossians 4:15

> "It has been reported to me by Chloe's people that there is quarreling among you, my brethren. What I mean is that each one of you says, 'I belong to Paul,' one of you says, 'I belong to Apollos,' or 'I belong to Cephas,' or 'I belong to Christ.'"[432]

I have never heard anybody refer to this verse in the context of a discussion of the gender issue. The name "Chloe" is the name of a female, and it is in the possessive form. Perhaps it has not been appealed to because the exact nature of the possession is unclear. As observed in the chapter on 1 Corinthians, this church was deeply

---

[432] Interestingly, part of the reason for Apollos being around spiritually is because Priscilla and Aquila explained the way of God more clearly to him. Acts 18:26. So, like Timothy (1 Timothy 1:5), this male had been influenced spiritually by a female.

mired in a number of extremely unhealthy practices. One of them was arguing and developing personality cults and, as a result, feeling superior to others in the church, depending on whose group one was in. Paul heard about this from a group of people described by the Apostle as being "Chloe's people." Perhaps it was a women's coffee and discipleship group. Perhaps it was a mixed group of men and women and Chloe had some sort of responsibility for organizing them. Perhaps it was one of the several groups within the church who were identifying themselves as being followers of a certain person. It just is not clear. The situation was that there were people who claimed to belong to Paul, some who claimed to belong to Apollos, and some who claimed to belong to Cephas, and those who claimed to belong to Chloe tattled on the rest! Perhaps with a sense of superiority, but there is nothing in the text to indicate that.

So I am hesitant to make any conclusions about the nature of her position. But there was something about her relationship with what is described as "her" people that the genitive is used. It does not appear she was fulfilling the role of a passive follower.

In Colossians 4:15, we find Paul sending greetings to "the brothers at Laodicea and to Nympha and the church in her house." It is speculative exactly what role Nympha fulfilled in "the church at her house." It would certainly seem, however, that it was more than setting a beautiful table of refreshments and then sitting silently (as women should not speak in church) while everybody else, especially men, had church. It would seem she was a woman of influence in that church since it met in her house—at least that and maybe much more.

Romans 16:1–7

"I commend to you our sister Phoebe, a deaconess of the church at Cenchreae, that you may receive her in the Lord as befits the saints, and help her in whatever she may require from you, for she has been a helper of many and of myself as well. Greet Prisca and Aquila, my fellow workers in Christ Jesus, who risked their necks for my life, to whom not only I but also all the churches of the Gentiles give thanks; greet also the church in their house. Greet my beloved Epaenetus, who was the first convert in Asia for Christ. Greet Mary, who has worked hard among you. Greet Andronicus and Junias, my kinsmen and my fellow prisoners; they are men of note among the apostles, and they were in Christ before me. Greet Ampliatus, my beloved in the Lord. Greet Urbanus, our fellow worker in Christ, and my beloved Stachys. Greet Apelles, who is approved in Christ. Greet those who belong to the family of Aristobulus. Greet my kinsman Herodian. Greet those in the Lord who belong to the family of Narcissus. Greet those workers in the Lord, Tryphaena and Tryphosa. Greet the beloved Persis, who has worked hard in the Lord. Greet Rufus, eminent in the Lord, also his mother and mine. Greet Asyncritus, Phlegon, Hermes, Patrobas, Hermas, and the brethren who are with them. Greet Philologos, Julia, Nereus, and his sister, and Olympas and all the saints who are with them."

Remember that, in the chapter on Hermeneutics, I explained that one of the rules of interpreting Scripture is that we interpret narrative passages by the didactic. Just because Adam was a tiller of the Garden does not mean we all have to be farmers. Just because many Old Testament kings had lots of wives does not mean it is permissible to have lots of wives. Just because Jesus was single does not mean we all have to be single. Just because Jesus chose only male disciples does not mean only males can be leaders in the church. It may illustrate that principle or it may not be illustrative of any principle at all. But we have to look elsewhere to see what is taught, to see what the principle is, and then decide if the narrative example is normative or not.

It is a helpful interpretive tool to observe how the Apostle carried out his understanding of the gender issue that he taught about in other texts. So this text is a narrative text and does not teach, but it does model for us how the Apostle lived and thought. If we saw no women listed in his list of people whom he desires to send greetings to at the end of this significant letter, that would indicate that women did not play a very significant role in the life of the Christians at Rome or in the mindset of the Apostle. That decidedly is not the case! In fact, the very first person listed is a woman. I know that I am being repetitious, but we are at a large cultural distance from the Jewish mindset of the time and do not comprehend how unusual it was for a Jewish rabbi, a well known Jewish rabbi, when he constructs a list of people he appreciates as co-workers, to place as first on his list a woman.[433]

Remember how shocked the disciples were in John 4 when Jesus sat down to talk with the woman at the well.[434] Here Paul is listing his teammates and instead of just listing Aquila, Epaenetus, Andronicus, Ampliatus, Urbanus, Stachys, Herodion, Rufus, Asyncritus, Phlegon, Hermes, Patrobas, Hermas, Philologus, Nereus, Olympas, and all the others—instead of that list of all males, he starts out with Phoebe. A female. She is to be received in the Lord as befits the saints. And she is not a token female in a list of Paul's teammates. As Paul ends this wonderful book of Romans, he sends greetings to twenty-five individuals and five households. Of the twenty-five individuals, eight or possibly nine are females. Clearly, in Paul's mind the female gender played a very significant role in the building of God's kingdom.

As we go through the list, some are completely unknown. Some are partially known. Not all names in this text will help us understand the mindset of Paul on the issue of gender, but the fact that he named women as co-laborers is significant. They were not by-standers in the early construction of the Church of Jesus Christ, at home making supper, taking care of the kids, and welcoming home their men after a hard day building the church.

---

[433] In fact, it was normal for a rabbi to address a woman only as the wife of a certain man and not by name. In the list of people Paul sends greetings to at the end of this letter, there are eight or nine females addressed by name. They were persons in their own right, not just as wives of their husbands.

[434] "They marveled that He was talking with a woman...." John 4:27

Also, as I said in the introduction, I know no Greek. There was a professor at the college I attended who taught various New Testament courses, and he regularly stated that if one was serious about studying the New Testament, one had to learn Greek. I would have to say that I agree with him, and I guess that condemns me as not being serious about studying the New Testament. There are several places in this text where looking into the Greek is helpful, and, since I know none, I have to rely on what others say about it. And in at least one instance in this text, different experts come to the opposite conclusion. That leaves me scratching my head and somewhat at a loss as to making any firm conclusions.

There are some real difficulties in understanding some texts, and this one has some. God needs to help us to know ourselves to see whether we are unclear about a text because we don't like what it appears to teach or because it really is unclear.

In verse 1, Phoebe is mentioned as a deaconess of the church of Cenchreae. Paul writes to the church at Rome to "receive her in the Lord as befits the saints."[435] Probably Phoebe is carrying Paul's letter to the church, although that is not stated.

There are two words used to describe Phoebe in this text. One is the word "deaconess" in verse one and the other is the word, in the Revised Standard Version, "helper" in verse two. The word translated as "deaconess" is *diakonos*, and one can quickly see the similarity between our English word and the original Greek word.

Churches have different words for the hired person who leads the church and preaches on Sunday. Some call him the pastor. Some a teaching elder. Probably the most common is the term "minister." To many, this conjures up a slightly overweight older man in a black robe who is friendly, warm, and largely inoffensive. I apologize for that caricature, and perhaps is it unfounded. The point is that we tend to define the word "minister" as the paid professional who preaches on Sunday morning. Some of that confusion may come

---

[435] Romans 16:1

from the manner in which the King James translators translated our word *diakonos*.

"But it shall not be so among you, but whosoever will be great among you, let him be your minister."[436]

"Who then is Paul, and who is Apollos, but ministers by whom ye believed, even as the Lord gave to every man?"[437]

"Whereof I was made a minister according to the gift of the grace of God given unto me by the effectual working of his power."[438] (The apostle Paul writing.)

In all three of the above verses, the word translated "minister" is our word *diakonos*, and it is the word Paul uses to describe Phoebe. To "minister," used as a translation of *diakonos*, means to serve. Dr. Payne, when he talks of Phoebe as a *diakonos*, says she was a minister, that is, a regular leader in the church.[439] However, we need to understand that our English word "minister" represents something that *diakonos* does not necessarily represent. In reading these verses and seeing that the word translated as "minister" is used to describe Phoebe, it would be easy (and I believe mistaken) to quickly form the mental image of Phoebe in a black robe preaching on a Sunday morning. Our mistake has been to make the role of a *diakonos* into the professional paid role of a church preacher. The definition of a *diakonos* is a servant. In fact, in more recent translations of Matthew 20:26, the word is translated as "servant" instead of "minister." And Dr. Payne himself acknowledges the same: "Christian leadership is based upon love, willingness to serve and spiritual gifts, not on wisdom, strength or influence as the world sees these. Indeed, "deacon" means "servant."[440]

---

[436] Matthew 20:26 (KJV)

[437] 1 Corinthians 3:5 (KJV)

[438] Ephesians 3:7 (KJV)

[439] Phillip Payne, ibid., p. 61

[440] Phillip Payne, ibid., p. 70. I might beg to disagree just a little that there are some skills and other character qualities required, as listed in 1 Timothy 3 and Titus 2.

Here are some other uses of the same word, still in the King James version:

""His mother saith unto the *servants*, Whatsoever he saith unto you, do it."[441] The context is Jesus turning water into wine, and the mother of Jesus was telling the servants to do whatever Jesus told them to do.

"And he sat down, and called the twelve, and saith unto them, if any man desire to be first, the same shall be last of all and *servant* of all."[442]

"But he that is greatest among you shall be your *servant*."[443]

In all these texts, the word in italics, servant, is the word *diakonos*, but this time it is translated as "servant" rather than "minister." In fact, we are all called to be a *diakonos*. We are all called to be servants of one another. It does not necessarily describe a paid position of leadership. So to describe the current debate as being about "women in ministry" as many do, meaning "women in leadership" or "women as pastors" is confusing and misleading. Of course women may take on roles of "ministry" in the church. We are all called to be servants or "ministers." That is the meaning of the word. I have known at least one woman who left a church because women were not allowed to be elders. I have never known a woman to leave a church because women were not allowed to be janitors. That seems to imply *perhaps* that there are other underlying or unconscious issues than just denying women roles of leadership. *Perhaps* some are wanting the supposed status of being a leader. The Bible does not see leadership that way.

There was a position of being a deacon in the early church, as evidenced from the qualifications listed in 1 Timothy 3:8–12. It is a different word from the word used for "bishop" or "elder" in 1

---

[441] John 2:5 (KJV)
[442] Mark 9:35 (KJV)
[443] Matthew 23:11 (KJV)

Timothy 3:1–7, so it was apparently a different office. Traditionally, churches have observed the division of labor in Acts 6:1–6 between the apostles and another group traditionally called "deacons." The Apostles devoted themselves to prayer and the ministry of the Word, and this other group was directed to care for the daily needs of the people. In 1 Timothy 3:1–7, in a passage that describes the qualifications for elders or bishops, at least two of those qualities (those of being apt to teach and not being a recent convert) are not listed in the list required of deacons. Since a different word, *episcope*, is translated as bishop, while *diakonos* is translated as deacon, and since the requirements are different, it must really be a different office. There is not agreement among Bible-believing Christians as to whether or not Paul allowed women to function as deacons. The first deacons in Acts 6 were all men. One of the requirements for a bishop (or elder, as we would more normally call them) is that they must be "the husband of one wife."[444] The same phrase is used of deacons, as well: "Let deacons be the husband of one wife...."[445] It is also said in the list of requirements for deacons, "The women, likewise must be serious, no slanderers, but temperate, faithful in all things."[446] There is no such requirement of "the women" in the list of qualifications for elders. It seems to me that if Paul intended the office of deacon to be limited to men, why would he add the phrase about the required character of women in the list of requirements for deacons when he did *not* add that phrase for the office of bishop? I take that addition as significant and as evidence that Paul did not limit the office of deacon to men. We'll look at this passage in more detail below.

So the question before us is whether or not Phoebe was a normal, run-of-the-mill servant, which we are all called to be, or if she fulfilled the office of deacon, or even pastor, in the church at Cenchreae. I think it is a perfectly legitimate interpretation that

---

[444] 1 Timothy 3:2
[445] 1 Timothy 3:12
[446] 1 Timothy 3:11

she fulfilled the office of deacon in the church, since that office was probably not limited to men.

So our first lady mentioned in the list of teammates of Paul in Romans 16 is a female deacon of the church at Cenchreae, and she may well be carrying the letter from Paul to the church at Rome. They did not have e-mail. Paul trusted a woman with the book of Romans, just as Jesus trusted women with the Good News of His resurrection, to be carried to the disciples. I remind you that, in the Jewish culture of the time, women were not considered reliable witnesses in court. Such a commonly held belief of that culture, which was mistaken, invites us to examine what commonly held beliefs we might unconsciously hold that are also mistaken. It is easy to be molded into the thought patterns of your culture, or your church, and none of us are immune from that mistake.

The other word used to describe Phoebe is "succourer" (KJV) or "helper" (RSV). "For she [that is, Phoebe] has been a helper of many and of myself as well."[447] The word is *prostates*, and it is a significant word. It is used only here in the New Testament. It is the feminine form of the word *prostatis*, which means one who is 1) set over others, or 2) a protector or guardian or one who cares for and gives aid. It is derived from the word *proistemi*, which is sometimes translated "rules" in texts such as Rom 12:8, 1 Timothy 3:4, 12, and 1 Timothy 5:17, where it describes elders who rule well (1 Tim 5:17).[448] But it is not the same as *hegeomai*, which means to lead, go before, rule, command, have authority over, as in Hebrews 13:7,[449] 13:17,[450] and 13:24.[451]

Some have interpreted Paul's use of this word to describe Phoebe as evidence that she had some sort position of authority in the early church. That is probably not a conclusion that can be drawn from this word for the following reasons: 1) the word *hegeomai* is a

[447] Romans 16:2
[448] "Let the elders who *rule* well be considered worthy of double honor...."
[449] "Remember your *leaders*, those who spoke to you the word of God...."
[450] "Obey your *leaders* and submit to them for they are keeping watch over your souls."
[451] "Greet all your *leaders* and all the saints."

stronger word to describe one who rules, and Paul did not choose that word, and 2) that would mean that she at some point had authority over Paul himself, since he says she has functioned as a *prostates* to him. That is highly doubtful for two reasons: a) There is no other example of the Apostle Paul being under the authority of a woman, and b) Paul was quite clear in his understanding that, as an apostle, he was under *no* authority except God. He made that clear in the book of Galatians.

In addition, the reason that he asks the church to receive her and to help [*paristemi*] her is because she has been a *prostates* to him. The first word, the request of Paul to the church to "help" her, really means to help or assist. It makes no sense to ask the church to help her because she has been in authority over Paul. But it makes good sense to ask the church to help her because she has been a helper to Paul. In fact, it makes more sense than for Paul to ask them to help her because she has been in authority over him.

So while Phoebe is obviously a significant woman, the first one listed in this list of Paul's teammates that includes both men and women, it does not appear that she occupied a position equivalent to elder. She was a person who cared for people; she had helped Paul; she was a *trusted* courier for the profound book of Romans; she was to be received as befits the saints; and he was asking the church to help her in whatever her need was.

That brings us to the next person listed, which is actually two: "Greet Prisca and Aquila, my fellow workers in Christ Jesus, who risked their necks for my life, whom not only I but also all the churches of the Gentiles give thanks; greet also the church in their house."[452]

Prisca is the same name as Priscilla. They were a husband and wife team. We have met them before in Ephesus, but actually Paul first met them in Corinth. Paul had just left Athens, and, as they were both tentmakers and also believers, they teamed up together.

---

[452] Romans 16:3

When Paul left Corinth, he took them both with him to Ephesus. When he left Ephesus, he left Prisca and Aquila there. While they were there, a Jew named Apollos showed up. "He was an eloquent man, well versed in the scriptures, and instructed in the way of the Lord. He spoke and taught accurately the things concerning Jesus, though he knew only the baptism of John. When Priscilla and Aquila heard him, they took him and expounded to him the way of God more accurately. Later, he powerfully confuted the Jews in public, showing by the Scriptures that the Christ was Jesus."[453]

A couple of observations are in order:

1. When Luke first mentions the couple, they are Aquila and Priscilla.[454] Every time after that, they are Priscilla and Aquila. The woman is named first.[455] Paul follows Luke's example, naming Priscilla first. That may or may not have been significant. It was certainly unusual.

2. They obviously were quite astute theologically and did not hesitate to correct Apollo's lack of understanding of Jesus.

3. The text does not say that Aquila expounded to Apollos the way of God more accurately. It does not say that Priscilla expounded the way of God more accurately. It says, "He began to speak boldly in the synagogue, but when Priscilla and Aquila heard him, *they* took him and expounded to him the way of God more accurately.[456] It was a team effort.

4. The word "expounded" is a different word than the word "teach" in 1 Timothy. The word is actually *ektithemi*, which means to expose, to set out, and, by implication, to expound or clarify. It is the word used in Acts 7:21 in the middle of Peter's historical defense of Christianity, relating the story of Moses: "At this time Moses was born, and was beautiful

---

[453] Acts 18:24–28
[454] 1 Corinthians 18:2
[455] Acts 18: 2,18, 26
[456] Acts 18:26

389

before God. And he was brought up for three months in his father's house; and when he was *exposed*, Pharaoh's daughter adopted him and brought him up as her own son."[457] The word "exposed" is our word, *ektithemi*, describing how Moses was set out in the open. That is what Priscilla and Aquila did for Apollos. His learning was incomplete, so they completed it by exposing him to, as Paul Harvey would say, "the rest of the story." It is not the same word as Paul uses in 1 Timothy 2:11, when he says, "I do not permit a woman to teach or have authority over men." The word there is *didasko*, which is a technical term used often in 1 and 2 Timothy and Titus.

Having said that, let's not miss the fact that Paul addressed a woman as equal with a man in helping another man understand the gospel. It would seem that, whatever the prohibition against women teaching in 1 Timothy consists of, it does not prohibit an adult woman from explaining spiritual things to an adult male.

Prisca and Aquila are also addressed as fellow-workers with Paul. They would be teammates with Paul. There are others in this section who are addressed in the same way: Urbanus in verse 9 and Timothy in verse 21. Those are both males. It is the word used to describe Euodia and Syntyche in Philippians 4:2. Those are both feminine names. So in the building of the church of Jesus Christ, women as well as men seem to be equally involved.

One other observation is in order before we leave Priscilla and Aquila: it is twice mentioned that they hosted a church in their house, both here and in 1 Corinthians 16:19. So they were also willing to have their place of dwelling used to further the Kingdom of God. They were quite an amazing couple, and Paul's words about them are striking: "not only I but also all the churches of the Gentiles give thanks."[458] Their combination of hard work, risking their necks

---

[457] Acts 7:21–21
[458] Romans 16:4

for the Apostle, hospitality, recognizing lack of understanding and correcting it, mobility for the cause of Christ—all these added together present us with a picture of a very significant couple, a man and a woman, who were used mightily of God to build His church.

In verse five, we are introduced to Epaenetus. Nothing is said of him except that he apparently was the first convert in Asia. Paul labels him "beloved," a very understandable designation for a missionary. Anybody who has labored in evangelism in a particular area will understand the warm place in a person's heart for the first convert.

I remember well my first evangelistic talk as a staff worker with the college ministry I worked with. It was a terrible talk and, as I think back on it, I am amazed that the whole group did not get up and walk away. It was around a campfire and I gave a long, boring, intellectual lecture to a bunch of college guys. I am convinced most of them were bored out of their minds and were hoping it would end as soon as possible—and rightly so—but they politely sat there and listened to the end. When I finally made my appeal, I said I had no intention of having them bow their heads, close their eyes, and quietly slip up their hand if they wanted to become a Christian. No, with all eyes open, if anybody wanted to become a Christian, I wanted him to raise his hand and say out loud he wanted to become a Christian. (I still believe that way. I am not a fan of secret conversions.) One guy in the front row shot his hand in the air and said with crystal clarity that he wanted to become a Christian. I about fell over. I met with him afterward and we prayed. He went on to be a leader in the group, earn a PhD from Cornell, teach himself Chinese, marry a Chinese woman, and is now a missionary in China. I in no way relate that story as a feather in my hat. In fact, I am ashamed at what a poor job I did of presenting the gospel, at how intent I was on impressing people with my "knowledge," and how I was not free just to be who I was. Clearly, God was intent on doing something, and I just happened to be there. But Mike still has a warm place in my heart as a first convert, although, clearly, to call him "my" convert is totally wrong. So I understand Paul's phrase, "Greet my beloved Epaenetus, who was the first convert in Asia."

In verse 6 we meet Mary. "Greet Mary, who has worked hard among you." Nothing really is known of her, except that she was a female and a hard worker. The word is *kopiao* and means to grow weary and exhausted with working so hard. The same word is used of the sisters Tryphaena and Tryphosa in verse 12, as well as of Persis. Working hard in the service of the gospel was not a task limited to men.

Verse 7 introduces us to another couple (apparently) by the name of Andronicus and Junia. "Greet Andronicus and Junias, my kinsmen and my fellow prisoners; they are men of note among the apostles, and they were in Christ before me."[459] All five descriptions of them are difficult to interpret. 1. Paul calls them kinsmen. It is not known if he means by that that they were fellow Jews or actually blood relatives. 2. It is not known when they were in prison with Paul. 3. It is not known what exactly is meant by the phrase "men of note among the apostles." It could mean that they were to be considered as an addition to the original twelve apostles or that they were well known and respected by the original twelve.[460] 4. The word "men" in the phrase "men of note among the apostles" is actually not present in the Greek. It just says they were kinsmen and fellow prisoners and were of note among the apostles. 5. It is not known for sure if Junia is a feminine name or a masculine name. We'll assume at this point that Junia was a woman, as the evidence seems to indicate that is the case.

What does he mean by the phrase "of note among the apostles"? Does he mean they were known *as* apostles or well respected *by* the apostles? There are several issues to be noted here:

---

[459] Romans 16:7

[460] The plural masculine pronoun "men" is not in the original. It just says in the NIV, "They are outstanding among the apostles," or (in the KJV) "who are of note among the apostles."

1. From what I have read, the structure of the Greek does not support well the second interpretation—that they were well respected by the apostles but were not actually apostles themselves.[461]

2. The term "apostle "does not necessarily mean one of the original twelve apostles. There seemed to be a number of "messengers" sent out by a church for a particular missionary purpose, and the name "apostle" was also used to describe them. However, they were not one of the twelve and did not carry the same authority.[462]

3. It would be unusual for a "new apostle" on a par with the original twelve just to pop up in a friendly list of acquaintances and greetings at the end of a letter.

4. To be an apostle with the authority and reputation of the original twelve, there were certain requirements, including seeing the risen Lord.[463] Or again, in Acts 1:21, when Mathias is chosen to replace Judas, the requirements were listed as: a) accompanied us during all the time that the Lord Jesus went in and out among us, and b) be a witness to his resurrection. There is no mention of Junia having been a member of that group. Now, to be fair, there is also no mention of the Apostle Paul, but clearly his call and appointment by God himself is an exceptional case. It would seem extraordinary that another apostle named Junia, particularly if she were a woman, unlike the other twelve apostles, would just mysteriously appear without a

---

[461] James Hurley, Man and Woman in Biblical Perspective, Zondervan Publishing House, Grand Rapids, MI 49506, c. 1982, p. 121. "It is unlike Paul to make something like acquaintance with the apostles a matter of praise. It is therefore more likely that he intended to say that they were outstanding as apostles."

[462] 2 Cor 8:23: "and as for our brethren, they are messengers of the churches, the glory of Christ." Or Philippians 2:25: "I have thought it necessary to send to you Epaphroditus my brother and fellow worker and fellow soldier, and your messenger and minister to my need." In both cases, the word translated as "messenger" or "messengers" is the word for apostle.

[463] "Am I not an apostle? Have I not seen the risen Lord?" 1 Cor. 9:1, This was Paul's claim to the authority of an apostle.

similarly miraculous calling like that of the Apostle Paul. She would need a similarly profound calling to substantiate her call and authority and role as an apostle, just as Paul did. But there is no record of such.

5. If a woman apostle on a par with the original twelve were the case here, it raises the question of why Jesus did not appoint any women apostles. Unlike today, when a culture can radically change in the space of thirty or forty years, things did not change that quickly then. If Jesus avoided appointing a woman apostle due to cultural pressure, that would still have been the case at the time of the writing of the book of Romans. Besides, Jesus was no stranger to offending the culture of the time. To appoint a woman apostle later would condemn Jesus for caving in to cultural pressure.

The other major problem is that we really cannot tell if the name Junias or Junia is a masculine or feminine name. Because of the grammatical structure, it is impossible to tell for sure if the name is masculine or feminine. However, there are several points to be made:

1. There existed a name Junia that was a feminine name, like Sue.
2. The name Junias, which is a masculine name, like Bill, would consist of exactly the same letters as Junia in the particular sentence structure here.
3. The evidence available, while not conclusive, seems to point to Junia being a woman. Much of it is not from the time of writing of Paul's letter, unfortunately. John Chrysostom (AD 347–407) referred to Junia as follows: "How great is the devotion of this woman, that she should be even counted worthy of the appellation of apostle![464] Epiphanius

---

[464] John Chrysostom, *Homilies on the epistle of St. Paul the Apostle to the Romans, xxxi.7,* in *A Select Library of the Nicene and Post-Nicene Fathers of the Christian Church,* ed. Philip Schaff

(AD 347–407) wrote, "the bishop of Salamis in Cyprus, wrote an Index of Disciples, in which he includes this line: 'Iounias, of whom Paul makes mention, became the bishop of Apameia of Syria' (Index disciplulorum, 125.19–20). In Greek, the phrase 'of whom' is a masculine relative pronoun (*hou*) and shows that Epiphanius thought Iounias was a man." Interestingly, he also refers to Priscilla as a man, but we know her to be a woman, so that somewhat clouds his reliability. He may have been an early example of gender confusion![465]

4. There is some speculation that Junias could have been a contraction of the masculine name Junianus. From my reading, that seems highly speculative.

I commend the reader to do more research, but my conclusion is that Junia was an uncommonly used name (only three occurrences), and it was a feminine name.

The only thing that seems clear about this couple is that they were Christians before Paul. They were "in Christ before me." "In Christ" is a technical phrase describing the position of the Christian. It is not used to describe the position of an apostle, although, of course, an apostle must be a believer. So they were spiritually older than Paul.

What makes the most sense to me is that Junia was a woman, and she was one of the apostles sent out by a particular church for a particular mission, a "second tier" of apostles. There is no one else named among the second tier of apostles, and by that I mean, not one of the original twelve, who is a woman. Epaphroditus and Barnabus were also called apostles, but were not one of the twelve. So we must not miss the significance of Junia. Women, who previously in the Old Testament temple were allowed only one step

---

(Grand Rapids: Eerdmans, 1956) first series, vol. 11, p. 555. Quoted in <u>Recovering Biblical Manhood and Womanhood</u>, p. 79.

[465] Ibid., pp. 79, 80, 479

closer than Gentiles, who were considered unteachable by Jewish leaders contemporary with Paul, were now included with Barnabas, Epaphroditus, and other men who were co-laborers with Paul in the building of Christ's church.

Next we come to Urbanus and Stachys in verse nine. Nothing is known of either of these men. Perhaps a hint of the personality of Urbanus is that the name means "refined" or "elegant." We get out English word "urbane" from the same Latin root. His only description is that he was a fellow worker. Apparently being cool and refined (if that described him at all, which is speculative) does not hinder one from working in the Kingdom of God. Stachys's only description is that he was "beloved" of Paul.

Apelles in verse 10 is described as being "approved in Christ." That might indicate some unusual test or experience passed, but that is speculation.

It is not known for sure who the family of Aristobulus was. It is interesting that he himself is not addressed but instead his family or household, which might indicate that he himself was not a believer but his family was.

Herodion, described as "my kinsman" in verse 11, may possibly have been associated with King Herod, although that is speculation. The fact that he is called "my kinsman" may indicate that he was a Jewish believer.

Narcissus may have been a quite wealthy freedman of the time who is known from secular history, though that fact is not sure. Again, he himself is not greeted, but his family, which may indicate that he was not a believer but his family was.

That brings us to Tryphaena and Tryphosa in verse twelve. These are two feminine names, and they were probably either sisters or maybe even twins. It was not unusual then, as now, to name sisters or twins with similar names. I went through grade school with two twin girls names Carolyn and Marilyn, but I could tell the difference because one was heavier. Tryphaena and Tryphosa mean "dainty" and "delicate." Perhaps they were of the aristocratic class. However,

Paul describes them not as rich, nor beautiful, nor delicate, but as "workers in the Lord." They were apparently not afraid to get their hands dirty in the work of the Lord. Persis, in the same verse, is also a woman and is described as "beloved" and "worked hard in the Lord." So here we have three women in the same verse who are described as being "hard workers" in the Lord. The word is often translated as "toil" in the New Testament. It was what Peter said to Jesus expressing doubt when told to toss his nets onto the other side of the boat: "But Master, we toiled all night and have taken nothing."[466] It describes hard work, and it was used to describe the toil of these three ladies in the Lord. It was a word that Paul used of himself in Galatians 4:11, when he says, "I am afraid I have labored over you in vain" (RSV). As fits the pattern so far in this chapter, women were clearly highly involved in the building of the early church. They were not bench warmers who cheered the men on in their position of leadership.

In verse 13 we meet Rufus. The name means "red" or "red-haired" in Latin and was a very common name in Rome and Italy. There is a Rufus mentioned in Mark 15:21: "and they compelled a passer-by, Simon of Cyrene, who was coming from the country, the father of Alexander and Rufus, to carry his cross." It is pure speculation if this Rufus is the same. Paul describes him as "eminent" in the Lord. The interesting thing about Paul's greeting to Rufus is the mention of his mother, whom Paul describes as "his mother and mine." Surely this Rufus was not Paul's brother?! No, almost for sure, Rufus had a very caring and accepting mom who reached out to Paul in his loneliness, perhaps after his conversion, which would have cost him his whole social support system[467] and would have cared for him in a most profound way. She was mother-like to him. Her name is not mentioned but clearly she played a very significant

---

[466] Luke 5:5 (KJV)
[467] "For His sake I have suffered the loss of *all things*." Philippians 3:8

role in the apostle's life, just as women played a significant role in the life of Timothy.[468]

Paul ends his list of people to whom he sends greetings with an "all the rest" structure: "Greet Asyncritus, Phlegon, Hermes, Patrobas, Hermas, and the brethren who are with them. Greet Philologos, Julia, Nereus and his sister, and Olympas, and all the saints who are with them."[469] Very little can be said of them. But it is worth noting that at least two women are mentioned: Julia and the sister of Nereus.

In summary, several observations may be made:

1. The list of those greeted by the apostle was a very diverse list. Several names in the list appear in inscriptions at Rome as possibly being slaves of the imperial household. So, while several were slaves (although slaves of the period could be quite well educated), the household of the emperor was already infiltrated for the gospel.

2. There were a number of women in the list. As mentioned above, they were, judging from this list, quite influential in the building of the church of Jesus Christ. This situation appears to be normal, rather than abnormal.

3. The word for "hard worker" is a repeated word, both of women and of men. It is mentioned three times, describing Mary in verse six, Tryphaena and Tryphosa in verse twelve, and Persis also in verse twelve. It describes, as I mentioned above, not just work, but hard work. These people were not just coasting along fitting Christianity into their lives, but orienting their lives around Christ's ownership of everything about them.

4. The word for "fellow-worker" also appears three times, describing Prisca and Aquila in verse three, Timothy later

---

[468] "I am reminded of your sincere faith, a faith that dwelt first in your grandmother Lois and your mother Eunice and now, I am sure, dwells in you." 1 Timothy 2:5

[469] Romans 16:14, 15

on in verse twenty-one, and Urbanus in verse nine. It means to be a companion in work, or a fellow-worker, a teammate. Paul was obviously a team player, even though he was an apostle, and considered at least one woman, Priscilla, as part of that team.

5. The women fulfilled at least three roles and possibly four: 1) A deaconess, Phoebe, in verse one. 2) A wife to Aquila in the person of Priscilla in verse three. 3) A mother to Rufus and at least a pseudo-mother to Paul in verse thirteen, and 4) probably single women since Phoebe, Mary, Junia, Tryphaena and Tryphosa, Julia, and the sister of Nereus are not mentioned as having husbands. 5) Junia may have been a "secondary" apostle like Barnabas, James, and possibly several others. The only clear apostle who was comparable to the original twelve who walked with Jesus was Paul, and he made clear his qualifications as such—he had seen the risen Jesus. Junia does not seem to be the same as Paul.

It seems clear to me that, while Paul, in my opinion, taught hierarchy in the texts we have already looked at, he did not consider women as inferior to men, as incompetent, or as incapable of or ineffective in ministry. He even accepted "help" from one. If only we, as modern Christians, could maintain the Biblical view of a hierarchy of equals, without competition and without erasing gender differences which are created in by our Creator. Just as Paul did. He was quite radical for his time and upbringing. He was able to leave behind his cultural history and upbringing and then to think Biblically, being transformed by the renewal of his mind. The same should happen to us. Let's not be conformed to this world but be changed as we study. That is the purpose of Scripture. There has been nearly endless and sometimes very ugly debate over the topic of the trustworthiness and reliability of Scripture, but Scripture itself is clear about its purpose: it is for 1) teaching, 2) reproof, 3) correction, and 4) training in righteousness.[470] So we need to follow the example of Paul and allow God's powerful Word to change our souls just as Paul did.

1 Timothy 3:1–9 and Titus 1:5–9

"The saying is sure: if any one aspires to the office of bishop, he desires a noble task. Now a bishop must be above reproach, the husband of one wife, temperate, sensible, dignified, hospitable, an apt teacher, no drunkard, not violent but gentle, not quarrelsome, and no lover of money. He must manage his own household well, keeping his children submissive and respectful in every way, for if a man does not know how to manage his own household, how can he care for God's church? He must not be a recent convert, or he may be puffed up with conceit and fall into the condemnation of the devil; moreover he must be well thought of by outsiders, or he may fall into reproach and the snare of the devil.

"Deacons likewise must be serious, not double-tongued, not addicted to much wine, not greedy for gain; they must hold the mystery of the faith with a clear conscience. And let them also be tested first; then if they prove themselves blameless let them serve as deacons. The women likewise must be serious, no slanderers, but temperate, faithful in all things. Let deacons be the husband of one wife, and let them manage their children and their households well; for those who serve well as deacons gain a good standing for themselves and also great confidence in the faith which is in Christ Jesus." (1 Timothy 3:1–9)

"This is why I left you in Crete, that you might amend what was defective, and appoint elders in every town as I directed you, if any man is blameless, the husband of one wife, and his children are believers and not open to the charge of being profligate or

---

[470] 2 Timothy 3:16

insubordinate. For a bishop as God's steward, must be blameless; he must not be arrogant or quick-tempered or a drunkard or violent or greedy for gain, but hospitable, a lover of goodness, master of himself, upright, holy, and self-controlled; he must hold firm to the sure word as taught, so that he may be able to give instruction in sound doctrine and also to confute those who contradict it." (Titus 1:5–9)

There are many ways the question of gender roles in the Church comes up. When I was younger, the question was phrased in terms of whether or not women should be "ordained." At that particular time in my life, I had no idea what ordination actually meant or how it was accomplished. It turns out it is in many ways a cultural phenomenon and usually is a result of going to seminary, passing an exam, and then being "ordained" by your denomination. That means that the call of God into full-time Christian work is recognized. It is loosely based on the passage in Acts where the Holy Spirit called on the church at Antioch to "set apart for me Barnabas and Saul for the work to which I have called them."[471]

To say that women should not be ordained, then, would be saying that women should not be allowed to go into full-time Christian work. That seems to me to be unBiblically restrictive. Paul often describes women as "co-laborers" and refers to Phoebe as a deacon and Junia as an apostle. They may or may not have been full-time workers, but I think it is very difficult to make a strong case that women should never be in full-time Christian work and therefore never be ordained. Having said that, I think usually the question is asked in reference to whether or not women should be in a leadership position in the church, especially whether or not they should be elders or pastors.

There are two different words used in the texts above for the church office we usually call "elders." In 1 Timothy 3:1 and 2 and

---

[471] Acts 13:2

in Titus 1:7, the word is *episkopos*, which means overseer or elder. Their job description is found in Acts 20:28, when Paul is giving his farewell address to the elders of this very church. "Take heed to yourselves and to all the flock, in which the Holy Spirit has made you overseers (*episkopos*) to care for the church of God which he obtained with the blood of his own Son." The word for "care" is a shepherd term, *poimaino*, and means to feed and tend, as well as govern.[472] Their calling is critical because Paul predicts that fierce wolves—male wolves—would come into the church to draw away the disciples after them. As we saw in the chapter on 1 Timothy, that very thing did happen.

The other word is *presbyteros*, and it is used to refer to those who presided over assemblies or churches. The New Testament uses the two terms interchangeably. New Testament church members were called to submit to them and to respect them. Traditionally they have been men. It is a valid question whether or not women should function as elders or as deacons.

There are two passages that deal with the qualifications for elders, and they are quoted above. In both cases, Paul is giving directions on how to chose elders. In reading both texts, there are a couple of observations in order. First, most of the qualifications are issues of character, not skill. We are not to choose elders on the basis of what direction they will take the church. That is in stark contrast to our national political campaigns, which are all about the direction a particular candidate wants to take our country in and very little, unfortunately, about the character of the candidates. Again, the church is to be different. Second, in the 1 Timothy passage, there are two skills mentioned: he must be an apt teacher and he must manage his household well. In Titus, he must be able to give instruction in

---

[472] It is the same word Peter uses in 1 Peter 5:2, when he says the job of an elder is to "*tend* the flock." It is a shepherd term—he says to tend the <u>flock</u>, meaning the congregation. I find this exhortation or encouragement to be challenging. It means that elders are to be involved in the lives of the people in their congregation, investing in them to build Christian character in them. An elder board is not just a board of trustees, making policy decisions for the church. They are really pastors, but not full-time pastors probably.

sound doctrine and be able to confute those who contradict it. There is nothing said about being a successful businessman or a leader in the community or having a charismatic personality or any other of the assumed characteristics we are often attracted to in choosing spiritual leaders. I well remember once noticing the group of elders in my church standing up front to serve communion. One of them was vice-president of the Big Ten university in our town and another was a ditch digger. Both were wise and mature Christians, although they each had a different kind of wisdom. Both met the character qualities of an elder, even though their community standing was very different. In the church, they were equals.

One of the qualifications listed in both texts is "the husband of one wife." It is not clear if that was meant to disqualify single people, people who had been divorced, one who had been in "serial marriages," or if it just meant the spouse of one person. The word translated as "husband" is really *aner*. That means male, not just a person, which would have been *anthropos*. The word for wife is *gyne*, which means woman. So what Paul is saying is that the elder must be a man of one woman.

Some understanding of the context might be helpful here. Sometimes today we talk of a "double standard" when it comes to moral expectations of guys and girls. Today's practice is nothing compared to the blatant double standard in New Testament times. Husbands had legal authority over their wives so that any breach of sexual fidelity was an indictable offense—at least against the wife. That principle, however, did not apply to husbands. In fact, in speeches given at weddings, wives were often warned that they needed to be patient with their husband's sexual freedoms but that they, the wives, needed to be completely faithful to their husband.[473]

We are told the story in John 8:3–11 about an event where some scribes and Pharisees brought a woman who had been caught in

---

[473] Dr. Bruce Winter, After Paul Left Corinth. Wm B. Eerdmans Publishing Co., Grand Rapids, MI 49505, c. 2001, pp. 228ff.

the act of adultery to Jesus. They were wanting to trap him. They reminded him that the law of Moses said to stone such a woman. What did He think? Jesus stooped down and began to write in the sand with his finger. The accusers continued to bug him with the question. Jesus stood up and said, "Let him who is without sin cast the first stone." Then He bent down again and continued to write in the sand. One by one, beginning with the eldest, they silently turned and walked away. Since the context was sexual sin, and since they walked away rather than throw a single stone, it would seem that they recognized they were also guilty of the same thing and acknowledged that by turning around and silently walking away without throwing any stones.

More importantly, the whole incident shows the double standard of the time: if the woman was actually caught *in the act*, there must have been a man present also—right? It takes two. Why did the men who were so indignant at this woman not also bring the man? Because the man was not guilty in their eyes. Boys will be boys and men will be men. But women had to be faithful. Jesus clearly and embarrassingly shot that double standard down. There was one standard for both men and women. I wish the text told us what he was writing in the sand; I wonder if it was the names of the very men who were ready to throw stones, indicating that they had done the same thing they were accusing this woman of—and Jesus knew it. That is complete speculation, but I would not be surprised if it were true.[474]

---

[474] In Mark 10:1–12, we have recorded the incident when the Pharisees questioned Jesus about divorce. He gives them an answer and then answers more completely to his disciples in private. It is easy to miss His profoundly egalitarian response. In that culture, if a man had sexual relations with another man's wife, he actually committed adultery against the other woman's *husband*. But he was not considered to have committed adultery against his own wife. But that is exactly what Jesus said he is doing. In that culture, it was not considered possible for a man to commit adultery against his wife, no matter what he did, only a wife against her husband. Jesus blew that double standard out of the water when he said, "Anyone who divorces his wife and marries another woman commits adultery against *her*. And if she divorces her husband and marries another man, she commits adultery" (Mark 10:10–12. Note the completely egalitarian, but culturally unacceptable, view of divorce. In that culture, a woman could not divorce her

So in this text in 1 Timothy, it was necessary to say that an elder must be a man of one woman, thus eliminating the double standard. It went without saying that wives must be the wife of one man; legally they had to! Paul also could have eliminated the double standard just by saying that persons needed to be faithful to their spouses, but those are not the words he used. Had he said that, he would have left open the possibility that women could serve as elders. But he used the word *aner*, which as I said above refers to males, not persons. To me, that indicates that males should be elders. It also indicated that they were held to the exact same standard of sexual fidelity as women. There was one rule for everybody—men and women alike. Paul was egalitarian in the character standards for men and women.

There is another qualification that indicates that elders should be men. They are to be "apt to teach." Unfortunately, chapter divisions and verse divisions tend to divert the train of thought of the author of a text. The division between the end of chapter two and the beginning of chapter three is artificial; it is not in the author's original manuscript. As we have already seen, many disagree over what Paul meant in chapter two when he said, "I permit no woman to teach or have authority over men." But whatever he meant, it is fair to assume that he has the same definition in mind here in chapter three, some four verses later. The context is the same. The author is the same. The audience is the same. The time period is the same. Whatever the word meant, he says that it is not allowable for a woman to do it, but one of the qualifications for elder is that the person be "apt" to do it. That would eliminate a woman from the job. That seems harsh and makes me uncomfortable writing it, but I don't see how to get around it. It does not mean women are never allowed to teach anybody or are incompetent to teach; it just means

---

husband, but Jesus condemns that double standard. See also <u>The Expositor's Bible Commentary</u>, edited by Frank Gaebelein, c. 1984 by Zondervan, p. 710.

that women are not to be chosen for a job that entails an activity that Paul says he does not permit women to do.[475]

The Old Testament prescribed men as priests.[476] Only Aaron and his male descendants were to fulfill this office. One of the complications in this whole study is figuring out the degree to which God accommodates culture in His directives for His people. For example, clearly God hates divorce. But he not only allows it but gives parameters by which it was to be conducted. One could chalk up the exclusively male priesthood in Old Testament Israel to cultural accommodation, just like the parameters on divorce, which, we know, was clearly not part of God's original design. Jesus Himself tells us that.[477] But the consistent practice was clear: men, and men only, functioned as priests in the Old Testament.

The issue before us, however, is this: If women were to serve as New Testament equivalents in the office of elder, it is unthinkable that Paul would have ignored this enormous switch. He would have had to explain the change and the reasons for it. For those who support women elders, Paul's silence on this needs explanation.

As we have already seen, headship in marriage is consistently a male position. That is a term used only in marriage and only describing males. That relationship is a unique relationship of *one* man and *one* female. Headship is not a term used in the context of church government. Since an elder board is usually a group, it would be strange to talk of "head" in that context, as it would have to be a plural. However, it would make sense that the same principle would carry over into church government if the church is supposed to be characterized by Kingdom-of-God principles or as

---

[475] Remember the gender-neutral statement in 1 Corinthians 14:26: "When you come together *each one* has a hymn, a lesson (*didache*), a revelation, a tongue, or an interpretation. Let all things be done for edification." *Anybody* can teach a lesson. I believe what Paul has in mind here in 1 Timothy 3 is an office rather than an activity.

[476] Exodus 28:1. "Then bring near to you Aaron and your brother and his sons with him, from among the people of Israel to serve me as priests...."

[477] Matthew 19:1-3. "For your hardness of heart Moses allowed you to divorce your wives, but from the beginning it was not so."

the "Bride of Christ." In fact, Paul calls the church the "household of God." Three times in the same context as that phrase is used, the same word is also used of the family or extended family. One of the qualifications of an elder is that "he must manage his *household* well." "If a man does not know how to manage his own *household*, how can he care for God's church?" "Let deacons be the husband of one wife, and let them manage their children and their *households* well." "If I am delayed, you may know how one ought to behave in the *household* of God, which is the church of the living God, the pillar and bulwark of the truth."[478] Clearly, the author saw the church and the family as similar and therefore they should function under the same principles. In fact, the preferred training-ground for an elder is his own household. That must indicate that there are similar principles in each.[479]

So I see four reasons for the position of eldership being reserved for males. There is the phrase that he must be a "male of one female." There is the qualification that an elder be "apt to teach" and in the preceding paragraph Paul says he does not permit a woman to teach a man. There is the lack of explanation from Paul about the radical switch from male-only priests to both male and female elders in the New Testament churches. And there is the similarity between the family of God, where the male and the male only functions as the head, and the church of God, which is the family of God. I feel the need to remind us that this is not about competence, significance, importance, value, skill, or status in the Body of Christ. Every ministry for which an elder is responsible can be practiced in other venues in the church. Not being an elder in the church will not limit

---

[478] 1 Timothy 3:4, 5, 12, and 15

[479] I have talked with people who believe in role differentiation for men and women for marriage but not in the church, partly because the term "head" is never used in the context of the church or in reference to elders. But the office of elder is always a plural position, not a singular position. For there to be several "heads" because there are several elders might be confusing.... The fact that whether or not a potential candidate did a good job in his family is important in deciding whether or not he should fulfill a similar role in the church indicates the roles are similar.

your fulfillment or personhood or value in the Kingdom of God. We must not forget those principles.

The next section in 1 Timothy is about qualification for deacons. Traditionally, the deacons have cared for physical and emotional needs of the church membership. The qualifications are very similar, and the phrase "husband of one wife" also appears in this list. That might indicate that, again, only males are to be deacons. The word, again, is *aner*. But there is this mysterious phrase in verse eleven: "the women, likewise, must be serious, no slanderers...," etc. That phrase about "the women" is missing in the list of qualifications for elders. Some have said that all Paul is doing is making sure that wives of deacons are trustworthy and not gossips because they would be privy to a lot of personal information by virtue of being married to a deacon. But that surely would have also been true by virtue of being married to an elder. I think the absence of that phrase specifying the qualifications of "the women" in the qualifications for elders, but its presence in the qualifications for deacons, indicates that women could be and should be deacons. And, just as a reminder, it did not need to be said that the women must be "women of one man" because that freedom was not open to them. Because of the double standard in that culture, only men were allowed such sexual freedom.

To summarize, I think the evidence in this text is that the office of elder is reserved for men. That does not mean men are more competent or wise or less susceptible to deception. That is very important to understand. I take it as a principle that in the household of God there is a hierarchy of equals, just as there is in the Trinity. At the risk of repeating myself, in spite of this principle, in no way are women denied ministry in the church or are they in any way second-class or incompetent. I see no reason why a woman should be prohibited from preaching a sermon. The reason for that is because I do not equate "teach" with giving a public lecture. That is an assumption we tend to make in our culture. To put it another way, as I understand Scripture, I am led to be more open to women fulfilling various roles than most complementarians are.

That does bring up the question of women pastors. If the pastor's role is the same as the elder's role is described, then I think that role is reserved for men. Where there is a multi-pastoral staff, it may well be appropriate for a woman to serve as a pastor in that situation, depending on her responsibilities. We need humbly to ask for wisdom and guidance as we make these decisions, realizing that there is never a perfect doctrine or application of a doctrine in a fallen world.

Hebrews 5:8

This particular verse is not one like Galatians 3:28, which some see as a central text. In fact, it is rarely referred to. And it is not one that deals directly with the issue of gender relationships. However, it is one that tells us something of the relationships between the persons of the Trinity, particularly the Father and the Son, and it is one that some have referred to in trying to define the nature of that relationship. It is exceptionally difficult to interpret. The verse says, in the RSV, "Although he was a Son, he learned obedience through what he suffered...." The "he" refers to Jesus. Understanding what the author of Hebrews meant is not easy. For starters, let's not miss the first surprise: it is quite astounding that Jesus, who was God Incarnate, had to learn anything! Part of the mystery of the Incarnation is that the God of the universe, the Creator of everything that is, became completely part of His creation. C. S. Lewis said that it would be like Shakespeare writing himself into one of his plays. As he put it, "Hamlet could initiate nothing. If Shakespeare and Hamlet could ever meet, it must be Shakespeare's doing."[480] So the Creator of the Universe had to learn how to walk and how to talk. He who is

---

[480] C. S. Lewis, <u>Surprised by Joy</u>, Harcourt Brace and Company, New York, NY, c. 1955, p. 119. Used by permission.

described as the Logos, the Word, who is the same yesterday, today, and forever, had to learn how to form a word with His mouth and to talk. Such a bizarre and incomprehensible theology surely cannot be man's creation. We would create something a bit more "reasonable." It is so ridiculous that it must be true.

When a sentence begins with the word "although," that introduces the possibility that there are coming two propositions and one does not follow naturally from the other. "Although we were the better team, we got creamed." "Although the weatherman said it would be clear, it rained all day." So we have to ask what two propositions are stated and why one does not follow the other. Dr. Bilezikian says it is the fact that, although Jesus was a son, he had to become obedient. "Whenever Christ is said to act in obedience, he fulfills his self-assumed destiny as Suffering Servant rather than obeying orders. In so doing, he displays an obedience not required of him since he was a Son. He did not learn obedience because he was a Son but in spite of the fact that he was a Son. (Although he was a Son, he learned obedience [Heb. 5:8].)"[481]

It seems that Dr. Bilezikian's starting point is that it is not required of sons to be obedient to fathers. In fact, that seems to be the implication of his phrase "in spite of." Unless I am understanding him incorrectly, which is always a possibility, he seems to be saying that a son's obedience to his father is abnormal, not normal. I do not see how he arrives at that position. That certainly is not a principle taught in the Bible about the relationship of children to parents.

Note Dr. Bilezikian's commentary on Ephesians 6:1-4, which says, "Children, obey your parents in the Lord, for this is right. 'Honor your father and mother' (this is the first commandment with a promise), 'that it may be well with you and that you may live long on the earth.' Fathers, do not provoke your children to anger, but bring them up in the discipline and instruction of the Lord."

Here is his commentary on this text: "First, we should note the

---

[481] Gilbert Bilezikian, <u>Beyond Sex Roles</u>, Baker Academic, Grand Rapids, MI, 3rd edition, c. 2006, p. 228.

difference in the terminology used for spouses, on one hand, and for children, on the other. Whereas husbands were instructed to love their wives, and wives to submit to husbands, children are told to 'obey' their parents…. Obviously, the word obey does not belong in the dynamics of mutual subjection…. The apostle Paul uses the language of authority for parental relations but deliberately avoids its use in defining marital relationships."[482]

First, I agree with his observation that different words are used to describe marital relationships and parent-child relationships. And that the word "obey" does not describe mutual subjection, a phrase he uses to mean mutual submission. A wife's relationship to her husband is not like a child's to his parent. To be honest, some complementarians have presented the husband-wife relationship that way.

Second, it is noteworthy that he observes that children are to obey their parents. Third, it is also noteworthy that the text directs fathers specifically to bring up their children in the discipline and instruction of the Lord.

So it seems that Dr. Bilezikian really believes that children ought to obey their parents, and a natural subset of that concept would be that sons ought to obey their fathers. Since fathers are to bring up their children in the discipline and instruction of the Lord, it would seem that children (and sons, specifically) ought to obey their fathers in this.

In that light, since God has chosen the terms Father and Son, which are used before creation and after the end of the world, it seems strange to me that Dr. Bilezikian would see it as a *new* role for Jesus to be submissive to the Father. He seems to be saying that being submissive to the Father does not necessarily follow from His being a Son. In fact, Dr. Bilezikian even uses the phrase "in spite of" in the quotation from his book. It was "in spite of" His being a son that Jesus became obedient to the Father. This would make sense from

---

[482] Ibid., p. 130

his starting assumption that all persons of the Trinity are equally submissive to each other, but not from a Biblical understanding of sonship.

I have tried to make it clear that I do not think mutual submission is a legitimate description of the persons in the Trinity, even though complete equality *is* a perfect description of the persons in the Trinity. If mutual submission were the description of the persons in the Trinity, that raises for me, again, the question of why God would choose the terms Father and Son instead of Brother and Brother or Brother and Sister or Father and Mother. It seems quite misleading to choose terms that clearly and Biblically include submission of one party to another instead of terms that do not imply submission of one party to another. It seems that the submission of one party to another must have been intended. And since the Son is present at creation (Heb. 1:2b) and is seated on the throne of the Father (Rev. 3:21) at the end of time, it seems difficult to limit the Father-Son relationship only to the Incarnation.

I am not sure why Dr. Bilezikian left out the phrase "through what He suffered." That part of the sentence seems to me to be necessary to understand what the verse is saying. Learning obedience *through suffering* was a new experience for Jesus. There was no suffering in heaven. The suffering required of living a Godly life in a fallen world was new to Him, just as learning to talk was new to Him, even though He is the Logos, the word, of God.[483] This is why we struggle so much with the concept of a hierarchy of equals in a Fallen World. It is no longer perfect. It is no longer uninfected with selfishness, rebellion, and arrogance. Jesus had to experience this just as He had to experience every painful experience in this fallen world. I do not mean to imply that Jesus' relationship with the Father was anything less than perfect. That was not the suffering involved.

---

[483] I have to mention a humorous, true story. We used to have a Logos bookstore in our town that was owned by one of the elders in our church. He once mentioned that when a book salesman would come into the store and ask for Mr. Logos, that told him a lot about the man's spiritual condition.

What was new and had to be learned was not being obedient as a perfect Son of a perfect Father, but being obedient as a perfect Son to a perfect Father in a fallen world where He had to suffer for doing what was right.

This is carried to an unthinkable extreme as Jesus approached the cross, and even more so when "The Transfer" happened, and my sin was transferred to Jesus. He became sin for the whole world, including for me. And so He experienced separation from the Father for the first time in his life, a separation that we all live with and do not recognize as abnormal. This separation is evident in the unthinkable question, "Why have you forsaken me?" Significantly, this is the only recorded instance of there being discord among the persons of the Trinity, which shows how sin can affect a relationship. I recognize the heretical nature of the phrase of "discord among the Trinity." How could one person of the Trinity "forsake" another person of the Trinity? The word means to "leave helpless" or "totally abandon." Are you kidding me? How could this be—especially *for me*? I do not begin to understand. He became sin—*for me*? I think Jesus was still God incarnate, but somehow now infected with my sin. I'm not going to die on that mountain because I could be so wrong—it is so unthinkable. Jesus also did not know the date of His return, so there were some things that God knew but that Jesus, as a man, did not. But at this point the whole universe goes out of focus.

I don't think His question arises out of the depths of unbearable pain; I think it is an honest question because now, for the first time in his life, *He did not know.* It is significant, I think, that sin clouded His thinking in the area of the holiness of God. He apparently did not understand the separation from the Father that now was reality due to the presence of *my* sin on His back. Sin had so muddled His understanding that He now asked the Father why the he had forsaken Him. He was clueless. That is what sin does to us. Here is the Lord Jesus, the agent of creation of the universe, who claimed legitimately to be God, who said we must be *perfect* even as the

Father in heaven is perfect, now asking clarification of the situation. "Why, God? What's going on here?"

Like a tottering old man in a nursing home, trying to remember names, this Lord Jesus—"He is before all things and in him all things hold together—in him all the fullness of God was pleased to dwell"—this Lord Jesus is in the dark and confused about his own relationship with his Father and what exactly is going on. Our eyes blur. We look away in embarrassment. It is too painful to watch.

I'm not sure if there is any circumstance of the Incarnation that is more painful, more embarrassing, more difficult to comprehend than this: Jesus suffering for *me* on the Cross. And yet, all the time as Jesus walked to the point of His death, He went in obedience to the Father. And, as we saw in chapter three, He was even willing to be a servant to his mixed-up disciples as He walked toward the Cross.

Does this not cause our arrogant, busy minds to stop and look with wonder upon this astounding person? Look at not only the Son, but also the Father and the Spirit (who were also undoubtedly enduring searing pain by the loss of fellowship among the three of them) bearing the pain of loss of their fellowship and that due to the immense cost of the disobedience of the very beings they created. For this moment in History, things are upside-down, mixed up, confused beyond recognition, as the penalty for sin is somehow erased out of existence. How can we yawn at this profound event? How can we not worship? How can *you* not fall on your knees in wonder at this extraordinary act among the Triune God to assume the penalty for our sin? For my sin? For your sin?

Now, my point in referring to this text is to point out God's use of the terms Father and Son. They imply both hierarchy and equality among the persons of the Trinity. And since gender is created to reflect that, we should see both in gender relationships.

Judges 4:1–5:31

The period of the judges extends from the death of Joshua to the establishment of the monarchy in the person of Saul. It was a time of great instability and disobedience and, at times, chaos, as Israel repeatedly did what was right in their own eyes, not in God's eyes. In fact, the period is striking by its repeated cycles of disobedience, God sending a "deliverer" or a judge, and, through that person, delivering Israel. Then Israel goes back to its evil ways, and God again sends a deliverer. This cycle is repeated some six times. It is a striking picture of God's unfailing love for His people and His people's conscious ignorance and disobedience.

Eventually Israel gets the picture. Sort of. They recognize that there is a problem here, but they propose the wrong solution because they diagnose the problem wrongly. They go to the last judge, Samuel, and say to him, "Behold, you are old and your sons do not walk in your ways; now appoint for us a king to govern us like all the nations.[484] Samuel's response was wise: He prayed to God. And God told him that, in essence, they were not rejecting Samuel, but God. Those are applicable words for any spiritual leader or parent. We should not be surprised when people reject Godly leadership or parenting. If people reject God, if people saw Jesus face to face and then reject both (as they did), why should we be surprised if people rebel against good parenting and leadership? It happens.

Israel's concern for the behavior of Samuel's sons was legitimate. The text tells us that his sons, Joel and Abijah, whom Samuel himself appointed to be judges, did not live a life appropriate for judges.[485]

But part of Israel's diagnosis was incorrect. They wanted a "king to govern us like all the other nations."[486] Perhaps, had they acted correctly and lived corporately a Godly life, they would not have had

---

[484] 1 Samuel 8:5
[485] This is a problem for Samuel. How could he have appointed his sons who, Scripture says, turned aside after gain? They took bribes and perverted justice. (I Samuel 8:3)
[486] 1 Samuel 8:5

the problems they did. But perhaps (and this is what I believe) they were half-correct: they did need a king. They needed hierarchy to function. As I observed in chapter four on the Trinity, Hierarchy, and Equality, even egalitarians observe that in order to function as a society, human beings need hierarchy. They need some sort of authority structure. They are not like a flock of birds that can magically all fly the same direction, turning this way and that, as if obeying some mysterious inner voice. So the chaos of the period of the Judges should teach us a dual lesson: 1) We should do, corporately, what God wants us to do. It is disastrous not to. 2) Leadership, or hierarchy, is necessary for a society to function. And it should be Godly leadership. And one of the ways to recognize Godly leadership is by the behavior of the children. That is one of the marks of an elder: "he must manage his own household well, keeping his children submissive and respectful in every way."[487]

I want to look at the account of one amazing female judge— Deborah. She was instrumental, along with Barak, in an enormous victory for Israel. Chapter five, verse two, in Judges, a very difficult verse to translate, begins the song of Victory of Deborah and Barak. Since it is so difficult to translate, I don't want to put too much weight on what the translators say it means. The RSV puts it this way: "That the leaders took the lead in Israel, that the people offered themselves willingly, bless the Lord!" That may give us some help in interpreting what went on between Deborah and Barak: 1) It is important for leaders to lead and for the people to follow. It is good for that to happen. That is the way we are designed. Otherwise chaos will result. 2) That this is the way that the song of Victory begins

---

[487] 1 Timothy 3:4. However, this raises a question for me. God's own children, as we have seen, were not "submissive and respectful in every way." How can God expect something of us, as parents, that He was not able to do? I am in the process of raising four kids, and they are not always "submissive and respectful in every way"! However, I am convinced that they will be after they go through their tough times of growing up in a very secular culture. And that will be because of God's faithfulness, not mine nor my wife's. I suspect that this qualification is more a mark of the humility of praying parents who put their trust in God rather than of the latest techniques of child-rearing. It is a mark of God's answering their prayers and of being old enough to see the results of their prayers. Age has a lot in its favor to qualify a person to lead.

may indicate that what was missing was leaders leading and the people following. But more on that later.

Let's have a look at this amazing woman, Deborah, wife of Lappidoth. The story begins in Judges 4:1 with the statement of the situation. "And the people of Israel again did what was evil in the sight of the Lord, after Ehud died. And the Lord sold them into the hand of Jabin king of Canaan, who reigned in Hazor.... Then the people of Israel cried to the Lord for help; for he [Jabin] had nine hundred chariots of iron and oppressed the people of Israel cruelly for twenty years." The narrative ends with a long victory song running from 5:1 to 5:31 and ends with the peaceful verse: "And the land had rest for forty years."[488] In between is the story of Deborah and her cohort Barak.

Deborah is introduced to us not primarily as a judge, but as a prophetess. She is not alone in that role in the Old Testament: there are also Miriam (Exodus 15:20), Huldah (2 Kings 22:14), Nadia (Nehemiah 6:14), and, in the New Testament, Anna (Luke 2:26), as well as the daughters of Phillip (Acts 21:9). Deborah also judged the people. The text says the "people came to her for her judgment"[489]

Without any transitional statement, verse six says that she sent and summoned Barak and told him, "The LORD, the God of Israel, commands you, 'Go, gather your men at Mount Tabor, taking ten thousand from the tribe of Naphtali and the tribe of Zebulun. And I will draw out Sisera, the general of Jabin's army, to meet you by the river Kishon with his chariots and his troops; and I will give him into your hand.'" Notice that Deborah is fulfilling her role as a prophetess. She is telling Barak what God is telling him to do. It's is God's authority to which Barak needs to submit, not Deborah's. But it is Deborah's word he needs to trust. Barak, unfortunately, trusts Deborah too much: "If you will go with me, I will go; but if you will not go with me, I will not go."[490] Perhaps he trusted Deborah's

---

[488] Judges 5:31b
[489] Judges 4:5
[490] Judges 4:8

presence like others trusted in the Ark of God: it represented the presence and power of God. Or perhaps Barak wanted her continued guidance from God. That can be very handy in a battle. The text does not tell us. But it does tell us that Deborah, as well as God, sees his response as negative, even though she submits to his request: "I will surely go with you; nevertheless, the road on which you are going will not lead to your glory, for the LORD will sell Sisera into the hand of a woman."[491]

One of the problems with reading a narrative text is that we have to decide if the events narrated are good or bad. Are they an example to follow or an example to avoid? That is not always clear. But is seems clear that Deborah, whose word from God to Barak was clearly trustworthy, saw Barak's response as negative. As a result of Barak's unwillingness to go unless Deborah went with him, the glory of victory would not be his: it would belong to another man. No, that's not what it says: "The Lord will sell Sisera into the hand of a woman."[492] Is it significant that it is into the hand of a woman that Sisera is sold? Difficult to answer. Yet it seems that, if it were irrelevant, not only would God have not specifically chosen a woman to do the final work of victory, but also God would not have specifically mentioned that it would be a woman. It seems to me difficult to avoid the conclusion that God was not happy that Barak would not follow God's direction unless Deborah went with him. Apparently, God was not sufficient in Barak's mind.

The Israelites tended to inhabit the mountainous areas of Canaan and the Canaanites the flat plains. The Canaanites were armed with a new technology-chariots of iron-some 900 of them. Those chariots did fine on the flat lands but were not as useful in the mountains.

Deborah gave Barak the word, "Up! For this is the day in which

---

[491] Judges 4:9
[492] Sisera was the commander of King Jabin's army. He was king of Canaan.

the LORD has given Sisera into your hand. Does not the LORD go out before you?"[493]

Barak obeyed the word of the Lord given to him through Deborah, and, as a result, the Lord routed Sisera and all his chariots and all his army. It may well be, even though the text does not tell us, that a storm came up and the plains became muddy and the chariots bogged down in the mud and so were unusable. Their technology failed. Whatever exactly happened, Sisera gets out of his chariot and runs, which seems to imply that running was faster than his chariot, which would be true if the chariot were bogged down in mud. Barak pursued him. Sisera kept on running and came upon the tent of Jael. She came out to meet him and, being the hospitable woman that she was, invited him in and told him not to be afraid. He went in and lay down, and she covered him up and gave him a drink, probably goat's milk. He told her that if anyone came by asking for him she was to lie—she was to say, "No—he is not here." Being dead tired and exhausted from the battle and then from running and being in what he supposed to be a safe place, covered with a blanket and having drunk some warm milk, he was out like a light.

In that culture where people lived in tents and were regularly moving on, putting up the tent and taking down the tent was woman's work. Women were quite skilled at handling hammers and tent pegs. They were familiar tools to Jael. She adeptly took one of each and probably, in one fell swoop, nailed Sisera to the ground. The text tells us specifically that the peg went through his temple and into the ground. When Barak arrives, Jael invites him into the tent so he can see the man he is seeking. He is already dead. She nailed him.

The summary of the story, in typical fashion, which is the truth, is that "on that day, God subdued Jabin the king of Canaan before the people of Israel."[494] The reason I use the word "typical" is that, even though Barak and his men fought the battle, ultimately it was God's doing and that is God's normal pattern of work. Ultimately, it was

---

[493] Judges 4:14
[494] Judges 4:24

God who won the battle; but in his typical mysterious partnership method, He used people like you and me to fight His battle.

Deborah and Barak sing a song together about God's victory. All of chapter five is the duet that Deborah and Barak sing. Verse two is translated something like, "That the leaders took the lead in Israel, that the people offered themselves willingly, bless the LORD!" and, as I said, it is difficult to translate. It literally says something like, "in the breaking forth of the breakers of Israel," or "When long locks of hair hung loose in Israel," which may refer to the custom of soldiers not cutting their hair when involved in a holy battle. As I said before, I do not want to put too much weight on a verse that seems so difficult to translate, but it may well imply that when leaders lead and people follow, it is a good thing. Obviously it is assumed that it is good leaders leading in a direction that is good in God's eyes. In the context of the whole book of Judges, where there is the repeated cycle of chaos and the result is that the people see the need of a leader in the person of a king and where Deborah, who is a prophetess, tells Barak that he needs to lead the people into battle and even tells him the precise day when he needs to get moving, this understanding of the text seems to make sense. It fits with what seems to be the nature of the human condition: that we need hierarchy to function.

As I write this, modern Egypt is in chaos, as the people are rebelling against a repressive government. History is stocked with instances of rebellion against repressive governments. But such a repressive government is always replaced with another government, sometimes just as bad and sometimes better. But it is never replaced with nothing. We are inescapably hierarchical.

And we function, at least as well as possible in a fallen world, with sinful leaders and sinful people, when the leaders lead and the people follow. This is true whatever the organization is, from a childhood club to an athletic team, to a large corporation, to the army, to the government, to the Universe. It is a hierarchical creation we live in.

I want to make just a couple of observations before we leave Deborah:

1. She was very competent. People came to her for judgment. The text does not say if they were compelled by any authority to obey her judgment. But the fact that people came to her seems to imply that people needed help to resolve disputes and that they trusted her.

2. She functioned as a prophetess to Barak. She was very clear that it was God who was calling him to go to battle, not her. She said, "The LORD, the God of Israel, commands you. Go . . . ."[495] So I scratch my head at authors who claim that here we have an instance of a man submitting to a woman's authority. That is just not what the text says.[496]

---

[495] Judges 4:6

[496] Dr. Stanley Grenz puts it this way: "Deborah also fulfilled her political role when she commanded Barak to assemble Israel's army to repel the foreign oppressors (4:6). ...Deborah also directed the plans for the military expedition against the Canaanites, including the day of the attack (Judges 4:14). ...After defeating Sisera's army, she—like Miriam generations earlier—praised God in song for the victory." From Women in the Church by Dr. Stanley Grenz and Denise Kjesbo, p. 69. "She"—that is, Deborah—did not defeat Sisera's army. Barak, with God's help, did that. The text actually says, "Up! For this is the day in which the Lord has given Sisera into your hand. Does not the Lord go out before you?" "So Barak went down from Mount Tabor with ten thousand men following him. And the Lord routed Sisera and all his chariots and all his army before Barak at the edge of the sword." It was Barak who led the men into battle. "The Lord routed Sisera... before Barak." Not Barak and not Deborah. She also did not direct the plans for the military expedition. The "I" in those verses is God, not Deborah, although it is Deborah relating them to Barak as a prophetess. Read them for yourself. Dr. Catherine Kroeger puts it this way: "When the enemies obstructed the roads so that it was impossible for the people to assemble before the Lord, she [Deborah] decided upon military action. The male general was afraid to lead the hosts of Israel against so formidable a foe, and so Deborah marched with him at the head of the troops. As promised, God accomplished the destruction of the enemy general at the hand of a woman (Judges. 4:9, 21–22). The entire story emphasizes the superior wisdom and resourcefulness of the woman." That quotation is from I Suffer Not a Woman by Catherine Kroeger, pp. 18, 19. When Dr. Kroeger says, "God accomplished the destruction of the enemy general at the hand of a woman," it sounds as if Deborah was the one whom God used to accomplish the destruction of the enemy, that is, *she* led the army into battle. That is just plainly not what the text says. The Biblical text also says nothing about the roads being clogged or that it was Deborah's "superior wisdom and resourcefulness" that solved the issue. The text actually says that it was another woman (not Deborah, which is implied in the quotation from Dr. Kroeger) into whose hands Sisera was delivered, and that was a punishment upon Barak for not being willing to go into battle himself without Deborah. Deborah's answer to Barak's

3. And so Barak obeyed God's authority, not hers.

4. God's will was communicated to a man through a woman prophet. There is no comment in the text as to whether this is good or bad. The only word of condemnation is to Barak, who is unwilling to go by himself but requires Deborah to go with him.

5. There is surely some significance in the fact that Sisera is given, by the Lord's hand, into the hand of a woman. The glory of victory for Barak is not just given to another person, but specifically to a woman. If the problem were lack of faith in God or there needed to be present some piece of matter through which God's power was present, like the Ark of the Covenant or Deborah herself, then it would seem that God would have punished Barak by just giving Sisera over to another man. But no, it is over to a woman specifically that God gives Sisera. That seems to imply that Barak's requirement of Deborah's presence was not pleasing to God. It may well be that the skeleton of the story can be seen beginning with Deborah's functioning as a judge and prophetess. Then she tells Barak what to do, and he balks but needs her for courage. The result is that the victory belongs to another woman, not him. And the summary is that when the leaders finally lead and the people follow, it is good. Barak, after all, finally did the job that God had called him to do; but he seems conspicuously reticent until Deborah kicks him in the seat of his pants.

---

request for her presence in battle is this: "I will surely go with you. Nevertheless, the road on which you are going will not lead to your glory, for the Lord will sell Sisera into the hand of a woman" (Judges 4:9). The text presents Deborah as a prophetess, not a commander-in-chief. She says to Barak, "The Lord, the God of Israel, commands you...." Barak responded to her prophecy from God, not to her personal authority or even her wisdom, although undoubtedly she was a wise woman. He responded to God's authority, not hers. Such shameless misreading of the text is not a small issue for those of us who hold a high view of Scripture. We must not make the text say something it does not.

Again, narrative texts are not always easy to interpret, and this is a perfect example. It is very easy for all of us to use this text to approve the prejudice we bring to the text. Perhaps I have done that. I hope not. But it seems that, while Deborah was certainly competent, it was Barak, a male, who was supposed to do the job God wanted, and God punished Barak for his hesitancy to do the job by having a female finish the job and get the glory.

It is a significant interpretive question for us why Deborah (or God) called Barak to lead and she did not do it herself. Of course, the first possibility that springs to mind is that in a culture as patriarchal as Old Testament Israel, no army of men would ever follow a woman leader into battle. And that, certainly, is quite true. However, God can, of course, cause anything to happen, and if God really wanted to make the case for women in leadership positions, He could have made an overwhelming case by having Deborah lead the army into victory, and the victory song would have been about egalitarian leadership, even in the Old Testament. Just as Jesus could have made an overwhelming case for egalitarian leadership by choosing six men and six women as disciples. But neither happens. It is, I think, insufficient just to attribute these events to merely bowing to cultural norms.

However, we must not miss the competence and reputation of Deborah. When the text says, "the people of Israel came to her for judgment,"[497] I find it highly doubtful that it was women only who came to her. In much of the literature I have read by complementarians, almost any kind of asking a woman for help or wisdom by a man is frowned upon as submitting to the leadership of women. Or the answer of a woman to the man must be done in such a way as not to impinge on the male's dominance. As if his ego is so fragile that it must be protected. Let's recognize the gifts God has given to both men and women and utilize them for the building of God's kingdom.

---

[497] Judges 4:5

Huldah
2 Kings 22:1 through 20

If you've ever played Bible trivia, this question is sure to come up: Who was the boy king?" The reason I know this is because I have stumbled on that one. It was Josiah. He was eight years old when he became king of Judah. Can you imagine an eight-year-old lad being president? The comparison is probably unfair: our world is immensely more complex than the world of Old Testament Judah. Yet an eight-year-old boy seems awfully young to be king. It was not unheard of, however; his grandfather, the evil Manasseh, became king when he was twelve.

It was a time of immense political instability and spiritual apostasy. It may be read as a slap in the face of the "open-minded" spiritual leaders that they should be led by an eight-year-old. It turns out he was much more spiritually astute than they.

In the eighteenth year of his reign, Josiah sent Shaphan to go up to the house of the Lord and ask Hilkiah, the high priest, to get the money together that people had brought into the temple treasury. It was time to get to work on repairing the house of the Lord and to pay those who were doing it. While in the temple, Hilkiah came across a dusty old book and, upon examining it, found it to be the Book of the Law. (It is unknown how much of what we now call the Old Testament was included, and probably it was just parts or the whole of what we now call the book of Deuteronomy.) Shaphan came back to King Josiah and told him that the money was given to the workmen working on the temple and—oh, by the way—look at this book that was found. And he read from it to the king.

The king's response was unmistakable: he rent his clothes and wept. And he told Hilkiah, the high priest, to go inquire of the LORD. His wrath against his people had been kindled.

That is our situation in 2 Kings 22:14. It begins with the word "so" in the RSV (though that word is absent in the NIV, but the sense seems to be the same). That word implies cause and effect. King Josiah told Hilkiah to inquire of the Lord. "So Hilkiah, the priest, and Achbor, and Shaphan and Asaiah went to Huldah the prophetess... and they talked with her."[498] His response is to go talk to a woman. Her name is Hulda. Only here in the whole Bible is she named. There is some evidence from where she lived that she was of humble means. It is interesting that a high priest, when asked to inquire of the Lord, would respond by going to a woman. It would seem to be a fair conclusion that she had a reputation for speaking the words of Lord. It is probably safe to assume that Hilkiah did not just open the phone book and point to a name. He went to a known quantity. And her response justifies Hilkiah's choice of her. She minces no words as she responds to Hilkiah's request.

"And she said to them, 'Thus says the LORD, the God of Israel: 'Tell the man who sent you to me, 'Thus says the LORD, Behold, I will bring evil upon this place and upon its inhabitants, all the words of the book which the king of Judah has read. Because they have forsaken me and have burned incense to other gods, that they might provoke me to anger with all the work of their hands, therefore, my wrath will be kindled against this place, and it will not be quenched. But as to the king of Judah, who sent you to inquire of the LORD, thus shall you say to him, 'Thus says the LORD, the God of Israel: Regarding the words which you have heard, because your heart was penitent, and you humbled yourself before the LORD when you heard how I spoke against this place, and against its inhabitants, that they should become a desolation and a curse, and you have rent your clothes and wept before me, I have also heard you, says the LORD. Therefore, behold, I will gather you to your fathers, and you shall be gathered to your grave in peace, and your eyes shall not see all the evil which I will bring upon this place.'"[499]

---

[498] 2 Kings 22:14
[499] 2 Kings 22:15–20a

425

There are a number of scenes in the Bible that I would like to have paintings of. One (which I do have as a gift from my wife) is of Peter telling Jesus that it is a waste of time to throw the nets onto the other side of the boat because they have been fishing all night and have taken nothing. They, after all, were the professional fishermen. Yet, as he said that, there were fish teeming under the boat, just inches from his feet, which, in a short time, were in their nets and on the boats. And the boats nearly sank because there were so many of them!

Another is the picture of Elijah, after the contest on Mount Carmel and after a long period of drought, when he commanded King Ahab to get in his chariot and take off, lest it become bogged down in mud from the coming rain. This is said when the ground is tinder dry due to some three years without rain. Ahab gets in his chariot as directed, and it says, "the hand of the LORD was on Elijah, and he girded up his loins and ran before Ahab"[500] I love the image of this strong man, running so fast he could outrun the King's chariot, with the sky darkening in the background as the rainstorms approach.

A third image is this one, of these ranking political and religious leaders listening to Hulda tell them what the Lord thinks. How ironic! The text does not record that they had to think very long before deciding to go to Hulda. It gives us no hint as to why they chose her, but it would seem reasonable that she already had a reputation for speaking the words of the Lord to a particular situation. That, after all, is what a prophet or a prophetess does. Their response is straightforward. The text tells us simply that they brought back the word to the King.

But his response, true to his character, is stunning. What follows in chapter twenty-three is twenty-four verses listing all the reforms of Josiah, as a result of hearing what this woman said. He tore this monument down and he removed that abomination from the

---

[500] 1 Kings 18:46

Temple of the Lord and he burnt down this altar to another god and he removed this and deposed that and broke down this and broke in pieces that and on and on. The testimony of Scripture about him is simple: "Before him there was no king like him, who turned to the LORD with all his heart and with all his soul and with all his might."[501]

All this as a result of listening to a woman who spoke the Word of the Lord to him!

Look carefully at what she said. Four times she says, "Thus says the Lord." There is not one verb of which Huldah is the subject. Clearly, she was not assuming the role of an authority over these men. But just as clearly, she was assuming to tell them the Word of the Lord. If they did not go back and do what she had told them, it was not her they were disobeying, but the Lord. To point to Huldah as an example of a woman with authority over a man, I think, is not what the text says.

However, don't miss the example of Huldah. She apparently was known as a woman of God, as a woman who spoke the words of God and spoke them to men, even to a high priest.

It seems as if several applications follow, though applications of a narrative text must always be influenced by the didactic texts on the same topic.

1. It seems to me that the example of Hulda renders the interpretation of certain New Testament passages that women should be silent in church and not say anything as overly literalistic. If an Old Testament woman could speak the word of the Lord to an Old Testament king and an Old Testament high priest, it would not make much sense that in the New Testament, with God's Spirit poured out on men and women alike, that they are prohibited from speaking in church.

[501] 2 Kings 23:25

2. There can be little doubt that Huldah did speak correctly the word of the Lord to these inquiring men. Therefore, it would seem that men should not be afraid of or avoid seeking advice, even spiritual advice, from women. I chaired a committee in our church that examined the issue of "women in leadership" and made a recommendation to the board of elders. I very strenuously pushed for having women on that committee. I said at the time, and still think, that it would be an affront to God to say that women have no ability to think theologically and have spiritual input on a subject for the good of the church. Huldah is a shining example of a woman's ability to hear the Word of the Lord and speak that word, even to men.

3. That raises the interpretive question of whether or not Huldah "taught" these men, which included the King of Judah and the high priest Hilkiah. I do not think so, because she did not fulfill the definition of teaching, as I understand it, from 1 Timothy and the general New Testament context of the word. She was a prophetess, not a teacher. And so the Bible does not contradict itself on this topic. However, it needs to be recognized that Huldah spoke the word of the Lord to men, to a king and a high priest. The men listening to her and responding to what she said were responding to the Word of the Lord spoken through her, not her authority. I think that means the New Testament prohibition against women teaching men is not about women teaching *men*.

Acts 16:11–18:28

One of my daughters had the privilege of taking a one-month course in her college that studied the churches of Paul. It involved actually visiting the historical places where these churches began in Greece and Italy. As she would text us each day which church she was visiting, my wife and I would read the corresponding passages in the book of Acts. As I had been thinking about this gender issue for some time and the particular culture in which Paul lived, I noticed some new details in the texts I had never seen, even though I had read them many times. One has to remember that a Jewish rabbi, such as Paul was, would never think of teaching theological truths to women. The common Jewish prayer of a man was to thank God that he was not a Gentile, a dog, or a woman. In that context, read the following excerpts from the text we are looking at:

At Philippi: "We remained in this city some days; and on the Sabbath day we went outside the gate to the riverside, where we supposed there was a place of prayer; and we sat down and spoke to the women who had come together. One who heard us was a woman named Lydia, from the city of Thyatira, a seller of purple goods, who was a worshiper of God. The Lord opened her heart to give heed to what was said by Paul. And when she was baptized, with her household, she besought us, saying, "If you have judged me to be faithful to the Lord, come to my house and stay." And she prevailed upon us." (Acts 16:12b–15)

At Thessalonica: "And Paul went in, as was his custom, and for three weeks he argued with them from the scriptures, explaining and proving that it was necessary for the Christ to suffer and to rise from the dead, saying, 'This Jesus, whom I proclaim to you, is the Christ.' And some of them were persuaded, and joined Paul and Silas; as did not a few of the leading women." (Acts 17:2–4)

At Beroea: "The brethren immediately sent Paul and Silas away by night to Beroea, and when they arrived they went into the Jewish synagogue. Now these Jews were more noble than those in Thessalonica, for they received the word with all eagerness, examining the scriptures daily to see if these things were so. Many of them therefore believed, with not a few Greek women of high standing as well as men." (Acts 17:10–12)

At Corinth: "After this he left Athens and went to Corinth. And he found a Jew named Aquila, a native of Pontus, lately come from

Italy with his wife Priscilla, because Claudius had commanded all the Jews to leave Rome. And he went to see them; and because he was of the same trade he stayed with them, and they worked for by trade they were tentmakers. ...After this Paul stayed many days longer, and then took leave of the brethren and sailed for Syria, and with him Priscilla and Aquila. ...And they came to Ephesus, and he left them there; but he himself went into the synagogue and argued with the Jews. ...Now a Jew named Apollos, a native of Alexandria, came to Ephesus. He was an eloquent man, well versed in the scriptures. He had been instructed in the way of the Lord; and being fervent in spirit, he spoke and taught accurately the things concerning Jesus, though he knew only the baptism of John. He began to speak boldly in the synagogue; but when Priscilla and Aquila heard him, they took him and expounded to him the way of God more accurately. And when he wished to cross to Achaia, the brethren encouraged him, and wrote to the disciples to receive him. When he arrived, he greatly helped those who through grace had believed, for he powerfully confuted the Jews in public showing by the scriptures that the Christ was Jesus." (Acts 18:1–28)

A couple of observations are in order:

1. Paul did not hesitate to teach theological truths to women, contrary to his upbringing or contemporary Jewish culture.
2. Women were not secondary in the forming of the new church. As Paul, recently released from prison in Philippi, left the town, the only person named whom he visited was Lydia, the first convert in that city. She was a woman.
3. Paul stayed with Aquila and Priscilla in Corinth. When he left, he took them both with him and ended up leaving them at Ephesus. When a Jew named Apollos came to Ephesus and started teaching the things of Jesus there, but apparently not completely correctly, they both "expounded to him the way of God more accurately." I don't think it is a fair reading

of this passage to say that Priscilla taught Apollos, that a woman taught a man. That is just not what the words say. But neither is it a fair reading to say that she was uninvolved in the correction of this man's theological understanding. It is a third person plural. That means they both did it.

The only thing I remember from my eighth grade government class is a strange Latin phrase: *post hoc ergo propter hoc*. It means "after this, therefore because of this." It describes a very common error in logic that assumes that just because something happens after something else, it was caused by the something else. It's a common mistake that people make with medicine. Just because you take a high dose of vitamin C and get better doesn't mean the vitamin C caused you to get better.

Here is Priscilla, after spending considerable time with the Apostle Paul, feeling very free, with her husband, to correct a man's theological understanding. It may not be fair to *assume* that her freedom to correct a man's theology was *caused* by being around Paul; on the other hand, if Paul had followed the culture of his day, it seems she would not have felt free to correct Apollos. There does seem to be a pattern here in the narrative passages in Acts, that Paul considered women as teachable, equal partners in the Gospel, and Priscilla felt free to help another man to understand the things of God after having spent considerable time with Paul. The pattern seems to be that Paul had a much higher view of women than the Jewish culture of his time, which considered women as pretty much unteachable.

It seems to me in looking at these isolated narrative texts that women, both in the Old and the New Testaments, were profoundly involved in doing God's work. I shake my head at the current debate concerning women's roles in the church as being about "women in ministry." The clear Biblical account and, I believe, Biblical teaching is that women have been and should be involved in ministry. As I said above, it is unfortunate that we describe the person who preaches on Sunday morning as the "minister." Does that mean that only the "minister" does the work of ministry? I think not. I hope not! To characterize the question of whether or not women should be elders or fulfill the role in marriage described as "headship" as synonymous with "women in ministry" is not a legitimate characterization. It is a worldview that belongs to this fallen world and sees being a leader as making one a more significant and important person. We need to understand the teaching in Ephesians 4:11 through 13, that the gifts of the Spirit are for the equipping of the saints *for the work of the ministry,* for the building up of the Body of Christ. Ministry is for *everybody,* and the gifts of the Holy Spirit are to accomplish the ministry. The end result is that we all attain to the unity of the faith and of the knowledge of the Son of God. The fact that there is a diversity of roles among the church as we work toward that goal does not mean there is a diversity of importance.

As I have read the debate about women in ministry, I have never read anybody referring to the issue as women in the position of headship. I wonder why that is. I suspect it is because the references to headship in the New Testament refer to males. So it would be difficult to talk about women in a position of headship, because that phrase does not occur in the New Testament.

Maybe the most important lesson for us to learn is that the fact that there is a diversity of roles in the church does *not* mean there is a diversity of importance. That is a uniquely Christian concept. This world does not understand it. I referred to Dr. Sarah Sumner's use of the "s-word" on page 100 in reference to roles of leadership. It's the word "status." We need to re-orient our thinking so that we do *not* associate status with certain roles, especially roles of leadership in the church. That concept will be left behind when we walk into heaven's door.

And that will be very good.

10

FINAL WORDS

As I said in the introduction, I am attracted to puzzles. It was puzzling to me that a chemistry professor would be studying the Bible and doing it with students. I needed to figure that out. It also has been puzzling to me to see the apparent contradictions in the Bible on the gender issue and so I needed to figure that out also. Even though I was initially skeptical about the usefulness of the Bible before I became a Christian, I have since come to see that I was wrong and now see the Bible as providing us reliable Truth from our Creator. And so searching the Scriptures is like going on a treasure hunt. But understanding them is complicated because our glasses are colored by living in a Fallen World, not to mention living in a culture very different from the cultures of the Bible or the simple fact that it was written in a different language. So if we are serious about finding Truth in the Scriptures we must do our homework in order to understand what the Bible says and pray for God's help in order to apply it to our lives. Following is a summary of what I believe the Bible says about the complicated gender issue.

There is a truckload of theology in the opening sentence of the Bible. The name of God in that first sentence, Elohim, is a plural name but always takes a singular verb. So we observe a plural being who always acts as "one," as if he were a singular being, not plural.

But He is plural. That plural being creates everything that is, all kinds of *different* things. The creation is *diverse*.

In chapter one of Genesis, the crowning act of creation is the creation of human beings, created as male and female—two *different* beings. Three times in as many verses we are told that they are created in the image of God. That implies, I take it, that the *different* beings who make up humanity reflect the *different* beings who make up their creator, who we later learn is a Trinity.

Interestingly, in chapter two of Genesis, which tells a different story of creation in order to emphasize some different aspects of creation, when the male and female are created separately, there is no mention of being created in the image of God. That difference between chapter one and chapter two seems to indicate that the male and female together, the male and female *relationship* in chapter one, is what reflects God. By that I mean that the relationship of the two different human beings reflects something of the relationship of the three different persons of the Trinity. That makes sense since, in the verses immediately preceding, God is portrayed as making a "plural" decision to create the humans and, when they are created, they are created as plural—male and female, as different beings.

Interestingly, also, when this plural God creates two beings who relate to one another as this plural God relates among himself, these two beings are not the same. They are diverse.

And also, interestingly, in chapter two, they become "one." As we will see later, Elohim is also "one."

Even though the creation of the male and female are portrayed in chapter one as the crowning activity of God, there is a lot of creation activity that precedes their creation. Lots. And the results of that preceding creation are very diverse. Morning and evening. Heaven and earth. Light and darkness. Water and dry land. Sun and moon. Differing kinds of plants. Different kinds of animals. And last of all, differing kinds of humans—male and female.

A work of art or a creation usually reveals something of the person who made it. It would seem, then, that the Creator in Genesis is a diverse being. He creates lots of different stuff. And mysteriously, for us at least, part of that diversity is a diversity of authority. It is hinted at in Genesis chapters one through three but not clearly revealed until much later when God became man.

From the very beginning, God's perfect creation, before it had been infected with sin, bristles with hierarchy. The words "dominion," "over," and "rule" are there and they are there before the Fall. God could have made a creation with no hierarchy present—it was not necessary for order.

From what we see later in the Bible, there is hierarchy in the Trinity. Even though that is most obvious in the Incarnation, as we saw in the chapter on the Trinity, Hierarchy, and Equality, the terms Father and Son are used both before the universe was made and at the end of time. So the hierarchy is not limited to the Incarnation. When Jesus came to the earth as a human, He came because He was "sent" and said that He would send the Spirit. He called God "Father," which implies authority (as compared to "brother"), and said that He could do *nothing* on his own authority. He was always submissive not to God but to part of God, the Father. But when He called God "Father" He ended up dodging stones. When He asked the stone throwers why they heaving stones at Him, they replied, "Because you call God 'Father,' thereby making yourself equal with God." *And He did not correct them.*[502] In other words, He knowingly called God Father, which implies authority and *also* sameness and equality. Those who heard Him tried to stone Him because they understood, correctly, that He was also claiming to be of the same substance as God and so to be equal with God. But at the same time *He* said He could do nothing on His own authority. In our fallen world, we have trouble comprehending a hierarchy of equals, but that is what the evidence points to: a Triune God, a plural, *diverse* God, who always acts as One yet where all the persons are completely

---

[502] John 5:18

equal. Not three gods but one God who exists as three persons who always act in complete unity and equality.

I think sometimes we miss the legitimate difficulty the people of Jesus' time had comprehending who Jesus was.

The Jews of the Bible would not even say the name of God because they thought God was so holy and so Other. Yet here is a man standing before them who went to the bathroom just as they did and probably had body odor just as they did and yet he was claiming to be Jehovah Elohim. Their problem was huge. Here is a normal person standing before them whose name they could not even say with their lips because He was so holy and yet He looked just like them. C. S. Lewis offers a profound insight here: "Among these Jews there suddenly turns up a man who goes about talking as if He was God. He claims to forgive sins. He says He has always existed. He says He is coming to judge the world at the end of time. Now, let us get this clear. Among Pantheists, like the Indians, anyone might say that he was a part of God, or one with God: there would be nothing very odd about it. But this man, since He was a Jew, could not mean that kind of God. God, in their language, meant the Being outside the world who had made it and was infinitely different from anything else. And when you have grasped that, you will see that what this man said was, quite simply, the most shocking thing that has ever been uttered by human lips."[503]

So let's not be too hard on those who struggled to comprehend who Jesus was—God the Son, the creator of everything that is, who was somehow always submissive to God the Father. We would have struggled also.

And we still do. Let's be honest: in our fallen world, we have trouble comprehending a hierarchy of equals. Remember in chapter four, titled "The Trinity, Hierarchy, and Equality," I surveyed no fewer than 28 different quotations by very intelligent authors who promoted the idea that hierarchy eliminates equality. Remember in

[503] C. S. Lewis, <u>Mere Christianity.</u> Macmillan Publishing Co., New York, NY, c.1952, pp. 54, 55. Used by permission.

the same chapter when I quoted Susan Sumner when she let the "s" word slip out. Status. She said "Men have exclusive access to higher status leadership solely on the basis of their gender."[504] Or Nicholas Walterstorff said, "Gender is simply not relevant to the assignment of benefits and deprivations...."[505] I pointed out how the words "status" and "benefits and deprivations" are not neutral words. They reveal how we view hierarchy—that being "higher" in the hierarchy offers "benefits" and "status." But I believe that is because we live in a fallen world. The Biblical view of hierarchy is that leadership does *not* impute status or benefits. It does *not* make you a more significant person.[506] In the Trinity, the Father does *not* have more "status" than the Son or the Spirit, nor is he "supreme," as some have said. In 1 Corinthians 12, it is said that we confer the *same* care on our more "unpresentable" parts. This, I believe, is where we profoundly need to change our thinking.

There are three social relationships in Scripture where the word "one" is used to describe them. The Trinity, Christian marriage, and the body of Christ. In Deuteronomy 6:4, Moses says, "Hear, O Israel: The LORD our God is one LORD." The word for "one" is an interesting word. It does not always mean "one" in the sense of a monolithic unity, but a "one" made up of parts, as "one" bunch of grapes or the people gathering as "one." There is a different word for "one" that really means one as a unity, like our number "one," but that is not the word used in Deuteronomy 6:4.

In John 17, Jesus prays three times that His disciples (and by extension His church) would be "one" *just as* He and the Father are "one." In 1 Corinthians 11:3, headship describes both the relationship of Jesus to God and that of husband to wife. So certain relationships among the followers of Jesus should mirror the relationships among the Trinity. In Genesis 2, the first man and woman became *one*. In

---

[504] Sarah Sumner, <u>Men and Women in the Church</u>. InterVarsity Press, p. 278.
[505] Nicholas Wolterstorff, <u>Women, Authority, and the Bible</u>, p. 291.
[506] But I need to say again that we should choose leaders on the basis of character and maturity. Spiritual maturity does matter when we choose leaders.

Ephesians 5, the apostle Paul describes how the husband and wife, by God's design, became *one* in a mystical re-union reminiscent of the first man and woman in Genesis 2. Since the Trinity is portrayed as a hierarchy of completely equal persons, it would seem to follow that the same concept would apply to the Body of Christ and Christian marriage.

We know from Scripture that the church is a *diverse* body of people. "There are varieties of gifts, but the same Lord. There are varieties of service but the same Lord. There are varieties of working but it is the same God who inspires them all. To each is given the manifestation of the Spirit for the common good."[507] In Revelation 7:9, the perfected church is gathered before the Throne and the Lamb, and it consisted of a "great multitude" from "every nation, from all tribes and peoples and tongues… clothed in white robes." So the design of the church is that it would be diverse but still "one," made up of *different* kinds of people who speak *different* languages and have *different* skin colors, yet all clad in the same color robes. They are a diverse group, just like God, their creator and redeemer.

So we should not be surprised that this strangely plural God who acts as *one* is mysteriously *diverse* and called by *different* names. Father, Son, and Holy Spirit is who they are, but still *one*. They are not revealed as Person A, Person A, and Person A. The names Father and Son imply both authority and sameness. Significantly, Jesus says that He always obeys the Father and then He sends the spirit. There is consistency in how authority is practiced in the New Testament— Father to the Son to the Spirit, and yet there is complete equality.

I cannot emphasize enough that this is a *different* kind of social arrangement from anything we might experience in this world. Its source is the diversity and equality in the Trinity. So what I believe the Bible teaches about the Trinity, about gender relationships, and about relationships in the Body of Christ might be called an

---

[507] 1 Corinthians 12:4–7

egalitarian hierarchy.[508] By that I mean that no position or role confers more status or value to the person who fulfills that role. The idea of a hierarchy where the person in the position of authority acts as a *servant* and uses that non-superior but authoritative position to *serve* and benefit others, *even sacrificing self* to serve others, is unworldly. (That is also a definition of what the Bible calls headship.) But that is the model to which we are called, even as sinners. I know it is easy to say we cannot do that because we are still sinners living in a fallen world, but the consistent pattern in the Bible is that we are called to live, even to think, what is correct, in our fallen world. And our Creator and Designer defines what is correct for us. Not we ourselves. The ideal is the goal, even though we may never achieve it. "Be perfect, even as your Father in heaven is perfect."[509] What that high standard of behavior and thought does for us is cause us to see our failures and draw near to God for grace.

This all comes from the first two chapters of Genesis. They introduce to us the twin truths of the complete equality of the genders (in Genesis 1) and the perfect egalitarian hierarchy of equals (in Genesis 2). That concept is central to my understanding of the gender issue and everything else flows from that. Those two chapters are my "window text." They lay the foundation of complete equality, though not interchangeability, of the genders, and yet a hierarchy of equals. The source of that structure is the Trinity itself. All the

---

[508] I would put it this way: I believe the Bible teaches hierarchy but not patriarchy. By that I mean that the Bible does not teach about male superiority in any way—innate intelligence, wisdom, fitness for leadership or whatever. It does not teach superiority of males over females. It does not each "Father knows Best," like the '50s television show. It *does* teach, however, male headship. In Ephesians 5 and 6 or Colossians 3:18-4:1, where, I believe, the Bible does teach hierarchy, it corrects the effects of the fall of man on hierarchy. It is truly stunning to me (it probably should not be) how people who called themselves Christians said the Bible supported slavery because it told slaves to obey their masters but ignored verses like Colossians 4:1 that told masters to treat their slaves "justly and fairly." It would seem that applying those verses would eliminate the horrors of slavery.

[509] Matthew 5:48

other texts coming later in the Bible expand upon and explain that foundation laid in those two chapters.

But something went terribly wrong in chapter three of Genesis, and the consequences of that disobedience, committed equally by both the man and the woman, affect everything that follows. None of the consequences of the Fall were new creations, just parts of the old perfect creation, but now *bent*. One of those consequences was that the male would "rule" over the female. As a result, the perfect hierarchy of the Creation, the perfect design of headship, became infected with assumed superiority, assumed inferiority, assumed "status," assumed selfishness in how the role is practiced, and assumed inequality. But it was not so from the beginning. All the New Testament passages that teach on gender contain teaching on both hierarchy and equality of the genders.

My son played football in high school and college and was a wide receiver. I grimace when I hear people talk of the positions of quarterback, running-back or receiver, as being the "skill" positions. It is the elephants on the offensive line who enable those "skill" positions to do their thing. If it were not for the linemen, who, by implication, are not fulfilling "skill" positions, the team would not be successful. And that happens. *All* the positions are "skill" positions, and *all* are necessary for the team to function. That is what C. S. Lewis was referring to when he described the Body of Christ as a "unity of unlikes" fulfilling different but *equally important* roles. Remove one, he says, and you have done more than reduce the number. Merely reducing the number would be a legitimate description if all the roles were the same. But instead he says you have inflicted *injury* on the *structure*.[510] So in the Body of Christ, we need all the members to fulfill their ministry. *Every* role is a ministry

[510] C. S. Lewis, "Membership," an essay included in the collection titled The Weight of Glory and Other Addresses. Wm. Eerdmans Publishing Company, Grand Rapids, MI, c. 1965, p. 34. Used by permission.

and *every* member has one. To talk about women being excluded from ministry makes no sense unless you mean by that they can do *nothing* in terms of ministry. That, of course, is as ridiculous as it is unBiblical. What a waste of gifted women that would be! There is no one who is excluded from ministry on the basis of gender. All roles are important. It is, however, an example of the mistaken thinking to believe that certain roles confer more *status* to the person fulfilling them. I am egalitarian in my understanding that all roles are equal in terms of status or conferring personal value or identity. And all are different. None makes you a more significant person in God's eyes or, hopefully, in the eyes of others. No one role is more helpful than any other in helping you "reach your potential." That's what "*oneness*" is all about. That makes the church of Jesus Christ, and marriage, different from the world around us.

And it should be.

Sometimes when you read a passage of Scripture you can miss the forest for the trees. Re-read the great priestly prayer of Jesus as He turns his face from his disciples who were with Him toward the Cross that was before Him and would save them. (And me.) This passage is packed with references to the mysterious hierarchy among the persons of the Trinity: over and over (some ten times), He refers to the Father who *sent* him, who *gave* him the disciples. Jesus then *sent* this disciples *as* the Father sent him. At the same time, He refers to the quality of relationships among His followers, the Body of Christ, as a *mirror* of the relationships among the persons of the Trinity: re-read just five verses from this prayer and look for this theme: "As thou didst send me into the world, so I have sent them into the world. And for their sake I consecrate myself, that they also may be consecrated in truth. I do not pray for these only but also for those who believe in me through their word, that they may all be one; *even as* thou, Father, art in me and I in thee, that they also may be in us, so that the world may believe that thou hast sent me. The glory which thou hast given me I have given to them, that they may be one *even as* we are one, I in them and thou in me, that they may become perfectly one, so that the world may know that thou has sent me."[511] Notice three things: 1) the repetition (which indicates what is important to an author) of Jesus' desire that his disciples be "one" *just as* He and the Father are "one," *so that* the world would know that the Father had *sent* Him. That "oneness" is not a monolithic unity where everybody is the same. He wants the world to see the quality of our relationships, not only our unconditional love for each other but also the perfect hierarchy of equals, where nobody is more significant or important because of the role they fulfill. Both should be visible in His church. That should convince the world, He says, that the Father sent Him. 2) He sent His disciples into the world "even as" He was sent into the world by the Father. The "sending" was the same in two ways: a) the target—which was our fallen and dangerous world, not some safe fortress of Christian community, and b) the authority of the sending one—the Father to Jesus and Jesus to the disciples. The perfect hierarchy of equals among the members of the Body of Christ, a hierarchy of equals who are diverse and not homogeneous, as is the Trinity as revealed in Scripture, should *help the world* to know that Jesus was *sent* from the *Father*. 3) Jesus prays that the relationship among His disciples would mirror the relationship among the persons of the Trinity. That is the weight of the italicized words "just as" in His prayer for His people remaining on earth. That's what Jesus wants for the community of His followers, the Body of Christ, as well as, I believe, a marriage between a man and a woman. At the risk of repeating myself, it's a hierarchy of complete equals, of beings who are different, even different in authority, but still equal, just as it is in the Trinity. That's what the world should see in us.

Now, notice something very significant: Jesus prays in John 17:21 and 23 that this quality of relationship in the Trinity, a hierarchy

---

[511] John 17:18–23

God, Gender, and a Fallen World

of equals, would also be in His church, and that it would convince the world that the Father had sent Him and loved them even as the Father had loved Him. Let that sit in your mind a bit. I have heard people say today if there is hierarchy in the church, especially a hierarchy based on gender that would hurt our evangelistic outreach. Jesus is saying just the opposite here, is He not? I think the problem is we do not have a Christian view of hierarchy when the head is a servant, and not just a self-serving boss.

Again, I say, that's what makes the church of Jesus Christ, and marriage, different from the world around us.

And it should be.

The church, and many Bible believing Christians today, need to repent of the unBiblically low view of women evident in some of the quotations at the beginning of some of the chapters in this book. Hierarchy does not eliminate equality, but many have assumed it does. This misunderstanding of hierarchy, which has its source in the fallen world instead of the Kingdom of God, needs to be corrected.

The church also needs to change its understanding of "headship" as being synonymous with leadership. Or synonymous with "authority." To say that the husband is the "leader" in the marriage relationship is mistaken. The husband is never called the "leader" in the Bible. To say that "male leadership" is the design of God's church is mistaken. To say that women must submit to and encourage "male leadership" is mistaken, although we should all encourage each other in our respective ministries. What I take issue with is the word "leadership." Headship *is* a male position and it is presented that way *consistently* in the Scriptures. But it is not synonymous with "leadership," although there are some similarities. Nor does it mean merely the one who has authority or is "in charge." The Biblical concept of headship belongs to the Kingdom of Heaven, and we, as citizens of this fallen world, struggle to comprehend it just as Nicodemus struggled to comprehend being born again. Headship is a position of authority, and that authority is used to love, serve, and feed another person, or group of persons, as elders should do. It does not make one superior or of elevated status. It is not self-serving. That is important.

Remember our topical study on how authority is exercised in the Kingdom of Heaven in the chapter on fingerprints and appetizers? Jesus exercised His *authority* to serve and to love His disciples. Even though much energy has gone into trying to prove that headship is synonymous with authority, which I believe is *partially* true, that part of the Biblical definition that includes serving, loving, and *sacrificing self* to benefit others is often mentioned only as an afterthought, even though it is really central, just as authority is also central. It has been taught by some that the real definition of headship is "authority." The men are in charge and the women need to submit to and encourage them in their position of leadership. That definition does not belong to the Kingdom of Heaven but instead to this fallen world where "ruling" is a result of the Fall.

Remember the authentic examples I gave of married couples and how they struggled to have the husband function as the "head"? One example involved the husband demanding the toilet paper be rolled from the top rather than the bottom to establish him as the "head." Another involved the couple having a dog that the husband wanted but the wife did not because she would have to take care of it. They got the dog. And she took care of it. Another involved the husband getting the hot shower before the hot water ran out so the wife got the cold shower. Those examples are *not* examples of what "headship" looks like. They all really happened.

However, I don't want to be misunderstood as thinking the Bible teaches mutual submission as a summary of gender relationships. It does not. In marriage, it is only the husband who is ever referred to as the head. As unpopular as it is, I think it is only males who should be elders—not because of inherently better qualifications because they are males—but because of a reflection of the hierarchy of equals in the Trinity. Males are not superior, just as the Father is not superior to the Son. I want to make it clear that I do not believe males to be superior to females. Nor is the Father superior to the Son in the Trinity.

What the world needs to see in us, the church of Jesus Christ, is a living example of how hierarchy functions in the kingdom of God. It is there. But it is there without providing "status" or "benefits and deprivations," as Dr. Sumner and Dr. Wolterstorff both observed. And it is exercised by those in the position of leadership (or, more properly, headship) by using their position sacrificially to serve others. Hopefully that will be so peculiar, especially in comparison to the world around us, that people will be attracted to us because of its peculiarity.

Since the relationship of the genders is an image of the relationship of the persons of the Trinity, it follows that any understanding of male headship that, even unconsciously, implies female inequality or incompetence or shallowness or gullibility or "unfitness for leadership" will also imply the same about the persons of the Trinity. Of course, that cannot be true. Any understanding of gender relationships that considers women as less than equal in *any* way, even unconsciously, is an insult to her Creator. But men and women *are* different, just as the persons in the Trinity are different.

As I have read numerous books on the issue of how the genders relate in marriage and in the Body of Christ, I have seen some blind spots.

In the books written from a complementarian perspective, I have seen very little, if any, emphasis on the equally important issue of the equality of women to men. It's all been on submission and women's "unfitness" for leadership in the church. I hope I have made it clear that the Bible teaches and demonstrates the equality of the feminine gender, as well as the hierarchical nature of gender relationships.

I have not seen a Christian understanding of hierarchy. We live after the fall where the understanding of hierarchy in the culture around us, like many other issues, is not a Biblical understanding.

There is a thundering silence on the problem of abuse of women by males.

I have not seen in the books written from a complementarian perspective reference to examples from Scripture where women do teach, even teach men. While Huldah technically did not teach, she did give the Word of the Lord to an Old Testament king and even to an Old Testament high priest. Deborah gave the Word of the Lord to a military leader. In 1 Corinthians 14:26, if "anyone" has a hymn, a "lesson" (which is the word *didache*), it needs to be done in an orderly manner. The word for "anyone" is not a translator's interpretation but is in the original. So there a woman may "teach," and since it is in church, presumably it would be before an audience of men and women. But eight verses later we are told that women need to be "silent" in church. As I take those verses, given the context, they are about being orderly in church. It's about women, who were new to co-ed church services, wanting to *learn* from their husbands, and they are *encouraged* to do so, but not in a way that would be disorderly during the service. We need to remember how important it was, in that context, for Christian services to be starkly different from the chaotic services of worship to Dionysus. Even though I am a complementarian, I think women are much more free to speak publicly and fulfill roles of leadership than most complementarians would allow.

As I said in the introduction, I am not a theologian. I have no seminary or theological training. I find myself disagreeing with people who have far more training than I have, and that makes me very uncomfortable. I encourage any and all readers to be like the Beroeans[512] and examine the Scriptures yourselves. But as much as possible try not to read the Scriptures through glasses shaded by this world's values.

---

[512] Acts 17:11

My goal in writing this book is to shed some light on what I believe are two blind spots in the discussion of gender in the church. One is a Christian understanding of hierarchy. That understanding is grounded in the nature of the Trinity, which I believe is revealed to us as a hierarchy of equals. The other blind spot is the fact of our living in a fallen world where the value system that surrounds us, which we grew up in, which is "normal" to us, is not the value system of the Kingdom of God, where being a servant is the highest position one can fulfill. Does that make the hair stand up on my neck? Yes, it does. Not only because I fall so far short of it but also because it is *so* different from what I am used to.

Now that you've read the whole book I'm going to try and summarize it in a couple of sentences. I believe the God of the Bible, the Trinity, is revealed to us as a hierarchy of equals. *Equals.* I believe there are two kinds of relationship in our fallen, secular world which are to function in the same way-because humans are created in the image of God. Those two types of relationship are the Body of Christ and Christian marriage. In both of those I see in the Bible a structure which is a reflection of the Trinity-a hierarchy of equals. But we have failed miserably in accomplishing the *equal* part, I think Paul does not try to eliminate hierarchy-in the Body of Christ, in marriage, or even in the horrible institution of slavery. But there are texts which eliminate the *evil* which has infected those institutions in our fallen world.

I recently watched the movie *Caste*, which is based on a book of the same name by Isabel Wilkerson. I have not read the book. From what I understand, the theme of the book and the movie is that all caste systems, including American racism and slavery, Nazi hatred of the Jews, sexism, the Indian system of castes, are related. The root cause, the author says, is endogamy, which is the prohibition of marrying and having children with someone outside of your caste, or class, or race. With all due humility, I think she is wrong. There must be some prior prejudice to prevent marriage outside your class or race. And so endogamy is a symptom rather than a cause. The cause is, I believe, hierarchy that has gone horribly wrong in a fallen world. So we invent somebody or some class to be "better than." We need to feel "better" than somebody. The real root cause is sin and an ugly rejection of the values of the Kingdom of God.

I have quoted C. S. Lewis before in this book. One of my favorites statements of his is this: "I believe in Christianity as I believe the sun rises; not only because I see it but because by it I see everything else." In other words, the Christian worldview is necessary to understand the world we live in. The *fallen* world we live in. The reason for the caste system, for racial prejudice, for slavery, for sexism, and for oppression, is that, in this fallen world where we live, the perfect hierarchy of equals designed into humans as a result of being created in the image of a hierarchy of equals in the Trinity, has been decimated. We need to find, or create, someone to whom we are superior. And then judge ourselves as "better". If I understand the Bible correctly, our calling is not to eliminate hierarchy but to heal it—to bring it back to the original design where everybody is of equal value and significance. And where leadership, or more properly headship, is not a position of self-serving domination but of service to others—even though it includes authority.

As I get older, I see the Design of God in my personal life and also in the Big Picture, and I am thankful for it. I also become more and more saddened by the unthinkable amount of pain in this fallen world and the unthinkable amount of pain that our Father has to view in His Creation because of *us*. We sinners have introduced so much chaos and suffering into His world.

I long to be at Home in heaven where all the appetizers injected into this world will be fulfilled and we will all be at peace. In no way does that imply a cheap lack of involvement with needy people who are hurting in this world, proving ourselves to be "so heavenly minded we are no earthly good." In fact, just the opposite is true:

it frees us up to minister and to give materially to the hurting and underprivileged in this world. We can do that because this world is *not* our home, and it makes no sense to build our kingdom and castles *here* while ignoring hurting people *here*. That is true for every person who really understands the amazing love of the Father who sent His Son to die as a substitute on the Cross for us sinners.

But until we reach our Permanent Home where all things will be made Right again, we live by *faith*, as sojourners in this present world, as members of the Dispersion, living *increasingly* as we grow by the values of the Kingdom of God and *decreasingly* by the values of this fallen world where we live, waiting for and hastening the inheritance kept for us in heaven. When we receive that inheritance, as adopted children receive an inheritance from their adoptive parents, unearned, that will be a glorious day indeed. All the appetizers given us by God with the purpose of helping us both to *hunger* and to *wait*, all the present but incomplete joy, delight, and temporary personal fulfillment—what Larry Crabb describes as being "prematurely happy"—will then pale in comparison to the final peace and wholeness that we will inherit in heaven.[513]

And that will be beautiful beyond comprehension. I hope I will see you there.

---

[513] Sixty-Six Love Letters, by Larry Crabb, Thomas Nelson, Dallas, TX, c 2009, p. xxvii.

100% of the royalties from this book will be donated to World Vision. I do not say that to brag but to make clear I have enough. As I said in the book why build castles here when there are starving people here and this is not my home? I hope I am setting an example for others to follow.

Printed in the United States
by Baker & Taylor Publisher Services